Pathways to Peacebuilding

American Society of Missiology
Monograph Series

Chair of Series Editorial Committee, James R. Krabill

The ASM Monograph Series provides a forum for publishing quality dissertations and studies in the field of missiology. Collaborating with Pickwick Publications—a division of Wipf and Stock Publishers of Eugene, Oregon—the American Society of Missiology selects high quality dissertations and other monographic studies that offer research materials in mission studies for scholars, mission and church leaders, and the academic community at large. The ASM seeks scholarly work for publication in the series that throws light on issues confronting Christian world mission in its cultural, social, historical, biblical, and theological dimensions.

Missiology is an academic field that brings together scholars whose professional training ranges from doctoral-level preparation in areas such as Scripture, history and sociology of religions, anthropology, theology, international relations, interreligious interchange, mission history, inculturation, and church law. The American Society of Missiology, which sponsors this series, is an ecumenical body drawing members from Independent and Ecumenical Protestant, Catholic, Orthodox, and other traditions. Members of the ASM are united by their commitment to reflect on and do scholarly work relating to both mission history and the present-day mission of the church. The ASM Monograph Series aims to publish works of exceptional merit on specialized topics, with particular attention given to work by younger scholars, the dissemination and publication of which is difficult under the economic pressures of standard publishing models.

Persons seeking information about the ASM or the guidelines for having their dissertations considered for publication in the ASM Monograph Series should consult the Society's website—www.asmweb.org.

Members of the ASM Monograph Committee who approved this book are:

Margaret E. Guider, OSF, Associate Professor of Missiology, Boston College School of Theology and Ministry

William P. Gregory, Associate Professor of Religious Studies, Clarke University

RECENTLY PUBLISHED IN THE ASM MONOGRAPH SERIES

George Shakwelele, *Explaining the Practice of Elevating an Ancestor for Veneration*

Peter T. Lee, *Hybridizing Mission: Intercultural Social Dynamics among Christian Workers on Multicultural Teams in North Africa*

Pathways to Peacebuilding

Staurocentric Theology in Nigeria's Context of Acute Violence

UCHENNA D. ANYANWU

FOREWORD BY
AMOS YONG

⌘PICKWICK *Publications* • Eugene, Oregon

PATHWAYS TO PEACEBUILDING
Staurocentric Theology in Nigeria's Context of Acute Violence

American Society of Missiology Scholarly Monograph Series 61

Copyright © 2022 Uchenna D. Anyanwu. All rights reserved. Except for brief quotations in critical publications or reviews, no part of this book may be reproduced in any manner without prior written permission from the publisher. Write: Permissions, Wipf and Stock Publishers, 199 W. 8th Ave., Suite 3, Eugene, OR 97401.

Pickwick Publications
An Imprint of Wipf and Stock Publishers
199 W. 8th Ave., Suite 3
Eugene, OR 97401

www.wipfandstock.com

PAPERBACK ISBN: 978-1-6667-3807-0
HARDCOVER ISBN: 978-1-6667-9833-3
EBOOK ISBN: 978-1-6667-9834-0

Cataloguing-in-Publication data:

Names: Anyanwu, Uchenna D., author. | Yong, Amos, foreword.

Title: Pathways to peacebuilding: staurocentric theology in Nigeria's context of acute violence / by Uchenna D. Anyanwu ; foreword by Amos Yong.

Description: Eugene, OR: Pickwick Publications, 2022 | American Society of Missiology Scholarly Monograph Series 61 | **Includes bibliographical references and index.**

Identifiers: ISBN 978-1-6667-3807-0 (paperback) | ISBN 978-1-6667-9833-3 (hardcover) | ISBN 978-1-6667-9834-0 (ebook)

Subjects: LCSH: Theology of the cross. | Violence—Nigeria. | Peacebuilding—Nigeria.

Classification: LCC HN831.Z9 A59 2022 (print) | LCC HN831.Z9 (ebook)

11/28/22

Unless otherwise indicated, all Scripture quotations are from the *ESV® Bible (The Holy Bible, English Standard Version®)*, Copyright © 2001 by Crossway, a publishing ministry of Good News Publishers. Used by permission. All rights reserved.

Map 1 is used with permission from The Economist Group—License Number 5207780435049

Map 2 is used with permission of Open Doors UK/Ireland

Map 3 is from open source.

The Poem, *Two Rows by the Sea*, is used with the permission of The Bible Society of Egypt.

To my dad,
Pa Philip Ndumeihechere Anyanwu,

and

My mom,
Mama Charity Agwawelem Anyanwu
(née Okorochukwu).

(Both of blessed memory).
For their sacrificial and self-giving love.

Contents

List of Maps | viii
Foreword by Amos Yong | ix
Preface | xiii
Acknowledgments | xvii
List of Abbreviations | xx

1. Introduction | 1
2. An Overview of Nigeria's Political and Religious Histories | 23
3. Contextual Theology and Nonviolence Peacebuilding Ethics | 70
4. Peacebuilding Concepts from Islamic and Muslim Perspectives | 96
5. African Concepts for Peacebuilding-Contextual Theology | 144
6. Peacebuilding Concepts from Nigeria's Ethnolinguistic Cultures | 170
7. *Staurocentric* Pathways to Peacebuilding-Contextual Theology | 194
8. Peacebuilding Carrefour: *Staurocentric* Contextual Theology and Praxis for African Contexts of Acute Violence | 236

Reference List | 279
Index | 297

List of Maps

Map 1   Map of Nigeria showing areas of major Islamists Acute Violence | 12

Map 2   Map of Nigeria: States Worst Hit by Boko Haram and the Sharia States of Northern Nigeria | 37

Map 3   Map of Nigeria showing the Oil Producing States in Niger-Delta Region | 59

Foreword

ALTHOUGH DR. UCHENNA D. Anyanwu finished his PhD thesis—which revised and now published version you are holding in your hands—under my supervision, I want to take a moment to pay tribute to Dr. Evelyne Reisacher who was the initial lead mentor. Uchenna's matriculation to the PhD Intercultural Studies program housed within Fuller Seminary's Center for Missiological Research (CMR) in the Fall of 2015 was at the invitation of Fuller's Professor of Islamic Studies at that time, who welcomed his basic idea of researching peacebuilding in a West African context fraught with Christian-Muslim tensions if not outright hostilities over recent decades. Evelyne had then completed the first draft of her groundbreaking manuscript, published in the Fall of 2016 by Baker Academic as *Joyful Witness in the Muslim World: Sharing the Gospel in Everyday Encounters*, which was one of the main reasons why she was eager to work with Uchenna to assist in nurturing his research theme into doctoral reality. Unfortunately, toward the end of the second year of Uchenna's course of study, medical doctors discovered reappearance of the cancer Evelyne had about eight years prior and which went into remission. Over the next two years, she continued to meet when she could with Uchenna, while undergoing chemotherapy and radiation treatments, until overcome by the disease 30 March 2019 when she passed away in Paris.

As the director of the PhD program, I had left Uchenna under the guidance of his mentor and working committee, which included my brotherly-colleague Dr. Veli-Matti Kärkkäinen. Over the course of Evelyne's last year, as it had become evident that she was no longer in a position to work with her doctoral mentees, we began to explore alternative committee assignments and considerations. In January 2019, the CMR-academic committee asked me to consider assuming lead responsibilities for Uchenna, and I agreed when it was clear Veli-Matti would continue in his role as a member of the committee. Uchenna passed his comprehensive examinations later that spring and then began working earnestly, and furiously, on writing his dissertation. From September through December of the same year, I received one-after-another of what amounted finally to eight chapters, a good number of which I would provide some extensive comments, to which he always attended to in meticulous detail in revising the thesis. I have no doubts that the same intensity with which Uchenna engaged the comments, edits, and questions I posed in response to the various chapter drafts he submitted was at work throughout his program of study, including in his interactions with his committee members and first mentor.

Uchenna's successful defense of the dissertation on Easter Monday, 13 April 2020 (awarded *with distinction* by the committee), broke new ground in three ways, reflective I believe of the ways he engaged with both Evelyne and Veli-Matti, especially. From Evelyne, he recognized the central role of affectivity in all interfaith relations, now with its own particular opportunities and challenges when applied to the West African Christian-Muslim environment; this meant, among other things, that orthodoxy and orthopraxis needed to include orthopathos, being rightly impassioned in our postures and approaches to people of other faiths, which Uchenna explicated in his thesis in terms of Christian forgiveness as lived out in hospitable community funded by open-heartedness, not only by right ideas or expected practices. Then, Veli-Matti's comparative theological method, one honed by this mentor and advisor over the last two decades in a range of works in constructive theology for a pluralistic world, was brought to bear in thinking about peacebuilding in Christian and Islamic traditions; yet Uchenna extended Kärkkäinen's comparative method across two overlapping and mutually informing registers that considered Muslim views along with indigenous West and sub-Saharan African perspectives on peacebuilding. What emerges is a theological trialogue between Christianity, Islam, and African religious and cultural traditions that exemplifies the fruitfulness of comparativism when unfolded across a more complex and complicated triadic frame. Now in relationship to the African traditional front especially, one dominated by oral rather than literary sources, Uchenna's comparative work is informed by data derived from the kind of ethnographic research long promoted in CMR. Not for no reason, then, the external examiner of the thesis noted that one of the original contributions herein is in Uchenna's "drawing readers' attention to ideas/concepts which are native to Africa and then relating these to Christological pathways towards peacebuilding. These concepts include the contextualized Islamic notions (since these are being reviewed and outlined by an African writer and mined from Africans and hence translated) but, more importantly, the concepts that are drawn by the researcher from the diverse ethno-linguistic background of Nigeria."

Yet all of this work, however methodologically sophisticated and rich, depends on a core theological and missiological presupposition: the centrality of the cross of Jesus Christ. This is the fundamental contribution that holds together the affective and comparative dimensions of the project: it is the death of Christ that invites us to empathize with the pain of others, surely also and even religious others, in a pluralistic world. This crucicentrism is surely a major theme in the Lutheran theological tradition within which Veli-Matti is ordained as a minister of the gospel, yet Uchenna's adoption of Luther's crucial notion is refracted through the lens of affectivity imbibed from the legacy left by his first mentor. In another context St. Paul originally wrote of a new relationship between Jews and Gentiles in this way: "he is our peace; in his flesh he has made both groups into one and has broken down the dividing wall, that is, the hostility between us" (Eph. 2:14, NRSV). Yet to the degree that the Ephesian context sought to reimagine the church catholic and universal under the Fatherhood of God, "from whom every family in heaven and on earth takes its name" (3:15), to that same degree Jesus remains the peace between all divided peoples, nations, tribes, and languages, even Christians and Muslims in the West African region. Further, Jesus-as-our-peace is possible only as this slain-buried-resurrected-and-ascended Christ "dwell[s] in your hearts through faith, as you are being rooted and grounded in love," so that Paul can only "pray that you may have the power to comprehend, with all the saints, what is the breadth and length and height and depth, and to know the love of Christ that surpasses knowledge, so that you may be filled with all the fullness of God" (3:17-19). Thus, the peace of Christ is accessed affectively, in and through the love of God in Christ, by the power of the Spirit.

Although I am the one writing this foreword, I hope we can see how the author of this book has worked closely with his other internationally renowned mentors at every stage. I am delighted therefore to recommend unreservedly and enthusiastically the *staurocentric* peacebuilding thesis of our West African Anglican priest, theologian, and missiologist that I pray can herald of "post-terrorist" world in which Christians and Muslims can bear witness to the living Christ and the Fatherhood of God for the shalom of the world!

Amos Yong, PhD

Dean of the School of Mission and Theology,
and Professor of Theology and Mission
Fuller Theological Seminary

Preface

THE WORK YOU ARE reading is a revised version of my PhD dissertation at Fuller Theological Seminary, which I successfully defended on Easter Monday, April 13, 2020. After the defense, my PhD Guidance Committee and Defense Jury (Professors Amos Yong, Veli-Matti Kärkkäinen, and Akintunde Akinade) encouraged me to seek channels for its possible publication. I first sent the manuscript to William (Bill) Burrows–the veteran Managing Editor of Orbis Books. After reading the work, Bill recommended the American Society of Missiology (ASM) Monograph Series. Hence, I sent it to Dr. James R. Krabill, the Chair of the ASM Monograph Series, who (after months of review by the Committee) informed me that the Committee had accepted the manuscript for publication in the series under Pickwick Publications, one of the imprints of Wipf and Stock Publishers. Thus, the present work comes to you from the crucible of the revisions of my doctoral dissertation manuscript.

I deem it necessary to point readers to certain salient details regarding the voice, translations, and transliterations employed in the body of this work. Being an African raised in a culture and context where we say: *umunna bu ike*—father's children as a unit is force or strength, I have the proclivity to often speak or write with a plural voice in recognition that it is not about the individual but the community—a theme you will encounter in this book. Hence, you will often notice the use of the first person plural pronouns (we, us, our) and sparsely the first person singular pronouns (I, me, my). I generally use the first person plural pronouns to portray my African-ness depicting my thought that we are in community even while you are reading this work. Where the subject or object has to do with me or where an assertion or emphasis is mine, however, I employ the first person singular pronouns.

Insofar as references to the Bible are concerned, all citations, unless otherwise stated, are taken from the *English Standard Version* (ESV), (Wheaton, IL: Crossway, 2008).

Citations from the Qur'ān, except otherwise indicated, are taken from *Al-Qur'an al-Kareem -* القرآن الكريم *Sahih International Translation* (Jeddah, Saudi Arabia: Saheeh International, 1997). *The Sahih International Translation* is a widely accepted English translation and has received widespread acceptance by English-speaking Muslim scholars from core Muslim Arab countries and beyond. References from the *Aḥādith* are taken from https://sunnah.com/. Three underlying rationales for using this website are: (a) There is a parallel reading of the *aḥādith* in both the original Arabic texts and in English. Such presentation is helpful for reading in the original language (Arabic) and comparing with the translation; (b) It provides the different major Hadiths from the widely accepted traditions.; and (c) It also gives Hadith numbers as referenced in their respective printed versions. This website is an authentic digital copy of and a one-spot call for all the widely accepted hadiths. The Book and *Ḥadith* numbers conform to the references in the English translations and reference numbers.

Transliteration of Arabic words follow the standards recommended by the *International Journal of Middle East Studies* (IJMES)[1]. Nevertheless, transliterations used in cited works are retained as they appear in the cited work even when they do not conform to the IJMES standards. The word *al-majiri*, for example is composed of the Arabic article (*al*) and the noun (*majiri*). In this book, the Arabic article (*al*) is separated from the noun with a dash (*al-majiri*), unlike what readers may find in many other writings in literature where the two words are written together (*almajiri*). In addition, transliterated Arabic words not generally known to be present in the English language registry are italicized. But such words are left as they appear in cited works where they were not italicized.

Whenever you read between the lines of any author, you may discern that the author's life experiences and journey find their way into his or her writing(s). You will certainly do the same reading this work. I have lived and served in four linguistic and cultural, and two religious contexts. In regard to educational formation, I came from a building and structural engineering background before diving into missiology and theology. All these widened my perspectives. Thus, as you read this work, you will find

---

1. https://www.tandf.co.uk//journals/authors/RJAB-TransliterationChart.pdf (accessed: Dec. 9, 2019).

footprint-expressions from these various contexts and formational perspectives. I implore you the reader to consider the footprint-expressions that may sound unfamiliar as part of my life journey. I have, nonetheless, made every effort to provide sufficient elucidation where necessary. Hence, I do not count it needful to reframe these expressions, as some reviewers may suggest. I entreat you to be gracious toward me and please count it as a ride with me through my life journey so far—a journey that I can neither deny nor divest.

Lastly, being keenly aware of my humanness that is devoid of perfection, I take responsibility of any mistakes or errors that might be found in this book.

Uchenna D. Anyanwu
South Hamilton, Massachusetts
Winter 2021/2022.

Acknowledgments

It is said that wherever you see a turtle on a fencepost, you know that it did not get there by itself. This work and its author are, indeed, a turtle on a fencepost. Evidently, I did not get to this fencepost by myself. Many labored to bring this work to this fencepost.

I am deeply grateful to Professor Amos Yong who took over the baton of guidance when my first doctoral advisor, Dr. Evelyne A. Reisacher (d. March 30, 2019), went home to be with Jesus after a long battle with cancer. Without Dr. Yong's prompt, constructive and substantive feedbacks and his deep scholarly insights, I would not have arrived at this fencepost.

Similarly, I acknowledge and appreciate the support and guidance that Dr. Evelyne Reisacher, provided from the onset of my doctoral journey at Fuller Seminary, even though this is coming postmortem. I am deeply grateful to Professor Veli-Matti Kärkkäinen who, right from the time my first PhD Guidance Committee was constituted, came on board, mentored, and tutored me in the theological aspects of my studies. The same expression of gratitude goes to Professor Akintunde E. Akinade who accepted to join the Committee when Dr. Reisacher's dwindling health necessitated its reconstitution. I also thank Dr. John Azumah and Dr. Johnny Ramírez-Johnson for their scholarly support in my doctoral journey. I greatly appreciate you all—my mentors and tutors for your accompaniment.

I am also indebted to the entire faculty at Fuller Seminary's Center for Missiological Research (CMR) for their support and input, especially Dr. Diane B. Obenchain whom the Lord providentially used to knock at doors that ultimately led to my receiving the Robert and Dorothy King PhD Fellowship—a fellowship without which I may not have commenced doctoral studies at Fuller Seminary, and Dr. David H. Scott for his meticulous academic support.

I express my gratitude to my colleagues at Fuller's Center for Missiological Research (CMR) with whom I started doctoral studies in the same cohort and those who started after our cohort. Their critiques of my seminars or colloquium presentations, their prayers, and moral encouragement meant a lot to me. I am immensely thankful to Johnny Ching whose guidance in procedural logistics of the CMR PhD program helped to keep me on track of the administrative requirements.

Daniell Whittington of the David Allan Hubbard Library (DAHL) at Fuller was such a great blessing to me, helping to acquire resources I desperately needed during the course of my research and writing. Thank you, Daniell, and all the DAHL personnel. You all are a blessing!

I am grateful to Dr. Chris Spinks, Stephanie Hough, Calvin Jaffarian, Dr. Savanah N. Landerholm, Matt Wimer, and all the editorial and typesetting team at Wipf and Stocks Publishers for their meticulous editorial guidance for the present volume.

Through the financial support of a host of friends (for my family and me), this turtle was put on a fencepost. My family and I appreciate particularly the following brothers and sisters in the Lord: Sonny and Chioma Wogu, Jack and Anne Wald, Peter and Favour Akpe, Mike and Anne Spiger, Alex and Chioma Onuegbu, Tunde and Bola Oyekola, Mary Nkagieneme, Sola Osunsami, Seyi and Foluwake Ajayi, Anthony and Funmi Adetayo, Jimmy and Florence Adegoke, Jon and Kim Raines, and Gene and Elaine Pierce. Thank you all for your faithfulness and love.

Many other friends stood with me in different ways. The Bereans Class at Lake Avenue Congregational Church Pasadena stood with me in prayers and other forms of support. There I found a dear friend in Matt Sanders and his spouse, Diana. The Bereans prayed regularly for me when I was in the field doing the ethnographic research and all through the months of writing. I also thank two special friends whom I met through leading Vocation and Formation Groups at Fuller—Daniel Fong and James Lee. I thank Dr. Patience M. Ahmed and Dr. Sheila Konyu Muchemi who supported me in different ways especially when I arrived in Pasadena in 2015 to begin my doctoral journey. A shout of appreciation goes also to Dr. David Muthukumar S. with whom I shared an apartment during our first year of doctoral work and who has become a dear friend and a systematic theology scholar in his own rights.

A shout of thanksgiving goes to all my interview participants whom I cannot name here, and to the faculty and students of Jos ECWA Theological Seminary, COCIN Theological Seminary, Gindiri, and EYN Kulp

Theological Seminary, Kwarhi. Thank you all for your hospitality and the help you provided me during my fieldwork.

Evidently, without the support and prayers of my spouse, Dolapo (*Nkemhurunanya*), and our two sons—Ezeanyinabia and Ozioma-Jesus—neither this book nor I would have arrived at this fencepost. Thank you so much my beloved *Judeopolis* Family. You're an awesome "clan"!

I leave the best for the last. I thank you, God, our Heavenly Father; Jesus Christ, my Lord and Savior; and the Holy Spirit, my Teacher and indeed my unseen but ever-present Counselor and Advisor. Without God's guidance, provisions and blessings, I certainly would not have been set on this fencepost even with all the human support and encouragement of the hosts mentioned and unmentioned. Therefore, unto you, O Lord God, who is able to establish your *shalom* upon our broken and violent world through the power of Jesus's death and resurrection life and the outpouring of the Holy Spirit, and place us upon a heavenly post, to you, O Lord, be all the glory and honor and praise forever and ever! Amen!

Abbreviations

ACW	A Common Word
API	Adamawa Peacemakers Initiative
AUN	American University of Nigeria
CAPRO	Calvary Ministries (CAPRO)
CMR	Center for Missiological Research (at Fuller Theological Seminary)
CMS	Church Missionary Society
COCIN	Church of Christ in Nations (formerly: The Church of Christ in Nigeria)
DSS	(Nigerian) Directorate of State Services
ECWA	Evangelical Church Winning All (formerly: Evangelical Church of West Africa)
EKAN	Ekklesiyar Kristi a Nigeria (former name of COCIN churches)
EKAS	Ekklesiyar Kristi a Sudan (initial name of COCIN churches)
EYN	Ekklesiyar Yan'uwa a Nigeria (the Church of the Brethren in Nigeria)
HOHVIPAD	Horn of Hope Vision for Peace Community Development of Nigeria

HSRC	Human Subject Research Committee
IDPs	Internally Displaced Persons
IJMES	International Journal of Middle East Studies
IPOB	Indigenous People of Biafra
IRB	Institutional Review Board
IT	Information Technology
MASSOB	Movement for the Actualization of the Sovereign State of Biafra
MCDF	Muslim-Christian Dialogue Forum
MEND	Movement for the Emancipation of Niger Delta
MSOP	Movement for the Survival of Ogoni People
NGO(s)	Non-Governmental Organization(s)
POD	People Oriented Development (a humanitarian agency of ECWA)
RCM	Roman Catholic Mission
SIM	Sudan Interior Mission (now known as Serving in Missions)
SUM	Sudan United Missions
TCNN	Theological College of Northern Nigeria
TEKAN	Tarrayar Ekklesiyoyin Kristi a Nigeria (Fellowship of Churches of Christ in Nigeria (FCCN)
VVF	Vesicovaginal Fistula
WIC	Women's Interfaith Council (also known as: Interfaith Forum of Muslim and Christian Women's Association)

1

Introduction

1.1 BACKGROUND TO THE STUDY

ETHNIC, POLITICAL, AND RELIGIOUS acute violence have remained a challenge to Nigeria since the country gained its independence from Britain in 1960. Among these three categories of violence, the latter (religious violence) occupies the top rank of Nigeria's history and timeline of acute violent incidents. Richard Bourne and Nigerian-born distinguished historian, Toyin Falola, chronicle some of Nigeria's incidents of violence in their respective works.[1] Another researcher, Ioannis Mantzikos, in an article particularly chronicles Boko Haram's attacks in Nigeria and her neighbors.[2] The onus for resolving such violent conflicts in Nigeria has often rested solely upon the Nigerian governing authorities. As may be expected of the political authorities of most countries, the Nigerian government is known to have the proclivity toward the use of military force for quelling such violence. Kenyan-born scholar, John Mwaruvie, underscores the same observation asserting that the proclivity to call on the government for intervention "is based on the notion that the government has the resources and coercive machinery that can be used to solve the conflict . . . [and that] [t]he government's intervention in most cases involves sending the armed forces to fight those assumed to cause trouble."[3] The use of military force has, however, often produced only momentary solutions to conflicts, thus making sustainable peace elusive. Furthermore, complications are introduced "when

---

1. Bourne, *Nigeria*; Falola, *Violence in Nigeria*; Falola, *Colonialism and Violence in Nigeria*.
2. Mantzikos, "Boko Haram Attacks in Nigeria and Neighbouring Countries."
3. Mwaruvie, "Mission of the Church in Africa," 270.

the aggressor also happens to come from the ruling ethnic group and the government becomes reluctant to respond to the crisis to safe [sic] the victims"[4] —a scenario that is indeed the case in Nigeria's contemporary experience of acute violence because the aggressors (Islamist groups like Boko Haram and Muslim Fulani herdsmen) belong to the same religious group as Muhammadu Buhari—the current Nigerian President. It is widely acclaimed in Nigeria that Muhammadu Buhari's government and his security apparatus have not demonstrated much concern to intervene in the silent mayhem and jihad being perpetrated by Fulani herdsmen in the country. In the face of such a scenario, government actors must, therefore, not be the only actors to depend upon for peacebuilding actions.

Allan Gerson, a scholar in the field of conflict resolution, argues that in order to reduce the challenges of acute violence, "[n]ew players—particularly the private sector, as well as nongovernmental organizations (NGOs)—must be enlisted in a new approach to. . . peace building."[5] Here, "private sector" and "nongovernmental organizations" include all non-state actors in the society. In this optic, therefore, the involvement of the church in Nigeria needs be encouraged and harnessed in order for the church in Nigeria to become a major contributor toward peacebuilding in a country that has been beleaguered with acute violence.

Undeniably, religion is strongly engrained and plays a vital role in the life of many Nigerians. Whereas, there are cases of conflict in Nigeria that are religious, there exist others which are ethnic or political or a *mélange* of two or more of those elements. One of the factors that trigger ethnic conflicts, for example, is dispute over land for cattle grazing and agriculture.[6] But in cases of acute violence orchestrated by Islamists in Nigeria, the influence of religious convictions has often been one of the underlying factors that birth them. If the church in Nigeria will become involved in any meaningful way in peacebuilding within its borders and beyond, then articulating and enacting a robust peacebuilding-contextual theology cannot be ignored. Moreover, in becoming agents and catalysts of peacebuilding, the church will not only reflect the peace of Jesus Christ whom she professes and confesses as Lord, but also will be fulfilling the less traveled road (in matters concerning peacemaking and peacebuilding) of its calling to be a "sacrament, a sign and an instrument" of the missionary triune God.[7]

---

4. Mwaruvie, "Mission of the Church in Africa," 270.
5. Gerson, "Peace Building," 102.
6. Ploughshares, "Nigeria (1990—First Combat Deaths)."
7. Bosch, *Transforming Mission*, 217, 381, 383–85.

Since the beginning of the twenty-first century, Boko Haram (self-identified as: *Jama'atu Ahl as-Sunnah li-Da'awati wal-Jihād*) has been the Islamist group in Nigeria that has occasioned incidents of Islamists' acute violence in the country. Boko Haram is, however, not the only Islamists group in Nigeria that has lashed out series of acute violent incidents in Nigeria's history. In the 1980s it was the *Maitatsine* group[8] and in the 2000s and 2010s it has been Boko Haram. The *Ansaru* group is another Islamists organization splintered out of Boko Haram and lashing its own genre of acute violence in Nigeria.[9] Since 2016, Nigerian news reports have been highlighting attacks and killings in many Nigerian villages by Fulani herdsmen in Benue, Enugu, Kaduna, and Nasarawa States of Nigeria.[10] These attacks have wasted and murderously terminated scores of lives. Conclusively, we may then assert that should the current active Islamists violent groups be quelled by means of military action, other groups would most likely emerge in the future. In the 2030s or 2040s it could be another Islamist group morphing into a different form, name, and structure. Thus employing military apparatus to swash Islamist insurgent groups in Nigeria will not ensure sustainable peace.

The foregoing background forms the basis from which the research question being posed in this study emerges. The question is: In what ways can the church in Nigeria articulate a *staurocenteric* peacebuilding-contextual theology in its context of acute violence to contribute toward transformational peacebuilding within the country? As will be later defined, *staurocentric* peacebuilding theology refers to a peacebuilding-contextual theological model of the cross—*stauros*, a word derived from Koiné Greek σταυρός meaning "cross." Put differently, given the context of Islamist acute violence, particularly in northeastern Nigeria, what *staurocenteric* peacebuilding-contextual pathways can the church in Nigeria adopt in order to position herself as God's sacrament, sign and instrument for catalyzing transformational peacebuilding? Thus, this study focuses primarily on three church denominations that have been worst-hit by Islamist acute violence in northeastern Nigeria namely: The Church of Christ in Nations in Nigeria (COCIN); the Evangelical Church Winning All (ECWA); and the Ekklesiyar Yan'uwa a Nigeria (EYN), which is the Church of the Brethren in Nigeria. We will attempt a succinct historical review of the emergence

---

8. Danjibo, "Islamic Fundamentalism and Sectarian Violence."

9. Comolli, *Boko Haram*, 65.

10. Mikailu, "Making Sense of Nigeria's Fulani-Farmer Conflict"; Gabriel, "Genocide in Southern Kaduna."

of each of these three denominations in Nigeria later in the next chapter.[11] *Staurocentric* pathways to peacebuilding-contextual will be proposed. Methodologically, recourse is given to the analysis of ethnographic in-depth individual interviews with leaders, theologians, and seminary students, and focus group interviews of participants from the three denominations—one focus group interview per denomination.

1.2. STATEMENT OF RESEARCH PROBLEM: RESEARCH SUBPROBLEMS AND PROPOSITIONS

Finnish-born constructive systematic theologian, Veli-Matti Kärkkäinen, affirms that the pervasive phenomenon of plurality creates several challenges, and that it is hard to "fathom the uttermost difficulty of doing theology in and for the 'post-' world."[12] Islamist acute violence—epitomized in contemporary times by Islamists' acts of violence—is one of the myriad of the challenges created by the pervasive phenomenon of plurality in our twenty-first century world. Artisans of peace in such contexts of Islamist violence and, indeed, within other non-Christian religious contexts will, therefore, have to grapple with and unravel the complexity of engaging the "other" in a pluralistic world. Insofar as it concerns the church in Nigeria, this challenge to engage the "other" within the context of Islamist violence forms the grounds for this study. Evidently, missiologists cannot turn a blind eye to issues in our world and society—issues that engender violence, human suffering, injustice, *inter alia*. As a follower of Jesus from Nigeria, the violent killings of several hundreds of people by the Islamist jihadist group globally known as Boko Haram, the attacks, sacking and ravaging of villages in some parts of Nigeria by Muslim Fulani herdsmen (also known as Miyetti Allah), and the displacement of tens of thousands from their homes, villages, places of work, farmlands and schools, have been of deep personal concern.

Thus, the research problem, to which this study seeks to make contribution, is posed by the question: In what ways can the church in Nigeria articulate a *staurocenteric* peacebuilding-contextual theology in its context of acute violence to contribute toward transformational peacebuilding within the country? In other words, given the context of Islamist acute violence, particularly in northeastern Nigeria, what *staurocenteric* peacebuilding-contextual pathways can the church in Nigeria adopt in order to position herself as God's sacrament, sign and instrument for catalyzing transformational peacebuilding? As will be defined shortly, Islamist acute violence has affected both Muslims and non-Muslims in Nigeria. It is not violence

---

11. See subsections 2.2.5–7.
12. Kärkkäinen, *Christ and Reconciliation*, 1:3.

against non-Muslims alone. Rather, both Muslims and non-Muslims in Nigeria all suffer the devastation such violence perpetrate.

The scope of the study is limited to peacebuilding-contextual theology within Nigeria's context of violence orchestrated by Islamists in northeastern Nigeria. The theologico-theoretical framework for this study is the *staurocentric* model of Jesus's death on the cross and resurrection with a critical and constructive integration of African concepts of peacebuilding and resources of peacebuilding from Islamic perspective. Before we define our terms, we first delineate the research problem stated above and break it down into manageable "smaller units."[13] We identify five subproblems in the research design for this study namely: a review of Nigeria's political and religious histories insofar as they contribute to Nigeria's context of acute violence (especially as orchestrated by Islamists); contextual theologies and peacebuilding; Islamic concepts and Muslims' perspectives for peacebuilding; African concepts of peacebuilding; and *staurocentric* peacebuilding model.

1.2.1 Subproblem 1: Evaluating Nigeria's Political and Religious Histories

The question the first subproblem seeks to answer is: How do Nigeria's political and religious histories interact and contribute to acute violence in the country?

> Proposition 1: Nigeria's Political and Religious histories contribute to acute violence.

> Two historical elements mesh to exacerbate acute violence in Nigeria namely political and religious histories. The political axis consists of the British colonial infringement, while the religious consists of the forceful establishment of Islam in northern Nigeria through Usman dan Fodio's jihad and the encounter of Islam with Christianity. An inquiry into this subproblem is undertaken in chapter 2: An Overview of Nigeria's Political and Religious Histories.

1.2.2 Subproblem 2: Contextual Theologies and Peacebuilding

For the second subproblem, the investigation seeks answers to the question: What current contextual theologies exist in African contexts and which of them (if any) may drive peacebuilding in the context of Islamist acute violence?

---

13. Leedy and Ormrod, *Practical Research: Planning and Design*, 36.

Proposition 2: African contextual theologies exist but a peacebuilding-contextual theology that constructively and critically integrates African concepts is yet to be articulated.

There are existing contextual theologies in Africa but a peacebuilding-contextual theology is yet to emerge. The Anabaptists' nonviolence peacebuilding ethics can serve as pointers to an African peacebuilding-contextual theology. This is the task we undertake in chapter 3: Contextual Theology and Nonviolence Peacebuilding Ethics.

1.2.3 Subproblem 3: Islamic Concepts and Muslims' Perspectives for Peacebuilding

The third subproblem seeks to answer the question: What peacebuilding resources or tools exist in Islam and from the perspective of Muslim artisans of peace that can be integrated and employed in formulating a peacebuilding-contextual theology in context of acute violence?

Proposition 3: Peacebuilding concepts from Islamic and Muslim Perspectives exist and can be harnessed for peacebuilding in the context of acute violence.

There are concepts for peacebuilding in Islam and from the perspective of some Muslim artisans of peace. These concepts are resources or tools that can be constructively and critically integrated into formulating peacebuilding-contextual theology and this forms the focus of chapter 4: Peacebuilding Concepts from Islamic and Muslims' Perspectives.

1.2.4 Subproblem 4: African Concepts for Peacebuilding

The forth subproblem sets to respond to the question: What are the African concepts for peacebuilding that may be critically and constructively integrated and employed for conceptualizing a peacebuilding-contextual theology in contexts of acute violence?

Proposition 4: A number of Africans concepts for peacebuilding exist.

There are a number of African concepts for peacebuilding that are already being employed in Africa for peacebuilding in contexts of acute violence. Chapter 5, "African Concepts for Peacebuilding-Contextual Theology", and chapter 6, "Peacebuilding Concepts from Nigeria's Ethnolinguistic Cultures", make a modest attempt to provide an answer to the question of this research subproblem.

1.2.5 Subproblem 5: Staurocentric Peacebuilding model

The question this subproblem seeks to find answer is: What model can the church in Nigeria adopt for peacebuilding in the country's context of Islamist-orchestrated acute violence?

> Proposition 5: The triune God's model of Jesus's cross is God's method and means for triumphing over evil, sin and violence, and can be adopted by Jesus's followers in contexts of violence. This forms the subject of focus in chapter 7: *Staurocentric* Pathways to Peacebuilding-Contextual Theology. A constructive integration of this model with Islamic and African concepts of peacebuilding is then attempted in the final chapter: Peacebuilding Carrefour: *Staurocentric* Contextual Theology and Praxis in African Contexts of Acute Violence.

Bibliographical and ethnographic research data from the investigation defined by the above subproblems crystalize into the formulation of *staurocentric* pathways put forth in this study. But before diving into that investigation, it is fitting we define our terms; outline the scope, limitations, and assumptions; and state the missiological and personal significance of the study.

1.3 DEFINING THE TERMS

It is fitting we define a few of the principal terms used in this book. They include: peacebuilding, σταυρός–*stauros* and *staurocentric* pathways, peacebuilding-contextual theology, Islamist acute violence, and the church in Nigeria.

1.3.1 Peacebuilding

Different terms or expressions are being used in scholarly circles to refer to peace actions. Among them are peacemaking, conflict resolution and peacebuilding. The question is: Is there a dividing line between these terms? For example, Kenyan-born scholar John Mwaniki Mwaruvie points to the difference between peacemaking and peacebuilding, observing that "[p]eacemaking is concerned with ending specific conflicts, but peacebuilding objective is to address the underlying causes of the conflict in the society."[14] On his part, renowned peacebuilding scholar, John Lederach, employs the term conflict transformation—what Johan Galtung

---

14. Mwaruvie, "Mission of the Church in Africa," 272; See also: Paffenholz and Lundqvist, *Community-Based Bottom-up Peacebuilding*, 14–15.

calls peacebuilding.[15] Abraham Adu Berinyuu holds that peacebuilding has to do with "post conflict settlement process . . . [which entails] the stage by stage as well as sector by sector process of embedding and nesting changes."[16] Catherine Morris provides the historical emergence of the term peacebuilding, linking it to "the widespread use after 1992 when Boutros Boutros-Ghali, then United Nations Secretary-General, announced his *Agenda for Peace*."[17] Morris's one definition of peacebuilding is rather a description of what it involves namely:

> building the capacity of non-governmental organizations (including religious institutions) for peacemaking and peacebuilding . . ., emphasis on . . . structural transformation, with a primary focus on institutional reform . . . a full range of approaches, processes, and stages needed for transformation toward more sustainable, peaceful relationships and governance modes and structures . . . building legal and human rights institutions as well as fair and effective governance and dispute resolution processes and systems.[18]

With these reflections in mind, I have come to define peacebuilding as "the proactive, conscious and structured efforts geared toward establishing the parameters that create a peace ("שָׁלוֹם"—*shalom*) culture and prevent conflict, acute violence, or war. It is preventive, intentional, and is not a reaction or response to crisis that has already begun, which is the domain of peacemaking. Peacebuilding does not wait for a context of conflict before it begins."[19] In my definition of peacebuilding, I underscore the intrinsic purpose of the triune God to redeem, restore, and re-instate his creation into a *shalom* relationship, not only along the human–God axis of relationship, but also along the human–human and human–creation axes in their multifaceted forms.[20] Hence, peacebuilding must be understood as encompassing contexts of conflict as well as where there is none. It is broader than conflict resolution and peacemaking because it seeks to create a culture that will prevent potential conflict. However, where a conflict situation already exists, peacebuilding works towards reconciliation, resolution, and peacemaking, but does not stop at that. The goal of peacebuilding is not limited to

---

15. Lederach, *Preparing for Peace: Conflict Transformation Across Cultures*, 127–30.
16. Berinyuu, "Peace Building in Africa," 24.
17. Boutros-Ghali, "An Agenda for Peace"; Morris, "What Is Peacebuilding?"
18. Morris, "What Is Peacebuilding?"
19. Anyanwu, "Pneumatological Considerations," 337.
20. For a brief discussion on the multifaceted forms of human-human broken relationships see Section 7.4 (in chapter 7).

resolving an existing conflict but to install a culture that will prevent further aggression and conflict between parties.

1.3.2 σταυρός—Stauros *(the cross)* and Staurocentric *Pathways*

The Greek word "σταυρός"—*stauros* is defined as (a). "pale, stake, erected for a palisade . . . [or] used for a foundation; [and (b).] stake used as an instrument of punishment."[21] Figuratively, it refers to the "crucifixion [of] Christ, whose suffering on the cross became a means of salvation and redemption of human sin."[22] Thus, "σταυρός"—*stauros* "is an instrument of torture for serious offences."[23] Symbolically, it was represented by the Greek letter τ (tau) ~ T.[24]

In this volume, we use the term σταυρός—*stauros* to refer to the cross of Jesus Christ and the resurrection life it produces, not only in regard to it as an instrument employed for Jesus's crucifixion for the redemption of humans and for the reconciliation of the human–God relationship, but also as the triune God's instrument and method for defeating death, evil, sin, and violence, and for redeeming, restoring and re-instating God's entire creation from all dimensions of broken relationships. Thus, by extension "*staurocentric* pathways" refers to postures and actions that cohere with Jesus's attitude when he faced the cross-event. Elements of *staurocentric* pathways will include, for example (but not limited to), forgiveness, demonstration of God's self-giving love (*agape*) in practice, compassion and praying for (not against) and blessing agents and perpetrators of violence and injustice, et cetera. In the light of the above definition, therefore, the *staurocentric* model is a trinitarian theological model that reflects the triune God's model of the cross (σταυρός—*stauros*) to overcome evil and violence. It is manifested in the *kenotic* model set by the incarnate Word—Jesus Christ. It is a model based on Jesus's giving of himself as a grain of wheat that fell to the ground, died and multiplied (John 12:24–25). It is a theological model of the cross built upon the *kenosis* principle.[25] This model requires a preparedness to die to oneself and a readiness to suffer in order that that the "other" may attain true life and peace.

---

21. Montanari, *Brill Dictionary of Ancient Greek*, 1954.
22. Montanari, *Brill Dictionary of Ancient Greek*, 1954.
23. Kittel and Friedrich, *Theological Dictionary of the NT*, 7:572.
24. See also http://stephanus.tlg.uci.edu/lsj/#eid=99117&context=lsj&action=from-search.
25. Martin, *Carmen Christi*.

1.3.3 Peacebuilding-Contextual Theology

Two elements are involved in our definition of peacebuilding-contextual theology. The first relates to the incarnational aspect, and the second to the attempt to apply contextual theology for peacebuilding. In regard to the first element, Wilbert Shenk maintains that "[t]he theological precedent for contextualization is the Incarnation—God in Christ entering history and culture . . . [and its] existential imperative is the *missio Dei*, in which the church is called to follow Jesus Christ in redemptive engagement with the world."[26] This incarnational aspect is further connected to the cross (σταυρός—*stauros*) because without Jesus's incarnation the cross-event would not have been possible. In the same manner that Jesus's incarnation prepared the grounds for his *stauros* event, peacebuilding-contextual theology must also take the incarnational aspect seriously.

In regard to the second element, peacebuilding-contextual theology seeks to apply the principles of coherence theory to search for a contextual theology for transformational peacebuilding, by engaging "not only theological resources but also cultural, religious, sociopolitical, and other resources."[27]

Thus, we define peacebuilding-contextual theology as incarnational contextual theology for peacebuilding within a given context that takes into consideration cultural contextual methods (in that context) reflecting biblical concepts—particularly the trinitarian model as demonstrated in the triune God's method for defeating evil, death, sin and violence through Jesus's incarnation, life, death on the cross, and his resurrection. Peacebuilding-contextual theology will also, in addition to the consideration of local cultural concepts, include historical elements which formed the foundations for the contexts and how those elements continue to impinge upon the present.

1.3.4 Islamist Acute Violence

Scholars have defined violence in different ways. Finnish-born constructive systematic theologian, Veli-Matti Kärkkäinen, puts forth "a minimum definition of violence . . . [as] harm done to another human being (or group of people or even the whole humanity) with evil intentions or at least without thinking of the best of the other."[28] Norwegian sociologist and peacebuilding scholar, Johan Galtung, defines it as "harming and/or

---

26. Shenk, "Contextual Theology," 207–8.
27. Kärkkäinen, *Christ and Reconciliation*, 1:15.
28. Kärkkäinen, *Christ and Reconciliation*, 1:322.

hurting,"[29] and underscores the assumption upon which that definition holds as "the existence of something that can experience being harmed and being hurt."[30] Violence can be physical, psychological, and/or systemic and it can manifest in social, political and economic structures—forms of violence Galtung calls "indirect violence."[31] Along the same perspective, Roman Catholic scholar, Robert J. Schreiter, asserts that there are various forms of violence of which "direct physical violence, which involves assault on an individual or a group"[32] is the most evident.

Drawing from the understanding of violence enunciated by these scholars, we point to the dimension of violence whose perpetrators possess a religious Islamic vision. Islamist acute violence is a re-rendering of acts of violence undertaken by militant Islamic extremists. It is a phenomenon of violence encompassing human bloodshed, suicide bombing, destruction of properties, burning of villages, kidnapping/abduction of people et cetera. Islamists are Muslims who tie "*din* (religion) with *dawla* (state) in a shari'a-based political order."[33] One of the leading authorities on Islamic law and Islam, Khaled Abou El Fadl uses the term "Muslim puritans"[34] to refer to Islamists.[35]

In this study, Islamists are extremist Muslims consumed with the vision of seeing the establishment of *Allahcracy*[36] (*hikimiyyat Allah*—Allah's control or rule) in the entire world. Their commitment to this vision situates them to employ all means including acute violence even when that implies laying down their own lives in the process of shedding the blood of others, to see the fulfillment of that vision because they are convinced that Allah will honor them for striving in his path. Islamists must not be confused with peace-loving Muslims who are equally committed to the vision of Islam's rule in the world but reject violence and espouse peacemaking as alternative approach.

29. Galtung, *Peace by Peaceful Means*, 2.
30. Galtung, *Peace by Peaceful Means*, 2.
31. Galtung, *Peace by Peaceful Means*, 2.
32. Schreiter, *Reconciliation*, 30.
33. Tibi, *Islamism and Islam*, 2.
34. Abou El Fadl, *Great Theft*, 5.

35. Other terms current in literature to refer to Islamists include: ""militant", "extremist," "radical," "zealot," and "fundamentalist... used loosely and interchangeably... often functioning as synonyms for "terrorist"" Appleby, *Ambivalence of the Sacred*, 11. These terms are, however, employed by non-Muslim authors.

36. The English word similar to this word—*Allahcracy*, (which I coined), is "theocracy." Instead of resorting entirely to the Greek words, θεος (*theos*—God) and κρατέω (*krateo* -to take control, hold). The Arabic word for God (Allah) is here co-joined to the Greek for "to take control." If Arabic is solely to be use, we would be saying "*hukumaat Allah* or *hakimiyyat Allah*." See Tibi, *Islamism and Islam*, 15.

1.3.5 THE CHURCH IN NIGERIA

For the purpose of this study, three church denominations (Church of Christ in Nations (COCIN) of Nigeria; the Evangelical Church Winning All (ECWA); and the Ekklesiyar Yan'uwa a Nigeria (EYN)—the Church of the Brethren in Nigeria) form the primary focus of research. These three have been delineated to be representative of the church in Nigeria. The rationale underlying their choice for research is undergirded by the fact that they are predominant in northeastern Nigeria where Boko Haram-orchestrated acute violence has been most felt. We undertake a brief historical review of each of these three church denominations (COCIN, ECWA, and EYN) in chapter 2 to outline their emergence in Nigeria's religious history.

Northeastern Nigeria is the region in Nigeria that has been adversely affected by Islamist acute violence. Three states particularly worst-hit by the violence are Adamawa, Borno, and Yobe States (see Map 1).

Map1: Map of Nigeria showing areas of major Islamists Acute Violence

State capital cities of the worst-hit States in northeastern Nigeria: Damaturu, Maiduguri and Yola

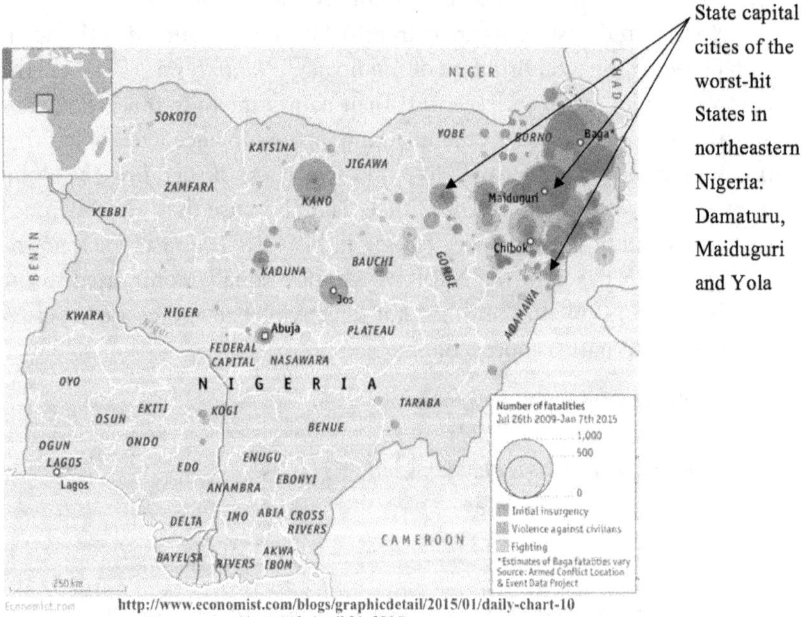

http://www.economist.com/blogs/graphicdetail/2015/01/daily-chart-10
(Accessed: April 21, 2016)

This study focuses on the context of these three states. There are, however, other states in northern Nigeria that have also been affected by Islamists' acute violence, such as Bauchi, Kaduna, Kano, Plateau, Taraba—see Map 1. The state capitals of Adamawa, Borno and Yobe where the COCIN, ECWA and EYN churches are located are respectively Yola, Maiduguri and Damaturu.

1.4 SCOPE OF STUDY, LIMITATIONS, AND ASSUMPTIONS

The study resulting in this monograph is not an investigation of the sociological, political, economic or psychological undertones of the phenomenon of Islamists' acute violence on Muslim and non-Muslim communities in Nigeria. There are reports and works that have done some work in this domain.[37] The scope of the present study is confined to theological reflection and articulation of peacebuilding taking contextuality into consideration.

Peacemaking initiatives may take political factors into consideration. This study, however, primarily focuses on the contextual theological elements that may inform and shape the formulation of a Christian theology that will drive peacebuilding in the context of acute violence in northeastern Nigeria. The study does not so much delve into socio-political elements of peacebuilding, not because they are irrelevant, rather its focus is on contextual theology that will position the church in Nigeria to contribute to the gains which socio-political factors bring to the table of peacebuilding.

The church in Nigeria is made up of a mosaic of denominations and independent initiated churches and organizations. The scope of this study is primarily limited to three church denominations—COCIN, ECWA and EYN. Secondarily, participants whose church denominations are none of these aforementioned church denominations whom we happen to have met during our fieldwork and considered their contribution relevant were also interviewed. Focus groups participants in the study were a mixture of members of the three denominations of primary focus as well as from other denominations.

The study seeks a contextual theological approach for peacebuilding that may be consistent with the *staurocentric* model in the context of acute violence in northeastern Nigeria.

A limitation imposed on this study is that Muslim participants were not interviewed given the focus on Christian theological perspectives. Nonetheless, one participant in our study is a follower of Jesus from a Muslim background, whose knowledge and familiarity with Islamic concepts are indeed substantive. In addition, bibliographical research undertaken in chapter 4 provides insightful sketches from some Muslim scholars' concepts of peacebuilding from Islamic scriptural texts.

37. Falola, *Violence in Nigeria*; Williams and Guttschuss, "Spiraling Violence"; Institute for Economics and Peace, "Global Terrorism Index 2015." Ahmed, "Impact of Terror on Internally Displaced Persons in Nigeria."

A basic assumption in this study is that contextual theological approach that entails the integration of African concepts for peacebuilding in the context of acute violence in northeastern Nigeria has not been a priority in the ranks of many churches in Nigeria. This is not to say that there have not been efforts at conflict resolution in the region. What is evident, however, is that the quest for peacebuilding only surfaces when conflicts occur. This study seeks to propose pathways for peacebuilding that go beyond incidences of conflict or violence.

Furthermore, given recent regional demands for political restructuring of Nigeria, this study assumes that Nigeria will remain a unified political entity. In other words, Nigeria as a political entity will not disintegrate into two or more countries. This assumption is necessary because in the event of a secession, such as has happened in the Balkans, what will become of northeastern Nigeria—to which part of a disintegrated Nigeria it may fall— can only be left to mere conjecture. Moreover, in the event of disintegration, some northern states in Nigeria are most likely to declare themselves an Islamic State under strict *shariʿa* (Islamic law).

1.5 SIGNIFICANCE OF THE STUDY AND CONTRIBUTION TO KNOWLEDGE

This study is personally significant in some respects. First, Boko Haram Islamists killed one of my colleagues in cold blood in a village in Borno State. This colleague (whom we can call Marcus[38]) had completed a discipleship class with new believers in the village where he was serving among an unreached peoples group. After the new believers left the place of meeting, the Islamists swamped upon him with machetes and killed him. Marcus's death left behind his widow with two young children. There are other missionaries from other organizations serving in the same region who have paid the ultimate price, dying as a result of Islamists' acute violence in northeastern Nigeria.

Secondly, there are several Muslims who have lost members of their families to Islamists' acute violence as well. According to a global report on terrorism released at the end of 2015 "Boko Haram [alone] was responsible for 6,644 deaths . . . [and it is considered] the deadliest terrorist group in 2014."[39] The pain and suffering of fellows affected by such acute violence have also become mine. A contextual theological model for peacebuilding that the church in Nigeria could employ to inform peacebuilding engagement in Nigeria will be an enormous benefit to future generations of

---

38. Not his real name.
39. Institute for Economics and Peace, "Global Terrorism Index 2015," 14.

Christians and Muslims alike in the country. And lastly, such peacebuilding engagement will reduce the phenomenon of Internally Displacement of Persons (IDPs) that has resulted from acute violence.

In regard to missiological and theological significance, the theological framework of this study is grounded upon its missiological relevance and significance. Nigeria, being the most populous nation in Africa has regularly experienced ethnic, political, and religious acute violence since its independence in 1960. Until now, the onus of resolving such violent conflicts has often rested solely upon the shoulders of the governing authorities. God's mission, however, entails the involvement of the church in God's intrinsic purpose to redeem, restore and reinstate his creation into a relationship of *shalom* with the triune God. As we posit in chapter 7, the redemption, restoration and reinstating into a relationship of *shalom* is three-dimensional— between humans and the triune God, between humans themselves, and also between humans and other creation. James R. Krabill asserts in this optic that it is God's vision to reconcile all things and set them right.[40]

Thus, the missiological significance of this study lies in the fact that it provides a peacebuilding-contextual theological model germane to the Nigerian context. Beyond providing such a model, churches in Nigeria can employ it as they "interact with the practices of the [Nigerian Muslim communities] with a view to ensuring and enabling faithful participation in God's redemptive practices in, to and for the world."[41] With such a model, the church in Nigeria will also play its role as God's instrument, sign and sacrament in a context beleaguered with acute violence.

The church will remain handicapped in its participation in God's mission where acute violence continues to prevail. A contextual model that informs, installs and promotes peacebuilding (*shalom*) will be missiologically significant (1Tim 2:1–4). Its relatedness to *missio Dei* is evident since God's purpose to redeem, restore and reinstate his creation into a relationship of *shalom* with the triune God is three-dimensional—restoration, redemption and reinstating of relationship of *shalom* between humans and the triune God; between humans (or peoples or nations); and also between humans and creation (ecological relationship). These facets of relationships are encapsulated within the mission of God (*missio Dei*). Redemption, restoration and renewal of *shalom* are concepts within that mission. Jesus, upon whose *staurocentric* model this theological framework is based, experienced violence on the cross (σταυρός— *stauros*), and yet he brought *shalom*.

---

40. Krabill, "Biblical Approaches to Peace," 88.
41. Swinton and Mowat, *Practical Theology and Qualitative Research*, 7.

That said, the theological framework that serves as a roadmap for this study is the trinitarian model of *staurocentric* peacebuilding. Justification for selecting this model lies in the historical and theological evidence of its efficacy. The *staurocentric* model has been employed by the missionary triune God in overcoming violence and death, as argued in chapter 7. A longitudinal phenomenological perusal of how it has transformed lives, communities and peoples since the historical and spiritual event of Jesus's death on the cross (σταυρός) and his resurrection, attests to its validity. It may then be argued that the triune God has left the *staurocentric* model as a model for Jesus's followers to emulate, but, hardly have we appreciated its efficacy and potency in overcoming evil and violence. There are overwhelming historical evidence that support the model. Jesus's death on the cross has resulted in the transformation of people's lives, people groups, and nations in diverse ways. Iconic missiologist and the father of the church growth movement, Donald McGavran, argued that the gospel of Jesus Christ brings to people both "redemption and lift."[42] This "lift" arguably includes the peace, love, forgiveness and a sense of belongingness to one family,[43] which Jesus Christ imprints upon the lives of his followers through the Holy Spirit and the written word of God.

With that said, what might be the contribution of this study to knowledge? The response to Islamists' acute violence in Nigeria from the part of the Nigerian ruling authorities and the Nigerian church has often been majorly reactionary and retaliatory.[44] Certainly, there have been several efforts of peacemaking in Nigeria's contexts of acute violence. Preventive peacebuilding that integrate contextual African concepts for peacebuilding are, however, yet to become praxis both in the society and in the church—not only in Nigeria, but also in many African countries. The lack of such preventive peacebuilding methods, at least from the side of the church in Nigeria, may be informed by the lack of a peacebuilding-contextual theology required to drive it. Furthermore, the theology of most churches in Nigeria has remained a mere replication of model inherited from the house

---

42. McGavran, *Understanding Church Growth*, 260–75; Zunkel, "Church Growth," 228–29.

43. An example of what is meant here by "a sense of belongingness to one family" (i.e. God's family) is the peace and love that has been attested to exist between Jesus's followers of Jewish and Arab origin. Naturally, (at least, as we know from the media), Israeli Jews and Arab Muslims have been brutal enemies. But when Jesus comes into their lives, all the enmity and hatred dissolve and peace is installed. http://www.israel-today.co.il/NewsItem/tabid/178/nid/24739/Default.aspx. and https://www.youtube.com/watch?v=BT50-Kuj2UY.

44. Williams and Guttschuss, "Spiraling Violence"; Agbiboa, "Boko-Haram and the Global Jihad"; Okoro, "Terrorism and Governance Crisis"; Comolli, *Boko Haram*.

of Western theologies. Thus, this study is a contribution to knowledge to bring to the fore a peacebuilding-contextual theology that constructively and critically integrates African concepts of peacebuilding and that coheres with Jesus's *staurocentric* model.

1.6 RESEARCH METHODOLOGY

What follows is the synopsis of the methodology adopted for this study, explaining very briefly the research procedure used during the fieldwork and the reasons justifying the choice of the adopted methodology. A short discussion on the procedure of narrative data analysis and integration of the concepts are also laid out in this section.

1.6.1 Synopsis of Methodology

This study involved human participants majorly from three Nigerian church denominations geographically located in northern Nigeria. Methodologically, in-depth ethnographic unstructured[45] individual and focus group[46] interviews were employed and combined with field-notes taken during the fieldwork. The period of fieldwork was from mid-Sept to mid-November 2018. There were two sets of interviews—individual and focus groups. A total of eighteen individual interviews were conducted as well as three focus groups, each group consisting of between 7 and 12 participants. Scholars identify three methods commonly used for Grounded Theory research namely: participant observation, interviews and collection of texts and artifacts.[47] During the fieldwork, method was limited to interviewing and collection of texts. Participant observation is a method that requires long period of field work for substantial data to emerge and be collected. Since the length of time in the field did not exceed two months, participant observation was, therefore, not employed for this study. Thus, the ethnographic aspect of the research is restricted to narrative data extracted from individual and focus group interviews and from bibliographical data.

Before outlining how I undertook the fieldwork, it is necessarily to acknowledge that I, the principal investigator for this study, I am a Nigerian follower of Jesus from a Christian background. As it is required of every researcher, I sought to keep in mind the chances of biases and

---

45. Bernard, *Research Methods in Anthropology*, 157.
46. Stewart and Shamdasani, *Focus Groups*.
47. Strauss and Corbin, "Grounded Theory Methodology"; Corbin and Strauss, "Grounded Theory Research"; Cohen and Crabtree, "Qualitative Research Guidelines Project."

endeavored to be as objective and fair as possible in my judgment and interpretation of data in this study.

1.6.2 The Research Procedure

I laid down the research procedure in the Institutional Review Board (IRB) protocol submitted, vetted and approved by the Human Subject Research Committee (HSRC) at Fuller Theological Seminary. For brevity, I outline the key outlines from that document.

The key focus of the study involved three church denominations in northeastern Nigeria: The Church of Christ in Nations of Nigeria (COCIN); The Evangelical Church Winning All (ECWA); and The Ekklesiyar Yan'uwa a Nigeria (EYN). Given their context of Boko Haram-orchestrated violence, I sought to find out how they have responded to the violence in relation to Jesus's teaching and model. These three church denominations (COCIN, ECWA and EYN) are among the church denominations worst-hit by Islamist acute violence in northeastern Nigeria.

Method 1 of the study involved bibliographical research. Method 2 focused on conducting ethnographic in-depth individual interviews with leaders, pastors and laypersons. For Method 3, I conducted three focus group interviews, one group per church denomination. The three focus grops were conducted at the respective theological seminaries beloging to the three denominations, namely: Gindiri Theological Seminary (COCIN), Jos ECWA Theological Seminary (JETS), and EYN Kulp Theological Seminary, Kwarhi. Focus group participants were randomly recruited in the three theological seminaries. All participants were at least 21 years old or above, and included both male and female participants. I personally moderated the three focus groups. English language was used for all interviews. A breakdown of the number of participants are shown in the table below.

Table showing the Distribution of Interview Participants

Individual Interviews		
	Reference	Number of Participants
Denomination 1	D1	5
Denomination 2	D2	3
Denomination 3	D3	5
Denomination 4	D4	5
Total Number of Individual Interviews		18
Focus Groups Interviews		
	Reference	Number of Participants
Focus Group 1	Focus Group#1	7
Focus Group 2	Focus Group#2	10
Focus Group 3	Focus Group#3	11
Total Number of Focus Group Participants		28

Participants for the unstructured individual interviews included church leaders, pastors, teachers and missionaries who have lived experiences of peacebuilding within the context under study. Focus group participants consisted of seminary students.

The narrative data for this study was collected from Nigerian Christians who come from states in northern Nigeria—particularly but not limited to the three states worst-hit by Boko Haram's activities of acute violence. The key states of focus were Adamawa, Borno and Yobe States (Map 1). However, during the fieldwork I observed that due to incessant Islamist attacks many Christians and Muslims from Yobe and Borno states (particularly) had relocated to Abuja, Plateau State, and other locations in the country. Thus, some participants interviewed are no longer resident in their States of origin due to displacement caused by violence. Some participants were also included who do not necessarily belong to the three key church denominations of focus but who have equally experienced the context of violence and are involved in responding to it. This group of participants are categorized as D4 in the table above.

I developed a list of interview questions used in the interviews. Interviews were in-depth non-structured interviews. Clarifying questions not included in the list were asked during each in-depth interview. Experience from initial pilot interviews conducted to refine the interview questions for this study revealed that an investigator may forget to ask some questions during a given interview—questions Bernard referred to as "probing."[48] In order to make up for such gaps, I followed-up participants later and responses to probing questions (where necessary) were received using information communication systems that included telephone calls, email, and WhatsApp.[49] The idea of follow-up is attested to be used more to improve response rates when questionnaires are used as the method.[50]

Each interview session was audio-recorded and later transcribed. All recorded interviews (individual and focus groups) were securely stored and kept in an encrypted Online Dropbox folder. From the transcribed texts of the interviews, analytical categories or themes were extracted and coded. The process of extracting recurring structural themes in narrative/text analysis is referred to as coding themes.[51] Important themes extracted from the transcribed texts were then highlighted—"a technique [Corbin and Strauss] call **in vivo** coding."[52] I analyzed the narrative data gathered by extracting such themes. The consistency and connectedness of these themes were compared to the *staurocentric* theological model. Similarly, African concepts for peacebuilding extracted from the narrative data were critically evaluated to determine *staurocentric* elements (if any) and how they might be constructively integrated into peacebuilding in the context of acute violence.

In respect to citation from transcribed interviews, the following annotation is followed: Tyriaka, D1#4, is the code name for Participant Number 4 in Denomination 1. The fieldwork consists of both individual interviews and three different focus groups. References to narrative data from either individual interview participants or from focus groups interview participants are indicated as the case may be. Pseudonyms are

---

48. Bernard, *Research Methods in Anthropology*, 161–65.

49. I kept a meticulous list of participants and their respective contact information. In the Informed Consent letter, which they signed, they accepted to be contacted if need be.

50. Bernard, *Research Methods in Anthropology*, 213.

51. Bernard, *Research Methods in Anthropology*, 429.

52. Bernard, *Research Methods in Anthropology*, 430 (emphasis in original). The techniques for locating/finding themes or categories are discussed in Bernard, *Research Methods in Anthropology*, 430–31. Those techniques are employed in the text analysis of the transcribed interviews.

adopted for participants alongside the code number for either the denomination or focus group. This is done to conform with the Human Subject Research requirements for this study.

Citations from transcribed individual interviews are, therefore, referenced according to the church denomination of the participant interviewed, order of interviews, and line numbers of the transcribed text. For example: "Tyriaka D1#4:150–156" refers to an individual interview with a participant to whom I assigned a pseudonym, Tyriaka. D1 indicates that this individual is from Denomination 1, and #4 indicates that he or she is the fourth participant from Denomination #1 interviewed. The range of numbers "150–156" indicates the line numbers of the transcribed interview. In conformity with the 'Informed Content Letter' and the document approved by the Human Subject Research Committee (HSRC), pseudonyms of all interviewed participants are used for the purpose of their security. Denomination numbers—D1, D2, D3, and D4—are randomly assigned. The same principle is employed in the citation from transcribed texts of focus group interviews. Since we had three focus groups, "Focus Group 1:340–346" (for example) will imply that the text is taken from Focus Group Number 1, lines 340–346. With these annotations in place, we proceed in the next segment to present the justification for the methodology adopted in this study.

1.6.3 Justifying the Methodology: Why Individual and Focus Group Interviews?

According to H. Russell Bernard, unstructured interviewing "is used equally by scholars who identify with the hermeneutic tradition and by those who identify with the positivist tradition. It is used in studies that require only textual data and in studies that require both textual and numerical data."[53] When one wants to understand "the lived experience"[54] of people this method is recommended. On another note, "at the heart of most ethnographic research"[55] lies the matter of understanding the insiders' perspective of reality. This is the emic perspective. Both Bernard and David Fetterman agree that one of the tools ethnographers employ for this kind of research is in-depth unstructured interviews.[56] Thus, the grounds for the use of this method for the study, I believe, is hereby justified.

---

53. Bernard, *Research Methods in Anthropology*, 158.
54. Bernard, *Research Methods in Anthropology*, 158.
55. Fetterman, *Ethnography*, 20.
56. Bernard, *Research Methods in Anthropology*; Fetterman, *Ethnography*, 22, 40.

In same vein, the use of focus groups has been found to be a fruitful research tool across the borders of behavioral sciences. Stewart and Shamdasani maintain that "focus groups have become an important research tool for applied social scientists who work in program evaluation, marketing, public policy, education, the health sciences, advertising and communications."[57] The use of focus groups, therefore, commends itself to this study to broaden the ethnographic inquiry which individual interviews will provide.

Having succinctly described our research methodology and procedure, we now briefly outline what follows in the rest of this monograph. Chapter 2 presents an overview of Nigeria's political and religious histories, therein arguing that Nigeria's political and religious histories interact together to form a complex tapestry that engenders contexts of violence. In chapter 3, we posit that the contexts of acute violence that beleaguer Nigeria require contextual means and methods for peacebuilding which will help followers of Jesus and participants in God's mission in Nigeria to contextually engage in peacebuilding given the context of violence. The focus of chapter 4 pertains to concepts and perspectives for peacebuilding that may be garnered from Islamic texts and Muslim artisans of peace. The chapter concludes that there exist within Islam concepts, resources, and tools that can be harnessed and employed in constructing pathways to peace. The argument of chapters 5 and 6 is that African concepts of peacebuilding are models that should be studied and understood, and then constructively and critically integrated into peacebuilding-contextual theology, not only in African contexts of violence but also in other non-African contexts of violence. The penultimate chapter (7) explores the intersection of the *staurocentric* approach and peacebuilding and maintains that the *staurocentric* model is God's instrument for triumphing over violence, and therefore, should be employed by Jesus's followers in every era and context for responding to violence. The last chapter, 8, ties together the trajectories of the preceding chapters and discusses the emerging peacebuilding-contextual theology and practices from the intersection of the *staurocentric* model. The last segment of chapter 8 synthesizes the concluding reflections.

---

57. Stewart and Shamdasani, *Focus Groups*, 39.

2

An Overview of Nigeria's Political and Religious Histories

STUDYING PEACEBUILDING IN THE context of violence in contemporary Nigeria requires an understanding of the contexts that produced today's Federal Republic of Nigeria. Thus, we seek to answer the research question: How do Nigeria's political and religious histories interact and contribute to acute violence in the country? Two principal historical axes—political and religious—are paramount for that understanding. We engage in our discussion on these two principal axes, not in a historically chronological order, but rather in the order of the political emergence of Nigeria as a political nation. There is no doubt that historically Nigeria's religious history preceded its political history because all the various ethno-linguistic people groups in Nigeria had their respective religious history before the country's birth as a political nation. We do not, however, follow the historical chronology here, instead we begin with the political elements that gave birth to the political unit that is today called Nigeria. In addition, we do not dive into the deep oceans of Nigeria's political history, but simply highlight the major historical elements in that history that contribute to violence today. It seems reasonable, therefore, to move from the general (that is: the political) to the more substantive (religious) history. This is the rationale for the order of our navigation in this chapter.

Thus, we first take a historical glance at the country's political history and secondly review the two-sided coin of Nigeria's religious history. This is followed by an overview of how the contexts created by these two axes of Nigeria's history invigorate violence, particularly in northern Nigeria. We also engage in a short assessment of the two axes of Nigeria's history (political and religious) while highlighting the connections they have with violence in contemporary Nigeria. Our argument in this chapter is that Nigeria's political and religious histories interact together to form a complex tapestry that engenders contexts of violence.

2.1 A GLANCE AT NIGERIA'S POLITICAL HISTORY

Today's Federal Republic of Nigeria is an unnatural and forced amalgamation of several self-governing, regional, and ethno-traditional states made up of various peoples. Prior to the coming of the British colonialists, these various peoples existed primarily as ethno-linguistic states. The principal ones in terms of demographic dominance and influence were the Fulani, the Hausa, the Igbo and the Yoruba. Language was a primary binding force and served as a demarcation line, even though inter-ethnic trade continued between surrounding peoples.[1] All began to change in the mid-nineteenth century when the Europeans began their infamous "scramble for Africa."[2] The "European ambitions and rivalries in West Africa [led to the creation of] final boundaries negotiated by Britain, France and Germany."[3] The British created two colonial protectorates—Northern and Southern colonies. On January 1, 1914, the British Governor-General of these protectorates, Sir Frederick John Dealtry Lugard, amalgamated the two to form what we know today as Nigeria. The name "Nigeria" was coined by Miss Flora Shaw (later married to Sir Frederick Lugard in 1902), who worked for *The Times* of London and had suggested the name in an article she wrote for *The Times*—an article published on January 8, 1897.[4]

The architects of the Nigerian amalgamation experiment hardly considered the existing stark differences between the various peoples. The British colonial powers installed structures of governance alien to the various ethnic peoples of Nigeria. The amalgamation in 1914 to form what is today's Nigeria and the ignoring of the "people's history and institutions"[5] by the British colonialists produced various problems and crises. Based on a critical historical analysis, eminent Nigerian historian and scholar, Toyin Falola asserts that:

---

1. Isichei, *History of Nigeria*, 5.

2. See for example: Pakenham, *Scramble for Africa*; Nutting, *Scramble for Africa* and Gann and Duignan, *Burden of Empire*, chapter 13, "The Scramble for Africa".

3. Crowder, *Short History of Nigeria*, 21.

4. Omoruyi, "Origin of Nigeria"; Perham, "Frederick Lugard"; Crowder, *Short History of Nigeria*, 21.

5. Falola, *Violence in Nigeria*, 51.

> The colonial state was coercive, primarily in order to establish power and attain narrow economic objectives . . . Colonial Nigeria was nothing more than an artificially constructed agglomeration of diverse and other loosely united groups. Built by conquest and subjugation, the state never acquired any enduring legitimacy or trust from the various indigenous groups and nationalities."[6]

In the same vein, Matthew Hassan Kukah (Catholic Bishop of Sokoto in northwestern Nigeria) and Kathleen McGarvey (who founded the Interfaith Council of Muslim and Christian Women's Associations in Kaduna, Nigeria), in their contribution to the volume, *Fractured Spectrum,* affirm that colonialism exacerbated tensions that existed between various ethnic peoples, particularly in northern Nigeria.[7]

About a decade after World War II, African national movements began to sprout—movements that ultimately birthed political independence of most of the African states from their colonial lords. In Nigeria's case, the pundits of such movements from the north (the Hausa/Fulani oligarchy), the southwest (the Yoruba political juggernauts) and southeast (the Igbo men of timber and caliber) teamed up, ignoring their differences, in order to wrench themselves out from the rule, control and domination of the British imperial powers. Thus, on October 1, 1960, Nigeria became an independent political state, ostensibly free from the grips of colonial rule. The declaration of independence did not, however, erase the differences and cracks that exist within Nigeria's peoples, polity and politics.

Less than a decade after the Nigerian independence, the country gravitated into a civil war (1967–1970)—a war that claimed the lives of about three million people (majority of whom were Igbos of the southeast) and devastated parts of the fledging nation. Over half a century after Nigeria gained its independence from Britain, the overwhelming differences that testify against the amalgamation experiment remain evident through agitations and violence. As Richard Bourne asks: "How could they [the British] create a modern nation out of the 250 or so ethnicities[8] in the region with three large cultural and religious blocs [that is Yoruba, Hausa/Fulani and Igbo], and a major

---

6. Falola, *Violence in Nigeria*, 52.
7. Kukah and McGarvey, "Christian-Muslim Dialogue in Nigeria," 14.
8. A query on *World Christian Database* shows that there exist 374 ethnic peoples in Nigeria, each with a population greater than 10,000. All of these people groups possess their respective distinct language and culture. There are 164 other people groups in Nigeria with a population of less than 10,000. Johnson and Zurlo, "World Christian Database."

dysfunctionality between a numerous, poor and largely Muslim north, and an increasingly educated, Christian, and richer south?"[9]

More than half a century since the start of the Nigerian civil war and the declaration of Biafra's secession from the amalgamation experiment, wounds are far from being healed. There exists a growing movement agitating for the realization of the Republic of Biafra and demanding for a referendum of auto-determination. This movement is currently gathering international momentum in view of the mobilization of many Igbos in diaspora. One may think the problem is peculiar to only the movements seeking the independence of Biafra, such as Movement for the Actualization of the Sovereign State of Biafra (MASSOB) and Indigenous People of Biafra (IPOB). Nigerians from oil-rich Niger Delta are grossly marginalized—their fishing waters and agricultural lands destroyed by oil spills. Irrespective of the fact that the Nigerian oil wealth is extracted from their lands, they in return receive nothing from the Federal Government to alleviate their predicament. Such marginalization has engendered the peoples of the Niger-Delta clamoring for emancipation. Movements such as Movement for the Emancipation of Niger Delta (MEND), Movement for the Survival of Ogoni People (MSOP) both emerged as an aftermath of the gross neglect and injustice meted out to a region that provides the wealth upon which the entire country depends, and yet themselves, have long been neglected and de-robed of their means of sustenance—fishing and agriculture. These examples are highlighted to illustrate that the quest for peacebuilding, at least, in Nigeria's context of violence must factor in, among other causalities, the contexts of violence created by Nigeria's political history.

It is evident in contemporary Nigeria that some of the conflicts the country grapples with owe their roots to the colonial jostling and amalgamation of incongruous peoples to form a state—a move made by the colonial lords, whose imperial and economic avarice outweighed and overshadowed genuine humanness and common good of the Nigerian people. There is no doubt that colonialization, as a historical element, continues to define and shape African contexts in general, and Nigeria in particular. Andrew Walls's discussion on its significance as it pertains to Africa is poignant. Walls maintains,t

> [T]he boundaries of African states were determined outside Africa, on the basis of the perceived interests of European powers. The colonial period represents a very short interlude in the history of Africa, but its creation of a new type of state is a landmark in that history. The map of Africa is still in essentials the

9. Bourne, *Nigeria*, 4.

final draft of that "map of Africa by treaty" produced between about 1880 and the First World War by the jostling of a handful of European powers enforced locally by the possession of technologically based firepower.[10]

Walls further asserts: "The new state boundaries usually took little account of ethnic considerations, or the special 'belongingness' of African societies. In the case of the larger-scale traditional states, where these were a threat to the colonial state, as in the case of the Zulu, they were broken up . . ."[11] Falola's assessment earlier cited concurs with Walls's. Falola maintains that "[t]he colonial state [in Nigeria] was coercive, primarily in order to establish power and attain narrow economic objectives."[12] In a similar vein, Ogbu Kalu argues that "forms of European nationalism changed the character of the contact with Africa from informal commercial relations into formal colonial hegemony by mid-nineteenth century."[13] The partitioning of Africa at the Berlin Conference of 1884–1885 introduced a forced occupation of African lands, and the impact of that coercion and force continues to inform some of the difficulties and crises in African lands till date.

An outspoken Nigerian attorney, Femi Fani-Kayode, has pointed the attention of contemporary Nigerians to an alleged letter which Lord Lugard wrote to the British authorities in 1914 just before the amalgamation wherein Lugard wrote:

> What we often call the Northern Protectorate of Nigeria today can be better described as the poor husband whilst it's southern counterpart can be fairly described as the rich wife or the woman of substance and means. A forced union of marriage between the two will undoubtedly result in peace, prosperity and marital bliss for both husband and wife for many years to come. It is my prayer that that union will last forever.[14]

These are pregnant words. First, British colonial lords at the time were grossly racially biased. Second, they applied theories of racial superiority which was the prevailing mid-Victorian mindset. Their mindset "was suffused with a vivid sense of superiority and self-righteousness . . ."[15] Britons considered nations and races as a ladder of which "the British [were] at the

10. Walls, *Cross-Cultural Process in Christian History*, 102.
11. Walls, *Cross-Cultural Process in Christian History*, 102.
12. Falola, *Violence in Nigeria*, 52.
13. Kalu, "Christianity in Africa," 10; Kalu, *African Christianity*, 33.
14. Fani-Kayode, "Lord Lugard's Magic and Flora Shaw's Spell."
15. Robinson et al., *Africa and the Victorians*, 2.

top, followed by the Americans and other striving . . . Anglo-Saxons . . . Lowest [in the echelon] stood the aborigines who it was thought had never learned enough social discipline to pass from the family and tribe to the making of a state."[16] This same mid-Victorian outlook exudes in Lugard's own writing in the volume, *The Dual Mandate in British Tropical Africa*. Lugard's taxonomy of sub-Saharan Africans fall into three categories, namely: Europeanized Africans, advanced communities and primitive tribes.[17] In describing the peoples of Nigeria, he ascribed superior status to Muslims of northern Nigeria. He held that:

> the creed of Islam . . . has been the more potent as a creative and regenerating force, because it brought with it an admixture of Aryan or Hamitic blood, and the races which introduced it settled in the country and became identified with its inhabitants. They possessed greater powers of social organisation than the negro aborigines, and may therefore claim to be of a superior race-type.
>
> The conquests of the Arabs and Berbers from the north-east introduced the creed of Islam in the belt bordering the southern edge of the Sahara early in the eighth century. The modern history of the advanced communities of Hausaland and Bornu in Nigeria . . . founded kingdoms which, in the zenith of their prosperity, rivalled the civilisation of Europe of that day. Their descendants, the Fulani, still form the dominant caste, and rule the Moslem States of Nigeria.[18]

Lugard classified the Hausa/Fulani people among his "advanced communities" and believed they were racially superior to other races of today's Nigeria because of "an admixture of Aryan or Hamitic blood." It is no doubt he gave Muslims preferential treatment and described the Northern Protectorate of Nigeria "as the poor husband" because they had no resources and were less educated, except in Islamic religion, while the Southern Protectorate he classed as the "rich wife or the woman of substance and means." Toyin Falola affirms that the British colonial lords regarded "Muslims as more intelligent and civilized than adherents to traditional religions . . . [and] the Muslim elite was also preferred over Western-educated Nigerians."[19] These Western-educated Nigerians were the fruit of Western Christian missionary enterprise who obtained education in the

---

16. Robinson et al., *Africa and the Victorians*, 2–3.
17. Lugard, *Dual Mandate in British Tropical Africa*, 72.
18. Lugard, *Dual Mandate in British Tropical Africa*, 76.
19. Falola, *Violence in Nigeria*, 27.

south through the work of missionaries. Lugard and his British colonialist compatriots considered them "arrogant and impatient."[20] This prejudiced judgment came to be perceived by Muslim leaders in northern Nigerian as having given them the sole right of leadership in Nigeria. That legacy and perception subsists till date. Furthermore, that legacy serves as one of the salient reasons behind some politically-orchestrated violence because some Muslims hold that power must remain in the hands of northern Muslims who are committed to establishing and maintaining Islam as the dominant religion and the Shari'a legal system.

Lastly, Lugard believed that "[a] forced union of marriage between the [Northern and Southern Protectorates] will undoubtedly result in peace, prosperity and marital bliss for both husband and wife for many years to come."[21] How myopic Lord Lugard was—believing that "a forced" union will produce "peace, prosperity and marital bliss . . . for many years"! And how incongruent as well! It must be surprising to the modern reader to perceive the incongruity in a notion of forced marriage with an expectation that it will result to a peaceful and happy union. On the contrary, acrimonious domestic violence is the best that has so far resulted from such a union in Nigeria's experience.

Nigerian Pentecostal and social ethics scholar, Nimi Wariboko, succinctly brings this to the fore in his contribution to the volume, *Dynamics of Muslim Worlds*, wherein he asserts that the system introduced by the colonialists "denied Nigerians political freedom and choice of state managers. Colonization in Nigeria did not provide liberal democracy, as the political correlate of capitalism instead imposed a state that was not a product of society."[22] Wariboko further enumerates some of the assumptions the British colonial administrators had which motivated such odd imposition.[23] The imposition of a state on Nigeria that was strange to the mosaic of Nigerian peoples remains a legacy that produces violence today in lieu of "peace, prosperity, and marital bliss" that Lugard hoped, affirming Wariboko's assertion that the British ". . . colonial administration . . . planted seeds of conflict and division between Islam and Christianity."[24] The product of this legacy left by the British in Nigeria continues to produce violence in various forms as may be expected of violence in a "forced [marriage] union" (to use

20. Falola, *Violence in Nigeria*, 27.

21. Fani-Kayode, "Lord Lugard's Magic and Flora Shaw's Spell."

22. Wariboko, "Christian-Muslim Relations and the Ethos of State Formation," 67.

23. Wariboko, "Christian-Muslim Relations and the Ethos of State Formation," 68–70.

24. Wariboko, "Christian-Muslim Relations and the Ethos of State Formation," 69.

the words of the British colonial master, Lord Lugard, who was the architect of the forced union). We must point out that there exists, at least, one contemporary case of murder in a forced marriage in Nigeria where a child bride of 14 poisoned the man upon whom she was forced to marry at such a young age.[25] Thus, the incessant eruption of violence in Nigeria is, indeed, analogous to similar dangers characteristic of a "forced union."

Such political legacy, left behind by the British colonialists, co-joins with Nigeria's two-sided religious history to nourish and invigorate the eruption of violence, particularly in northern Nigeria. Thus, we turn to grasp the role the two-sided Nigeria's religious history plays in creating violence within Nigeria's context.

2.2 ISLAM AND CHRISTIANITY IN NIGERIA'S RELIGIOUS HISTORY

Insofar as Nigeria's religious history tied to violence is concerned, it can be viewed as a two-sided coin. The first side relates to Islam in northern Nigeria with its associated elements. This first side of Nigeria's religious history (Islam) displays three major historical elements that have always had ties to violence, namely: (a) Islam's entry into northern Nigeria and Usman dan Fodio's jihad; (b) Nigeria's Islamist violence and the emergence of Boko Haram; and (c) the challenge of the *al-majiri* phenomenon and its contribution to Islamist violence in Nigeria. The second side of the coin of Nigeria's religious history is the entrance of Christianity and its encounter with Islam in northern Nigeria. These four elements form the core of our review in this section. But before we dive into the discussion, a caveat is necessary.

Identifying Islam and Christianity as the two sides of the coin of contemporary violence in Nigeria does not in any case obliterate the existence of African traditional religions. Evidently, before the entry of Islam and Christianity into today's Nigeria, there existed different and diverse ethno-religions among the different ethnic people groups within the country. Africans are undeniably very religious and therefore have always had strong religious lives even before the entry of Islam and Christianity within the African context. John S. Mbiti puts this forcefully in his seminal volume maintaining that "Africans are notoriously religious, and each people has its own religious system with a set of beliefs and practices."[26] Benjamin C.

---

25. "Wasilu Umar [14 years of age at the time of the incident] admitted killing her husband, who was more than twice her age, by concealing rat poison in his food, . . . in Kano"; BBC, "Nigerian Child Bride 'Poisons Groom'"; Voice of America, "Nigerian Child Bride Accused of Killing Husband."

26. Mbiti, *African Religions and Philosophy*, 1.

Ray, in his erudite work—*African Religions: Symbol, Ritual, and Community*—discusses some African "religious traditions in terms of [their] broad unifying themes . . . "[27] Therein, Ray acknowledges that intense diversity and profound similarity prevail in African religious life. Nimi Wariboko pointedly reminds us that both Islam and Christianity drew their adherents from African ethno-religionists.[28] Thus, the existence of African ethno-religious dimension is an irrefutable fact, but insofar as contemporary violence orchestrated by the religious axis of Nigeria's history is concerned, Islam and Christianity remain the principal sides of the religious historical coin that is undeniably linked to the violence. Thus, our focus on the two—Islam and Christianity in Nigeria's religious history.

We review, first, Islam in northern Nigeria and the role of Usman Dan Fodio's jihad and, second, Nigeria's Islamist violence and the emergence of Boko Haram. The *al-majiri* phenomenon and its challenges and contribution to Islamist violence takes third place in our review of Nigeria's religious history. The last four subsections focus on Christianity in Nigeria's religious history. Given that our fieldwork delineated three principal church denominations in Northern Nigeria (COCIN, ECWA and EYN) worst-hit by Islamists-orchestrated violence, a short historical background of the emergence of these church denominations within Nigeria's religious landscape is also fitting.

2.2.1 Islam in Nigeria and Usman Dan Fodio's Jihad

The entry of Islam constitutes the first side of the coin of Nigeria's religious history linked to contemporary violence. Islam preceded Christianity in Nigeria. Originally, through trade and merchants Islam found its route into northern Nigeria. Toyin Falola observes that it was through the Kanem-Borno empire that Islam first found its foot in today's Nigeria.[29] Sir Alan Burns highlights that the armies of the Kanem-Borno ruler in the twelfth century received military support from Tunis in order to subdue most of the regions in the Sahara under its empire.[30]

Islam was introduced during this early contact between the Kanem-Borno rulers and the Muslim powers in North Africa. Historians widely maintain that sufficient evidence demonstrate that Islam began to spread to

---

27. Ray, *African Religions*, x.
28. Wariboko, "Christian-Muslim Relations and the Ethos of State Formation," 63.
29. Falola, *Violence in Nigeria*, 24.
30. Burns, *History of Nigeria*, 55.

the Sahel (regions south of the Sahara) beginning from the eleventh century.[31] The Kanem empire was ruled by *Mais* or kings of the Saifawa dynasty established by nomadic Berbers called the Zaghawa. These nomads came from North Africa and established the Saifawa dynasty in a region north of Lake Chad. But when the Kanem empire began to decline owing to wars, the Saifawa dynasty fled from Kanem to Borno and established its capital at Gazargamu within the Borno region in today's Nigeria.

Rulers in the Saifawa dynasty with their roots and connections to North Africa were Muslims. Thus, they based their government on Islamic law and way of life. Being the dominant power at that time, Islam began to percolate into the Hausa hinterlands, first among the elites. The first Hausa ruler to convert to Islam was Yaji of Kano—one of the Hausa city-states, and this was in 1370.[32] Gradually, other Hausa city-states rulers followed in Yaji's steps turning also to Islam. It was, however, during the reign of King Idris Aloma that many of the ruling class in Hausa city-states professed Islam. King Idris Aloma is regarded to be the most renowned of all the Saifawa rulers.[33] Herbert R. Palmer underscores the fact that even though the kings of Borno professed Islam, it was not until the reign of King Idris Aloma (1571–1603) that majority of "the notable people became Muslims."[34] The Borno empire reached the zenith of its power during Aloma's time, but after his demise, the empire began declining during the seventeenth and eighteenth centuries.[35] From Borno, Islam spread to Hausa city-states in today's Northern Nigeria. Following the decline of the Borno empire, the Fulani rose to power by the beginning of the nineteenth century. It was at this turn in history that Usman dan Fodio emerged in the scene.

Ibraheem Sulaiman, in his *A Revolution in History: The Jihad of Usman Dan Fodio*, presents a Muslim's perspective on dan Fodio's life and impact on Islam's history in Northern Nigeria.[36] Mervyn Hiskett, on his part, simply tells the story describing Usman dan Fodio's life and context while avoiding unwarranted interpretations, in his volume *The Sword of Truth*.[37] From the historical accounts, it is evident that Islam became forcefully entrenched in northern Nigeria through Usman dan Fodio's jihad (1804 -1808). Usman

---

31. Hogben, *Introduction to the History of the Islamic States of Northern Nigeria*, 50; Falola, *History of Nigeria*, 29.

32. Falola, *History of Nigeria*, 29.

33. Hogben, *Introduction to the History of the Islamic States of Northern Nigeria*, 49.

34. Palmer, *Sudanese Memoirs*, 18; Kenny, "Sharīa and Christianity in Nigeria," 338.

35. Hogben, *Introduction to the History of the Islamic States of Northern Nigeria*, 49; See also: Kenny, *Spread of Islam through North to West Africa*, 132–43.

36. Sulaiman, *Revolution in History*.

37. Hiskett, *Sword of Truth*.

dan Fodio led his companions to fight and overthrow rulers of Hausa city-states instilling and establishing Islamic rule of law. These city-states became forcibly unified under the Sokoto Caliphate. Dan Fodio's jihad occasioned the shedding of lots of human blood on the grounds of instilling Islamic reform and revolution. Hiskett describes the terrain, the armies, and the battles of dan Fodio's jihad.[38] Sulaiman, on his part, gives the account of dan Fodio's declaration of jihad, its commencement, and the laws that guided it.[39] In that account, Sulaiman presents dan Fodio's war manifesto (*Wathiqat ahl al-Sudan*) wherein the following were stipulated:

> 1. To fight against an unbelieving king who has never in his life declared 'There is no deity but Allah', and to take the reins of government from him.
>
> 2. To fight against an unbelieving king who declares 'There is no deity but Allah' for the mere purpose of satisfying the established custom of the country but who in reality does not profess Islam, and to take the reins of government from him.
>
> 3. To fight against an apostate king who abandons Islam and reverts to unbelief, and to take the reins of government from him.
>
> 4. To fight against an apostate king who outwardly remains within the fold of Islam but who, nevertheless, syncretizes the practices of Islam with the practices of unbelief (like most of the Hausa kings), and to take the reins of government from him.[40]

These were the grounds upon which dan Fodio embarked on his jihad leading to the blood flow of many lives in the regions within today's northern Nigeria. Following the jihad, Muslim leaders from among the companions of dan Fodio were installed as Emirs of the conquered Hausa city-states. They came under the authority of the Sokoto Caliphate of which dan Fodio himself was the Shehu and the commander of the faithful, and later succeeded by his son, Muhammad Bello.

In Virginia Comolli's research (2015), she focuses on the Nigerian Islamist group that self-identifies itself as "Jama'atu Ahlis Sunnah Lidda'awati w'al Jihad,"[41] which the global media refer to as Boko Haram and of which we will discuss more later. Comolli, first, outlines a brief historical survey of Islam in Nigeria, tracing its pre-British colonial history in Nigeria,

---

38. Hiskett, *Sword of Truth*, 81–104.
39. Sulaiman, *Revolution in History*, 122–38.
40. Sulaiman, *Revolution in History*, 124.
41. *Jama'atu Ahl as-Sunnah li-Da'awati wal-Jihād* is a better orthography for the transliteration.

particularly as Usman dan Fodio unified the majority of the various northern Nigerian Hausa-Fulani city-states under the singular banner of Islam. She outlines how this came about.

> Up until the nineteenth century the region now known as northern Nigeria was dominated by city-states and kingdoms whose leaders were largely drawn from the Hausa ethnic group. Internecine and internal wars were the norm as kings constantly tried to expand their dominions . . . Whereas Christianity and Islam are by far the two most dominant faiths in Nigeria, Islam has a much older heritage in the region. In fact, the history of Islam in Nigeria dates back to the fifteenth century when the rulers of the Hausaland converted to Islam . . . The Fulani preacher Usman dan Fodio, considered to be the founder of Islam in Nigeria, made it possible for this 'new' faith to spread across the northern part of Nigeria *through his call to wage holy war against the infidels in 1804.*[42]

Thus, the Sokoto Caliphate dominated what is today's northern Nigeria until the coming of the British in the nineteenth century. Roman Loimeier, who "has built an impressive expertise on Muslim societies in sub-Saharan Africa"[43] observes that "the Sokoto empire with its emirates dominated the political and economic development of the [northern Nigeria] subregion in the nineteenth century."[44] The emergence and spread of different *maḏāhib* (Islamic schools of thought) accompanied Islam's spread in northern Nigeria. The phenomenon of conflict between different Islamic *maḏāhib* undoubtedly introduces further complexities into contemporary religious-orchestrated violence in Nigeria. The phenomenon of conflict within the house of Islam in Nigeria reflects similar scenario that prevailed during Usman dan Fodio's time, which ultimately resulted to his jihad against Hausa city-states who, themselves, were also Muslims.

Falola and Loimeier independently outline the historical development of the major Islamic groups in northern Nigeria and their push for various reforms. Falola notes that there exists some power struggle between the different Muslim factions in northern Nigeria. Such struggles have often led to "violence among the divided Muslim communities."[45] For his part, Loimeier points to four major Islamic factions in northern Nigeria—the Qādiriya, the Tijāniya, the Yan Izala and the Shi'ite. The Qādiriya and the

42. Comolli, *Boko Haram*, 13. Emphasis in italics is mine
43. https://www.uni-goettingen.de/en/123856.html.
44. Loimeier, *Islamic Reform and Political Change in Northern Nigeria*, 3.
45. Falola, *Violence in Nigeria*, 227.

Tijāniya are Sufi brotherhoods. Both were engrossed in serious conflicts pre-Nigerian independence era, but toward the end of the 1970s and following the rise and attack of Abubakar Gumi's emerging group, the Yan Izala, the Qādiriya and the Tijāniya united against the Yan Izala—which they considered a common enemy.[46] Abubakar Gumi, who founded the Yan Izala group, began his fight against the two Sufi brotherhoods—Qādiriya and Tijāniya—in 1978 through grassroots movement.

Later, the Sufi brotherhoods fought back accusing Gumi of various misappropriation and wrong teachings—among which include: "practicing *tafsīr* in a self-styled fashion, basing his interpretation on his own views instead of the Sunna, giving *zakat* to the wrong persons, destroying the peaceful coexistence between Muslims and non-Muslims . . . falsifying *ḥadīths*, and monopolizing the mass media with evil intentions."[47] Loimeier's conclusion after a careful examination of historical facts is that "the realization of political, social, and personal ambitions was an important motivating factor"[48] that underlines the various religious conflicts.

Another element of Nigeria's religious history intrinsically connected to contemporary violence in the country is the institution of Islamic law—the *Shari'a* legal system. This remains an issue in some states in northern Nigeria. It is an issue of debate in view of the glaring fact that within those states that opted for the installation of Islamic law despite Nigeria's secular constitution, there exists indigenous non-Muslims. Joseph Kenny traces the historical root of Islam and the institution of the *Shari'a* legal system in northern Nigeria beginning from the pre-colonial times up to Nigeria's second republic.[49] As Kenny points out, before Usman dan Fodio's jihad began in 1804 even though most of the kings of the city-states in northern Nigeria had submitted to Islam, they nevertheless did not prevail upon non-Muslims to submit to Islamic rituals, but rather tolerated traditional ethno-religious rituals depending on necessities of circumstances.[50]

According to Ibraheem Sulaiman, Usman dan Fodio's major contention was with the majority of the leading class who alongside African ethno-religious practices professed and practiced Islam—a situation dan Fodio could not bear.[51] In view of such prevailing syncretistic practices,

---

46. Loimeier, *Islamic Reform and Political Change in Northern Nigeria*, 19–103 and 207–324.
47. Loimeier, *Islamic Reform and Political Change in Northern Nigeria*, 210.
48. Loimeier, *Islamic Reform and Political Change in Northern Nigeria*, 328.
49. Kenny, "Sharīa and Christianity in Nigeria."
50. Kenny, "Sharīa and Christianity in Nigeria," 339.
51. Sulaiman, *Revolution in History*, xvii.

Usman dan Fodio charged the kings of the city-states to adopt the strict Islamic law in their respective domains. Following the refusal of the latter, dan Fodio embarked on his jihad, conquering the kings who ruled the majority of the Hausa city-states.

It is important to note that the Hausa-city states against whom dan Fodio initially directed his jihad were Muslim rulers (although the jihad later was also extended to city states that were not under Muslim kings). In dan Fodio's war manifesto (already pointed out above), his contentions included:

> To fight against an unbelieving king who declares 'There is no deity but Allah' for the mere purpose of satisfying the established custom of the country but who in reality does not profess Islam, and to take the reins of government from him . . . [and]

> To fight against an apostate king who outwardly remains within the fold of Islam but who, nevertheless, syncretizes the practices of Islam with the practices of unbelief (like most of the Hausa kings), and to take the reins of government from him.[52]

The definition of "an unbelieving king who declares 'There is no deity but Allah'" (that is the *shahāda*) remained dan Fodio's. The *shahāda* (declaring 'There is no deity but Allah') is the basic formulary of submission to Islam. Thus, one major difference between the rulers of the Muslim Hausa-city states and dan Fodio was that the latter did not consider the practice of Islam of the former as pure and in conformity with strict Islamic laws.

Dan Fodio's jihad introduced large scale shedding of human blood into the equation of Islam in what is today northern Nigeria. It orchestrated the death of many people under the guise of seeking to establish the Islamic legal system—*Shari'a*. Undisputedly, it is, however, evident that the installation of a religious law as the *Shari'a* has remained powerless in deterring northern Nigeria Muslims (being fallen humans like others humans on earth) from engaging in those conducts which the Islamic law and tenets were intended to deter. One may, therefore, pose the question: Why so? Ibraheem Sulaiman, in his assessment of Usman dan Fodio's ideals, posits,

> For any movement with the goal to bring about a society superior to the one it abhors and challenges, the test of its sincerity lies in its ability to develop individuals who are the very embodiment of its message and vision. No movement can be taken seriously if the character and behaviour of the core members do not set them clearly above others. That was precisely the challenge before the Shehu [that is Usman dan Fodio]. His responsibility was not only to preach the truth and to attack evil, but more

---

52. Sulaiman, *Revolution in History*, 124.

fundamentally, to produce men and women who believed in that truth and whose general disposition was a clear testimony to their faith in that truth.[53]

Usman dan Fodio's dream—to preach and attack evil—was noble according to human standards. He sought to overcome the prevailing evil he found in the society and went about training his companions to embody truth as he knew it in Islam. Dan Fodio's miss-step lies, however, in his resort to jihad that resulted to human bloodshed. We will attempt an assessment of dan Fodio's jihad in a later section in this chapter. But before we get there, we underscore another important point which Thaddeus Byimui Umaru highlights in his volume *Christian-Muslim Dialogue in Northern Nigeria*. Umaru maintains that until the present time "Nigeria continues to grapple with the question of Islamic sharia amidst economic, social, political, and ethnic problems."[54] Currently twelve states in northern Nigerian have adopted the Shari'a legal system (see Map 2 below), and the issue continues to generate debate and remains a potential source of conflict.

Map 2: Map of Nigeria: States Worst Hit by Boko Haram and the Sharia States of Northern Nigeria

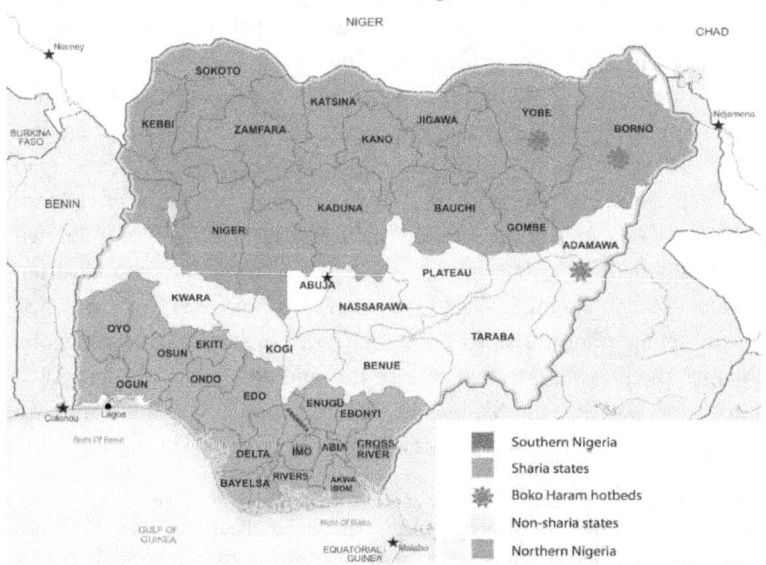

http://www.opendoorsuk.org/persecution/worldwatch/nigeria/documents/nigeria-report-48.pdf p. 9. (Accessed: May 7, 2016)

---

53. Sulaiman, *Revolution in History*, 32.
54. Umaru, *Christian-Muslim Dialogue in Northern Nigeria*, 69.

Before turning our flashlight on Christianity in Nigeria's religious history, it is fitting to briefly survey two other elements that are intrinsically linked to Islam in northern Nigeria, namely: Islamist violence in Nigeria and the emergence of Boko Haram; and the *al-majiri* phenomenon with its complications, challenges and contribution to violence.

2.2.2 Nigeria's Islamist Violence and the Emergence of Boko Haram

Before engaging in the discussion, it is fitting to first indicate that what has become a quasi-proper name—Boko Haram—is a colloquial Hausa expression derived from the Hausa word for book (*boko*) or western education and the Arabic word حرام—*harām* meaning forbidden, prohibited, interdicted. In Hausa language, '*boko haram*' will literally mean 'western education is prohibited, or is an abomination, not permitted.' As we have already indicated, Boko Haram, self-identifies as *Jama'atu ahl as-Sunnah li-Da'awati wal-Jihād* which is a transliterated Arabic name meaning "People Committed to the Propagation of the Prophet's Teachings and Jihad." Indeed, a plethora of scholarly articles and volumes has already been written on Boko Haram and its emergence.[55] In view of that, we do not deem it needful to recap the details that are already published. Instead we focus our discussion here on the primary developments.

It is also fitting to point out that Boko Haram is not the first Islamist insurgent group that Nigeria has witnessed since independence. There has been "a plethora of radical Islamist groups [that have] over time emerged in northern Nigeria."[56] In the 1980s, Nigeria experienced waves of violence and heinous atrocities undertaken by the Islamist insurgent group known as Maitatsine led by Muhammad Marwa. At that time, the then Nigerian President—Alhaji Shehu Shagari (1925–2018), a northern Nigerian Muslim—did set up a Commission of inquiry headed by Justice A. N. Aniagolu. Nathaniel Danjibo reports that one of the findings of Justice Aniagolu's Commission was that the Maitatsine Islamist group had a "build-up of a contingent of armed disciples, especially the Almajeris [sic]."[57]

---

55. Adesoji, "Boko Haram Uprising and Islamic Revivalism in Nigeria"; Agbiboa, "Boko-Haram and the Global Jihad"; Campbell, "Boko Haram"; Mantzikos, "Boko Haram Attacks in Nigeria and Neighbouring Countries"; Azumah, "Boko Haram in Retrospect"; Comolli, *Boko Haram*; Muir, "Nigeria's Boko Haram Pledges Allegiance to Islamic State"; Odo, "Boko Haram and Insecurity in Nigeria"; Kendhammer and McCain, *Boko Haram*; Thurston, *Boko Haram*.

56. Comolli, *Boko Haram*, 25.

57. Danjibo, "Islamic Fundamentalism and Sectarian Violence," 11. Discussion on the *al-majiri* phenomenon is taken up in the next subsection, 2.23.

An Overview of Nigeria's Political and Religious Histories 39

Irrespective of whatever differences in ideology and their respective *modus operandi*, political Islam remains a denominator that is common to Islamist violent groups in Northern Nigeria. In Comolli's own words: "they have instrumentalised religion as a political tool since their emergence,"[58] a position which Roman Loimeier also maintains.[59]

In the previous segment, we highlighted Usman dan Fodio's jihad as part of Nigeria's religious history. Historically, dan Fodio's jihad is considered to have introduced acute violence into the equation of Islam's presence in Nigeria. On the one hand, many northern Nigerian Muslims consider it as the foundation upon which Islam in northern Nigeria became established and they revere dan Fodio for such achievement. On the other hand, dan Fodio's jihad can also be viewed as the bedrock upon which subsequent Islamist violence in northern Nigeria and the surrounding regions is posed. Muslims in northern Nigeria consider Usman dan Fodio as the most influential Muslim leader in Nigeria that Islam has produced till date. That affirmation is, of course, not only owing to dan Fodio's jihad but also to his passion to establish puritanical Islam and to eradicate syncretistic *mélange* of Islam with African ethno-religious practices.

Northern Nigerian Muslims, therefore, proudly identify themselves with dan Fodio's legacies. J. N. Paden rightly asserts that dan Fodio's jihad which northern Nigeria Muslims considered as a "purification movement . . . has set a Nigerian precedent for claiming that rulers may be considered non-Muslims if they are unjust, even though the rulers may consider themselves Muslims."[60] This assertion is made knowing that dan Fodio's jihad was essentially a war he waged against leaders of Hausa city-states who on their part were also Muslims. Hence, this legacy, which dan Fodio left behind, continues to impact both the identity that northern Nigerian Muslims want to be known for and also inspires Islamist reformers who aspire to tread on the path dan Fodio walked.

The Nigerian Islamist group which self-identifies as *Jama'atu Ahl as-Sunnah li-Da'awati wal-Jihād*, but globally know as Boko Haram, is the most prominent form of dan Fodio-inspired Islamist aspiration in Nigeria today. The religiously-driven context of acute violence the group creates epitomizes an *Islamist-acute-violence context* in contemporary Nigeria. Geographically, this context is prevalent in northeastern states of Nigeria (see Map 2 above), but its sociopolitical and economic impacts are not limited to those states alone. There are reports of Boko Haram attacks in

58. Comolli, *Boko Haram*, 25.
59. Loimeier, *Islamic Reform and Political Change in Northern Nigeria*, 328.
60. Paden, *Muslim Civic Cultures and Conflict Resolution*, 57.

states other than northeastern states of Nigeria. Besides the thousands of lives that have been lost and over a million Internally Displaced Persons (IDPs), villages and towns have been ravaged, farmlands, barns and telecommunication equipment destroyed. Included among these devastating impacts is also the abduction of school girls from two secondary schools in Chibok and Dapchi towns respectively in Borno and Yobe States. One can only imagine the trauma all these have birthed at all levels.[61] The context posed by this religiously-driven context is glaring, challenging, and obviously linked to religious identity.

Regarding religious identity, Virginia Comolli, in reference to Paden,[62] notes that "[r]eligious identity has been defined as a determinant of, among other factors: orientation towards authority; tendency to conflict; and the possibility of conflict resolution."[63] Whereas on a local level villages and individual Muslims may self-identify themselves with a particular stream of Islamic school of thought or ideology, *par contre*, on a national level it has been suggested that "religious identity [is] being defined more along the broader lines of faith and politics."[64] Thus, Islamists' identity with dan Fodio's jihad inspires and drives them to re-enact similar history. We maintain, therefore, that dan Fodio's jihad is the bedrock upon which subsequent Islamist violence in northern Nigeria is posed.

In addition to aspirations to re-enact dan Fodio's legacy, there are other external factors which also contribute to the emergence of Islamist violence in northern Nigeria. Comolli makes that point, highlighting the clandestine involvement of Saudi Arabia through the provision of support to the likes of Abubakar Gumi, who aligns, as will be expected, with Wahhabi Islam with roots in Saudi Arabia.[65] Saudi Arabia's tacit support and sponsorship of violence for the propagation of Islam in other lands is undeniable. It introduces a dimension of political complexity in Nigeria's context.

As per how interference and support from Islamic powers and groups external to Nigeria impinges upon the contemporary Islamist violence in Nigeria orchestrated by Boko Haram, Ghanaian-born scholar of world

---

61. For some reports, and articles on Boko Haram's brutal attacks, impact and ripples, see "Threat to the Entire Country"; Maiangwa, "Killing in the Name of God?"; Agbiboa, "Boko-Haram and the Global Jihad"; Awojobi, "Socio-Economic Implications of Boko Haram Insurgency"; Nkwede et al., "Effects of Boko Haram Insurgency"; Mulders, "Crushed but Not Defeated."

62. Paden, *Muslim Civic Cultures and Conflict Resolution*.

63. Comolli, *Boko Haram*, 21.

64. Falola, *Violence in Nigeria*, 69; Comolli, *Boko Haram*, 21.

65. Comolli, *Boko Haram*, 20,23. Comolli cited Harnischfeger, *Democratization and Islamic Law*, 74–75.

Christianity and Islam, John Azumah, in an excellent retrospective assessment, concludes that "Boko Haram has to be seen and tackled as part of the global jihadist franchise and not a local Nigerian problem."[66] Azumah's conclusion is indeed incontestable seeing that countries sharing boundaries with Nigeria in the north and northeast—Cameroun, Chad and Niger Republic—are all experiencing in certain degrees the aftermaths of the conflict engendered by Boko Haram.[67] Furthermore, in March 2015 many international credible media reported Boko Haram's declaration of their allegiance to the Islamic State in Syria and Iraq (ISIS). The BBC News online, for example, reported the words of Boko Haram's leader, Abubakar Shekau, who purportedly said: "We announce our allegiance to the caliph [referring to Abu Bakr al-Baghdadi, the leader of ISIS] . . . and will hear and obey in times of difficulty and prosperity. We call on Muslims everywhere to pledge allegiance to the caliph."[68] This supports Azumah's conclusion that the conflict created by Boko Haram is far from being a local Nigerian concern. On the contrary, there is an international dimension to it.

The vision to establish Islam as the ruling polity lies at the core of the emergence of Boko Haram. As we have already noted, a number of published works[69] have highlighted the historical emergence of Boko Haram as an Islamist organization. One element underlying the emergence of Boko Haram's acts of violence that, hitherto and as far as I am aware, has not yet appeared in literature, is worthy of mention. This element was flagged by one of the participants in my research interviews.

Muhammed Yusuf is credited to have been the leader who brought Boko Haram to the limelight. There were other leaders before him, but Yusuf's charismatic leadership propelled the group toward growth and ultimately into violence. My interview with a former scholar of Islam, Ahmed[70] who personally knew Muhammad Yusuf and some of his companions, revealed some background elements that heightened Boko Haram's resort to violence.

66. Azumah, "Boko Haram in Retrospect," 50.

67. Mantzikos, "Boko Haram Attacks in Nigeria and Neighbouring Countries"; Campbell and Page, *Nigeria*, 8.

68. March 7, 2015.

69. Adesoji, "Boko Haram Uprising and Islamic Revivalism in Nigeria"; Agbiboa, "Boko-Haram and the Global Jihad"; Campbell, "Boko Haram"; Odo, "Boko Haram and Insecurity in Nigeria"; Comolli, *Boko Haram*, 45–84; Okoro, "Terrorism and Governance Crisis."

70. In accordance with the informed consent for my research, pseudonyms for all interviewed participants are used. "Ahmed" had a personal encounter with Jesus in Saudi Arabia, where he was an associate professor of Islamic law at a university there, and following that encounter, he currently identifies himself as a follower of Jesus.

According to Ahmed's account, Yusuf started a private school and a mosque in Maiduguri, in Borno State, northeast of Nigeria. Enrollment into the school grew. On the other hand, there was another top private school in Maiduguri owned by the son of Al-Kameni, the Emir of Maiduguri. This school incorporated Western method of education in their curricula. Yusuf's school, on the contrary, rejected all forms of Western education and taught puritanical Islamic ethics and standards. Thus, Yusuf's school attracted many Muslim parents to enroll their wards, thereby, depleting the enrollment for the school owned by the Emir's son. With the political connections of the Emir's son, Ahmed said Yusuf's "school was closed by the government . . . and then he [Yusuf] started teaching in the mosque" (D4#1 Ahmed:182–183). This stirred up rivalry between Yusuf and the Emir's son but the latter leveraged on his father's political position using government forces to oppress Yusuf's efforts and work. Ultimately, Yusuf's extrajudicial killing in 2009 spiraled into chains of Boko Haram-orchestrated violence. This account reveals the manner in which the actions of political and government figures exacerbate violence.

Another political element connected to Boko Haram's emergence and actions of violence is also worthy of mention. Femi Falana, a senior advocate in the Nigerian legal guild in a 2014 article pointed out that a former Governor of Borno state, Alhaji Ali Modu Sherriff, recruited a militia group composed of over a million youth of whom majority of them "gravitated towards religious extremism."[71] John Campbell, who was formerly the United States ambassador to Nigeria (2004 to 2007), in his recent book co-authored with Matthew T. Page, *Nigeria: What Everyone Needs to Know*, highlights this same point stating that in 2003 in Borno State, "politicians recruited armed thugs to rig elections and intimidate political opponents."[72] These thugs were radicalized Muslim youths who later joined Muhammad Yusuf and became part of Boko Haram's force. We discuss this phenomenon of recruiting Muslims youths in the next section because it is a pertinent religious element linked to Islamic structures, ubiquitous in Muslim regions in northern Nigeria, and contributes to Nigeria's religiously-orchestrated violence.

---

71. Falana, "How Ex-Gov Modu Sheriff Sponsored Boko Haram."
72. Campbell and Page, *Nigeria*, 13.

2.2.3 The Al-majiri Phenomenon: Challenges and Contribution to Islamist Violence

Al-majiri is a Hausa word derived from the Arabic word *al-muhajir* (migrant, plural in Arabic is *al-muhajirun*, and the plural in Hausa is *al-majirai*). The original meaning of the word is one who had immigrated (away from the comfort of home) into another land, city or place in search of knowledge—often to acquire Islamic education and Quranic instruction. Muslims generally affirm it is hinged on the concept of the early Muslims who migrated from Mecca to Yathrib (later renamed Medina).

The *al-majiri* concept is a way of re-enacting and identifying with the prophet of Islam's migration during the *hijra*. "This sentiment prompted [the most radical young Muslims at the Alhaji Muhammadu Ndimi Mosque in Maiduguri] to isolate themselves, replicating Prophet Mohammed's *hijra* when he left Mecca to retreat to Medina..."[73] In northern Nigeria, the *al-majiri* system of education is one meant, usually for young male children (often between the ages of 4 and early twenties)[74] who enroll in a Quranic school in cities away from their home under the tutelage of an Islamic teacher and master (*mālam*, plural *mālamai* in Hausa). They roam the streets begging and combing the waste bins seeking for food they could garner to feed themselves.[75] The parents of these *al-majirai* send them away without any form of sustenance. Their masters task them to bring in a certain amount of money or food which they receive from their daily mendicant street life. This system of *al-majiri* education is called *al-majirci* in Hausa.[76]

Virginia Comolli evokes the part that "the . . . almajiri syndrome"[77] plays in regard to the emergence of Islamist insurgent groups in northern Nigeria. In Nigeria, it is a widely known fact that *al-majirai* are ubiquitous in northern Nigerian cities and towns. There exists a complexity and a complication that the *al-majiri* phenomenon introduces, not only into the education of young children in northern Nigeria, but also into the framework of Islamist insurgency and much of politically motivated violence in that region of the country. Danjibo observed how evident it was that the leader of the Maitatsine group, "[Muhammad] Marwa[,] exploited the dwindling economic situation and the Almajeri [sic] system and was able to attract

---

73. Comolli, *Boko Haram*, 26.
74. Hoechner, *Searching for Knowledge and Recognition*.
75. Danjibo, "Islamic Fundamentalism and Sectarian Violence," 15.
76. For further studies on *al-majirai*, see: Taiwo, *How Colonialism Preempted Modernity in Africa*, Hoechner, *Searching for Knowledge and Recognition* and Mahmud, "Almajiri."
77. Comolli, *Boko Haram*, 25.

large followers amongst the commoners, who, unable to afford the basic necessities of life, became die-hard patriots of the sect and Marwa himself."[78] The same is true of Muhammad Yusuf and Boko Haram.

Because these children are abandoned to what ought to have been a place of acquiring knowledge (the Quranic *madrasas*) at the mercy of their masters (*mālamai*), they become vulnerable tools for those inclined to violence, for they use them to achieve their objectives—the use of violence, arson and other forms of societal disturbance to score points of control, for religious or political authority. Comolli asserts, "there is a well-established body of literature[79] that breathlessly identifies the *almajirai* as the critical mass behind social disturbances . . . ."[80] Danjibo attests that "a good number of almajirai . . . come from very wealthy homes but are subjected to the mendicant way of life . . . Parents, society and the government do not find it disturbing that the almajirai roam in the streets. *It often makes them vulnerable to social vices including being a ready-made army that can be recruited to perpetrate violence.*"[81]

It is evident, therefore, that the ubiquitous presence of and readily available *al-majirai* provide a standing army easily recruited by Islamist insurgent founders or leaders. These *al-majirai* are homeless. Their Quranic *madrasas* are their only points of reference. They could be referred to as street kids and children at risk. They are not only at risk in regard to their own very lives, but also in regard to the entire society. It would seem as if *al-majirai* have no aspiration for their own very lives. Little monetary offers leave them at the wimps and caprices of the insurgent recruiting apparatus, and then turns them into an army ready to strike and instill terror. There is sufficient evidence that these *al-majirai* receive little monetary offers from Islamic insurgent recruiters in order to be used as tools for violence. Danjibo, narrated the account of an *al-majiri* in a hospital in one of the major cities in northern Nigeria (Kaduna) who had lost a limb in a violent encounter. When the boy was interviewed, he said: "why has this happened to me. Now I have lost my life because of N200."[82] The same *al-majiri* who was questioned avowed that many of his colleagues were offered some money in order to "perpetrate violence."[83]

---

78. Danjibo, "Islamic Fundamentalism and Sectarian Violence," 6.

79. There are only a few references to the "body of literature" inferred to by Comolli.

80. Comolli, *Boko Haram*, 72.

81. Danjibo, "Islamic Fundamentalism and Sectarian Violence," 8. Emphasis in italics is mine.

82. Danjibo, "Islamic Fundamentalism and Sectarian Violence," 16. The market value of N200 (two hundred Naira) was equivalent to about 1 US dollar at that time.

83. Danjibo, "Islamic Fundamentalism and Sectarian Violence," 16.

Thus, neither the Muslim authorities nor the Nigerian government pay meaningful attention to the menace that the *al-majiri* phenomenon poses not only to the lives of these children at risk, but also the society. The Nigerian church, on its part, has stood aloof in regard to this matter. To my knowledge, Nigerian Christians have not made much effort to engage this societal complication and challenge. It would seem that for Nigerian Christians, the *al-majiri* phenomenon is regarded as "it is not our problem. It is the Muslims' cup of tea."[84] But events of, not only the Maitatsine insurgent crisis of the 1980s, but more pertinently also the havoc unleashed by Boko Haram since 2009 have shown that the matter is not just the "Muslims' cup of tea."

Thus, we argue that the Nigerian church can become proactive both in engaging Nigerian Muslim leaders and in seeking ways to bring about transformation of the *al-majiri* phenomenon. We further maintain that the Islamist or Jihadist movements together with their insurgent violence and terrorist activities further compound the challenge of the church's task of participating in Jesus's liberating mission. For the Nigerian context, the challenge is further compounded in northern Nigeria, not only by the *al-majiri* phenomenon, but also by a failure of political probity. There is, therefore, no doubt that the *al-majiri* phenomenon is complex, challenging, contributes to, and fuels Islamist jihadism in northern Nigeria.

Having surveyed the pertinent elements linked to Islam in Nigeria that contribute to violence, which form the first side of the coin of Nigeria's religious history, we now turn to the second side of that coin—Christianity in Nigeria's history, particularly its encounter with Islam in northern part of the country.

2.2.4 Christianity in Nigeria's Religious History

The second side of the coin of Nigeria's religious history pertains to the entry of Christianity. In regard to the history of the implanting of the church in Nigeria, which both African and Western church historians have well documented,[85] Western missionaries followed the model used by their colonialist compatriots. Western missionaries (from Europe and North America) operated with the same worldview as their colonialist compatriots, though

---

84. The expression "it is your cup of tea" is a widely known expression used in Nigeria to mean: "that concerns you." In other words, "it is your business, it does not concern me."

85. Ajayi, *Christian Missions in Nigeria*; Kalu, *History of Christianity in West Africa*; Hastings, *Church in Africa 1450–1950*; Sanneh and Carpenter, *Changing Face of Christianity*.

their goals differed. Falola maintains that "Christianity in Nigeria is part of the larger history of European incursions into Africa, beginning in the mid-fifteenth century."[86] Boston University-trained scholar and one of the pioneers and founding faculty of the ECWA Theological Seminary in Jos, Nigeria, Yusuf Turaki, notes that colonialism and the mission enterprise in Nigeria from the West were "both . . . products of the same society sharing the same socio-political roots, worldview and ethos but each differs from the other in its primary motif, goals, objectives and interests . . ."[87]

Initially, Christian missionary efforts were primarily focused on the southern and middle-belt regions of Nigeria, understandably because of access through the waters (the Atlantic and the two major rivers—the Niger and the Benue) which provided navigation routes. This initial effort to establish Christianity in Nigeria did not, however, yield feasible enduring results. It was not until the mid-nineteenth century that the ventures of Western missionaries, following in the shadows of their colonialist compatriots and the trend of abolition of slave trade, led to an emergence of enduring Christian presence. Beginning from the southwest toward the southeast, then to the middle-belt region, and later to the north, Christianity spread.[88] Historians have outlined the means and methods employed by missionaries to achieve the rapid spread of Christianity in the southern regions of Nigeria,[89] some of which include the establishment of schools and hospitals.[90] The missionary efforts of the Church Missionary Society (CMS)—the missionary apparatus of the Church of England—led to the implanting of what is today the Church of Nigeria (Anglican Communion), which accounts for about 23 percent of all Anglicans worldwide.[91] The Roman Catholic, Presbyterian, Methodist and Lutheran Churches in Nigeria all locate their roots in the missionary toil of European and North American missionaries. Whereas the Church of Christ in Nations—which was until 2013 the Church of Christ in Nigeria (COCIN) is the product of the missionary labors of the Sudan United Mission,[92] on its part, what is today the Evangelical Church Winning All—originally the Evangelical Church of West Africa (ECWA) —remains the fruit of missionary labors

---

86. Falola, *Violence in Nigeria*, 31.

87. Turaki, *Introduction to the History of SIM/ECWA in Nigeria*, 6.

88. Falola, *Violence in Nigeria*, 32–36.

89. Ajayi, *Christian Missions in Nigeria*; Ekechi, *Missionary Enterprise and Rivalry in Igboland*; Tasie, *Christian Missionary Enterprise in the Niger Delta*; Ekechi, "Medical Factor in Christian Conversion in Africa."

90. Falola, *Violence in Nigeria*, 33.

91. Johnson and Zurlo, "World Christian Database."

92. Boer, *Missionary Messengers of Liberation in a Colonial Context*.

of the Sudan Interior Mission (SIM).[93] Similarly, the missionary efforts of the Church of the Brethren from the United States yielded what we have today as Ekklesiyar Yan'uwa a Nigeria (EYN).[94] It is noteworthy to mention that church denominations like COCIN, ECWA, EYN, and Lutherans were geographically concentrated in northern Nigeria. Given that this study delineates COCIN, ECWA, and EYN as representative of the church in Nigeria worst-hit by Islamists-orchestrated violence, a brief historical background of their placement on the Nigerian Christian map is fitting. So we attempt a succinct historical review of their emergence in the following three subsections. Among these three denominations, ECWA was the first to be placed on the landscape of Nigeria's religious history, followed by COCIN, and lastly by EYN. Our review of these three denominations below follows that order.

2.2.5 A Succinct Review of the Emergence ECWA in Nigeria

The Evangelical Church Winning All, which until 2011 was the Evangelical Church of West Africa (ECWA), is a product of the missionary labors of the Sudan Interior Mission—currently known as Serving in Missions (SIM). Two Canadian missionaries (respectively of Scottish Presbyterian and English Salvation Army immigrant roots), Walter Gowans and Rowland V Bingham, and one American, Thomas Kent of Congregational Baptist roots, were the first pioneers of SIM. Even though the first missionary attempt (1893–1895) was met with deaths, discouragement, dangers of disease, of inclement weather, and of slave-raiding armies, SIM did not give up what one of SIM pioneers, Rowland V. Bingham, called the "Burden of the Sudan."[95] Yusufu Turaki provides an introductory historical account of the establishment of SIM and of the conglomeration of churches—ECWA—resulting from the SIM missionary enterprise in Nigeria.[96]

Truly, the pioneer history of ECWA and SIM will be incomplete without mentioning the role that Mrs. Margaret Craig Gowans (the mother of Walter Gowans) played. It was Mrs. Gowans who had the overwhelming burden for the Sudan. She prayed fervently that the gospel gets to

93. Turaki, *Introduction to the History of SIM/ECWA in Nigeria*.

94. Durnbaugh, *Brethren Encyclopedia*, vols. 1–2; Church of Christ in the Sudan, *Fifty Years in Lardin Gabas*.

95. Bingham, *Seven Sevens of Years and a Jubilee*, 14, 17; Turaki, *Introduction to the History of SIM/ECWA in Nigeria*, 73–76. The Sudan (formerly written as Soudan) was the name used to refer to sub-Saharan Africa in the late nineteenth century, particularly African regions southwest of the Sahel. It should not be confused with the country known today as Sudan.

96. Turaki, *Introduction to the History of SIM/ECWA in Nigeria*.

sub-Saharan Africa, and she shared the burden with people. Turaki notes that Margaret's son, Walter, "was the first of the three SIM Pioneers upon whom God laid the burden of the unreached millions in Africa's Central Sudan."[97] Through Mrs. Gowans's passionate sharing of her burden for the unreached peoples of the Sudan, both Thomas Kent (a friend and fellow student with Walter Gowans at New York Missionary Training College[98]) and Rowland Bingham also caught the vision.

The trio—Walter Gowans, Thomas Kent, and Rowland Bingham—arrived Lagos, Nigeria, on December 4, 1893.[99] Shortly after their arrival, Bingham took ill with malaria. Gowans and Kent went ahead of Bingham northward arriving in Bida (in today's Niger State in northern Nigeria) on May 6, 1894. However, Gowans took ill later and died on November 17, or 18, 1894 "in the little town of Girku [sic]."[100] Thomas Kent was also struck with malaria and died in Bida on December 8, 1894.[101] Both Gowans and Kent died barely a year after their arrival to the field of their call and mission. Rowland Bingham himself who had been struck down with malaria on their arrival in Lagos, remained in Lagos and later recovered. Bingham did not learn of the death of his two colleagues until early 1895.

In May 1895, he returned to Canada via England. On his arrival in Canada he broke the news of Thomas and Walter's death. On hearing this news, Walter's mother, Margaret, was silent for a while and then said: "*Well, Mr. Bingham, I would rather have Walter go out to the Sudan and die there, all alone, than have him home today, disobeying his Lord.*"[102] Bingham attests that Mrs. Gowans "ever prayed that God would raise up a witness in the little village where her boy [Walter] had died."[103]

---

97. Turaki, *Introduction to the History of SIM/ECWA in Nigeria*, 46. See also "SIM/ECWA History" at http://www.ecwa.org.ng/about-ecwa/ecwa-history/.

98. New York Missionary Training College (founded by Dr. Albert Benjamin Simpson) was later renamed Nyack College. See "A Little History" at https://www.nyack.edu/site/who-we-are/. Dr. Simpson also founded the Christian and Missionary Alliance. http://www.bu.edu/missiology/missionary-biography/r-s/simpson-albert-benjamin-1843-1919/.

99. Bingham, *Seven Sevens of Years and a Jubilee*, 18.

100. Bingham, *Seven Sevens of Years and a Jubilee*, 24. Ghirku is a small town in Niger State of Nigeria, about 40 miles (65 km) from Zaria Turaki, *Introduction to the History of SIM/ECWA in Nigeria*, 55.

101. Bingham, *Seven Sevens of Years and a Jubilee*, 24; Turaki, *Introduction to the History of SIM/ECWA in Nigeria*, 55.

102. Bingham, *Seven Sevens of Years and a Jubilee*, 25. Emphasis in italics is Bingham's.

103. Bingham, 28.

One would think that the glaring dangers of disease and death, inclement weather, lack of easy means of transportation, and even slave-raiding armies would have deterred Bingham from pursuing the vision and the "Burden of the Sudan." On the contrary, he later returned to the field in company of other pioneers. The first attempt (1893–1895) was met with stiff challenges and discouragement. The second attempt (1899–1900) was unsuccessful in terms of establishing a mission station. A third attempt in 1901 resulted to the first mission station located in Pategi in today's Kwara State of Nigeria and Dr. Andrew P. Stirrett was instrumental in that venture alongside four other pioneers (E. A. Anthony, Alex W Banfield, Albert Taylor, and Charles Robinson). From Pategi, several mission stations saw the light of day in many parts of northern Nigeria. The conglomeration of churches born from the labors of SIM missionaries adopted the legal name Evangelical Church of West Africa (ECWA) in 1954 at the first General Assembly held in Egbe (in today's Kogi State) with thirty-one delegates from seven districts in attendance.[104] Today, ECWA in Nigeria boasts of about 6 million members in more than 6,000 local churches administratively organized in 84 church districts. The majority of these churches are located in northern Nigeria.

One pertinent fact from the above short overview pertains to the resilience and resoluteness of the SIM pioneers amid the dangers of death—a fact that resonates with the thesis of this study. Dangers of disease and death did not deter them. Retrospectively, the sacrifices coupled with obedience that those pioneers made (some with their own lives) have no doubt produced resurrection life in many millions today in Nigeria and continue to do so beyond the frontiers of Nigeria where indigenous Nigerian ECWA missionaries continue in the steps of their founding fathers and mothers.

2.2.6 A Succinct Review of the Emergence COCIN in Nigeria

As we have already pointed out above, COCIN as a church denomination in northern Nigeria resulted from the labors of the Sudan United Mission (SUM) missionaries who arrived Nigeria by the autumn of 1904. COCIN history attests that four pioneer missionaries from the British branch of the SUM were the founding fathers of the denomination in Nigeria, namely Karl W. Kumm, Ambrose Bateman, John Burt and Lowry Maxwell. "The four pioneer missionaries . . . led by Dr. Karl Kumm arrived Wase, [a] town in Plateau State of Nigeria on 8th. October 1904."[105] The SUM was made

---

104. Turaki, *Introduction to the History of SIM/ECWA in Nigeria*, 274.
105. Gutip, *Church of Christ in Nations*, 24.

up of Christians from different "denominations in Europe, North America, South Africa, Australia and New Zealand."[106]

As the need to reach the various ethnic peoples in the Nigeria middle-belt region and the Plateau became more evident to the SUM pioneers, they mobilized more workers to join the work from Norway, the United States, and Canada. This led to the opening of mission stations in a number of districts in northern Nigeria—particularly in Langtang (among the Taroh people); in Wukari, Donga and Dampar (among the Jukun people); and in Bukuru (among the Berom people). Missionary labors later produced churches, schools and hospitals. The missionaries' search to meet the health needs that beleaguered the population led to the establishment "of dispensaries in most of the Mission stations, the establishment of Vom Christian Hospital in early 1923, Molai Leprosy Settlement in 1938 and Mangu Leprosy Settlement (now Mangu COCIN Hospital and Rehabilitation Centre)."[107] The health centers doubled as evangelization centers. Conversions to Christ led to formation of local churches. Growth was initially gradual until the early 1970s when, following the end of the civil war (1967–1970), the revival that occurred in most parts of Nigeria touched COCIN churches as well leading to exponential growth. Nanwul Gutip documents some of the narratives and testimonies of the mass movement of people turning to Christ witnessed in COCIN churches, particularly in Gindiri and Boi areas in Plateau State.[108]

The SUM missionaries were inclined to involve local believers right early. So, as early as 1934, an educational center was established in Gindiri to train local leaders. Today, Gindiri town in Plateau State hosts the COCIN Theological Seminary alongside other educational training schools. One important fact that must be mentioned in this very brief history of the emergence of COCIN pertains to the locations of their missionary enterprise in northern Nigeria. Jan Harm Boer observes that "the missionary community focused increasingly on the need to halt Islam's onward march. . . This circumstance became the very *raison d'être* of the S.U.M, according to Kumm's explanation to the government"[109] of Lord Lugard who aided Islam. In pursuance with the SUM policy of involving local followers of Jesus and in consonance with postcolonial trends, Nigerian local

---

106. Gutip, *Church of Christ in Nations*, 24, 26; see also: Boer, *Missionary Messengers of Liberation in a Colonial Context*, 112–18.

107. Gutip, *Church of Christ in Nations*, 3, 70–85.

108. Gutip, *Church of Christ in Nations*, 226–42.

109. Boer, *Missionary Messengers of Liberation in a Colonial Context*, 115.

members of "COCIN took over all the responsibilities of the SUM British Branch of the Mission in Nigeria"[110] on January 1, 1977.

The churches planted through the work of the SUM missionaries became incorporated under the name Ekklesiyar Kristi a Sudan (EKAS) in 1958. The name was later changed to Ekklesiyar Kristi a Nigeria (EKAN). In 1975 another name change followed, becoming the Church of Christ in Nigeria (COCIN). And most recently, following their expansion beyond the frontiers of Nigeria, they adopted the name Church of Christ in Nations in 2013—retaining the acronym, COCIN. Currently, COCIN has about 4 million members in 2,500 congregations. COCIN is a member of an ecumenical organization in Nigeria called Tarrayar Ekklesiyoyin Kristi a Nigeria (TEKAN), which stands for the Fellowship of the Churches of Christ in Nigeria—a conglomeration of fifteen church denominations in northern Nigeria with about 30 million members. TEKAN member churches jointly own the Theological College of northern Nigeria (TCNN) founded in 1958 and currently located in Bukuru, Plateau State of Nigeria.

2.2.7 A Succinct Review of the Emergence EYN in Nigeria

Harold Stover Kulp (1894–1964) and Albert David Hesler (1897–1969) were the pioneer missionaries of the Church of the Brethren from the United States who "arrived in Nigeria [o]n December [29,] 1922 to establish the first mission work of the Church of the Brethren in Africa."[111] They located their first mission station in Garkida (in today's Adamawa State), having arrived there on March 8, 1923.[112] The following year, 1923, their spouses (respectively Ruth Royer Kulp and Lola B. Helser) joined them. They first started their work using medical mission and education and in 1924, Dr. Homer L. Burke and his spouse, Marguerite, joined and opened a dispensary in Garkida. Dr. Burke was the first physician in the mission but other medical workers joined the team later.

Harold and Ruth started learning Bura, "writing some books in Bura language such as Bura Primer, Bura Hymn Book and Bura New Testament etc."[113] On June 13, 1924, Ruth Kulp gave birth to a child who died a few days later. Ruth herself also died. Isheku P. K. Mbaya writes that before Ruth's death, she "recited Psalm 23, and then prayed, 'Oh God! Save Bura

---

110. Gutip, *Church of Christ in Nations*, 2.
111. Durnbaugh, *Brethren Encyclopedia*, 2:936.
112. Durnbaugh, *Brethren Encyclopedia*, 1:305.
113. Mbaya, "Brief History of the Coming of the Church of the Brethren Mission into Lardin Gabas," 5.

people.'"[114] Harold Kulp remarried on December 8, 1926 to a Scottish lady, Christiana Masterton, whom he met at an "International Conference on the Christian Mission in Africa held in . . . Belgium."[115]

In 1927 four local believers were baptized in Garkida. That same year, the Kulps moved to Dille and later to Lassa—both being Margi[116] towns. Other missionaries who joined were stationed in other locations. A leprosarium was founded in 1929 at Virgwi, near Garkida and was managed by Dr. R.L. Robertson (a physician from the Church of the Brethren in the United States).

Following some differences between Kulp and Hesler, Albert Hesler with his wife, Lola, joined "the Sudan Interior Mission (SIM) [in 1936]."[117] Helser and Lola moved on to serve with SIM. In 1950, a pastors' training school started in Chibok (in today's Borno State) enrolled 6 local believers for training. With the training of local believers, the number of local pastors and churches grew. With time, the pastor's training school could no longer meet the growing need for local pastors and church leaders. In response to that growing need, Kulp Bible College was established, initially located at Mubi, and later moved to Kwarhi, to train more pastors and local leaders. (Today, the institution is Kulp Theological Seminary). Increasing growth of churches led the General Assembly of the Church of the Brethren in the United States to approve on June 26, 1972 the independence of the mission in Nigeria, which at that time had about 18,000 members in a number of congregations scattered around northeastern Nigeria.[118] Such move resulted in further growth and planting of new churches. A decade later (1982), according to *The Brethren Encyclopedia*, the number of members reached 40,000 worshipping in 96 organized congregations. In addition to these congregations were 400 preaching stations.[119]

The first official name of EYN was Ekklesiyar Kristi a Sudan, Lardin Gabas (EKAS, Lardin Gabas)—meaning Church of Christ in the Sudan, Eastern District. "Later the name was changed to *Ekklesiyar 'Yan'uwa*

---

114. Mbaya, "Brief History of the Coming of the Church of the Brethren Mission into Lardin Gabas," 5.

115. Mbaya, "Brief History of the Coming of the Church of the Brethren Mission into Lardin Gabas," 5.

116. The Margi is a people group found in today's Adamawa and Borno States of northeastern Nigeria. See http://www.oxfordreference.com.fuller.idm.oclc.org/view/10.1093/acref/9780195337709.001.0001/acref-9780195337709-e-2523 or the "Margi" entry in Gates and Kwame, *Encyclopedia of Africa*.

117. Durnbaugh, *Brethren Encyclopedia*, 1:596.

118. Biu, "Brief History of Evangelism in the Eastern District," 106.

119. Durnbaugh, *Brethren Encyclopedia*, 2:937.

a Nigeria [EYN], a Hausa phrase meaning 'Church of the Brethren in Nigeria.'"[120] According to one of the participants interviewed during our fieldwork, EYN has hundreds of congregations organized in 50 district church councils[121] with about 160,000 members. EYN is reckoned to have suffered the greatest loss of both lives and property to Boko Haram attacks. Estimates of EYN members who have lost their lives to Boko Haram attacks or as a result of the aftermath of such attacks stand at about 10,000. About 26,000 are reckoned to have fled to Cameroun as refugees, and many more thousands are in Internally Displaced Persons' (IDP) camps. More than half of EYN church buildings were burnt and many have been abandoned. In 2014, Boko Haram occupied the large property in Kwarhi where the EYN Headquarters, the Kulp Theological Seminary, and other educational institutions are sited and proclaimed it the headquarter of their caliphate. The property was recovered by the intervention of the Nigerian military in 2016.

Having briefly reviewed the emergence of the three church denominations that form the focus of our study, we now underline three principal elements pertinent to our study that are common to these three denominations. First, all the three are geographically located in northern Nigeria where Islam previously had sought to establish control. On the one hand, ECWA and COCIN first focused their missionary enterprise around the middle-belt region to check further penetration of Islam beyond the boundaries it had gained. EYN on the other hand, was planted in some regions within the old Borno province where the hold of Islam was firmly established. Thus, after the departure of the colonialists and following post-colonial trends, Islam's expansionist agenda was seemingly resuscitated—a fact that began to birth the rise of Islamists and subsequently their acute violent activities. It is no doubt, therefore, that Jesus's followers living in these northern regions have remained the primary victims of Islamist acute violence more than those in southeastern and southwestern Nigeria.

The second element we underline pertains to contextuality and it is not only common to the three churches we reviewed but to all mainline churches in Nigeria that are products of Western missionary enterprise. They uncritically adopted ecclesial forms, structures and theology bequeathed to them by Western missionaries who came with their cultural accouterments not part of the gospel. Local cultural forms and structures,

---

120. Durnbaugh, *Brethren Encyclopedia*, 1:307.

121. One EYN District Church Council (DCC) must have at least 5 Local Church Councils (LCC) and each local council must have not less than 100 baptized communicants. On average, a local church council will be made up of about 500 people counting children (Yohanna, D3#3: 34–45).

for example, were *mal-vu* by missionaries and they discouraged the locals from their use. Practically, little or no efforts were expended to incarnate or contextualize the gospel into Nigerian multi-cultural contexts. For example, hymns and canticles of Western origin were translated and used—thus missing out the wealth of contribution that the triune God had implanted in Nigerians' cultures well before the arrival of the missionaries. This only reflects how theology was also done and passed on to Nigerian churches planted by Western missionaries.[122]

Lastly, but not the least, local leadership resulted to growth and establishment of more and more local churches. Following de-colonization, Nigerian Christians majorly from the south began to engage in missionary enterprise themselves. Post-civil war revival in Nigeria ultimately birthed indigenous mission organizations. Thus, from the mid-1970s, Nigerian Christians themselves began to spearhead Christian missionary work in parts of Nigeria whose population consists of either majorly Muslims or adherents to African ethno-religions. Calvary Ministries (CAPRO) is a vivid example of such African indigenous missionary movement among others.[123]

From the above observations, we maintain that Nigeria's political and religious histories must, therefore, be put into consideration in seeking to construct peacebuilding-contextual theology in Nigeria's context of violence. Doing so will inform an appropriate conceptualization of a peacebuilding-contextual theology germane for Nigeria's context of acute violence. At the end of our review of Nigeria's political history we held that the legacy left behind by the British colonial masters serves as one of the salient reasons behind some politically-orchestrated violence because some Muslims hold that power must remain in the hands of northern Nigerian Muslims who are committed to establishing and maintaining Islam as the dominant religion and the Shari'a legal system. Thus, such a political legacy combines with Nigeria's religious history to form a tapestry creating contexts of violence in the country. It is rational at this point that we elucidate some of these contexts of violence, each of which is a context that begs for peacebuilding.

---

122. Mbefo, "Theology and Inculturation," 393–403.

123. The CAPRO story has been locally published in Nigeria CAPRO Media, *From Africa to the World*; See also: Fiedler, *Story of Faith Missions*, 375–77; Oyebamiji, *Travail and Triumph*, and has been the focus of a couple of unpublished dissertations or masters' theses in Nigeria.

2.3 CONTEXTS OF ACUTE VIOLENCE FOR PEACEBUILDING IN NIGERIA

There are some examples of peacebuilding contexts created by a combination of political and religious factors within Nigeria's landscape. Before we expound on these contexts, we first pose the question: what is context, and what contexts are to be considered for peacebuilding, particularly in Nigeria's context? "*Context* . . . most commonly refers to the environment or setting in which something (whether words or events) exists. When we say that something is contextualized, we mean that it is placed in an appropriate setting, one in which it may be properly considered."[124] Context takes into consideration how perceptions, events, words, approaches, values, dispositions, methods, etc. are weaved together to form a coherent whole. Context, arguably, is akin to German *Sitz im Leben* (setting in life), used in Form Criticism.[125] Contexts can be broad and as varied as weather from one location to another.

When engaging in peacebuilding, both the cultural ambience and socio-religious environment or a *mélange* of both and more should be brought into perspective and married. What applies in a Christian-Muslim engagement in North Africa may not be tenable or applicable in West or East Africa due to the variation in context. To 'copy-paste' what may have been found workable and fruitful in a Euro-American context unto an African context without considering the contextual peculiarities appropriate to the latter will be a misjudgment. Although ideas and methods could be borrowed from a given context, yet their application to another has to put the recipient context into consideration in order to adjust accordingly. Akintunde Akinade rightly observed that ". . . the tendency to strip Christian-Muslim engagements from their contextual situations has led to facile generalizations and hasty conclusions. It is, therefore, imperative to study Christian-Muslim relations as they are experienced indigenously within specific contexts and situations."[126] In view of this, contexts must be taken seriously. What contexts, then, must we consider for peacebuilding-contextual theology, particularly in the Nigeria? The following few paragraphs shade some light.

Christian-Muslim engagement cannot be monolithic. It is as varied as both Christianity and Islam. Evangelical Christian engagement with Sunni Muslims will certainly differ from engagement with Shi'ites, Sufis,

---

124. http://www.merriam-webster.com/dictionary/context.

125. For a simple definition of *Sitz im Leben*, see http://www.oxfordbiblicalstudies.com/article/opr/t94/e1778.

126. Akinade, "Christian-Muslim Relations in Contemporary Nigeria," 399–340.

and certainly Islamists[127] as well. Thus in considering contexts, primary questions such as the following arise: Which stream of Muslims are we seeking to engage in peacebuilding initiatives? What makes their geopolitical and sociocultural setting distinctive, and how could it be factored into peacebuilding initiatives germane to that context? Seeing that these play significant roles in peacebuilding engagement we limit the scope of our contexts for consideration to Nigeria alone. Whatever we are able to glean from Nigeria's perspective, can also be contextually modified and used to suit similar contexts, particularly in Africa.

Insofar as Nigeria is concerned, the first context for consideration is where violence and conflict are connected to Islamic religious-motives. I refer to this context as the *Islamist-acute-violence context* because in all the cases Islamist Muslims remain the leading actors. Such contexts are certainly neither peculiar to Nigeria nor to Africa. The case of contemporary insurgent Islamist groups such are Boko Haram in Nigeria and Al-Shabaab in Somalia are typical African examples. The Islamic State in Iraq and Syria (ISIS) and other militant Islamic religious groups enflaming violence and human suffering fall within this category as well. In *Political Islam: Revolution, Radicalism or Reform?*, Lisa Anderson, looking at the contexts in North Africa and the Middle East, maintains that despotic and authoritarian political regimes breed violence. Islamist opposition movements resort to violence using political Islam as tool. Anderson posits that beyond "the content of putatively Islamic political doctrines [motivating] a willingness to embrace violent means to desired end [lies also the] political circumstances, or institutional environment, that breeds political radicalism, extremism, or violence independent of the content of the doctrine."[128]

Besides Boko Haram already described above, another *Islamist-acute-violence context* is created by Muslim Fulani herdsmen.[129] These Muslim Fulani herdsmen identify themselves as *Miyetti Allah*—an association

---

127. Bassam Tibi distinguishes ordinary Muslims—who are committed to their Islamic faith and want to lead their normal daily lives, from Islamists—who are Muslims driven by their vision of "political order not faith... [and having] an ideology that connects *din* (religion) with *dawla* (state) in a shari'a-based political order" Tibi, *Islamism and Islam*, 1–2. Tibi underscores the fact that: "... all Islamists have a common commitment to a remaking of the world." Islamists consider Muslims who do not share in this view as unpatriotic to Islam, enemies to Islam and enemies of Allah.

128. Anderson, "Fulfilling Prophecies," 18.

129. More on Fulani herdsmen attacks and killings is discussed in chapter 3. See, for example: http://www.cnsnews.com/news/article/amy-furr/muslim-herdsmen-slaughter-dozens-christians-nigerian-village and http://www.christianpost.com/news/new-islamic-terror-in-nigeria-kills-800-christians-muslims-destroyed-16-churches-172554/.

of Fulani herdsmen.[130] Even though some have allegedly posited that the Fulani herdsmen situation is an ethnic conflict between nomadic Fulani pastoralists in search of pasturelands for their cattle and various ethnic peoples in the middle-belt and southeast Nigeria where they have predominantly killed people, yet the fact still remains that these Fulani herdsmen are Muslims who identify themselves as continuing the work of their hero and tribesman—Usman dan Fodio. As we have already pointed out, northern Nigerian Muslims highly value dan Fodio and consider him a Muslim hero of whom no northern Nigerian Muslim is yet to surpass his achievement and contribution toward establishing Islam in Nigeria. The interlude introduced by the British colonial era is regarded as a hiatus to the aspiration to take dan Fodio's jihad down south until Muslims have dipped the Qur'ān into the Atlantic Ocean—an expression by which Muslims mean a complete Islamization of southern Nigeria. The assertions of a renown Nigerian Islamic scholar—Ibraheem Sulaiman whom we cited in our historical review— and others like him are sufficient evidence that indeed this is the dream of many northern Nigerian Muslims, especially the Islamists.

Another Nigerian context for consideration is *ethnic*. *Ethnologue: Languages of the World 16th Edition* lists 527 distinct ethnic language groups in Nigeria. Of these 527 languages "520 are living and 7 are extinct. Of the living languages, 510 are indigenous and 10 are non-indigenous. Furthermore, 20 are institutional, 78 are developing, 351 are vigorous, 27 are in trouble and 44 are dying."[131] Each of these ethnolinguistic groups are characterized by distinctive cultural differences and in some cases these differences may create occasions of conflict. Where animosity and hatred breed between two or more ethnic groups, the prospect of eruption of violence becomes amplified. Nigeria reflects the multiethnic, multicultural and multi-religious nature of most African states. These elements were not factored into the colonial partitioning of African states. In view of this, political power imbalance at the corridors of power, unfair sharing of the national economic resources and lopsided development within any given African state can metamorphose into land mines for violence, conflict, and sometimes war. The Rwandan genocide epitomizes this genre of context.[132]

Violence within intra-religious formations creates another context. A starring example is the contemporary and pervasive Sunni-Shi'ite divide that propels conflicts within majority Muslim lands composed of an unbalanced Shi'ite population as against the Sunnis or vice-versa. That is

---

130. See for example: http://saharareporters.com/2018/01/18/miyetti-allah-privileged-terrorist-organization-rights-activist-slams-buhari-over.

131. https://www.ethnologue.com/country/NG.

132. A number of works have been published on the Rwandan genocide. See for example Wallis, *Silent Accomplice*.

the case in Syria, Iraq and Iran. Nigeria has its own share of this genre of *intra-religious context* between Sunni and Shi'ite Muslims. Clashes in two northern Nigerian cities (Kano and Kaduna) are examples of this Sunni-Shi'ite divide.[133] The Council for Foreign Affairs distills the situation in the following words:

> Sectarian conflict is becoming entrenched in a growing number of Muslim countries and is threatening to fracture Iraq and Syria. Tensions between Sunnis and Shias, exploited by regional rivals Saudi Arabia and Iran, could reshape the future Middle East . . . Sunni-Shia tensions contribute to multiple flash points in Muslim countries that are viewed as growing threats to international peace and security.[134]

The *Niger-Delta context* is yet another context requiring peacebuilding in Nigeria. Subordination of one ethnic group to another is not the only possible cause of ethnic conflicts. Other causes may include: land dispute, social injustice or marginalization and discrimination meted toward one group in distribution of resource and participation in governance. Hence, in peacebuilding efforts in such contexts, the artisans of peace are faced with the challenge of, first, unraveling the hidden causes of violence and conflict, and second, finding pathways that reflect the cultural contextual methods of building peace. A case study on the Niger-Delta region of Nigeria provides a stark example.

Nigeria's Niger-Delta is the country's region rich in crude oil (see Map 3 below). Before the discovery and extraction of petroleum from the region, the people relied on fishing and farming for sustenance. But when multinational oil-drilling companies installed themselves, fishing and farming became hampered and consequently dwindled. Oil spills destroyed the ecological habitats, rendering the waters and farmlands useless for farming and fishing. Whereas the Nigerian government and the oil companies made gains from the crude oil, the local people lost everything. They lost their lands, their fishing waters and their occupation. Neither the government nor the oil companies provided infrastructures and alternative means of livelihood for theses peasants and fishermen and women. A journal article based on research on the environmental damage that has been done in the Niger-Delta region affirms that "[d]ischarges of petroleum hydrocarbon and petroleum–derived waste streams have caused environmental

---

133. Obasi, "New Risks on Nigeria's Shiite Fault Line"; Muhammad, "Four Killed as Youth Attack Shiites in Kaduna."

134. http://www.cfr.org/peace-conflict-and-human-rights/sunni-shia-divide/p33176#!/.

pollution, adverse human health effects, socio-economic problems and degradation of host communities in the 9 oil-producing states in the Niger Delta region."[135] On another note, Bolanle Adetoun, who conducted a case study research on the Niger-Delta and the conflict (resulting from the degradation of host communities) in the region, noted that historically, the conflict situation in the region "reached boiling point in 1990 when the region's elite and its youth formed various organizations to protest against the marginalization, neglect, oppression, and exploitation of their people and resources."[136] He observed that "[l]ack of development has been at the core of the various conflicts in the Niger-Delta, with many issues concerning access to resources and fairness in resource sharing."[137]

Map 3: Map of Nigeria showing the Oil Producing States in Niger-Delta Region

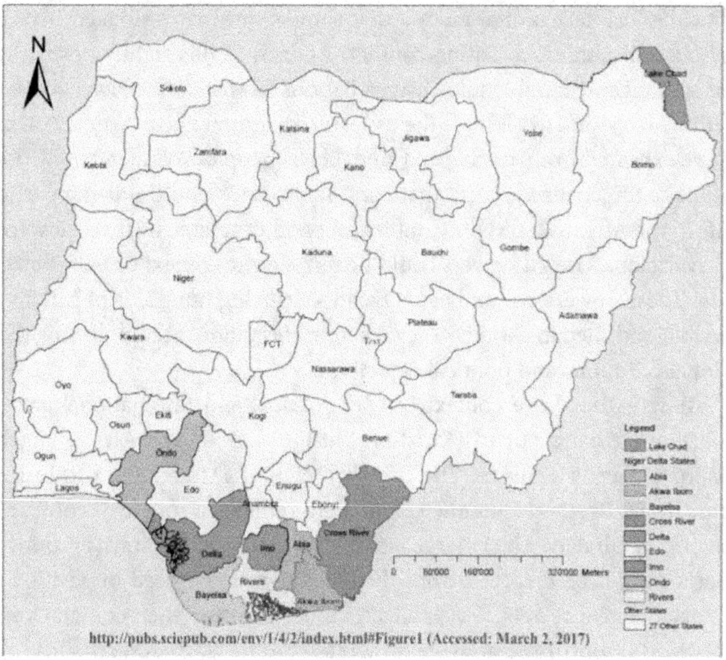

http://pubs.sciepub.com/env/1/4/2/index.html#Figure1 (Accessed: March 2, 2017)

An even more complicated context is one I refer to as *'merchants of death'*. Africa and its states do not perch as lonely birds on the global tree.[138] More often than not, the conflicts and wars within African states

135. Ite et al., "Petroleum Exploration and Production."
136. Adetoun, "Role and Function of Research in a Divided Society," 47.
137. Adetoun, "Role and Function of Research in a Divided Society," 48.
138. The theme of globalization is briefly explored in chapter 3.

are spurred by powerful international actors — whose economic avarice, foreign policies, and interest in Africa's natural and human resources trump their humaneness. Thus, some conflicts in Africa are set within certain political contexts manipulated by these powerful non-African international actors. It is unfortunate that most of these international actors and powers are Western countries occupying permanent positions in the United Nations Security Council. They reflect an Igbo idiom: a man who enters a bush, cuts down branches, and then steps out of the bush path asking "Who is cutting down those branches?" Examples abound. The world is still reeling with the dregs and dangers caused by the trading of Africans as slaves. The Berlin Conference of 1884–1885 where European powers partitioned Africa as morsels of meat and the ensuing colonization remain a source of conflict today in many parts of Africa. In seeking to build peace, there exist political and international factors that should not be overlooked because they play roles in exacerbating conflict. Andrew Wallis rightly posits that: "It is no longer excusable for Western nations to write off African conflicts as 'ethnic wars', and to rekindle the usual racist arguments that such violence is to be expected from 'uncivilized' and 'black' peoples. What, after all, does that make the civilized 'West' that continually arms and trains the participants in the African wars?"[139] Contexts of conflict created by these powerful and avaricious foreign powers could be termed the context of *merchants of death*. These powers do not bat an eyelid sacrificing hundreds of gallons of human blood shed in conflicts they create at the altar of accomplishing their national economic and political objectives.

Why is the above context (set by political and international actors) important? It plays out in Christian-Muslim conflicts in Africa. Nigeria remains a glaring example. The British preferential treatment of Muslims in northern Nigeria during the colonial era remains a source of conflict in the country till date. The emergence of some insurgent Islamists groups in Nigeria cannot be divorced from their reaction to a forced imposition of Western *manière de faire*, which Nigeria inherited from their colonial lords.

In addition to the above enumerated contexts, there exists also the problem of *porosity of borders* between Nigeria and her Francophone neighbors—Cameroun on the east side, Chad by the northeast, and Niger Republic in the north.[140] Freedom Onuoha in his paper, for example, concluded that Boko Haram's "access to sophisticated arms have enabled its fighters to continue to occasionally mount deadly attacks. The porosity of

---

139. Wallis, *Silent Accomplice*, x.

140. Examples of scholarly works on this matter include: James, "Lake Chad as an Instrument of International Co-Operation"; Spencer, "Border and State Insecurity"; Onuoha, "Porous Borders and Boko Haram's Arms Smuggling Operations in Nigeria."

Nigeria's borders is an important factor in its survival, offering it a lifeline to external support from transnational groups in the form of weapons, training, radicalisation, and funding."[141]

We need to reiterate that contexts are dynamic. In other words, contexts change with changing times and circumstances. Therefore, the contexts identified above are by no means exhaustive. Basically, our interest lies more in contexts tied to political and religious factors that exacerbate conflict within Nigeria's landscape. We posit that the contexts of acute violence that impinge upon Africa in general and upon Nigeria in particular, define the necessity to employ contextual means and methods for peacebuilding to help followers of Jesus and participants in God's mission to effectively and contextually engage in peacebuilding given those contexts. We will pursue this argument further in chapter 3. In the meanwhile, we turn to an assessment of the two historical axes of Nigeria's history that together form a violence-tapestry in the country.

2.4 CARREFOUR OF NIGERIA'S POLITICAL AND RELIGIOUS HISTORIES AND THEIR CONTRIBUTION TO VIOLENCE

A *carrefour* is simply an intersection or crossroads. Roads may merge or meet at a carrefour. Carrefour also refers to a marketplace with the sense of a place where, not only sellers and buyers converge but also different merchandise and commodities are brought to converge. I use the term '*carrefour*' here to portray the resulting crossroad that emerges from the political and religious histories profiled above, as well as the ensuing violence they produce in contemporary Nigeria.[142] The goal is to delineate the issues common to the trajectories that cross paths (in this particular case, the political/religious histories and how they contribute to violence).

With that said, we ask: What are the implications of the British colonial infringement into Nigeria's history, and how does that inform religiously-orchestrated violence in Nigeria today? And, as a follower of Jesus, how do I understand the historical undertones of the two sides of Nigeria's religious history? Our response to these questions forms the carrefour of the political and religious histories and their contribution to violence in Nigeria's context. We identify three principal elements related to this carrefour namely: (a) political imbalance created by British colonial legacy and made complex

---

141. Onuoha, "Porous Borders and Boko Haram's Arms Smuggling Operations in Nigeria," 7.

142. I employ this same language in other chapters to also depict the emerging crossroad of Muslims' perspectives of peacebuilding and of similar peacebuilding concepts existing in the Christian tradition.

by ethno-religious diversity; (b) resort to religious teachings and symbols as tools for attaining political and economic goals; (c) the encounter of Islam with Christianity. What follows elaborates these elements.

Firstly, as we saw from our survey of Nigeria's political history, colonial domination and economic interests pushed the colonial powers to construct unnatural "agglomeration of diverse ethnicities and other loosely united groups . . ."[143] Insofar as we know it today, this forced union has not acquired lasting legitimacy from the coercively amalgamated states. The Nigerian context is not only made complex by the "diverse ethnicities and loosely united groups", as Falola points out, but much more so by the religious topography wherein the majority Muslim north is poised against the majority Christian south. Furthermore, religious diversity in northern Nigeria is taken even to a higher degree of complexity because at least "a third of the population [of northern Nigeria is] not Muslim."[144] One of the implications of this fact is the creation of political imbalance, which often stirs agitation for fair participation in governance and for appropriation of national revenue. Obviously, a mere "balkanization" of Nigeria into, say Northern, Southwest and Southeast Nigeria may not become the pathway to peace. So we are confronted with several layers of complexity within the Nigerian context.

The legacy left behind by British colonial rule, therefore, continues to haunt Nigeria, particularly the fact that northern Nigerian Muslims from the Hausa/Fulani stock appropriate unto themselves to be the "poor husband" who must rule and control the substance and means of the "rich wife" of the south. Thus, Nigeria continues to grapple with this political history bedeviled with violence and laced with both political and ethno-religious intricacies.

The second element, which warrants a longer discussion, concerns Nigeria's religious history and the proclivity to resort to religious teachings and symbols as tools for attaining political and economic goals. Insofar as conflict in northern Nigerian is concerned, many Islamic groups in northern Nigeria—whether Islamist or non-Islamist—employ Islamic teachings, arguments and Islam's symbolic system of controlling the masses as tools to attain political and economic goals. As we have already alluded above, dan Fodio's jihad introduced human bloodshed into the equation of Islam's entrance in what we know today as northern Nigeria. It orchestrated the death of many people on the grounds of establishing Islamic reform with Islamic legal system—*Shari'a*. How do we assess this historical element? On the one hand, the installation of the *Shari'a* legal system has remained powerless

---

143. Falola, *Violence in Nigeria*, 52.
144. Bourne, *Nigeria*, 32.

An Overview of Nigeria's Political and Religious Histories 63

in deterring northern Nigerian Muslims (being fallen humans like others humans on earth) from engaging in those conducts which the Islamic law and tenets were intended to deter. Social injustice and corruption continue to prevail within the same fabric of Islamic hegemony which was installed with the hope of eliminating such societal evil.

On the other hand, as we highlighted in our historical review, many northern Nigerian Muslims revere Usman dan Fodio and have high regards for his accomplishment through his jihad of 1804 to 1808. What northern Nigerian Muslims have failed to point out, however, is the implications of the human bloodshed which the jihad produced. Looking beyond the surface, one is poised to ask: What is the aftermath of the blood of innocent people shed during those years and what are the implications of the bloodshed that continue to occur under the guise of religion?

As we briefly noted, the jihad was initially a war between dan Fodio's armies against Hausa city-states, who themselves were also Muslims. The blood of people, especially of innocent non-combatants, women, and children, shed to enforce a cause against the people's voluntary conviction may stand crying out for vindication. It is probable, therefore, that there exists a co-relationship between the spirit[145] of conflict in today's northern Nigeria and the "base animal drives"[146] that spurred and drove Usman dan Fodio's jihad of the early nineteenth century in which thousands of people were killed in the name of religious reform and revolution. Thus, this issue ought not be ignored. The implication pertaining to the blood of people shed during dan Fodio's jihad and similar wars which Muslims in northern Nigeria have embarked upon on the grounds of fighting for the cause of Allah (في سبيل الله *fī sabīli llāhi*) is indeed grave.

In our discussion on Islam in Nigeria, we pointed to Ibraheem Sulaiman's evaluation of Usman dan Fodio's jihad. Sulaiman justifies dan Fodio's *jihad* and affirms it was for the cause of eradicating evil. Human history is, however, replete with evidence that no one defeats evil by resorting to evil. Muslims in northern Nigeria may not have viewed dan Fodio's resort to jihad as a resort to evil to triumph over evil. A retrospective view and the argument of certain contemporary Muslim scholars speak out, however, against the

---

145. By "spirit" here, I mean the unseen spiritual dimensions of spiritual powers working through culture and society which influence both societies and structures. From an African cosmological point of view, we Africans–whether Christians, Muslims or African ethno-religionists–are often aware that there is a spiritual dimension to a lot of things that happen within our material cosmos.

146. Ṭāhā, *Second Message of Islam*, 161. What *Ustadh* Mahmoud Taha refers to as "base animal drives" is what I render as "spirit(s)". Further explanation of Taha's position from which I am drawing upon here in a preliminary manner will be discussed later in chapter 4.

resort to bloodshed. Muslim scholars such as Naṣr Ḥāmid Abū Zayd,[147] have called for tolerance and reinterpretation of the Qurʾān, of Muslim history and of Muslim traditions[148] upon which Muslims base their argument for waging wars for the cause of Allah (في سبيل الله *fī sabīli llāhi*).

From a Christian perspective, Miroslav Volf in his *End of Memory* encapsulates the idea concerning means of defeating evil. Volf maintains that for evil "to triumph fully, [it] needs two victories, not one. The first victory happens when an evil deed is perpetrated; the second victory, when evil is returned. After the first victory, evil would die if the second victory did not infuse it with new life."[149] By infusing the evil in northern Nigerian societies of the nineteenth century with the second victory which that evil needed to be triumphant by way of human bloodshed (jihad), Usman dan Fodio delivered the victory to evil. More than two centuries after dan Fodio's jihad, the trend of human bloodshed continues in today's northern Nigeria. The goal of the present work from a Christian missiological perspective is to point to a pathway—the *staurocentric* pathway—that can make significant contribution toward overturning the table over the evil of violence and bloodshed in Nigeria—especially religiously-orchestrated violence.

Furthermore, we also alluded to Comolli's observation that "Usman Dan Fodio... made it possible for [Islam] to spread across the northern part of Nigeria *through his call to wage holy war against the infidels in 1804.*"[150] One question that begs for response in regard to Usman dan Fodio's jihad[151] is: Could it be the same "base animal drives"[152] that animated the seventh century fathers of Islam (the prophet of Islam and his companions), propelling them to spread Islam with the sword which stirred and supported

---

147. More views of Dr. Naṣr Ḥāmid Abū Zayd (1943–2010) will be discussed in chapter 4.

148. See Naṣr Ḥāmid Abū Zayd's inaugural lecture delivered on May 27, 2004 for Ibn Rushd Academic Chair, for Islam and Humanism, established by the University of Humanistics, Utrecht, The Netherlands (https://ia801405.us.archive.org/12/items/RethinkingTheQurAnTowardsAHumanisticHermeneutics/Rethinking-the-Qur-an-Towards-a-Humanistic-Hermeneutics.pdf); his published book Abū Zayd, *Rethinking the Qurʾān*; and an interview he granted in The Netherlands (https://www.youtube.com/watch?v=n61uo3Gqhy8).

149. Volf, *End of Memory*, 9.

150. Comolli, *Boko Haram*, 13. Emphasis in italics is mine.

151. Sulaiman, *Revolution in History*; Kenny, "Sharīa and Christianity in Nigeria"; Kenny, *Philosophy of the Muslim World*; Azumah, *The Legacy of Arab-Islam in Africa*, 137–221. On the political changes and Islamic reforms in northern Nigeria, see: Loimeier, *Islamic Reform and Political Change in Northern Nigeria*.

152. Ṭāhā, *Second Message of Islam*, 161. As noted earlier, what *Ustadh* Mahmoud Taha refers to as "base animal drives" is what I render as "spirit(s)".

dan Fodio to wage war for the cause of Allah (في سبيل الله *fī sabīli llāhi*)? Evidently we are limited in the scope of our discussion to be in a position to attempt a response to that question here, but certain Muslim scholars, by their argument, are definitely calling for a reinterpretation of the violent language and culture of death which have been widely associated with the Qur'ān and Islamic traditions. Some modern-day Muslim scholars stand in a better position to critically and historically evaluate the impact the age-old Muslim tradition of engaging in war may have on contemporary Muslim insurgents and Islamists. Whatever position one may take, we posit, however, that resorting to bloodshed for the cause of seeking to establish common good betrays and mars the intended good. The substructures upon which things are built impact and influence whatever may become their superstructures, outcomes, and posterity—be it a religious faith, a lifestyle, a career, a physical building, et cetera.

Foundations matter! Jesus Christ's metaphorical statement flashes this truth. He asserted: ". . . for the tree is known by its fruit" (Matt 12:33b).[153] One of Job's friends, Eliphaz the Temanite posited that ". . . those who plow iniquity and sow trouble reap the same" (Job 4:8). The words of Paul to the Galatians also highlights it: "Do not be deceived: God is not mocked, for whatever one sows, that will he also reap" (Gal 6:7). On foundations, one may extend Paul's word to the Corinthians; which contextually refers to material generosity; to be equally applicable to methods people adopt to achieve their desired goals and aspirations. Paul wrote: "[t]he point is this: whoever sows sparingly will also reap sparingly, and whoever sows bountifully will also reap bountifully" (2 Cor 9:6).

It can be argued, therefore, that a kingdom or sphere of control and power established by human bloodshed will always require human blood to be maintained and sustained. In other words, spheres of control built by subjugating its subjects through terror leashed out by violence and human bloodshed may only be sustained by the continual shedding of blood and terror in order to keep the subjects under its control—whether the sphere of control be political or religious. It is also probable that the "base animal drives"[154] that inspired such a movement at its genesis will continue to inspire and revive certain subjects of the movement all along its historical trajectory to reenact, rebuild, and renew the age-old foundations upon which it was founded.

If this premise is anything to be reckoned with, one may then pose yet another question: Could the human blood-letting in northern Nigeria

---

153. See also Luke 6:44 "for each tree is known by its own fruit"
154. Ṭāhā, *Second Message of Islam*, 161.

through Islamists' acute violence be a reflection, continuation, and reenacting of the foundations upon which Islam in northern Nigeria was implanted? Two centuries of historical evidence seem to lend itself to support the hypothesis. Hence, the "base animal drives" of northern Nigerian Islamists may only be answering to the "base animal drives" that inspired Usman dan Fodio, who through human bloodshed (jihad) subjugated northern Nigerian Hausa city-states, unifying them under the Sokoto Sultanate. Put differently, the "spirit" inspiring northern Nigerian Islamists is simply in rhythm with the same "spirit" that inspired Usman dan Fodio, who through his jihad produced a lot of human bloodshed in order to subjugate northern Nigerian Hausa city-states to form the Sokoto Sultanate. The same "drives" or "spirits" that animated Usman dan Fodio continue to inspire Islamists, not only in northern Nigeria, to call for jihad in order to seek to restore the glories of Islam where they feel convinced those glories have waned, are waning, but also to establish it where it is yet to take root. Comolli added:

> Throughout the nineteenth century Fodio's warrior-scholars travelled east, west and south *bringing jihad* and expanding the territory of the caliphate. They managed *to conquer* territories beyond Hausaland expanding to the east into Bauchi and south in the Nupe and Yoruba territories that evolved into emirates that were vassals of the Caliph of Sokoto.[155]

Jesus said: "A disciple is not above his teacher, but everyone when he is fully trained will be like his teacher" (Luke 6:40). Usman dan Fodio's "warrior-scholars" referred to above[156] were only being true to the example they learned from their master—using jihad to conquer territories and subjugating the conquered to the authority of the Caliph (Usman dan Fodio). We posit, therefore, that shedding human blood to impose one's power and control always seems to answer to and engender more bloodshed. War engenders more war. A corollary proposition to this is that blood sacrificially shed for the good of others produces life and peace in people for whose benefit such self-offering is made and even also to benefit of the offender. We will explore this corollary proposition more extensively in chapter 7—*Staurocentric* Pathways. Thus, as war engenders war, conversely, peace will always engender peace.

Under the section sub-titled "*The path to* Sharia" Comolli briefly outlined some of her reflections on religious identity. According to a report

---

155. All emphases in italics are mine. Comolli, *Boko Haram*, 16; Quinn and Quinn, *Pride, Faith, and Fear*, 21.

156. Quinn and Quinn, *Pride, Faith, and Fear*, 21.

in a Nigerian daily, *The Guardian*,¹⁵⁷ the ultimate goal of the present-day Nigerian Islamist insurgent group, Boko Haram, is to Islamize Nigeria and make the nation come under the full governance of the Islamic law. Boko Haram is not the only Muslim group that makes this their goal. Several other Muslim leaders and Islamic groups in Nigeria have voiced the same vision. Toyin Falola points to an example from the words of the Nigerian Islamic scholar whom we have already cited, Ibraheem Suleiman, who asserts that Nigerian Muslims "will be betraying the cause of Islam and the integrity of the Muslim umma if [Muslims] fail to discharge [their] obligations as Muslims. These obligations entail, among other things, the establishment of Islam as a complete polity . . ." ¹⁵⁸ In addition, both Mervyn Miskett and John Azumah independently cite Sulaiman's "The 'Moment of Truth' in Nigeria" wherein the latter posits:

> that all the past efforts to solve Nigeria's problems without reference to Allah, without reference to the sacred Sharia and to Islam, have failed. Islam is Nigeria's most important, most entrenched system of life: to bypass it and attempt to grab the untenable colonial system and institutions is self-defeating and a blatant display of blindness to our very history.¹⁵⁹

In the same article, Sulaiman poses a rhetorical question to historians to assert that Islam is the only solution to Nigeria's problems: ". . . has there ever been more successful, more integrated, more disciplined states and governments in Africa, and on our own very soil [Nigeria], than the Islamic states and the Islamic governments?."¹⁶⁰ Azumah points out the flaw of Sulaiman's assertion and others like him. Azumah maintains that such assertions are based on narratives of the Muslim victors and that "those like Sulaiman and other Muslim activists who laud the jihadist *sharia* are not only uncritical but 'frequently untrue' omitting 'anything contentious or difficult' thereby degenerating into 'propaganda.'"¹⁶¹

In our historical survey of Islam in northern Nigeria, we also highlighted the complications, challenges and contribution of the *al-majiri* phenomenon and how it fuels Islamist jihadism. We posit that the problem of Islamist jihadism is not localized to a particular global region, wherever its

---

157. See Comolli, *Boko Haram*, 182n45 and http://www.theguardian.com/world/2012/jan/27/boko-haram-nigeria-sharia-law.

158. Falola, *Violence in Nigeria*, 69.

159. Sulaiman, "Moment of Truth in Nigeria"; Hiskett, *Sword of Truth*, xvii.

160. Sulaiman, "Moment of Truth in Nigeria," 10; Azumah, *Legacy of Arab-Islam in Africa*, 100.

161. Azumah, *Legacy of Arab-Islam in Africa*, 101.

genesis might be. It has become a pest upon our global village. It has not only distressed and displaced the Yazidis, Christians and Muslims in Iraq and Syria. It is not only a thorn in the flesh of Nigerians, nor does it concern only the Somalis and Kenyans of East Africa. Rather, it touches also those in Paris, France and even those in San Bernardino, California. The problem of heinous and atrocious destruction of lives and property by ISIS, Boko Haram, Hamas, and Al Shabbab militants now plagues our entire world. Anyone who imagines that it happened only to some three thousand New Yorkers on September 11, 2011, or to only some Parisians on November 13, 2015 or to a little above a dozen people at San Bernardino on December 2, 2015; then such one would be grossly mistaken. The next attack might just be next door to one's workplace, or a hotel one frequently uses when he or she travels for a conference or holiday, or the Café one frequently uses. Amos Yong succinctly summarizes this point it as follows:

> We have since [the event of September 11, 2001] realized that the war on terrorism in not just a war fought abroad, but it involves all human beings who care for peace, justice, and freedom. More to the point, the religious, ideological, political, social, and economic struggles in various places around the world have reverberating effects for every one of us."[162]

In that same optic, the Nigerian church of which the majority of believers are found in the south and middle-belt of Nigeria must no longer stand aloof in regard to whatever phenomenon that might only be prevalent in the north, particularly the *al-majiri* phenomenon—which supplies "*a ready-made army that can be recruited to perpetrate violence.*"[163] As we will show from the narrative data of our fieldwork, a few participants acknowledged the importance for the church in Nigeria to become involved in demonstrating care toward *al-majirai*.

Besides, the elements of political imbalance that stirs violence, and the proclivity to resort to religious teachings and symbols as tools for attaining political and economic goals; the third element of the carrefour of Nigeria's political and religious histories pertains to the evident encounter of Islam with Christianity in northern Nigeria. The meeting of Islam with Christianity in northern Nigeria introduced occasions of conflict and violence. Such encounters, having been interlaced with political undertones, introduce degrees of complexity in the equation of peacebuilding in Nigeria's context. We have briefly underscored the point that the Usman dan Fodio jihad was in essence a war between dan Fodio's community who sought to establish

---

162. Yong, *Hospitality and the Other*, 1.
163. Danjibo, "Islamic Fundamentalism and Sectarian Violence," 8.

puritanical Islam and rulers of Hausa city-states who themselves had professed Islam but nonetheless still left room for African ethno-religious practices. Thus, whether it was the encounter with Hausa-city states ruled by Muslim kings or Islam's encounter with Christianity in northern Nigeria, we find occasions of violence orchestrated by Islamists in both scenarios.

Contrastingly, when we consider the Christian side of Nigeria's religious history, we find a different scenario from the historical survey vis-à-vis Islam's side. Christianity entered Nigeria through the southwestern and southeastern parts of the country. Although there were missionary efforts from different Christian denominations/organizations—the Roman Catholic Mission (RCM) of the Roman Catholic Church, the Church Missionary Society (CMS) of the Church of England, the Methodists from the United Kingdom, the Sudan United Missions (SUM), the Sudan Interior Mission (SIM), the Presbyterians from Scotland and the United States, et cetera—yet there were no reports of intra-Christian violence degenerating into bloodshed in the southern regions of the country as it was the case between Muslims in northern Nigeria. Even though there were manifestations of rivalry between certain missionary apparatus (especially between the Roman Catholic missions and the Protestants), yet we find no historical evidence of human bloodshed in the south as a result of the encounter of Christianity with the existing African ethno-religious *status quo*. Where there were clashes between groups in southern Nigeria, such classes were rather tied to ethnic or political differences.

Our argument from both the political and religious histories of Nigeria is that these two axes interact together to form a complex tapestry that births contexts of violence in Nigeria. The question remains: How can the church in Nigeria, as participants in God's mission, address such matters to enact peacebuilding in such a complex context? The present work is poised to attempt a response to this question. But before we delve into that, we need to also survey contextual theology that might inform an appropriate response—peacebuilding-contextual theology—which is the focus of discussion in chapter 3.

3

Contextual Theology and Nonviolence Peacebuilding Ethics

WE BRIEFLY REVIEWED IN chapter 2 Nigeria's political and religious histories and ended with the thesis that these two historical trajectories interact together to form a complex tapestry that engender violence in Nigeria. In this chapter, we explore contextual theology and peacebuilding. Given that Nigeria's political and religious histories form a complex tapestry that births violence in the country, this chapter posits that the contexts of acute violence that beleaguer the country necessitate the use of contextual means and methods for peacebuilding which will help followers of Jesus and participants in God's mission in Nigeria to effectively and contextually engage in peacebuilding.

So this chapter begins with an exploration of contextual theology, explicating its connectedness with contextualization, and then moves on to define contextual theology. Given the impact that globalization creates on contexts, we go on to review very briefly the intersection that occurs when contexts encounter other cultures because of globalization. We further identify the major currents of African contextual theologies, and posit that peacebuilding-contextual theology be welcomed (as a stream) into the house of contextual theologies, not only in African contexts, but also across our globalizing world. Finally, we explore the principal elements that characterize the nonviolence peacebuilding ethics from the Anabaptist tradition, Glen Harold Stassen's Just Peacemaking theory, and the nonviolent resistance philosophy of Mahatma Gandhi and Martin Luther King Jr.

3.1 CONTEXTUAL THEOLOGY AND CONTEXTUALIZATION

Whereas in missiological circles the term 'contextualization' finds predominant currency *inter alia*,[1] 'contextual theology' or 'contextualized theology' is more dominant in the house of theology. In essence, both 'contextual theology' and 'contextualization', however, belong to the same semantic range. Contextual theology is essentially the theology that undergirds the practice of contextualization. It is unnecessary here to review the historical evolution of these terms.[2] It suffices to focus primarily here on its meaning and its possible implications in a globalizing world. Hence, we first attempt a response to two questions: what does contextual theology imply? and secondly what makes contextuality dynamic in view of a globalizing world?

3.1.1 *The Meaning of Contextual Theology*

The close tie between contextual theology and contextualization requires we first understand the latter before we turn to the former. Late Nigerian Catholic theologian, Justin Ukpong (1940–2011), posits that contextualization "... represents a new orientation in Christian practice and expression witnessed in [the 20th] century... [and that the concept] arose out of the realisation that all forms of Christian expression are tinted with the cultural context traits from which they originate."[3] Along the same optic, Darrell Whiteman, Cultural Anthropology scholar and erstwhile missionary in Papua New Guinea, affirms that "[c]oncern over issues of contextualization has been a part of the Christian church from its inception, even though the vocabulary of contextualization dates back only to the early 1970s."[4] Whiteman defines contextualization as being "concerned with how the Gospel and culture relate to one another across geographic space and down through time... [and maintains that it] captures in method and perspective the challenge of relating the Gospel to culture... [and] is part of an evolving stream of thought

---

1. Other terms used in missiological circles akin to contextualization include: inculturation, adaptation, accommodation, and indigenization. Bosch, *Transforming Mission*, 458; Whiteman, "Contextualization," 2.

2. For the historical evolution of the terms "contextual theology" and "contextualization," see Ukpong, *African Theologies Now*; Ukpong, "Contextualisation"; Bosch, *Transforming Mission*, 430–42; Küster, *Theologie im Kontext*, 39–45 cited in Pöntinen, *African Theology as Liberating Wisdom* 2; Pöntinen, *African Theology as Liberating Wisdom*, 2n12.

3. Ukpong, "Contextualisation," 278.

4. Whiteman, "Contextualization," 2.

that relates the Gospel and church to a local context."[5] The advance of the gospel from one geo-cultural sphere to another does not only necessitate theologizing but also contextualizing—that is: doing theology within the context of the recipient geo-cultural sphere. Consequently, theology is done in context. This is the process and practice of contextualization.

Doing theology in context (that is: contextual theologizing) is the brainchild of Christian mission. David Bosch attests that modern-day New Testament scholars now support Martin Kähler's dictum "Mission is the 'mother of theology.'"[6] "Kähler pointed to the fact (1899 and 1908!) that the church in mission over and over again encounters new situations which provoke questions which have never been asked before and which call for answers which are not available in the treasure of the tradition."[7] David Bosch's echo of Kähler's words, "Mission is the mother of theology"[8] implies that theology "always developed as the church crossed frontiers with the gospel."[9] The work of Christian mission will always birth the need to theologize within the sphere of the geo-cultural recipient. This is obvious because mission often entails crossing culture and context. Thus, when culture and context are crossed in order to implant the gospel, then theology necessitated by mission must strive toward a contextual *gestalt* (shape, form).

Having made the point above, here are a few other scholars' understanding of contextual theology. Eminent Roman Catholic missiologist, Stephen Bevans, defines it "as a way of doing theology in which one takes into account: the spirit of the gospel; the tradition of the Christian people; the culture in which one is theologizing; and social change in culture, whether brought about by western technological process or the grass-roots struggle for equality, justice, and liberation."[10] In the house of Western theology, theological insights from non-Western contexts and traditions are sometimes viewed as "contextual"—framed by the contexts from which they originate, whether they be African, Asian, Latin American, Feminist, *Minjung*, Black theologies et cetera. Veli-Matti Kärkkäinen, himself a distinguished Western systematic theologian, however, rightly contends that Western theologies

---

5. Whiteman, "Contextualization," 2.
6. Bosch, *Transforming Mission*, 16.
7. Werner et al., *Handbook of Theological Education in World Christianity*, 706.
8. Bosch, *Transforming Mission*, 16, 501.
9. Werner et al., *Handbook of Theological Education in World Christianity*, 716.
10. Bevans, *Models of Contextual Theology*, 1.

are as contextual as much as theologies originating from non-Western contexts.[11] To buttress his point Kärkkäinen asserts that:

> . . . theology is by nature contextual, whether theologians or theological movements acknowledge it or not. It is not the case that theology done by predominantly white male theologians would be "neutral" while, say, trinitarian theology of the Tanzanian Roman Catholic Charles Nyamiti, who takes as the framework African ancestral traditions, would be "contextual." They are both content-laden—just differently context-laden.[12]

Kärkkäinen is not alone on this. Bevans, for example, maintains that "every authentic theology has been very much rooted in a particular context in some implicit or real way."[13] Timothy C. Tennent, a respected missiologist and scholar, on his part, argues along the same line, asserting that "theological discussion emerging in these new global contexts [that is: the Global South] is not a 'mere squabble' among a bunch of new Christians with strange faces from even strange places, but rather the voices that are transforming the Christian church and changing the trajectory of human history."[14]

From these arguments, anyone who refuses to acknowledge the contextual nature of all theologies and ascribes contextuality to only non-Western theologies, would most likely be prone to contest their validity and authenticity. Wherever contextual theology is denigrated and opposed, the richness of God's creation hidden within the recipient culture stands the danger of extinction and the message of the gospel will often be treated as foreign. It is the recognition of the importance of doing theology in context that led Paul Hiebert (1932–2007), who was a distinguished Professor of Mission and Anthropology, to assert that ". . . importation of cultural practices from outside has made Christianity a foreign religion in many lands, and alienated Christians from their own peoples and cultures."[15] Hence, theology must not be

---

11. Kärkkäinen, *Christ and Reconciliation*, 1:xii. One of the reasons Veli-Matti Kärkkäinen's views stand out on this subject from many of his fellow white male Western colleagues is because of his substantial interaction and teaching among people of non-Western origins. He lived and taught in Asia and continues to teach in many non-Western contexts besides his many masters and doctoral students from Africa, Asia and Latin America at Fuller Theological Seminary, where he currently chairs the systematic theology program at Fuller Seminary's School of Theology.

12. Kärkkäinen, 1:19.

13. Bevans, *Models of Contextual Theology*, 3.

14. Tennent, *Theology in the Context of World Christianity*, 19.

15. Hiebert, "Critical Contextualization," 288.

considered to be "authentic theology"[16] only when it is brewed in the house of Western theology. Ukpong concludes in his article that contextualization "is a means of making the Christian message penetrate the fabric of society. . . [and that] authentic contextualization is the fruit of a genuine encounter between the Christian message and the local context. It is a cultural response to the challenge of the Good News."[17]

Having briefly surveyed above the understanding of contextualization and contextual theology, how do I define contextual theology? We noted above that it is the theology undergirding the process and practice of contextualization. I define contextual theology, therefore, as the theological epistemology and hermeneutics of the message of the gospel woven together with the threads of ethno-cultural, socioeconomic and geo-political habitat where the gospel is implanted. Why ethno-cultural, socioeconomic, and geo-political dynamics? Before we respond to this, it is fitting to underscore that the horizon of the above definition is expandable to suite other spheres other than the implanting of the gospel.

Islam, for example, is known to resist contextualization. Converts to Islam must say the *shahāda* (confession of faith) in Arabic (the language of Islam), and all Muslims irrespective of their language and culture do their *salāt* (prayer) in Arabic. Only seventh century Arab cultural norms in consonance with the early fathers of Islam are considered authentic norms in Islam. Muslims do not, however, deny that contextualization is indeed practiced within its fold in different forms. Folk Islam and the various forms of Islam in Africa (for example: Mouridism in Senegal) are examples of forms of Islam being forced into an African context. Contextualization is not, therefore, unique to implanting the gospel (read: Christianity). Similarly, contextualization can also be applied to other non-religious domains—whereby the bearers of a given message or makers of some commodity wanting to win adherents or gain marketability respectively in a locality and context different from its origin are forced to package their message or commodity (as the case may be) in such a manner that the recipient context can receive, identify with, and/or buy the message or commodity. We have no need to delve into that larger horizon of definition of contextualization since our concern is strictly within the house of Christian theology.

So we return to our question: why include ethno-cultural, socioeconomic, and geo-political dynamics in our definition? These are elements that get woven into every culture. Every culture possesses a cultural form that does not stand alone in itself. Within every culture there exists the linguistic

---

16. Bevans, *Models of Contextual Theology*, 3.
17. Ukpong, "Contextualisation," 285.

characteristics, the social dynamics which inform the economy of life and living within the culture under consideration. And every culture has a geographical habitat within which there exists its political *manière de faire*. In Morocco, for example, we cannot divorce the geo-political elements from the socioeconomic dynamics shaped by its Islamic religious culture. Within Morocco, we find people of Arab origin, the Berbers of the Rif (who speak Tarifit) and of Shilha (who speak Tachelhit), and the Tamazight-speaking Berbers of the central Atlas Mountains.[18] Each of these peoples, although within the same political nation, possesses cultural differences that are not only ethno-culturally and linguistically different, but also possess their respective socioeconomic and geo-political distinctiveness. The implication, insofar as understanding contextual theology and contextualization is concerned, is that the theological epistemology and hermeneutics of the message of the gospel must be woven without neglecting these elements when seeking to implant the gospel in any of the ethno-cultural landscapes. With the above said, we underscore the point that for Christian contextual theology to be authentic, it must remain faithful to the core message of the gospel. Failure of faithfulness to the Scriptures results to syncretism.[19] Insofar as contextual theology is therefore concerned, the gospel must remain the structural framework to which culture and context are woven.

An example will illustrate what we mean by culture and context woven around the gospel. Music, for example, is an art present in every human culture. It is as varied as much as cultures are diverse. Africans do not only possess their own musical rhymes and notes, but also have their own musical instruments created with their God-given materials present within their respective geographical habitats. The Igbos of southeastern Nigeria, for example have instruments such as *ekwe* (slit-drum), *udu* (drum) and *ogene* (gong). The Yorubas of southwestern Nigeria have *gangan* (talking drum) and the Hausas in northern Nigeria are known for their *kakaki* (long brass trumpet). When Western Christian missionaries arrived Nigeria and planted churches they demonized the use of these local instruments in church liturgy and worship, attaching pagan stigma to them. The Anglicans, Methodists, and Presbyterians brought their church organs and bells from England and Scotland, and the Roman Catholics from Rome. Besides musical instruments, clerical garments and elements for the Eucharist were all (and are still being) imported from the land of the white missionaries. Hardly was an attempt made to use the God-given materials, instruments and ideas

18. See: https://www.ethnologue.com/country/MA/languages and https://joshuaproject.net/countries/MO.

19. Ukpong, "Contextualisation," 285; Hiebert, "Critical Contextualization," 289, 295.

resident within the ethno-cultural contexts to weave the theology and liturgy of worship and praxis into the African context. Until today, a Nigerian Anglican church is not considered 'authentically Anglican' in its liturgy if they do not use a church organ to play and sing the hymns composed by Westerners but translated into the local tongues. Much of the richness of God-given talents and ideas that could have become significant contributions to the global Christian community today have seemingly been lost due to the lack of contextual theology relative to liturgical practice in many Western-missionary-implanted churches in Africa. Put differently, the wealth of the contribution that the triune God had implanted in most African cultures well before the arrival of Western missionaries have seemingly been lost in communities where Western Christianity implanted the gospel with Western cultural forms. This well-known fact is only a reflection of how theology was done and passed on to African churches planted by Western missionaries. We assert that it will not be tantamount to syncretistic practice or contrary to the gospel for Africans to use their own local musical instruments, local garments as clerical regalia, or local elements for the celebration of the Eucharist. Were these God-given elements woven into the gospel implanted in the African context, that would have been authentic contextual theology. Moreover, Africans will not have any sentiments of viewing Christianity as foreign or the religion of the white people.

We must underline, therefore, that a critique of Western missionaries' failure to have done contextual theology in Africa does not imply that their labors in Africa were in vain. That will be far from the truth. Many of those agents of mission in Africa actually laid down their lives in one way or the other for simply choosing to leave their homelands to serve in Africa. In fact, Africa was referred to in the nineteenth and the first half of the twentieth centuries as the "Whiteman's [and White-woman's] grave"[20] because of the high mortality rate of westerners in Africa during that period. The sacrifice those heroes of faith made in their bid to be agents of light and transformation must not be denigrated or disparaged on the ground that they failed to contextualize the gospel they brought to Africa. They must, instead, be lauded and hailed for their labors and for the love that compelled them.

With that said, we posit that it is necessary to point out that African cultures and contexts are not islands in themselves, untouched by the wind of our globalizing world. With the confluence of peoples from different cultures and lands in our globalizing world, contexts become dynamic. Hence, we have to look retrospectively—reviewing very succinctly some of the

---

20. Korieh and Njoku, *Missions, States, and European Expansion in Africa*, 128.

elements that shape present-day African contexts within which contextual theology for peacebuilding in contemporary Africa in general, and in the Nigeria in particular, must be articulated and constructed.

3.1.2 Intersection of Contextuality and Globalization

Globalization is a term that has been defined in different ways depending on the perspective from which it is viewed. There are some who are pro- and yet others anti-globalization.[21] Whereas Neil Ormerod and Shane Clifton define it based on "the most common understanding [in regard to] economic and technological structures,"[22] there are others who rather define it from a sociological perspective. On the basis of economics and technology, Ormerod and Clifton define globalization as relating to "modern capitalism and its relationship to process of the internationalization and liberalization of trade and capital, which are empowered by technological developments in communications, travel and commerce."[23] On the other hand, it is defined sociologically as referring "to the expansion of global linkages, the organization of social life on a global scale, and the growth of a global consciousness, hence to the consolidation of world society"[24] or as "*a social process in which the constraints of geography on economic, political, social and cultural arrangements recede, in which people become increasingly aware that they are receding and in which people act accordingly.*"[25]

What is of particular interest to us as far as the present investigation is concerned is the "*cultural*" dimension mentioned by Waters in his definition of globalization. Ormerod and Clifton observed that "[a]s our social organization takes on an increasingly global shape, so too must our culture take on such a shape, to help us make sense of, and direct, our emerging global existence."[26] Hence, in a world that is on a globalizing trail, African cultures and contexts are certainly not left aloof as though they are islands untouched by this wind. Far from that! We should be asking ourselves therefore: What might be the factors one must take into account while studying contextual theology in Africa, particularly in respect to peacebuilding? How does the receding of the constraints on culture placed upon geo-cultural

---

21. It is not needful to go into such discussion here. But for a succinct summary see: Ormerod and Clifton, *Globalization and the Mission of the Church*, 3–5.
22. Ormerod and Clifton, *Globalization and the Mission of the Church*, 4.
23. Ormerod and Clifton, *Globalization and the Mission of the Church*, 4.
24. Leong et al., *Internationalizing the Psychology Curriculum in the United States*, 2; Ajiboye, "Globalization and Africa's Development," 308.
25. Waters, *Globalization*, 5. Emphasis is the author's.
26. Ormerod and Clifton, *Globalization and the Mission of the Church*, 123.

contexts affect our contextual theologizing? Contextual theology, as we have seen above in Bevans's definition of contextual theology, is tied to "... the culture in which one is theologizing; and social change in culture ..."[27] Thus, whatever co-relation that might exist between contextual theology in a given context and the elements of globalization must not be ignored. Such co-relation should be brought into view as we seek the contextual path to peacebuilding. We flesh this out by drawing from an example.

The Igbo people of southeastern Nigeria had cultural ways of building peace with their non-Igbo neighbors in the pre-colonial age. An Igbo dictum says: "*Agbata obi mmadu bu nwanne ya*" (One's neighbor is also his/her brother or sister)."[28] Cajetan Ebuziem maintains that this dictum "summarizes how the Igbo relate to their neighbors or other people of the world ..."[29] Adiele E. Afigbo, late professor emeritus of History at University of Nigeria, Nsukka, writing on inter-group relationship of the Igbos in Nigeria asserted with evidence:

> [T]he most viable model for understanding the inter-group relationship that built up between the Igbo and their neighbours is one that postulates mutual dependence in harmony and equality rather than one that postulates the subordination of one group to the other. In this model the motive force of inter-group relations is free exchange—of ideas, institutions and usages, of goods and services, of populations through migration and marriages ...[30]

But what has become of this ancient Igbo model of inter-group relationship in post-colonial period? Collision with groups in northern Nigeria (particularly the Hausa-Fulani, forcefully Islamized through Usman dan Fodio's *jihad* of the early nineteenth century—a discussion we had in chapter 2) introduced the dynamics of conflict. Afigbo maintains that for the Igbos,

> exchange implies that one gives what one has in plenty and receives what one lacks. In short, people involved in inter-group relationship along the lines of this model do for, or give to, one another what each cannot either do for, or give to himself. This is the case at least for as long as those concerned want cordiality

---

27. Bevans, *Models of Contextual Theology*, 1.
28. Ebuziem, *Doing Ministry in the Igbo Context*, 12:40.
29. Ebuziem, *Doing Ministry in the Igbo Context*, 12:40.
30. Afigbo, "Age of Innocence"; Ebuziem, *Doing Ministry in the Igbo Context*, 12:40.

to be the dominant tone of such inter-group or inter-personal contact.[31]

All through the pre-colonial period the Igbos applied the principle of give-and-take in their inter-group relationships. The encounter with the Hausa-Fulani, whose over-riding aim (as historical events seem to adjudicate) has been forcibly Islamizing their non-Muslim neighbors, introduced different dynamics—that of antagonism and war. Here, what we want to illustrate is that the confluence of culture and context (a sociological dimension of globalization) between the Igbos and the Muslim Hausa-Fulani introduced a dynamic of conflict that now demands a contextual theology for peacebuilding. We refer to this as the intersection of contextuality with globalization.

Another example illustrating this matter relates to contemporary killings in Nigeria by so-called Muslim Fulani herdsmen.[32] Some Nigerians believe there exists a religious agenda of Islamization underlying the murderous acts. Three primary reasons seemingly give credence to such position. The first is that the current Nigerian President—Muhammad Buhari who himself is a Muslim Fulani—has hardly reacted to the killings by Fulani herdsmen until there is a public outcry. The second stems from the monetary compensation which the Kaduna State governor—Malam Nasir El-Rufai (another Muslim Fulani)—allegedly paid to Fulani herdsmen ostensibly to stop them from killing Christians in Southern Kaduna.[33] Thirdly, the government has failed to make arrests of Muslim Fulani people involved in the killings, whereas a Christian leader who spoke openly against the killings and told his congregation to kill any Muslim Fulani person coming into their area was menaced to be arrested by the Nigerian Directorate of State Services (DSS);[34] and southeastern leaders engaging in peaceful agitation for the independence of Biafra, on the one hand, are held in custody without indictment and are classified as terrorists by Muhammad Buhari's government, although, on the other hand, there has been no report or record of arrests of Fulani herdsmen ravaging, killing people in villages, and occupying their farmlands.

---

31. Afigbo, "Age of Innocence."

32. This has been in the news media since the last quarter of 2016. See, for example: http://www.cnsnews.com/news/article/amy-furr/muslim-herdsmen-slaughter-dozens-christians-nigerian-village and http://www.christianpost.com/news/new-islamic-terror-in-nigeria-kills-800-christians-muslims-destroyed-16-churches-172554/.

33. Gabriel, "Genocide in Southern Kaduna."

34. Omega Fire Ministries, *Apostle Suleman Speaks On Biafra, Southern Kaduna Killings*.

How does our second example co-relate with our discussion on globalization? First the Muslim Fulani are a semi-nomadic people and are often on the move in search of grazing fields for their herds. Their search for grazing fields leads them southward of Nigeria in view of drought that continue to menace the entire West African Sahel and the encroachment of the Sahara Desert. The herdsmen graze their cattle on farmlands of people as they move southward. Hence, the drive for economic flourishing and the ease of transportation (both being elements of globalization) pushing them southward occasion "*the constraints of geography on the economic and cultural arrangements. . . to recede*"[35]—not only for the Fulani themselves, but also for the various groups they are encountering beyond their former herding territories. In a globalizing world, therefore, interests collide and crash. Economics is not the only factor to be looked at when evaluating contexts in a globalizing Africa. There are also religious interests and agenda that groups may have which complicate the contexts. The two examples from Nigeria given above are only microcosmic representations of the macrocosmic dimension of what Samuel P. Huntington referred to as *The Clash of Civilizations*.[36]

In Patrick Chibuko's article, he argued that "[p]eace is a prerequisite for authentic and functional globalization . . . [and] is a *conditio sine qua non* for globalization to thrive and achieve its desired aims."[37] It is this need for peace within the varying contexts in Africa that makes imperative the need for such contextual theology, which will help create and install an enduring culture of peacebuilding. In view of Africa's position in our globalizing world the challenge remains, therefore, for participants in God's mission in Africa to confront the challenges of conflicts and create peace cultures through the gospel with a contextual theology for peacebuilding. It is in search for a pathway modeled after Jesus which can position Jesus's followers to face that challenge in Nigeria's context of violence, that this project is set to make contribution. Since it is needful to first understand the current forms of contextual theologies in Africa, we now turn to investigate the current streams of African contextual theologies. Is there any stream among them that can undergird contextual theologizing for peacebuilding? And if there is, can the impact of globalization render such a stream applicable to both African and other global contexts? We will find out.

---

35. Waters, *Globalization*, 5.
36. Huntington, *Clash of Civilizations and the Remaking of World Order*.
37. Chibuko, "Globalization," 6.

3.2 AFRICAN CONTEXTUAL THEOLOGIES AND PEACEBUILDING-CONTEXTUAL THEOLOGY

We have two objectives here. The first is to identify the current streams of African contextual theologies and tangentially what informs each stream. Secondly, we make a case for peacebuilding-contextual theology as a stream of contextual theology needed for African contexts of violence, while outlining the basis for it. Drawing from these two objectives, we then argue that peacebuilding-contextual theology as a stream for African local contexts of violence can also be applicable across global contexts—thus making it "glocal."

3.2.1 Streams of African Contextual Theologies

In his short dissertation on African contextual theologies, Justin Ukpong identifies three principal streams in African theology namely: inculturation theology, South African Black theology and liberation theology. Ukpong asserts that "African inculturation theology simply referred to as African theology" is the most prevalent and is ubiquitous in all regions of Africa.[38] According to Ukpong, what propels this first trend of African theology is "an attempt to give African expression to the Christian faith within a theological framework."[39] This is evidently due to the 'foreignness' of the "Christianity" implanted in Africa, undeniably through the non-contextual missionary approaches and methods of Western agents of mission in Africa. Thus, Africans seek to craft a contextual theology that could be considered germane to the African context and at the same time authentic to the Christian Scriptures. Ukpong maintains that this first stream of African contextual theology relates to establishing creative, constructive and contextual dialogue between theology on one part and African culture and philosophy on the other. Luke Mbefo writing on this same theme with particular reference to the Nigerian context asserts: "The theological motive force seems to be this thesis: if we could reclaim such a cultural originality, we would be able to develop within its structural outlines a theology that is authentically Christian and equally authentically Nigerian."[40]

We can indeed fuse Mbefo's thoughts referred to above with Ukpong's and extrapolate it to apply to Africa as a whole. In other words, African contextual theology, having been necessitated by the foreignness of Western theology implanted by missionaries, implies attempting to craft

---

38. Ukpong, *African Theologies Now*, 4.
39. Ukpong, *African Theologies Now*, 4.
40. Mbefo, "Theology and Inculturation," 394.

an African contextual theology that is authentically African in context and at the same time authentic and faithful to the Scriptures. This is the goal of African contextual theology.

The second stream of contextual theology which Ukpong identifies is the South African Black theology which reflects the African American Black theology. The goal of this trend is to relate the message of the gospel "to the social situation of segregation and oppression"[41] undeniably occasioned by and tied to the issue of skin color. This trend is not ubiquitous in Africa and is regionally limited to South Africa where apartheid was dominant. It is also found in the United States of America among African Americans in view of the segregation, oppression and racial injustice they experience on the grounds of skin color.

The third and last stream Ukpong identified is liberation theology which trifurcates into three tributaries. The first is grounded "on the indigenous socioeconomic system, the second takes after the Latin American model [of liberation theology], and the third involves a combination of elements from both approaches."[42] Whichever tributary is considered in this category of liberation theology; the goal remains the search for "genuine human promotion in the context of the poverty and political powerlessness of Africa. . . "[43]

What has not yet been incorporated among these streams of contextual theologies in Africa is what I call *peacebuilding-contextual theology*. Within Africa there have been widespread conflicts and wars—some, ethno-religious in essence; and yet others political or a complex *mélange* of ethnic, religious and political elements. Some contemporary examples include the continued Islamist violence in Nigeria, the Islamist acts of violence in Sahel Africa, in Eastern Africa and the Horn of Africa, and the Islamist resurgence in North Africa. Among them are also the various civil wars that some African countries have witnessed. Don't these conflicts require a form of contextual theology that African followers of Jesus and participants in God's mission should articulate, construct and craft to undergird contextual peacebuilding practices? Are there no practices of peacebuilding imbedded within African cultures that can be theologically harnessed for articulating contextual theology for peacebuilding? Our position is that the contexts of acute violence that beleaguer Nigeria as a country require the use of contextual means and methods for peacebuilding which will help followers of Jesus and participants in God's mission in Nigeria to effectively and contextually

---

41. Ukpong, *African Theologies Now*, 4.
42. Ukpong, *African Theologies Now*, 5.
43. Ukpong, *African Theologies Now*, 5.

engage in peacebuilding given those contexts. In chapter 5 we will attempt to proffer answers to some of the questions posed here. But before we jump into that boat, we make a case here that peacebuilding-contextual theology be admitted into the house of African contextual theologies, and that in view of the intersection of contextuality and globalization, such a stream can be constructively applied both in African and global contexts.

3.2.2 Peacebuilding-Contextual Theology as a Stream of Contextual Theology

Contextual theology scholars have not given sufficient attention to considering peacebuilding-contextual theology as a stream in the house of contextual theology. Matters of conflict resolution and peacemaking have instead often been left to political governing actors. Non-governmental actors, of which the Church must be in the forefront, must get on board as artisans of peace. Allan Gerson advocated for this citing Ibrahim A. Elbadawi's paper presented at a World Bank's Development and Research Group Conference held February 22 to 23, 1999. Gerson writes,

> Meeting the challenge of curbing such civil wars and preventing their re-ignition requires a radical readjustment. Restructuring must reach beyond traditional institutional mandates and methodologies. New players—particularly the private sector, as well as nongovernmental organizations (NGOs) must be enlisted in a new approach to economic peace building.[44]

Along the same optic, Kenyan scholar John Mwaniki Mwaruvie, puts it starkly, observing that "when internal or external conflicts arise, people more often than not are quick to call upon the government to intervene to solve the problem. This is based on the notion that the government has the resources and coercive machinery that can be used to solve the conflict."[45] Nonetheless, political authorities must not be left alone with the task of peacebuilding. Mwaruvie proffers reasons why it should not be left to the authorities alone. First, "government's intervention in most cases involves sending the armed forces to fight those assumed to cause trouble."[46] Second, the use of military force only pushes those involved in armed conflict into dens to regroup and later re-launch their attacks. Government's military intervention only puts off the conflict and does not resolve it.

---

44. Gerson, "Peace Building," 102.
45. Mwaruvie, "Mission of the Church in Africa," 270.
46. Mwaruvie, "Mission of the Church in Africa," 270.

Mwaruvie makes another important point. He maintains that in contexts of conflict, "the government . . . would be seen as another aggressor, out to undermine peoples' rights. . . [and that] armed intervention will be seen as the government's effort to protect the interest of a certain favoured ethnic group at the expense of the other."[47] Hence, in a situation where the aggressors are of the same ethno-religious group as those in the corridors of political power, then the latter are often unenthusiastic to intervene in favor of the victims. Mwaruvie's observation rightly reflects the current situation in Nigeria where the current political and government security apparatuses have not demonstrated commensurate concern and effort to intervene in the silent mayhem and jihad being perpetrated by Muslim Fulani herdsmen in Nigeria. Mwaruvie's position reinforces, Gerson's call for non-governmental organizations (including the church) to become actively involved in peacebuilding and not to leave the ball in the courts of the government authorities.

On his part, Wilson Maina, observed that one of the ways "African theology has responded to social issues is by appealing to methods of liberation and political theology. But one cannot avoid raising the question as to why African theologians are not coming up with a method that addresses social and political issues that are genuinely African other than appealing to foreign philosophical and theological systems of thought."[48] It is evident then that not much has been articulated in the area of peacebuilding-contextual theology as a stream of contextual theology, particularly in response to issues in various African contexts. The lacuna is, however, receiving some attention through various peacebuilding initiatives in Africa. We, nonetheless, maintain that a peacebuilding-contextual theology is needed to undergird such efforts, especially from a Christian missiological perspective. To further buttress our argument that peacebuilding-contextual theology be welcomed into the house of contextual theologies, we outline some basis for peacebuilding-contextual theology.

Diverse forms of plurality currently characterize our twenty-first century world. Whether one resides in Umudim (a town in Ikeduru Local Government Area of Imo State in Nigeria) or in a megacity[49] such as Beijing, London, New York, Paris, Tokyo, et cetera, she or he is bound to encounter

---

47. Mwaruvie, "Mission of the Church in Africa," 270.

48. Maina, *Historical and Social Dimensions in African Christian Theology*, 1.

49. The demographic threshold of cities considered "mega" varies depending on the study. The lowest threshold is one with a population greater than 1 million; Barrett, *World-Class Cities*, 20–21. Other studies peg the threshold to 5 million; Koonings and Kruijt, *Megacities*, 2, and yet others at 10 million; Liotta and Miskel, *Real Population Bomb*, 2. Thus, a megacity or an "urban agglomeration" can be defined as one having "more than five, eight, or ten million people. . . " https://www.schueco.com/web2/fi/architekten/magazine/sustainability/megacities.

Contextual Theology and Nonviolence Peacebuilding Ethics 85

and engage with plurality in one or more of its multifaceted forms.[50] This multidimensionality of plurality could be ethno-cultural, sociopolitical, economic, racial, or relating to issues of gender and sexual orientation, religious, or a complex combination of two or more of these facets. Renowned constructive systematic theologian, Veli-Matti Kärkkäinen, affirms that this pervasive phenomenon of plurality creates several challenges, and that it is hard to "fathom the uttermost difficulty of doing theology in and for the 'post-' world."[51] Acute violence happens to be one of the myriad of these challenges which our twenty-first century world[52] faces. In some contexts, Islamists' acts of violence epitomize this genre of violence. Thus, Christian artisans of peacebuilding in such contexts of Islamist violence and, indeed, within other non-Christian religious contexts would have to deal with and unravel the complexity of engaging the "other" in a pluralistic world.

In view of the foregoing, the theme of plurality defines, at least to a large degree, the essential framework within which contextual theology must be constructed in our twenty-first century world. In other words, widespread diversity and plurality in our twenty-first century world demands that peacebuilding-contextual theological engagement be taken seriously by missiologists and theologians alike. Kärkkäinen takes this theme seriously in framing his five-volume series of constructive theology, wherein he does not only take into consideration "the results, insights and materials of all theological disciplines, that is: biblical studies, church history and historical theology, philosophical theology... ministerial studies... related fields of religious studies, ethics, missiology,"[53] but also incorporates "nontheological and nonrelgous fields such as natural sciences, cultural studies, and... the study of living faiths..."[54] Among the living faiths Kärkkäinen broadly considers is, of course, Islam—viewed as one of the three Abrahamic faiths alongside Judaism and Christianity. Kärkkäinen erects his comparative theological project on coherence theory.[55] Along that same trajectory, we search for biblical and missiological coherence in order to propose a

---

50. Veli-Matti Kärkkäinen's introduction in the first volume to his five-volume *summa* discusses this multifaceted forms of plurality or diversity in a "Post-" world, see: Kärkkäinen, *Christ and Reconciliation*, 1:1–4.

51. Kärkkäinen, *Christ and Reconciliation*, 1:3.

52. A world Kärkkäinen succinctly refers to as a "post-" world Kärkkäinen (*Christ and Reconciliation*, 1–21). Prolific Pentecostal scholar of renown, Amos Yong, prefers the expression "late modern world" Yong, *Spirit Poured out on All Flesh*, 17, 18, 26, 30, 31ff.

53. Kärkkäinen, *Christ and Reconciliation*, 1:13.

54. Kärkkäinen, *Christ and Reconciliation*, 1:13.

55. For a brief discussion on "coherence theory", see Kärkkäinen, *Christ and Reconciliation*, 1:15.

peacebuilding-contextual theology in the context of acute violence, using Nigeria's experience of Islamist acute violence as a reference.

Insofar as peacebuilding-contextual theology is concerned, the basic idea behind the principle of coherence is that, in search for a contextual theology that will yield transforming peace, we seek to "engage not only theological resources but also cultural, religious, sociopolitical, and other resources"[56] that can be explored, studied and then constructively and critically integrated for peacebuilding. Besides these resources, historical elements through which the context in question has been shaped and which continue to impinge upon the present must also be considered. In regard to the scope of this study and our engagement with Islam, the implication, therefore, is that our search would incorporate resources in Islam that point to peacebuilding insofar as they relate to the African context and share commonality with the truth of Christian doctrine. This task, we will undertake in chapter 4—peacebuilding concepts from Islamic and Muslim perspectives. Besides, we also harness the ethno-cultural resources resident within the African contexts and culture in order to formulate our peacebuilding-contextual theology. Drawing from both literature and narrative data of our research interviews, we will discuss some of these African ethno-cultural resources or concepts for peacebuilding in chapter 5—African concepts for peacebuilding-contextual theology, and in chapter 6—Peacebuilding Concepts from Nigeria's Ethnolinguistic Cultures. Our conclusion is that given the contexts of acute violence that beleaguer Nigeria as a country, contextual means and methods for peacebuilding are necessary for followers of Jesus and participants in God's mission in Nigeria to effectively and contextually engage in peacebuilding given those contexts.

Before we proceed (in chapter 4) to explore the resources for peacebuilding that might be drawn from Islamic scriptural texts and Muslim traditions, it is important we make the connection between peacebuilding-contextual theology and globalization. After reviewing the meaning of contextual theology, we underscored the necessity to point out that African cultures and contexts do not stand as islands in themselves in our globalizing world. Although we have our local cultures and contexts in Africa, yet our contexts share the impact occasioned by globalization. Contexts are, therefore, local, and yet some take on a global character because of the relationship between contextuality and globalization.[57] Rick Love in the preface to his volume *Glocal* noted that "[w]e live in a 'glocal' world: what happens globally impacts us locally, and what happens locally

---

56. Kärkkäinen, *Christ and Reconciliation*, 1:15.
57. See our discussion in section 3.1.2

impacts things globally. What happens among the nations impacts our neighbors, and what happens among our neighbors impacts the nations."[58] We can then argue that contexts in our globalizing world are 'glocal'—a catchword scholars have fused together from 'global' and 'local' to refer to "being global and local at the same time."[59]

Given this intersection of contextuality and globalization, we posit that peacebuilding-contextual theology, which we have posited here to be welcomed as a stream in the house of African contextual theologies, possesses the same contextuality, thereby, making it applicable to both local African and global contexts. In other words, the constructive and critical integration that may be achieved by installing peacebuilding-contextual theology in Africa's contexts can also be employed across other global contexts while taking respective contextual peculiarities into consideration. Thus, peacebuilding-contextual theology will not only be gain for African contexts but also for our globalizing world. Wilber Shenk's idea supports this position. Shenk posits that the gains of contextual theology will not only be beneficial to the church of the Global South, but also might revitalize the "floundering"[60] Western church. He calls it "the Promise of Contextual theology" asserting that "[t]he quest for authentic expressions of the Christian faith in Asia, Africa, Latin America, and the Pacific Islands on the part of the so-called younger churches is having a 'reflexive' impact on the West as well."[61]

3.3 PEACEBUILDING TRADITIONS OF NONVIOLENCE ETHICS

One of the implications of the intersection of contextuality and globalization as we noted above is that peacebuilding-contextual theology, as stream of contextual theology in Africa, can also be constructively applied in other global contexts that are not necessarily African. This claim is validated by examples we now advance—examples based on the application of the Anabaptists' tradition of nonviolence, Glen H. Stassen's Just Peacemaking theory, and the nonviolent resistance philosophy of Mahatma Gandhi and Martin Luther King Jr.—all three being non-African models of peacebuilding ethics and yet applicable to African contexts. These examples also foreshadow the discussion we will engage in chapters 7 and

58. Love, *Glocal*, vii.

59. Engelsviken et al., *Church Going Glocal*, vii. See also Roland Robertson, "Glocalization" in Ashcroft et al., *Post-Colonial Studies Reader*, 477–80.

60. Shenk, "Contextual Theology," 208.

61. Shenk, "Contextual Theology," 208.

8, on a few traditions of peacebuilding that have advocated and practiced nonviolence ethics. Given that our thesis surrounds *staurocentric* peacebuilding-contextual theology, the historical understanding of these traditions provides support for our argument. Hence, we peer firstly into the Anabaptists (Mennonite and Amish) tradition of nonviolence, secondly into Glen Stassen's Just Peacemaking theory, and thirdly into Mahatma Gandhi and Martin Luther King Jr.'s nonviolence ethics.

3.3.1 *The Anabaptist Nonviolence Ethics*

Historically, the origins of the Anabaptists go back to the sixteenth century. In his concise volume *An Introduction to Mennonite History*, Cornelius J. Dyck outlines the historical origins that led to the birth of the ". . . movement with roots in religious, social, economic, and political conditions in most of Western Europe."[62] Former Dutch Roman Catholic dissenter priest, Menno Simons later emerged as a prominent leader in the movement and "because of [his] capable leadership the Anabaptists in East Friesland gained the name, "Mennites" (Mennonites)."[63] Two major groups or factions of the Anabaptist movement are the Mennonites and the Amish. The Amish is a splinter group from the Mennonites[64] but both belong to the Anabaptist movement. Among the core values of the movement is their peacebuilding ethics of nonviolence. The Anabaptists' nonviolence ethics is grounded on Jesus's model and takes the cross as its locus. John Howard Yoder well articulates it in his volume, *Nevertheless*, wherein he outlines a taxonomy of different forms of pacifism,[65] but zeros, at last, on what he called "the Pacifism of the Messianic Community."[66] Yoder maintains that the foundation of this genre of ethics affirms "its dependence upon the confession that Jesus is Christ and that Jesus Christ is Lord. . . Therefore, in the person and work of Jesus, in his teachings and his passion, this kind of pacifism finds its rootage, and in his resurrection it finds its enablement.[67] Rooted on this foundation,

---

62. Dyck, *Introduction to Mennonite History*, 33.

63. Dyck, *Introduction to Mennonite History*, 102, 105.

64. It was during the summer and fall of 1693 that Jakob Ammann demanded that the Swiss Mennonites separate themselves from worldly society and adhere to the practice of shunning. When the demand was not met, Jakob Ammann and his supporters separated from the Swiss Mennonites and came to be known as the "Ammann-ish" group. It was from that the name "Amish" was derived, but they are counted among "the wider Anabaptist community" Nolt, *Amish*, 18.

65. In older literature, some scholars use the term 'pacifism' to refer to nonviolence ethics, which is used interchangeably in latter works.

66. Yoder, *Nevertheless*, 133–38.

67. Yoder, *Nevertheless*, 133–34.

the Mennonite World Conference includes among the seven commitments that characterize the Mennonite church holding that: "The Spirit of Jesus empowers [them] to trust God in all areas of life so [they] become peacemakers who renounce violence, love [their] enemies, seek justice, and share [their] possessions with those in need."[68]

So regarding the Anabaptists' locus on the cross, Yoder in another volume, *The Politics of Jesus*, asserts that Jesus's call to his followers to take up their cross and follow him (Matt 10:38–39; Luke 9:23) implies "the inevitable suffering of those whose only goal is to be faithful to that love which puts one at the mercy of another's neighbor, which abandons claims to justice for oneself and for one's own in an overriding concern for the reconciling of the adversary and the estranged."[69] Yoder points out that the social consequences of such a stance draws from Jesus's example, who, "When he was reviled, . . . did not revile in return; when he suffered, he did not threaten but continued entrusting himself to him who judges justly" (1Pet 2:23).

This Anabaptist locus on the cross is particularly essential for *staurocentric* peacebuilding because as we will see a later chapter, it entails total reliance on the triune God to be the ultimate administrator of justice, thus positioning the *staurocentric* disciple of Jesus to love, to do good, to forgive, to bless, and to pray for (not against) the perpetrator of violence of which he or she is the object. Furthermore, the locus of the cross invites those who will submit to it to prepare their mind for the worst, even physical death. And where it would imply physical death, the cross invites the follower of Jesus to die blessing, forgiving, and praying for (not against) the one or those from whose hands that death is occasioned.

In *The War of the Lamb*, Yoder further presents a theological critique of violence to show that nonviolence entails life and love. He repudiates the "tit for tat" motif, maintaining that although it was "in the Mosaic corpus, Jesus set it aside. . . being the last high priest and the last victim."[70] Along the same optic, one of the leading voices of neo-Anabaptist movement, Gregory A. Boyd (who has adopted the Anabaptist theological position on this issue) posits that "[t]it for tat, eye for an eye, tooth for a tooth . . . is what makes the bloody kingdom of the world go around."[71] Boyd rightly argues that "peace achieved by violence is a peace forever threatened by violence, thus ensuring that the bloody game will be perpetuated."[72] Boyd makes the same point, in

---

68. Shenk, *Christian. Muslim. Friend.*, 186.
69. Yoder, *Politics of Jesus*, 236.
70. Yoder, *War of the Lamb*, 31.
71. Boyd, *Myth of a Christian Nation*, 24.
72. Boyd, *Myth of a Christian Nation*, 27.

his volume more recent than the former, convincingly showing that Jesus's "repudiating a law of the OT is his rejection of the foundational law of just retaliation (known as *the lex talionis*)"[73] is a model to be adopted by anyone who "follow[s] Jesus and [will] be considered a 'child of the Father,' . . . "[74] Boyd insists that "Jesus taught that to be considered a 'child of the Father,' a person has to commit to doing the exact opposite of what [the just retaliation[75]] law commands!"[76] This argument is further buttressed in Boyd's two volume set, wherein he maintains that adherence to the repudiation of this law is an important "criteria for being a child of the Father."[77] Thus, the onus rests upon those who identify themselves as Jesus's followers to embody for their societies and for the world the "hope that. . . lies in a kingdom that is not of this world, a kingdom that doesn't participate in tit for tat, a kingdom that operates with a completely different understanding of power. [And that] kingdom [is the one] established by Jesus Christ and. . . expanded by people committed to following him."[78] Such hope can only be embodied by walking the path that Jesus walked—the way of the cross, which Boyd calls "cruciform hermeneutic."[79] Besides the Anabaptists, there are other scholars and practitioners who have also stood with the nonviolence ethics. Glen Harold Stassen (1936–2014), a Southern Baptist theologian and the proponent of the Just Peacemaking theory, is in that company.

3.3.2 *The Just Peacemaking Theory of Glen Harold Stassen*

Glen H. Stassen put forth the Just Peacemaking theory as "a new paradigm that cuts between the just war theory and the pacifism" theories.[80] For Stassen, the just war and pacifism theories seek to answer the question: Is war justified? This, Stassen called the x-axis question. Whereas, on the negative end of this x-axis lies the pacifism theory that says: No, war is not justified whatever the form; on the positive end of the axis falls the just war theory that says: Yes, there are certain conditions or principles that must be applied to determine whether or not war could be justified. Stassen then proposed

---

73. Boyd, *Cross Vision*, 30.

74. Boyd, *Cross Vision*, 30.

75. The "just retaliation" law is based on the following OT passages: Exod 21:24; Lev 24:19–20; and Deut 19:21; and implies that "the severity of a person's punishment must correspond to the severity of their crime" Boyd, *Cross Vision*, 30.

76. Boyd, *Cross Vision*, 30.

77. Boyd, *Crucifixion of the Warrior God*, 70–73.

78. Boyd, *Myth of a Christian Nation*, 27.

79. Boyd, *Crucifixion of the Warrior God*, 1:xxxiv, 141–228, 417ff.

80. Cahill, "Just Peacemaking," 195.

that there is a y-axis question that has been left out. That y-axis question asks: Should we be taking just peacemaking practices to prevent war?[81] The just war and pacifism paradigms "focus attention on whether a war is justified rather than on effective preventive practices"[82]—an idea the Just Peacemaking paradigm advocates. Stassen's Just Peacemaking theory therefore "combines a biblical faith commitment with active political engagement. It aims to unite persons of many faiths and cultures to be proactive in diminishing war and other politically motivated violence."[83] Stassen clearly stated that this theory does not replace the just war theory and pacifism paradigm. He rather maintains that the theory cuts across both and seeks to fill the lacuna they create. But what is the core of Just Peacemaking theory?

The theory consists of the ten practices that should be proactively observed in order to prevent war. For brevity, we simply enumerate these ten practices, which are enunciated with details in Stassen's volumes, *Just Peacemaking: Ten Practices for Abolishing War* and *Just Peacemaking: The New Paradigm for the Ethics of Peace and War*.[84] They are:

1. Support nonviolent direct action;
2. Take independent initiatives to reduce threat;
3. Use cooperative conflict resolution;
4. Acknowledge responsibility for conflict and injustice, and seek repentance and forgiveness;
5. Advance democracy, human rights, Interdependence and religious liberty;
6. Foster just and sustainable economic development;
7. Work with emerging cooperative forces in the international system;
8. Strengthen the United Nations and international efforts for cooperation and human rights;
9. Reduce offensive weapons and weapons trade; and
10. Encourage grassroots peacemaking groups and voluntary associations.[85]

---

81. Stassen, "Unity, Realism, and Obligatoriness of Just Peacemaking Theory," 175–76; Ecuyer, *Dr. Glen Stassen on Just Peacemaking*.

82. Stassen, "Unity, Realism, and Obligatoriness of Just Peacemaking Theory," 172.

83. Cahill, "Just Peacemaking," 195.

84. Stassen, *Just Peacemaking*, 1998; Stassen, *Just Peacemaking*, 2008; see also: Cahill, "Just Peacemaking."

85. Stassen, *Just Peacemaking*, 1998; Stassen, *Just Peacemaking*, 2008.

The details of what each of these ten practices entail in pragmatic terms and the theological grounds for them are all outlined in the above-cited volumes. Stassen noted that these ten practices are "intended not merely as ten practices that effectively prevent wars, but as a new paradigm, alongside pacifism and just war theory."[86] He maintained that "[w]ars will still happen, and therefore pacifism and just war theory are still very much needed."[87] Lisa S. Cahill enumerates five key emphases that the practices of the Just Peacemaking theory seek to underline and unite.[88] First, it "is not only about ideas, theories, or principles."[89] It entails proactive participation of people within a community to build their community. The practice is not "about forbidding specific kinds of behavior, even killing."[90] It is about normative practices— "historically situated in practices."[91]

Second, it emphasizes the "need for mediating institutions that connect individual action to social change,"[92] which gives a new understanding in the view of the consequences of globalization. Cahill further notes that for this second emphasis, "social institutions, especially international and transnational institutions can offer persons of diverse cultures and religions the opportunity to share in common practices."[93]

The third key emphasis is that the practices seek to establish "in Christian and social ethics a salutary and overdue requirement that claims and mandates be grounded in fact in order to have practical legitimacy."[94] The point this emphasis tries to elucidate is that "Christian ethics cannot simply deduce obligations from abstract premises or ideals and [then] present them as though they can change behavior without investigating whether the conditions of possibility of change are in place."[95] The theory asserts that ten practices do indeed "enhance global conditions of peaceful coexistence."[96]

The fourth emphasis surrounds the "economics and the connection of both liberal capitalism and the avoidance of war to representative

---

86. Stassen, "Unity, Realism, and Obligatoriness of Just Peacemaking Theory," 171.
87. Stassen, "Unity, Realism, and Obligatoriness of Just Peacemaking Theory," 172.
88. Cahill, "Just Peacemaking," 196–99.
89. Cahill, "Just Peacemaking," 196.
90. Cahill, "Just Peacemaking," 197.
91. Cahill, "Just Peacemaking," 197.
92. Cahill, "Just Peacemaking," 197.
93. Cahill, "Just Peacemaking," 197.
94. Cahill, "Just Peacemaking," 197.
95. Cahill, "Just Peacemaking," 197.
96. Cahill, "Just Peacemaking," 198.

democracy."⁹⁷ Modern democracy promotes the development of cultural norms, which favor tolerance and nonviolent resolution of conflicts. Thus it is believed that economic interdependence creates a "democratic aversion to war."⁹⁸

Finally, the ten practices seek to emphasize, "that the global environment still remains an anarchic society."⁹⁹ Stassen does not claim or "maintain that all war will eventually be ended."¹⁰⁰ This position distances the theory from any hint the third emphasis might create on the effectiveness of peacemaking. On the other hand, what the theory seeks to assert is that "the historical incidence of war will be on the whole decreased."¹⁰¹

All things considered, Stassen's theory can be explored to find points of contextuality in African contexts of violence, particularly in Nigeria.

3.3.3 Mahatma Gandhi and Martin Luther King Jr.'s Nonviolence Ethics

Several biographical volumes exist on the nonviolence ethics of Mahatma Gandhi, whose principle of *ahimsa* (nonviolence) drove his struggle for India's independence from the British colonialists.¹⁰² Mark Bredin, drawing from Ignatius Jesudasan (an Indian Jesuit) and Thomas Merton's edited volume, *Gandhi on Non-violence*, provides a succinct introduction to Gandhi's *ahimsa* principle in the volume *Jesus, Revolutionary of Peace*. Ahimsa is an expression of nonviolent and suffering love. It "is the truth of humankind's nature which desires peace, justice, order, freedom and personal dignity."¹⁰³ In a selected works of Gandhi, Gandhi wrote: "I do claim to be a passionate seeker after Truth, which is but another name for God. In the course of that search the discovery of non-violence came to me. Its spread is my life mission. I have no interest in living except for the prosecution of that mission."¹⁰⁴ To showcase his stand for nonviolence, Gandhi challenged the British in a writing he captioned "To Every Briton" with the following words:

97. Cahill, "Just Peacemaking," 198.
98. Cahill, "Just Peacemaking," 198.
99. Cahill, "Just Peacemaking," 199.
100. Cahill, "Just Peacemaking," 199.
101. Cahill, "Just Peacemaking," 199.
102. Primary sources include the 100 volumes of Mohandas Karamchand Gandhi: Gandhi, *Collected Works of Mahatma Gandhi*, 1:100; Secondary sources include: Gandhi, *Gandhi on Non-Violence*; Jesudasan, *Gandhian Theology of Liberation*; Chatterjee, *Gandhi's Religious Thought*, and Tidrick, *Gandhi*.
103. Bredin, *Jesus, Revolutionary of Peace*, 5.
104. Gandhi, *Gandhi on Non-Violence*, 1:282.

> I do not want Britain to be defeated, nor do I want her to be victorious in a trial of brute strength, whether expressed through the muscle or the brain. Your muscular bravery is an established fact. Need you demonstrate that your brain is also as unrivalled in destructive power as your muscle? I hope you do not wish to enter into such an undignified competition with the Nazis. I venture to present you with a nobler and a braver way, worthy of the bravest soldier.[105]

The "nobler and a braver way" to which Gandhi referred is the way of nonviolence. It was in the course of Gandhi's search that he discovered non-violence. But what or who inspired him? From where may Gandhi have discovered his non-violence ethics? Indian Jesuit priest, Ignatius Jesudasan in his volume, *A Gandhian Theology of Liberation*, asserts that "Gandhi saw Christ as an ideal *satyagrahi* [truth force or love-force]."[106] Gandhi himself wrote: "Jesus. . . was the most active resister known perhaps to history. His was non-violence par excellence."[107] He also wrote: "Jesus to me [Gandhi] is a great world-teacher among others. He was to the devotees of his generation no doubt 'the only begotten son of God.'"[108] Furthermore, with his many references to the Sermon on the Mount, it is not doubtful that Gandhi was influenced by Jesus's teachings. In Gandhi, we find an example of nonviolence ethics in Indian context.

Martin Luther King Jr. is reckoned to have exemplified the nonviolence ethics within the contours of American socio-political scenes. King Jr. acknowledged he was "deeply fascinated by [Gandhi's] campaigns of nonviolent resistance. [He wrote:] As I delved deeper into the philosophy of Gandhi my skepticism concerning the power of love gradually diminished, and I came to see for the first time its potency in the area of social reform."[109] Prior to studying Mahatma Gandhi, King Jr held "that the ethics of Jesus were only effective in individual relationships. The 'turn the other cheek' philosophy and the 'love your enemies' philosophy were only valid, I [King Jr.] felt, when individuals were in conflict with other individuals; when racial groups and nations were in conflict a more realistic approach seemed necessary."[110] All that changed for King Jr. after he read Gandhi's works. In

---

105. Gandhi, *Gandhi on Non-Violence*, 1:281.

106. Jesudasan, *Gandhian Theology of Liberation*, 107.

107. Gandhi, *Gandhi on Non-Violence*, 2:16; cited in: Bredin, *Jesus, Revolutionary of P{eace*, 12.

108. Gandhi, *Collected Works of Mahatma Gandhi*, 62:333–334.

109. King, *Stride Toward Freedom*, 84.

110. King, *Stride Toward Freedom*, 84.

regard to nonviolence ethics, therefore, King Jr. outlines five elements that undergird his nonviolent resistance to evil in his work, *Stride Toward Freedom*, which we concisely summarize here.

- First . . . nonviolent resistance is not a method for cowards; it does resist . . .

- A second basic fact [is] that . . . nonviolence . . . does not seek to defeat or humiliate the opponent, but to win his friendship and understanding.

- A third characteristic . . . is that the attack is directed against forces of evil rather than against persons who happen to be doing the evil. It is evil that the nonviolent resister seeks to defeat, not the person victimized by evil.

- A fourth . . . [is] that . . . nonviolent resistance is a willingness to accept suffering without retaliation, to accept blows from the opponent without striking back.

- [And the] fifth . . . is that it avoids not only external physical violence but also internal violence of spirit.[111]

There are two principal takeaways for us from the concise reviews undertaken above. The first is that Jesus Christ is the epitome, the model par excellence in our quest to overcome violence, injustice and evil, whether it be on a micro-individual or macro-societal level. This point is established by the four trajectories nonviolence peacebuilding ethics we have reviewed—the Anabaptists' (Mennonite and Amish) tradition; Glen Stassen's Just Peacemaking theory; Mahatma Gandhi and Martin Luther King Jr.'s nonviolent resistance. Our second takeaway, is that nonviolence, particularly for Jesus's followers, must not be limited to the individual. It must translate to being the ethics of "the messianic community" (in the words of John H. Yoder). These two takeaways are very essential for our thesis because it hovers around Jesus's example through his death and resurrection and the power that a community fleshing out the *staurocentric* life can exude in order to vanquish violence. We will discuss the existing carrefour between these elements and the *staurocentric* model in our last chapter.

---

111. King, *Stride Toward Freedom*, 90–92; King, "Nonviolence and Racial Justice," 442–44.

4

Peacebuilding Concepts from Islamic and Muslim Perspectives

IN THE PREVIOUS CHAPTER, we reviewed the meaning of contextual theology and the principal streams of African contextual theologies. We argued that the contexts of acute violence that beleaguer Nigeria as a country necessitate contextual means and methods for peacebuilding that will help Jesus's followers and participants in God's mission in Nigeria to effectively and contextually engage in peacebuilding given those contexts. We posited that peacebuilding-contextual theology be admitted into the house of contextual theologies to undergird peacebuilding theologizing, not only in African local contexts but also in our globalizing world. Demographically, Nigeria is divided almost equally between followers of Jesus and followers of Muhammad. One implication for Nigerian followers of Jesus engaging in peacebuilding in contexts involving Muslims, therefore, is the need for respect and what Martin Accad, in his recent volume, *Sacred Misinterpretation*, calls a "kerygmatic approach."[1] Accad posits that Jesus's "followers who hold a kerygmatic understanding of Islam will engage with Muslims on two solid foundations: respect and trust."[2] Understanding the Muslims' position and locus on a matter is important if one must engage with respect and trust. Hence, insofar as peacebuilding in contexts involving Muslims is concerned, duty calls on the follower of Jesus to explore potential resources, means, and methods for peacebuilding within the Muslims' scripts of authority and tradition, and then envisage ways to constructively, critically, and respectfully employ those resources in peacebuilding engagement within that context.

1. Accad, *Sacred Misinterpretation*, 8–10.
2. Accad, *Sacred Misinterpretation*, 14.

This chapter, thus, explores the contours of peacebuilding resources resident in the two principal scriptural texts that define Islamic theology (*kalām*) namely: The Qur'ān and the Hadith. Secondly, we narrow down our exploration to hear the peacebuilding voices of some African Muslims. Thirdly, gleanings for peacebuilding from some Muslim artisans of peace both of non-African and African origins are also gathered. And lastly, we tie the knot to find points of commonality between the surveyed Muslims and Christians' peacebuilding perspectives—what I call "Christian-Muslim carrefour" for peacebuilding. The conclusion we draw from the parkour is that there exist within Islam concepts, resources, and tools that can be contextually and critically harnessed and employed in constructing pathways to peacebuilding.

4.1 PEACEBUILDING IN THE ISLAMIC SCRIPTURES

The Qur'ān and the Hadith form the two principal scriptural authorities in Islam.[3] From their corpus, Islamic law is derived and constructed. The Qur'ān is the primary source of Islamic law whereas the Hadith—the recordings of the traditions, the acts and the deeds of Muhammad—elucidates, elaborates and supports the Quranic texts. The Qur'ān remains, however, for Muslims a supreme authority in matters of faith and practice. Thus, in order to understand Muslims' perspectives on peacemaking and peacebuilding, it is necessary, first and foremost, to survey the Quranic texts on the theme of peace.

4.1.1 Witness to Peace in the Qur'ān

Egyptian-born Islamic Studies scholar, Muhammad Abel Haleem, asserts that "[t]he Islamic relationship between individuals and nations is one of peace. War is a contingency that becomes necessary at certain times and under certain conditions. Muslims learn from the Qur'ān that God's objective in creating the human race in different communities was that they should relate to each other peacefully."[4] God's objective mentioned here is based on Q. 49:13 "O mankind, indeed We have created you from male and female and made you peoples and tribes that you may know one another. Indeed, the most noble of you in the sight of Allah is the most righteous of you. Indeed, Allah

---

3. Abdel Haleem, *Understanding the Qur'an*, 59.
4. Abdel Haleem, *Understanding the Qur'an*, 60.

is Knowing and Acquainted."[5] The Arabic expression translated here as "that you may know one another" (لِتَعَارَفُوا—*li-taʿārafū*) is worthy of special note in a discussion on peace. In a commentary[6] on this verse, Tafsir al-Jalalayn, underscores the point that "one of the two *tā*' letters of *tataʿārafū* has been omitted that you may acquire knowledge of the customs of one another and not to boast to one another of whose is the more noble lineage for pride lies only in the extent to which you have fear of God."[7]

South African research scholar of Islamic Studies and Peacebuilding, Rashied Omar, takes up this theme of *taʿāraf* as an alternative and a higher concept and paradigm for "interracial and interreligious harmony that goes beyond the limitations of the idea of tolerance."[8] Omar posits that

> Through this verse [cited above] the Qur'an teaches that differences among humankind are not incidental and negative but rather than human diversity represents a God-willed, basic factor of human existence. The Qur'anic concept of *taʿaruf* is an alternative vision to that of the tolerance paradigm and represents for me [Omar] the litmus test of good religion: not how much I can tolerate the other but rather the extent to which I am able to embrace "the other" as an extension of myself.[9]

Omar goes further to assert that "Islamic paradigm of *taʿāruf*, intimately getting to know one another is a pathway to embracing the other as an extension of the self, whether we are Jew, Christian or of no faith."[10] This concept of embracing "the other" is also reflected in a narrative in the Hadith—to which we will turn in the next subsection.

In respect to the Quranic verse under our survey radar here (Q. 49:13), Khaled Abou El Fadl, one of the world's leading authorities on Islamic law, asserts that it is a Quranic discourse, which "not only expects,

---

5. As stated in the preface, all citations of the Qur'ān, except otherwise indicated, are taken from *Al-Qur'an al-Kareem—*القرآن الكريم*—The Sahih International Translation* Sahih International, *Al-Qur'an al-Kareem*. The abbreviation, Q. is used hereafter to refer to references in the Qur'ān. I have used chapter numbers (1, 2, 3, etc.) to refer to *sūrat* in the Qur'ān instead of their transcribed Arabic names. For example, instead of *Al-Fātiha*, the first Surah of the Qur'ān, I use Q. 1.

6. All commentaries to verses of the Qur'ān, except otherwise indicated, are taken from http://www.altafsir.com/ provided by Royal Aal al-Bayt Institute for Islamic Thought, Amman, Jordan http://www.aalalbayt.org 2016. This online resource provides various commentaries to the Qur'ān.

7. Al-Maḥallī and Al-Suyūṭī, *Tafsīr Al-Jalālayn*, 606.

8. Omar, "Islam Beyond Tolerance," 18.

9. Omar, "Islam Beyond Tolerance," 18.

10. Omar, "Islam Beyond Tolerance," 19–20.

but even accepts the reality of difference and diversity within human society."[11] He buttresses this point with another verse of the Qur'ān: "And if your Lord had willed, He could have made mankind one community; but they will not cease to differ" (Q. 11:118). El Fadl, admits, however, that both classical Muslim commentators and contemporary Muslim scholars have not fully explored the implications of this matter and therefore the theme of diversity in this verse of the Qur'ān remains "underdeveloped in Islamic theology."[12] He hopes that the outworking of the "implications of a commitment to human diversity and mutual knowledge [ta'āraf] under contemporary conditions requires moral reflection and attention to historical circumstances, [which he asserts is]–precisely what is missing from puritan theology and doctrine."[13]

Along the same optic, Q. 30:22 reads "And of His signs is the creation of the heavens and the earth and the diversity of your languages and your colors. Indeed, in that are signs for those of knowledge." Egyptian-born Islamic Studies scholar, Nasr Abū Zayd, who until his death in 2010 was an outspoken advocate for reform of Islamic thought, posits that Muslim thinkers "such as Nurcholis Madjid and others use 30:22 to argue that differences among humankind are the starting point for positive competition. [And that] In their view, the Quran expresses that pluralism must be taken for granted."[14] Abu Zayd is counted among African scholars who call for tolerance and reinterpretation of the Qur'ān, of Muslim history, and of Muslim traditions.[15] And such reinterpretations include the subject of diversity and democracy in Islam.

There exists an important connection between diversity and peacebuilding. This connection emerges when a group's recognition of diversity opens their hearts, heads and hands to "the other." Without the cognizance of diversity, it is impracticable (on one hand,) to accept and respect those who are different from us. On the other hand, where diversity is acknowledged and even valued as a blessing, the propensity to be open to learn and draw from the riches and knowledge that reside in "the other" will be present. Such proclivity provides the grounds for peacebuilding in the context of

---

11. Abou El Fadl, *Place of Tolerance in Islam*, 15.
12. Abou El Fadl, *Place of Tolerance in Islam*, 16.
13. Abou El Fadl, *Place of Tolerance in Islam*, 16.
14. Abū Zayd et al., *Reformation of Islamic Thought*, 61.
15. Abū Zayd, *Rethinking the Qur'ân*. Naṣr Ḥāmid Abū Zayd further elucidates his position in an inaugural lecture he delivered on May 27, 2004 for Ibn Rushd Academic Chair, for Islam and Humanism, established by the University of Humanistics, Utrecht, The Netherlands.

violence. Thus, drawing from Muslim scholars' exegesis of Q. 49:13 provides an important nexus to peacebuilding vis-à-vis diversity and difference.

Another passage in the Qurʾān that is noteworthy speaks of "maximum effort [that] must be made to advance the cause of peace."[16] In Q. 10:25 we read: "And Allah invites to the Home of Peace and guides whom He wills to a straight path." The Sahih International Translation renders the Arabic term: دَارِ السَّلَامِ (dār as-salām) as "Home of peace." A better rending for dār as-salām should be 'the house or abode of peace.' This notion of the house of peace introduces the dual Muslim house of Islam (dār al-Islām) and house of war (dār al-ḥarb). According to some Muslim commentators (mufāsirūn), the straight path (صِرَاطٍ مُسْتَقِيمٍ—ṣirāṭ mustaqīm) to which Allah makes this summon to the house or abode of peace and guides is no other but the house of Islam. Tafsīr al-Jalalayn comments on this verse (Q. 10:25) that "... God summons to the Abode of Peace[-]that is[-]the Abode of security which is Paradise by summoning people to faith and He guides whomever He wills that he be guided to a straight path[,] the religion of Islam."[17] In the commentary attributed to Muhammad's cousin, Ibn ʿAbbās, Tanwīr al-Miqbās min Tafsīr Ibn ʿAbbās, "the Peace (al-Salam) is Allah and His abode is Paradise"[18]; the straight path is "an established religion with which He [Allah] is pleased, i.e. Islam."[19] Drawing from these two commentaries mentioned here (Tafsīr al-Jalalayn and Tanwīr al-Miqbās min Tafsīr Ibn ʿAbbās), one can deduce the exclusivist interpretation that supports the prevailing current of Muslim thoughts of dualist worldview that divides humanity into dār al-Islām (house of Islam) and dār al-ḥarb (house of war).

We encounter, however, a more balanced and open interpretation in Tafsīr Al-Kāshanī wherein

> ... God summons to the Abode of Peace: He summons all to the abode of the peace of the spiritual world in which there is no calamity, no deficiency, no misery and no perishing, but instead there is safety from every defect and security from every fear, and He guides whomever He wills, of the prepared folk from among them, to the path of [His] Oneness.[20]

Here God's invitation is to "all"; the house of peace is the "spiritual world"; and the straight path (الصِّرَاطَ الْمُسْتَقِيمَ—ṣirāṭ al-mustaqīm) is "the

16. Gangat, "Islam."
17. Al-Maḥallī and Al-Suyūṭī, Tafsīr Al-Jalālayn, 216.
18. Ibn ʿAbbās and Al-Fīrūzabādī, Tafsīr Ibn ʾAbbās, 215.
19. Ibn ʿAbbās and Al-Fīrūzabādī, 215.
20. Al-Kāshānī, Tafsīr ʿAl-Kāshānī: Great Commentaries of the Holy Qurʾan Part 1 Surahs 1–18, 309.

path of God's Oneness." Al-Kāshānī's commentary on this verse (Q. 10:25) adopts a rather inclusive and open-minded approach as opposed to Al-Jalayan and Ibn 'Abbās. Wherever Muslims espouse and embrace such inclusive and open-minded approach in the light of *ta'āruf* (discussed briefly above), great doors to peacebuilding would be opened to artisans of peace from Muslims' perspectives. If, on the contrary, Muslims—particularly in Nigeria's context where this particular research is focused—stand by the exclusivist approach, then peacemaking and peacebuilding are bound to remain elusive. Thankfully, there is at least one example of a Muslim cleric in northern Nigeria—Imam Muhammad Ashafa— who subscribes to the inclusive and open-minded approach in the light of *ta'āruf*—to whom we shall return later in this chapter.

In the preceding paragraph we called attention to the theme of 'the straight path' (الصِّرَاطَ الْمُسْتَقِيمَ—*ṣirāṭ al-mustaqīm*). This theme has attracted much attention and volumes have been written around it.[21] In Q. 10:25 (mentioned above), the expression occurs in an indefinite form—صِرَاطٍ مُسْتَقِيمٍ *ṣirāṭ mustaqīm* —without the definite article "*alif-lam.*" But the first occurrence of the expression in the Qur'ān is in the opening *sūra- Al-Fātiḥah* (chapter 1 of the Qur'ān).

It is You we worship and You we ask for help. Q. 1:5	1:5 - إِيَّاكَ نَعْبُدُ وَإِيَّاكَ نَسْتَعِينُ
Guide us to the straight path—Q. 1:6	1:6 - اهْدِنَا الصِّرَاطَ الْمُسْتَقِيمَ
The path of those upon whom You have bestowed favor, not of those who have evoked [Your] anger or of those who are astray. Q. 1:7	1:7 - صِرَاطَ الَّذِينَ أَنْعَمْتَ عَلَيْهِمْ غَيْرِ الْمَغْضُوبِ عَلَيْهِمْ وَلَا الضَّالِّينَ

The Islamic philosophy and theology constructed around this theme of 'the straight path' plays a role that cannot be ignored in a discussion on peacemaking and peacebuilding from the Muslim perspective. How do Muslims generally understand and interpret this passage cited above? The straight path is sure understood to be the religion of Islam as we have already seen in a couple of Muslim commentaries (*tafāsir*). Those outside *dar al-Islam* are branded as people upon whom Allah's anger rests- الْمَغْضُوبِ عَلَيْهِمْ (*maghḍūbi 'alaihim*).

In many Muslim communities, this clause in verse 7, الْمَغْضُوبِ عَلَيْهِمْ (*maghḍūbi 'alaihim*)—"those upon whom [Your] wrath (anger) repose"[22]

---

21. See for example: Adamson, *Philosophy in the Islamic World* and Krawietz and Tamer, *Islamic Theology.*

22. The Arabic verb is in the passive voice.

(my translation) is often interpreted to mean Jews and Christians in particular and all other non-Muslims considered as the *kafirūn*—infidels in general. Children are breastfed with this teaching. Before they bring forth their first set of teeth, hatred against "the other" is implanted in the subconscious of many Muslim children. Such subtle implant of hatred against "the other" fertilizes and nourishes the culture of hatred in many Muslim communities in Nigeria and (from my personal experience) in North Africa as well. I was personally amazed the day my Muslim neighbor (in a North African city where I lived for about a decade) told me that this is their hermeneutics of this verse. His view is not unique.

A Bahraini intellectual and author, Dhiyaa Al-Musawi, brings this ideology to the fore, challenging his fellow Arab Muslims to change their language of hate and culture of death and make room for embracing the other. In an interview aired on Abu Dhabi TV on December 29, 2006, Al-Musawi did not mince his words. "We need to reform and to reshape religious thinking, because, in all honesty, the pulpits of our mosques have begun to 'booby trap' the people," he said.[23] When asked: "In what way?" Al-Musawi replied:

> They booby trap them by generating hatred towards 'the other.' We have claimed a monopoly over Paradise, and each of us has recorded it in the land registry in his name . . . This problem has political reasons, but who pays the price? The country, society, civil society, and the young man, who is being told that the black-eyed virgins await him at the gates of Paradise, and that all he has to do is kill himself, to slaughter himself. He might blow up his family and children to get the virgins of Paradise. This is the language and culture of death . . . We were not born into this world in order to die this way. The beauty of man lies in his living for the sake of his homeland, not in dying while booby trapping others.[24]

Al-Musawi went further to say:

> Some of us say: 'May Allah curse the Jews and the Christians, the offspring of apes and pigs.' Is this the language of progress? Is this the language of enlightenment and tolerance? If you had been born in Rome, you would have been Christian, if you had been born in Tehran, you would have been Shiite, and if you had been born in Saudi Arabia, you would have been Sunni, and so

---

23. Abu Dhabi TV, *Bahraini Liberal Author Dhiyaa Al-Musawi*.
24. Abu Dhabi TV, *Bahraini Liberal Author Dhiyaa Al-Musawi*.

on. How wonderful it would be if all these people could gather in love around the table of humanity.²⁵

The words of Dhiyaa Al Musawi challenge the *status quo* not only in the majority Arab Muslim world but also in all Muslim lands because the latter often look up to the former as being much closer to the Islamic faith, sometimes providing the Islamic model. Unfortunately, however, Muslim scholars among them who dare call for critical thinking and re-interpretation of age-old ideologies in Islam (in the words of Abu Nimer and Yilmaz—"reinterpretation of Qur'anic teachings or Muslim history and tradition"²⁶)—are often branded as heretics and menaced with death. That company includes the Egyptian-born scholar, Naṣr Ḥāmid Abū Zayd, who, due to threats of death on his life, left Cairo and lived in exile in the Netherlands. Abū Zayd's 'sin' was his call for tolerance and reinterpretation of the Qur'ān, of Muslim history, and of Muslim traditions.

What point are we seeking to underscore from these examples? They are to show that there exist some Muslim scholars and intellectuals who admit that seeds of death and hate have been sown and continue to be sown, which instills and catalyzes the zeal toward acute violence, especially in the hearts of Muslim youths²⁷; and that, certainly, some Islamic scriptures exist that could be reinterpreted and used as grounds for true peacebuilding with "the other". For an enduring peacebuilding in the context of Islamist acute violence, "the language and culture of death" (in the words of Dhiyaa Al Musawi) that continue to promote the culture of hatred for the "other" must be countered from within Muslim communities—not only in the Arab world, but also in the global Muslim community (*umma*)—and this has to be done by Muslims themselves. In Nigeria's context, the onus will fall upon Muslim artisans of peace to work towards this. (We will pursue further discussion on the pragmatic dimensions in the section on Christian-Muslim carrefour for peacebuilding). Before we get there, we highlight, yet, a couple more references in the Qur'ān that speaks to peacebuilding. The first is alluded to Cain and Abel, the sons of Adam and Eve (Q. 5:27–29), and the second to those who kindle fires of war (Q. 5:64).

Cain and Abel's narrative in the Qur'ān presents another insightful Islamic scriptural basis for peacemaking and peacebuilding. This narrative appears in Q. 5: 27–29, and reads:

---

25. Abu Dhabi TV, *Bahraini Liberal Author Dhiyaa Al-Musawi*, Counter 05:10–05:35.
26. Abu-Nimer and Yilmaz, "Islamic Resources for Peacebuilding," 47–48.
27. Abu Dhabi TV, *Bahraini Liberal Author Dhiyaa Al-Musawi*.

> Q. 5:27 And recite to them the story of Adam's two sons, in truth, when they both offered a sacrifice [to Allah], and it was accepted from one of them but was not accepted from the other. Said [the latter], "I will surely kill you." Said [the former], "Indeed, Allah only accepts from the righteous [who fear Him].
>
> Q. 5:28 If you should raise your hand against me to kill me—I shall not raise my hand against you to kill you. Indeed, I fear Allah, Lord of the worlds.
>
> Q. 5:29 Indeed I want you to obtain [thereby] my sin and your sin so you will be among the companions of the Fire. And that is the recompense of wrongdoers.[28]

Comparatively with the Genesis account, Jews and Christians do not have the details of this conversation between Cain and Abel in their Scriptures. (My goal here is neither a textual criticism of this text in the Qur'ān nor an investigation into the source of the account). Since we are discussing peacemaking and peacebuilding in the context of Islamist acute violence from Muslim perspectives, it suffices to resort to resources resident in the Islamic Scriptures to argue for such potentials and possibilities. Thus, Abel's response to Cain in verse 28 expresses what I refer to as a *staurocentric*[29] model of peacebuilding-contextual theology—which will be the focus of discussion in our penultimate chapter. What a challenge Abel presents to all those who resort to violence in the face of aggression to learn to be God-fearing and to abandon all judgment to the One who judges justly! In *Tanwīr al-Miqbās min Tafsīr Ibn 'Abbās*, the commentator notes on verse 29 as follows: "Lo! I would rather thou shouldst bear the punishment of the sin against me and thine own sin of shedding my blood (and become one of the owners of the Fire) of the dwellers of hell. (That is the reward of evil-doers) Hell is the reward of those who wrongfully transgress."[30] Ḥamid Enāyat affirms that Cain and Abel's "story has an obvious moral import, and has always been treated as such by religious commentators, Muslim or otherwise, who have seen in it nothing other than a condemnation of greed and murder, especially fratricide. [And

---

28. https://quran.com/5/27-29.

29. This expression describes the epistemological framework and theology of the cross for peacebuilding. It is built upon the *kenosis* principle (see Martin, *Carmen Christi*). It is based on Jesus's giving of himself as a grain of wheat that fell to the ground, died, and multiplied (John 12:24–25, cf. Phil 2:5–11—the Hymn of Christ).

30. Ibn 'Abbās and Al-Fīrūzabādī, *Tafsīr Ibn 'Abbās*, 115.

that] –Abel, [is] 'the man of faith, peaceable and self-sacrificing', and Cain, 'the voluptuous, the transgressor and the fratricide.'[31]

John Renard, Harvard-trained scholar in Islamic Studies, discusses briefly Cain's question thrown back to God when God encountered Cain after the latter had murdered his brother, Abel. Cain's answer to God's question ("Where is Abel your brother?") was "I do not know; am I my brother's keeper?" (Gen 4:9). Was Cain expecting God to give him an answer to the question? On Cain's question to God, Renard asserts that "[b]oth the Christian and Islamic traditions have in their distinctive ways, answered that question in the affirmative."[32] In other words, both Christians and Muslims would say: Yes, I am my brother's [or sister's] keeper. Nevertheless, this analysis becomes complexified when followed up with another question: Who is my brother? Who is my sister? — a question that is not novel. A Jewish lawyer posed a similar question, asking Jesus: "Who is my neighbor? (Luke 10:29).

In the field of peacebuilding, it is likely that both Christians and Muslims will restrict the answer to their respective communities of faith. In the field of international relations, political nations and regions are likely to restrict their response to include only those within their respective national, regional or ethnic boundaries. On the part of Christians, however, Jesus's narrative of the Good Samaritan (Luke 10: 25–37) debunks such a restriction, because the cultural and religious differences that existed between Jews and Samaritans could have debarred the Samaritan from coming to the aid of that traveler who "was going down from Jerusalem [an indication that he might have been a Jew] to Jericho [and who was waylaid by] robbers who stripped him and beat him and departed, leaving him half dead" (Luke 10:30). For Muslims, there will certainly be a varying spectrum of responses to the question—who is my brother or sister? or "who is my neighbor?" One thing remains, however, incontestable. And that is: all humans are created by God and we all live on this one planet we call Earth. John Renard argues further that

> For Muslims and Christians alike, divinely mandated responsibility for their fellow human beings and for their earthly home covers a broad spectrum, from stewardship for creation to upholding the dignity and God-originated rights of each person, from establishing just social and religious institutions to seeking

31. Enāyat, *Modern Islamic Political Thought*, 156–57. In Muslim *Shi'a* culture, particularly in Iran, the story of Abel and Cain has acquired an additional significance–that of martyrdom. For cursory reading on this see *Modern Islamic Political Thought*, 181.

32. Renard, *Islam and Christianity*, 179.

a religiously ideal world in which all people espouse the same system of beliefs.³³

Before moving away from *Sūra* 5 (Q. 5), God's desire for peace in the world³⁴ could be deduced as well from verse 64 of this *sūra*. "... Every time they³⁵ kindled the fire of war [against you], Allah extinguished it. And they strive throughout the land [causing] corruption, and Allah does not like corrupters." Although the words are addressed to Jews in this passage, yet it could actually refer also to all who "kindle the fire of war" (نَارًا لِّلْحَرْبِ) –*nāran al-ḥarb*)–whether they are Jews or non-Jews. Some Muslims will, however, disagree that there are Muslims who also kindle the fire of war just as the Jews were attested to do in this verse. But the point to be put in relief from this verse is that it does not please God to see physical wars which result in violence and human bloodshed; and that, historically, Muslims can strongly attest and affirm it is not only Jews who kindle the fires of war. This is supported to some degree by verse 32 of the same *sūra* 5, which reads in part: "... We decreed upon the Children of Israel that whoever kills a soul unless for a soul or for corruption [done] in the land—it is as if he had slain [hu]mankind entirely. And whoever saves one—it is as if he had saved [hu]mankind entirely..." (Q. 5:32).

Classical Muslim commentator, Ibn Kathir, commenting on the above verse says it "states that whoever kills a soul without justification—such as in retaliation for murder or for causing mischief on earth—will be as if he has killed all [hu]mankind, because there is no difference between one life and another."³⁶ Ibn Kathir's emphasis is on the sanctity of human lives. He argues that the expression, وَمَنْ أَحْيَاهَا فَكَأَنَّمَا أَحْيَا النَّاسَ جَمِيعًا — *wa man 'ḥyāha fakā'nnāmā 'ḥyā a-nas jamī'n*—implies that "by preventing its [human] blood from being shed and believing in its sanctity, then all people will have been saved from him, so أَحْيَا النَّاسَ جَمِيعًا (it would be as if he saved the life of all [hu]mankind)."³⁷ Thus from Muslims' perspective, unjustified acute violence resulting to human bloodshed is considered, indeed, as a desecration of the sanctity of human life.

33. Renard, *Islam and Christianity*, 179.

34. In his contribution to the volume *Resources for Peacemaking in Muslim-Christian Relations*, Tanory Ateek attests that "[a]ccording to the Qur'ān peace was the original intention of God for all humanity" (Ateek, "Nonviolence of the Strong: Muslim Resources for Resistance," 37–57). "According to the Qur'ān peace was the original intention of God for all humanity" (Woodberry and Basselin, *Resources for Peacemaking in Muslim-Christian Relations*, 39 see n49).

35. "They" in the text refers to the Jews—دُوَيْدُ ال—*al-Yahūd*.

36. Ibn Kathir, *Tafsīr Ibn Kathir*, 2:113.

37. Ibn Kathir, *Tafsīr Ibn Kathir*, 2:113.

The above brief survey of some verses of the Qurʾān relating to peace are certainly only representative and far from being exhaustive. So, before we proceed to equally survey similar resources for peacebuilding as they appear in the traditions of the prophet of Islam—the *Aḥādīth*—the assertion of Khaled Aboud El Fadl on the position of the Qurʾān on peace is worthy of note. El Fadl, in his contribution to the volume *Islam in Transition: Muslim Perspectives*, asserts that "*salam* (peace and tranquility) is a central tenet of Islamic belief, and safety and security are considered profound divine blessings to be cherished and vigilantly pursued. The absence of peace is identified in the Qurʾān as a largely negative condition."[38] From the perspective of Muslims who take the Qurʾān seriously in regard to the issue of peacebuilding, it suffices to assert that *there exists an unmined wealth of concepts, resources, and tools from the Islamic scriptures that Muslims can employ to engage in peacemaking and peacebuilding within Muslim communities, with non-Muslims and also in within contexts of Islamist acute violence* (emphasis here is mine). This is the primary argument in this chapter. Inasmuch as there exist some Muslim views ostensibly opposed to peacebuilding based upon certain hermeneutics of the Qurʾān, yet the truth remains that those views are grounded upon non-holistic or unwholesome hermeneutical methods, at least from the view of open-minded Muslim scholars and exegetes. In the light of the witness to peacebuilding surveyed above, there exists much more witness of the Qurʾān supporting the side of peace than could be argued to support the side of war and violence. We turn now to the *Aḥādīth* (traditions of the prophet of Islam) to also highlight some resources for peacebuilding therein.

4.1.2 Resources for Peacebuilding from the Aḥādīth

In the preceding section, we saw, though briefly, the Qurʾān's reference to the two sons of Adam (Q. 5:27–29). The principle of peacebuilding underscored in the Qurʾān from those verses are also alluded to in the *ḥadith*.[39] In *Sunan Abi Dawud*, it is narrated that Muhammad, the Messenger of Allah said:

> Before the Last Hour there will be commotions like pieces of a dark night in which a man will be a believer in the morning and an infidel in the evening, or a believer in the evening and infidel in the morning. He who sits during them will be better than he who gets up and he who walks during them is better than he who runs. *So break your bows, cut your bowstrings and strike*

---

38. Abou El Fadl, "Islam and Violence," 460.

39. As already noted in the preface, where the rationales are stated, all references from the *Aḥādīth* are taken from https://sunnah.com/.

> *your swords on stones. If people then come in to one of you, let him be like the better of Adam's two sons.*[40]

The last two sentences in this *hadith* narrative are noteworthy: "So break your bows, cut your bowstrings and strike your swords on stones. If people then come in to one of you, let him be like the better of Adam's two sons [that is: like Abel]." This *hadith* echoes a biblical prophecy in Isa 2:4b and Mic 4:3b:

> [2:4] . . . and they shall beat their swords into plowshares, and their spears into pruning hooks; nation shall not lift up sword against nation, neither shall they learn war anymore.

It is not my intension here to delve into an exegetical analysis of this passage. We simply want to point out that the *hadith* we have cited: "So break your bows, cut your bowstrings and strike your swords on stones" (Sunnan Abi Dawud, Book 36, Hadith 4246) echoes these Biblical passages. Hence, could not this *hadith* be a resource for peacemaking and peacebuilding from Muslims' perspectives? Tanory Ateek believes it is one of the basis of central beliefs in Islam which provides resources for nonviolence engagement.[41] According to the narrative in the Qur'ān, Abel was not retaliatory in the face of threat to his life, for his response to his brother was: "If you should raise your hand against me to kill me—I shall not raise my hand against you to kill you. . . "(Q. 5:28). The idea of not raising one's hand against another to kill is akin to beating one's sword into a plowshare, or one's spear into a pruning hook. In other words, it is nobler and better to convert one's instruments of revenge, of war, and of violence into agricultural equipment with which one can tend God's creation and forthwith provide bread to feed oneself, the hungry, and become a blessing to one's neighbor.

Sahih Al-Bukhari devotes an entire section to the traditions of Muhammad's peacemaking approaches—a section titled "Book of Peacemaking" (Sahih Al-Bukhari 2690 Book 53, Hadith 1). In one of the narrations attributed to Al-Bara, the account of Muhammad's peacemaking toward Meccans is recorded in Al-Bukhari Vol. 3, Book 49, Ḥadith 863. This *hadith* is about Muhammad's encounter with the Meccans who were against him and seeking to restrain him from performing the *'umra* (the pilgrimage to Mecca) in the month of *Dhul-Qada*. The Meccans only acknowledged Muhammad as the son of Abdullah, but not as a messenger of Allah. In this regard, Muhammad

---

40. "Sunnah.Com," Sunnan Abi Dawud Book 36, Hadith 4246. Emphasis in italics is mine.

41. Ateek, "Nonviolence of the Strong," 39–40.

took the document [of agreement] and wrote, 'This is what Muhammad bin 'Abdullah has agreed upon: No arms will be brought into Mecca except in their cases, and nobody from the people of Mecca will be allowed to go with him (i.e. the Prophet) even if he wished to follow him and he (the Prophet–will not prevent any of his companions from staying in Mecca if the latter wants to stay.'[42]

Muhammad dispensed of being recognized as messenger of Allah in order that peace might be established. In addition, he also did not insist that any of his companions who wished to desert him and remain with the Meccans be prevented to do so. This is in consonance with a verse in the second *sūra* of the Qur'ān, *Al-Baqarah*, verse 256: لَا إِكْرَاهَ فِي الدِّينِ—*la ikrāh fī dīn* —"There shall be no compulsion in [acceptance of] the religion ..." (Q. 2:256).

Furthermore, a *ḥadith* attributed to Jabir bin 'Abdullah records Muhammad's response to his followers who questioned his standing up while a funeral procession of a Jew was passing by. "... We said, 'O Allah's Messenger ...! This is the funeral procession of a Jew." He said, "Whenever you see a funeral procession, you should stand up."[43] This is buttressed by another *ḥadith* attributed to 'Abdur Rahman bin Abi Laila, who reports:

> Sahl bin Hunaif and Qais bin Sa'd were sitting in the city of Al-Qadisiya. A funeral procession passed in front of them and they stood up. They were told that funeral procession was of one of the inhabitants of the land i.e. of a non-believer, under the protection of Muslims. They said, "A funeral procession passed in front of the Prophet ... and he stood up. When he was told that it was the coffin of a Jew, he said, "Is it not a living being (soul)?"[44]

These two traditions cited above reiterate the theme of *taʿāruf* (embracing "the other") which we have earlier alluded to in the preceding subsection (4.1.1).[45] Muhammad honored the dead of "the other" whose corpse was being carried to his or her burial place and encouraged his followers to do the same. Muslim exegetes suggest three reasons behind the action of standing

---

42. "Sunnah.Com," Sahih Al-Bukhari Vol. 3, Book 49, Ḥadith 863.
43. Sahih Al-Bukhari Vol. 2 Book 23, Hadith 398.
44. Sahih Al-Bukhari Vol. 2, Book 23, Hadith 399.
45. This Hadith is also reported in Sahih Muslim Book 4, Hadith 2098.

up while the bier of a non-Muslim was passing. One of those reasons[46] is deduced from Muhammad's words in the last *ḥadith* cited above—"Is it not a living being (soul)?" It points to the importance of honoring the sanctity and dignity of human life irrespective of the person's religion or ethnicity. Rashied Omar argues that this same *aḥadith* cited here reinforces the "concept of *taāruf* [as] an alternative vision to that of the tolerance paradigm and represents for [him—Omar] the litmus test of good religion."[47]

Besides the above examples from the traditions of Muhammad, other principles exist upon which peacemaking and peacebuilding in Islam can be constructed. Mohammed Abu-Nimer argues that peacebuilding in Islam is grounded on such principles as "*'adl* (justice), *iḥsan* (beneficence), *raḥma* (compassion), and *ḥikmah* (wisdom)."[48] Among these four principles, the first three—*'adl, iḥsan* and *raḥma* (justice, beneficence and compassion respectively)—have particular nexus to peacemaking and peacebuilding. The fourth principle, wisdom–*ḥikma*–is interwoven into the other three because wisdom (*ḥikma*) is a necessary requirement to execute and apply justice (*'adl*), beneficence (*iḥsan*), and compassion (*raḥma*). Here, we focus primarily on the first three, searching for connections in the *aḥadith*.

On the principle of justice (*'adl*), the *aḥadith* have much to say. A *ḥadith* attributed to Abdullah bin Umar narrates that the Messenger of Allah said:

> Behold! the Dispensers of justice will be seated on the pulpits of light beside God, on the right side of the Merciful, Exalted and Glorious. Either side of the Being is the right side both being equally meritorious. (The Dispensers of justice are) those who do justice in their rules, in matters relating to their families and in all that they undertake to do."[49]

In another *ḥadith* it is narrated that Muhammad said "[t]he best fighting (*jihad*) in the path of Allah is (to speak) a word of justice to an oppressive ruler."[50] From these and many other *aḥadith*, we see that they speak pointedly to the theme of justice from the traditions of Muhammad. Those who dispense justice (*'adl*) would be reckoned to sit with God—an

---

46. The other two reasons suggested by Muslim exegetes are: (1) standing for the angels (see Sunan an-Nasa'I Vol. 3, Book 21, Hadith 1931 https://sunnah.com/nasai/21/113); and (2) standing in awe and fear of death (see Sunan Abi Dawud, Book 20, Hadith 3168 https://sunnah.com/abudawud/21/86).

47. Omar, "Islam Beyond Tolerance," 18.

48. Abu-Nimer, *Nonviolence and Peace Building in Islam*, 49.

49. "Sunnah.Com," Sahih Muslim Book 20, Hadith 4493.

50. "Sunnah.Com," Sunan Abi Dawud 4344; Book 38, Hadith 4330.

idea akin to Jesus's words "Blessed are the peacemakers, for they shall be called sons of God" (Matt 5:9).

Still on the principle of justice (*'adl*), Majid Khadduri in his volume, *The Islamic Conception of Justice*, asserts that Muslims continue "to pursue the path to justice as a duty for the good of the community"[51] and such a pursuit is determined by reason, revelation or even by social habits. On how justice is pursued remains a debate among Muslim scholars, and wisdom becomes an essential element for weaving the methodological approaches to justice. Khadduri observes that there exist "differences arising. . . from changing circumstances [but] one of the continuing causes of disagreement among scholars was methodological: failure to relate the theory of justice to practice."[52] In view of this, Muslim scholars are not in accord on how "[d]ivine justice would be realized on Earth, not to speak of the hereafter."[53] What is evident from the *aḥadith*, however, is that Muhammad ". . . stressed religious values. . . [,] was a social reformer and his decisions provided precedents on the strength of which the issues that were to arise in succeeding generations were resolved. The idea of justice was of particular interest to him, and he dealt with the problems of his day with uprightness, balance, and fairness."[54] The relationship between justice and peacebuilding is intrinsic, for in a society where justice flows like streams, the causes of oppression and violence will be kept at bay, reduced, and may even be absent. In a society where there is lack of justice, the chances of revolt, high degree of violence become pronounced. This might be the case in Nigeria's context of Islamist acute violence. Thus, we argue that the motif of justice (*'adl*)—present in the *aḥadith* is a resource that should be explored and employed for constructing pathways to peacemaking and peacebuilding.

Concerning beneficence (*iḥsan*) or doing/being good (*khayr*), the Muslim practice of *sadaqa* (charity) has its roots in the traditions of Muhammad. In a narrative attributed to Abu Huraira, it is reported that Muhammad "said, 'There is a Sadaqa to be given for every joint of the human body; and for every day on which the sun rises there is a reward of a Sadaqa (i.e. charitable gift) for the one who establishes justice among people."[55] This *ḥadith* occurs in Al-Bukhari's section, "Book of Peacemaking" already referred to above. Abu-Nimer makes reference to this particular *ḥadith* and

---

51. Khadduri, *Islamic Conception of Justice*, 227; cited in Abu-Nimer, *Nonviolence and Peace Building in Islam*, 50.

52. Khadduri, *Islamic Conception of Justice*, 193.

53. Khadduri, *Islamic Conception of Justice*, 11,193.

54. Khadduri, *Islamic Conception of Justice*, 10–11.

55. "Sunnah.Com," Sahih al-Bukhari 2707 Vol. 3, Book 49, Hadith 870.

maintains that the injunction on Muslims to practice *sadaqa* occurs in not less than "twenty-five Qur'anic verses. [And that those verses] encourage Muslims to take more responsibility for redressing social injustice in their communities."[56] Thus, *sadaqa* could be considered as a tool for peacemaking and peacebuilding from the Muslims' perspective.

The challenge, however, lies on whether or not all Muslim scholars may agree that non-Muslims could also be beneficiaries of *sadaqa* from the hands of Muslims. In other words, should Muslims' performance of *sadaqa* be restricted toward only Muslims in their communities or could it be extended as hospitality to non-Muslims? In regard to this seeming challenge, Middle Eastern Studies researcher, Egbert Harmsen, points out in his published doctoral dissertation that "Mahmoud Sartawi, lecturer in shari'ah and fiqh at the Shari'ah Faculty of Jordan University, concurs that sadaqah is a moral obligation that every Muslim ought to practice on an ongoing and regular basis."[57] But as to whether it is should be universal or restricted to the community of Muslims alone, he posits that "[s]ome parts of the Qur'an are universalistic and compassionate in tone regarding the well-being of humankind in general. [Whereas] others emphasize differences with non-Muslims, condemning the kufar and mushrikun outright. . . ."[58] Harmsen adds that "countless different interpretations of the Qur'anic message exist. [But that] Sartawi clearly advocates the universalistic line when he stresses that the shari'ah-based principle of mutual help and solidarity with people in need is boundless. Everybody in need deserves help, regardless of skin color, origin, nationality or religion."[59]

On his part, Khaleed Abou El Fadl, while discussing "What All Muslims Agree Upon" in one of his works, *The Great Theft*, maintains that "in addition to alms[giving–*zakat*] Muslims are strongly encouraged to give charity (*sadaqa*), each according to his or her wealth and ability."[60] And in regard to the question of to whom *sadaqa* should be performed, El Fadl asserts that the

> Qur'an mentions groups of people particularly deserving of charity [*sadaqa*]: the poor, the orphan, relatives in need, wayfarers and strangers or aliens in the land, and prisoners of war or other people in a state of bondage. . . Importantly, most Muslims

---

56. Abu-Nimer, *Nonviolence and Peace Building in Islam*, 56.
57. Harmsen, "Islam, Civil Society and Social Work," 176.
58. Harmsen, "Islam, Civil Society and Social Work," 176.
59. Harmsen, "Islam, Civil Society and Social Work," 176–77.
60. Abou El Fadl, *Great Theft*, 120.

scholars make no distinction between giving charity to non-Muslims or non-Muslims.[61]

From these arguments, one will, with a high degree of confidence, maintain that the practice of *sadaqa* in Islam can serve as a tool Muslims may employ for peacebuilding not only within Muslim communities, but also with non-Muslims. Furthermore, *sadaqa* (charity) can also be linked to hospitality.

In Sunan Abi Dawud, Abu Shuraih al-Ka'bi reports that messenger of Allah said: "He who believes in Allah and the Last Day should honour his guest [with] provisions for the road are what will serve for a day and night: hospitality extends for three days; what goes after that is sadaqah (charity): and it is not allowable that a guest should stay till he makes himself an encumbrance."[62] A similar ḥadith is found in Sahih Muslim. "It is narrated on the authority of Abu Shuraih al-Khuzai' that the Prophet [Muhammad] observed: He who believes in Allah and the Last Day should do good to his neighbour and he who believes in Allah and the Last Day should show hospitality to the guest and he who believes in Allah and the Last Day should either speak good or better remain silent."[63] The question one may then ask is: Is there a common ground between peacebuilding and the practices of *sadaqa* and hospitality? Their connection is evident in the fact that a Muslim, with an intention to live out the true import of these practices, will not perform the obligation of *sadaqa* or offer hospitality to a non-Muslims against whom he or she intend to harm. In other words, if one gives *sadaqa* and hospitality, then she or he is providing a platform for building peace.

The idea of "not harming" the other (to whom the obligation of *sadaqa* and hospitality may be performed) is made more glaring in Riyad as-Salihin's *sunna*. According to Abu Hurairah, Messenger of Allah said: "He who believes in Allah and the Last Day let him not harm his neighbour; and he who believes in Allah and the Last Day let him show hospitality to his guest..." (Al Bukhari Book 1, Hadith 308). The expression "let him not harm his neighbor" in the original text is "فلا يؤذِ جارَه . . . " (*falā yu'dhi jārihi*) (Sunnan Riyad as-Salihin Book 1, 308). The principles of hospitality (*diyāfa*) and charity (*sadaqa*) are, therefore, intertwined in Islam that they could both be harnessed as tools for peacebuilding. This is possible because *sadaqa* and hospitality create the space where dialogue, embrace of the other (*ta'āruf*), and consequently peacebuilding can be cultivated,

---

61. Abou El Fadl, *Great Theft*, 120.
62. "Sunnah.Com," Sunnan Abi Dawud Book 27, Hadith 3739.
63. Sunan Sahih Muslim 48, Book 1, Ḥadith 78. This ḥadith appears also in Riyad as-Salihin: Book 1 (The Book of Miscellany), Hadith 308, and Book 2 (Book of Good Manners), Hadith Book 2, Hadith 706.

given that a Muslim will offer neither sincere hospitality nor *sadaqa* to another of whom he or she intends to harm.[64] This said, it does not imply that one should undermine the reality of the differences in understanding and interpretation of who "the neighbor" may be from the perspective of Muslims. As we have earlier hinted, the complexity of this issue can be eased by emphasizing the sanctity of human life, which both the Qur'ān and the *aḥādīth* alike affirm. Thus, irrespective of the differences of understanding and interpretation, Muslim artisans of peace possess a wealth of resources that can be employed using these concepts.

In regard to the principle of compassion or mercy (*raḥma*), Anas bin Malik attributed the following words to Muhammad: "None of you truly believes until he loves for his brother" or he said "for his neighbour, what he loves for himself."[65] This *sunna* reinforces the Qur'ān's injunction in Q. 28:77 "And do good as Allah has done good to you. And desire not corruption in the land . . ." It also reflects what has come to be widely known as the Golden Rule—Do unto others as you would have them do unto you.[66] This rule owe its origin to Jesus's teaching — ". . . Whatever you wish that others would do to you, do also to them. . ." (Matt 7:12). It is on this premise that Abdullahi Ahmed An-Na'im based the thesis of his volume, *Toward an Islamic Reformation*, arguing that "the universal principle of reciprocity requires a person to treat others as he or she would like to be treated by them, that is, to claim and exercise their own individual and collective rights to self-determination, Muslims must concede and guarantee that same right to others."[67] The principle of compassion and mercy is bound to this rule and it is a concept that should not be ignored in peacebuilding, whether on a micro (inter-personal) or on a macro (inter-communal, inter-ethnic, inter-religious or inter-national) levels.

On compassion and mercy, both the Qur'ān and the traditions of Islam's Prophet have robust statements which can be employed for peacebuilding from the Muslims' perspective. In a chapter on weeping for the deceased, Usamah ibn Zaid narrated what the Messenger of Allah said when

---

64. This argument is based on the grounds that the best intensions lie beneath the practices, but does not deny the possibility that, given the brokenness and evil often resident in human hearts, some may employ a practice(s) intended for peace and turn it/them into a Trojan horse to do evil, and destroy.

65. "Sunnah.Com," Sunnan Ibn Majah, Book 1, Hadith 69. Sahih Muslim reports a similar ḥadith in The Book of Faith Book 1, Ḥadith 72 قَالَ أَيُّ مُحَمَّدٍ أَحَدُ كُمْ حَتَّى يُحِبَّ لِأَخِيهِ ". وَأَوْ قَالَ لِجَارِهِ — امَ يُحِبُّ لِنَفْسِهِ".

66. For a succinct philosophical reflection on the Golden Rule, see "Internet Encyclopedia of Philosophy—A Peer-Reviewed Academic Resource": http://www.iep.utm.edu/goldrule/.

67. An-Na'im, *Toward an Islamic Reformation*, 1.

the news of a dying person was brought to him and he was requested to go there. The *ḥadith* reflects the idea of compassion. It reads in part:

> What Allah has been taken [sic] belongs to Him, what He has given (belongs to Him), and He has appointed time for everything. She then sent a message adjuring him (to come to her). So he came to her and the child who was on the point of death was placed in the hearts of those whom He wished. Allah shows compassion only to those of His servants who are compassionate.[68]

Muhammad's favorite wife, Aisha, is reported to have narrated what the Messenger of Allah told her while she was on a "camel which was somewhat intractable and the Prophet remarked: 'You must be compassionate. Whenever there is compassion in something, it adorns it, and when it [compassion] is removed from something it disgraces it.'"[69]

The theme of compassion (*raḥma*) pervades the Islamic scriptures. Three epithets are attributed to Allah in the opening *sūra* of the Qu'ran and they also become the opening heading for all the other *sūrat* in the Muslim Holy Book, بِسْمِ اللهِ الرَّحْمَٰنِ الرَّحِيمِ (*bismi Llahi Raḥmān, Raḥīm* — in the name of Allah, the Most Compassionate, the Most Merciful). Compassion and mercy are, therefore, imbedded within Islamic tenets and can become points of departure for peacebuilding. Malaysian renowned scholar of Islamic Law and Jurisprudence, Mohammad Hashim Kamali, in one of his volumes, *The Dignity of Man*, makes a strong case based on the Qur'ān and the traditions of the Prophet of Islam that compassion to all humans (not just Muslims to Muslims, but also Muslims to non-Muslims) is what Muhammad stood for. Sufi and Quranic exegete, Reza Shah-Kazemi, citing Kamali, writes: "One of [Muhammad's] companions, Abū Mūsā al-Ashʿarī said to the Prophet: 'You remind us so frequently about *raḥma* (compassion), even though we actually think that we are compassionate toward one another.' The Prophet replied: 'But I mean *raḥma* to all! (*innamā urīd al-raḥma bi'l-kāffa*).'"[70] Furthermore, Kamali in his award-winning volume,[71] *The Middle Path of Moderation in Islam*, argues that the Muslim "... ummah [community] is also a

---

68. "Sunnah.Com," Sunan Abi Dawud Book 20, Hadith 3119. The same *ḥadith* is narrated also in Sunnan Sahih Muslim Book 4 (The Book of Prayers—Funerals), Ḥadith 208.

69. "Sunnah.Com," Al-Adab al Mufrad, Book 26, Hadith 46. See: Al-Adab Al-Mufrad, Book 26 (Book of Compassion) Ḥadith 469 https://sunnah.com/adab/26/8.

70. Shah-Kazemi, *Spirit of Tolerance in Islam*, 12; Kamali, *Dignity of Man*, 1–8, 70.

71. Mohammad Hashim Kamali's volume, *Middle Path of Moderation in Islam*, was named the 2016 best book of the year at the 24th Iran International Book Festival in Tehran on February 7, 2017.

compassionate and just community, with the capacity to mediate between people and demonstrate by its very existence the mercy and justice of God."[72] In Kamali's understanding the themes of justice, goodness and mercy (or compassion) are all tied and they form essential elements that the Muslim *umma* must espouse if they are to ensure a balanced community. Our argument is that these concepts should serve as foundations for peacemaking and peacebuilding from the Muslims' perspective.

King Solomon asserted in one of his words of wisdom that "The beginning of wisdom is this: Get wisdom, and whatever you get, get insight" (Prov 4:7). Wisdom is an essential element. From the foregoing succinct survey of three principal concepts (*'adl, iḥsan* and *raḥma*) in Islam, we maintain that peacemaking and peacebuilding can be grounded upon the Islamic scriptural witnesses that attest to them. One may also add that the fourth concept—*ḥikma* (wisdom)—is an interwoven element required to apply the aforementioned principles. Kamali underscores this assertion in his concluding remarks on the "Manifestations of *Wasaṭiyyah*" (moderation). He writes,

> Wisdom that is guided by revelation encompasses values of honesty and justice, compassion and kindness, avoidance of harm and prejudice to oneself and to others. *Wasaṭiyyah* is about real-life situations, which more often than not present one with a mixture of diverse elements and conflicting interests, and the challenge of *wasaṭiyyah* becomes one of practical wisdom that is also informed by the guidelines of custom, cumulative knowledge, and experience of one's own and other civilizations. Islam's vision of *wasaṭiyyah* makes practical wisdom an integral part of its messages and the way of life it has envisaged for its followers.[73]

It seems appropriate to conclude this discourse with the note that "The Peace" (*as-Salām*) is one of the ninety-nine names of Allah in Islam.[74] Peacemaking and peacebuilding engagement from a Muslim perspective must, therefore, keep these concepts in mind to provide both motivation and resolve in the face of conflicting terms that engender violence. From both the Qur'ān and the *Aḥādīth* there exist unmined concepts and tools that can be explored, exploited and employed for constructing pathways to

---

72. Kamali, *Middle Path of Moderation in Islam*, 16.

73. Kamali, *Middle Path of Moderation in Islam*, 58.

74. Woodberry and Basselin, *Resources for Peacemaking in Muslim-Christian Relations*, 39.

peacemaking and peacebuilding in the context of Islamist violence (emphasis is mine).

On the one hand, we must laud the existence of these concepts and tools in Islam that can be explored for constructive and critical pathways to peacebuilding. On the other hand, we must also acknowledge the challenges that artisans of peace may confront vis-à-vis resources from Islamic scriptural texts. One of such challenges pertains to the principle of *taqiyya* in Islam, which finds its basis from the Qur'ān and the *Aḥādīth*. Sami Mukaram's volume in Arabic, *At-Taqiyya fī'l-Islam*—Dissimulation in Islam— is the authoritative Islamic scholarly work on the theme of *taqiyya*. Briefly, it is a concept wherein Muslims hold that the Qur'ān and the *aḥādīth* give them the leave to lie, dissimulate and display friendship on the outside to non-Muslims but inwardly seeking to attain their own ultimate purpose or goal. Foundational passages upon which the concept is drawn include: Qur'ān 3:28 "Let not believers take disbelievers as allies rather than believers. And whoever [of you] does that has nothing with Allah, except when taking precaution against them in prudence. And Allah warns you of Himself, and to Allah is the [final] destination"[75]; and the *hadith* attributed to Um Kulthum bint ʿUqba: "... she heard Allah's Messenger saying, "He who makes peace between the people by inventing good information or saying good things, is not a liar."[76] Khaled Abou El Fadl was confronted with this matter during the 2016 U.S. Presidential elections when a Republican candidate, Ben Carson, raised the matter of *taqiyya* in Islam, and Washington Post published an article on the issue.[77] We argue, therefore, that for concepts and tools for peacebuilding from the Muslims' perspective to be of use in any peacebuilding process, there must be a reformulation and outright rejection of such concepts (such as *taqiyya*) that encourage people to dissimulate or lie intentionally to deceive "the other." Peacebuilding cannot be achieved using a 'Trojan horse' motif.

Having surveyed these concepts based on the witness of the Qur'ān and *Aḥādīth*, we turn our discussion then to peacebuilding pathways in Islam that can be gleaned from some African Muslims in general and from the Nigerian context in particular.

---

75. Sahih International, *Al-Qur'an al-Kareem*, 3:28.
76. Sahih al-Bukhari Vol. 3, Book 49 Hadith 857.
77. See: https://www.washingtonpost.com/news/fact-checker/wp/2015/09/22/ben-carsons-claim-that-taqiyya-encourages-muslims-to-lie-to-achieve-your-goals/?utm_term=.779792c14bdo. For Further reading see: Ibrahim, "Lies about Islamic Taqiyya."

4.2 PEACEBUILDING FROM AFRICAN MUSLIMS' PERSPECTIVES

It will be beneficial to cast a bird's eye view on African Muslims' perspectives in general while zeroing-in on the possible concepts that we can draw from their ideas which will enhance the construction of pathways for peacebuilding in the context of Islamist violence. In order to embark on this objective, we discuss the pathways in Islam from African Muslims' perspectives that can be harnessed to construct both the sub- and supper-structures necessary for peacebuilding within Nigeria's context of Islamist violence.

Some African Muslim scholars are probing into and challenging Islamists' interpretations of Muslim scriptural texts (the Qur'ān and Aḥādīth) upon which they—the Islamists—base their actions of acute violence against non-Muslims, whom they consider to be *kuffār* (infidels) and, of course, also against Muslims who do not subscribe to or support their views and whom they reckon as having backslidden into *jahiliyya* (pre-Islamic ignorance).[78] Farid Esack, a South African Muslim scholar, posed the foundation for his volume, *On Being a Muslim*, upon "a comprehensive commitment to personal growth through involvement alongside others in a struggle to create a more humane and just world where people are truly free to make Allah the centre of their lives."[79] Two clauses are of note from the foundation of Esack's thesis namely: "alongside others" and "to create a more humane and just world." As far as Esack is concerned, "alongside others" is not limited to Muslim involvement with other Muslims. It entails, in addition, finding "a space in [his—Esack's] own theology for those who are not Muslim, yet are deeply committed to seeing the grace and compassion of an All-Loving Creator expressed in the righteous and caring works of ordinary men and women."[80] Esack, in his discussion "on the self in a world of otherness,"[81] takes the route with the African philosophy of *ubuntu*, as he declares ". . . I know that with the passing on of every person something of me also passes on, and that the birth of a person is also in a sense my birth, that *I am because you are* (emphasis here is mine),[82] that otherness is

---

78. Bassam Tibi correctly asserts that "Islamists argue that Muslims have fallen into *jahiliyya*, ignorance, and lack political consciousness and so need a surrogate to act on behalf of the besieged and oppressed umma. . . " Tibi, *Islamism and Islam*, 145–46.

79. Esack, *On Being a Muslim*, 3.

80. Esack, *On Being a Muslim*, 5.

81. Esack, *On Being a Muslim*, 136–61.

82. Esack's phrase accords with John Mbiti's words: "I am because we are; and since we are, therefore I am." Mbiti, *African Religions and Philosophy*, 141. Cited in: Hord and Lee, *I Am Because We Are*, 8. We engage in a robust discussion on *ubuntu* as one of the African concepts for peacebuilding in chapter 5.

a condition of selfhood. I also know that celebrating and esteeming otherness is, in fact, a celebration of the self."[83] As an African Muslim scholar, Farid Esack is not a lone bird in espousing this principle, which we argue, should become a tool from African Muslims' perspective (in general) and Nigerian Muslims' perspective (in particular) for engaging in peacemaking and peacebuilding in the context of Islamist violence.

Sudanese *Ustadh* Mahmoud Mohammed Taha, whose life was unfortunately and unjustly cut short by hanging on January 18, 1984, presents another eloquent African Muslim example. One of *Ustadh* Taha's works, *The Second Message of Islam*, has been translated by one of his protégé, Abdullahi Ahmad An-Na'im, who in turn has been building upon the foundation laid by his teacher, Taha. Before outlining Taha's and An-Na'im's positions, a foundation for their paradigmatic shift argument is necessary.

The theme of abrogation[84] (*naskh*) is well-known among Muslim scholars—a theme that is a field of study in Islam. The crux of Quranic abrogation posits that certain later verses of the Qur'ān abrogate certain earlier revelations of Muhammad. This theology of abrogation is based primarily on Quranic verses such as: "Whenever We abrogate a verse or cause it to be forgotten, we bring one better than it or one equal to it. Do you not know that Allah is powerful over everything?"[85] as well as "And when We substitute a verse in place of a verse—and Allah is most knowing of what He sends down—they say, 'You, [O Muhammad], are but an inventor [of lies].' But most of them do not know."[86]

Most of the abrogating verses (*al-naskh*) are reputed to be revelations or verses received during the Medina period, whereas the abrogated verses (*al-mansūkh*) are tied to the Meccan period of Muhammad's revelations. For example in regard to the Quranic verses that approve the use of violence and force to oblige non-Muslims to submit to Islam,[87] Abdullahi Ahmad An-Na'im maintains that

---

83. Esack, *On Being a Muslim*, 142.

84. For a succinct introduction on abrogation in Islam see Christopher Lamb's essay "Abrogation," 16–26. See also Shāh Walī Allāh on the Causes of Abrogation in: Renard, *Islamic Theological Themes*, 65–70.

85. Sahih International, *Al-Qur'an al-Kareem*, 2:106.

86. Sahih International, 16:101. See also Q. 22:52 "And We did not send before you any messenger or prophet except that when he spoke [or recited], Satan threw into it [some misunderstanding]. But Allah abolishes that which Satan throws in; then Allah makes precise His verses. And Allah is Knowing and Wise." Sahih International, 22:52.

87. An example of such verses include what has come to be known as the Sword Verse, Q. 9:5 "And when the sacred months have passed, then kill the polytheists wherever you find them and capture them and besiege them and sit in wait for them at every place of ambush. But if they should repent, establish prayer, and give zakah, let them [go] on their way. Indeed, Allah is Forgiving and Merciful." Sahih International, *Al-Qur'an al-Kareem*, 9:5.

> All the verses of the Qurʾan and related Sunna that sanction the use of force in propagating Islam among [non]-Muslims and in upholding it among renegade Muslims were revealed and uttered by the Prophet during the Medina stage. In accordance with the principle of *naskh*, abrogation or repeal, the founding jurists have held that these subsequent texts and practices of the first Islamic state that was based on them must have legally abrogated or repealed all previous texts and practices that were inconsistent with what was perceived to be the final message of the Prophet in Medina. In this way, the earlier Meccan texts and practices were seen as a transitional stage, dictated by tactical considerations, namely, the small numbers and the relative weakness of Muslims during that stage. With the massive conversion of Arabs to Islam and the establishment of the Islamic state in Medina, it was perceived that the Muslims became strong enough to propagate their faith by force and subjugate all the enemies of the Islamic state, whether within or outside the Muslim community.[88]

Thus, Islamists base their propaganda for the use of violence and war on the abrogating verses of the Qurʾān. The late Osama bin Laden, for example, in his "World Islamic Front Declaration to wage *Jihad* Against the Jews and Crusaders"[89] on February 23, 1998 cited Q. 9:5 and buttressed it with a reference to Ḥadith Sahih Muslim, Book 1 Hadiths 33–36.

Now, in regard to the doctrine of abrogation, *Ustadh* Mahmoud Taha takes a rather novel and revolutionary position. Taha's position on the abrogated verses is "that the abrogation process (*naskh*) was in fact a postponement and not final and conclusive repeal."[90] He states that "[t]he primary texts were repealed or abrogated, in the sense of being postponed and suspended in relation to legislation until the proper time, which has dawned upon us now."[91] Taha posits that there is the First Message of Islam as well as the Second. He likens religion to a pyramid with "the peak being with God at infinity, and the base with humanity."[92] The First Message of Islam represents the base of the pyramid and the Second points toward the peak. He also maintains that a "good society is one that is based on three equalities: economic equality. . . ; political equality or democracy . . .; and

---

88. An-Naʿim, *Toward an Islamic Reformation*, 158.

89. For the full text of Osama bin Laden's declaration, see Bin Laden and Ẓawāhirī, *Al Qaeda Reader*, 11–14.

90. Ṭāhā, *Second Message of Islam*, 21.

91. Ṭāhā, *Second Message of Islam*, 137.

92. Ṭāhā, *Second Message of Islam*, 165.

social equality . . ."[93] But the First Message of Islam, according to Taha, was deficient in ensuring economic equality, was not democratic and not socialist.[94] He classifies the Sword verse of the Qur'ān (Q. 9:5) as one of the verses that represent the First Message of Islam and which became "the basis for the Shari'a of *jihad*, while the verse of Shura [consultation] provided the Shari'a of government, in accordance with the principle of guardianship of the mature individual [the Prophet] over the community."[95]

A careful analysis of Taha's work shows that those verses of the Qur'ān on which Islamists underpin their theological base to engage in violence and human bloodshed belong to Taha's First Message of Islam and, therefore, to the analogical base of his pyramid of religion. On the other hand, those verses of the Qur'ān that sue for equality and peace to ensure the good society—one "characterized by a lack of social classes and discrimination based on color, faith, race and sex"[96]—belong to the Second Message of Islam and closer to the peak of the pyramid of religion. It is toward this peak that "true submitters (*al-muslimin*)"[97] must strive, Taha insists.

With regard to perspectives for peacebuilding, Taha's message—although not yet widely received by Muslim orthodoxy—could become a revolutionary tool from the perspective of Muslims to build peace and denounce acts of violence and war in name of Allah and of Islam. Taha further posits that "economic and political equality are preludes to social equality, [and that] the latter has not yet been accomplished."[98] However, he holds that they would be accomplished

> when man moves away from his base animal drives and develops a superior moral character. The law of the jungle—the law of violence and oppressive force—will then be replaced by the law of justice, truth and compassion—thereby improving the equality of human relations. [And when that happens, then]

93. Ṭāhā, *Second Message of Islam*, 153.
94. Ṭāhā, *Second Message of Islam*, 166.
95. Ṭāhā, *Second Message of Islam*, 166.
96. Ṭāhā, *Second Message of Islam*, 153.
97. *Ustadh* Mahmoud Taha differentiates between *al-mu'minin* (believers) and *al-muslimin* (true submitters). He states: "Actually, present Muslim society is the nation of the *al-mu'minin* [believers]. No nation up to now has deserved the name *al-muslimin*. Any mention of Islam with respect to previous nations refers merely to initial Islam, excepts for the pioneers of humanity who achieved ultimate Islam, or rather a degree of the ultimate Islam, as the ultimate Islam can never be exhaustively achieved. Such pioneers are, therefore, the pioneers of the nation of *al-muslimin* which has not come yet" Ṭāhā, *Second Message of Islam*, 151.
98. Ṭāhā, *Second Message of Islam*, 161.

Consensus will replace force, justice exploitation, freedom oppression and intelligent community awareness selfish individual drives.[99]

Ustadh Mahmoud Taha's protégé, Abdullahi An-Na'im, follows in his footsteps. In his discussion on the "Universality of Human Rights" An-Na'im adopts the position "that there are certain universal standards of human rights which are binding under international law and that every effort should be made to enforce them in practice."[100] He goes further to maintain that the golden rule is "a common normative principle shared by all the major cultural traditions, which if construed in an enlightened manner, is capable of sustaining universal standards of human rights."[101] An-Na'im based the thesis of his volume on this principle. This principle, as we have earlier highlighted, although drawn from Jesus's teaching in Matt 7:12, is also reflected in the Islamic scriptures (in Qur'ān 28:77 and the Sunan Ibn Majah, The Book of the Sunnah, Book 1, Ḥadith 69). An-Na'im, maintains it is a "principle of reciprocity shared by all the major religious traditions of the world. [And that] the moral and logical force of this simple proposition can easily be appreciated by all human beings of whatever cultural tradition or philosophical persuasion."[102] He made the same point in an article he entitled "A Kinder, Gentler Islam?" where he argues that "the Islamic tradition must undergo its own reformation and develop a modern conception of Shari'a that can be implemented today."[103]

Based on the arguments of these African Muslim scholars—Esack, Taha, and An-Na'im—which we have briefly surveyed, we posit that *there exist concepts, resources, and concepts from the Muslims' perspectives that can be harnessed, used and applied for constructing pathways for peacemaking and peacebuilding within a context characterized by Islamist violence* as it is the case in Nigeria—a case orchestrated by Boko Haram's acute violence and being exacerbated by Muslim Fulani herdsmen.

Taking this matter closer to Nigeria's context, examples are sparse. Historical development in northern Nigeria attests to intra-Muslim conflicts and fight for legitimacy to gain both political and economic power. John Paden synthesizes this thought, asserting that what has been the "central issue within the Muslim community of Nigeria for the past two hundred years has been what degree of tolerance is necessary to sustain unity with

---

99. Ṭāhā, *Second Message of Islam*, 161–62.
100. An-Na'im, *Toward an Islamic Reformation*, 162.
101. An-Na'im, *Toward an Islamic Reformation*, 162.
102. An-Na'im, *Toward an Islamic Reformation*, 162–63.
103. An-Na'im, "Kinder, Gentler Islam?," 8.

diversity, without letting syncretism or cultural mixtures run riot in the local traditionalist communities."[104] This was what undergirded Usman dan Fodio in his jihad of the nineteenth century, and was the crux behind the conflicts between Abubakar Gumi's Yan Izala group and two principal Sufi brotherhoods earlier mentioned (Qādiriya and Tijāniya). The matter still remains the bottom line of conflicts in most intra-Muslim conflicts in northern Nigeria and also plays a role in religious and political appointments, such as the appointment of the Sultan of Sokoto.[105]

Insofar as I am aware, persuasive Nigerian Muslim scholars advocating Islamic reformation drawn from the Islamic scriptural grounds for peace with "the other", particularly with non-Muslim, are yet to emerge. One erudite Nigerian Muslim scholar, Professor Is-haq Olanrewaju Oloyede, who was formerly a professor of Islamic Studies and Vice-Chancellor at the University of Ilorin and currently[106] the Registrar and Executive Director of Nigeria's Joint Admissions and Matriculation Board (JAMB), has nonetheless presented papers and written on the subject of peace in Islam.[107] Peacebuilding engagement with non-Muslims drawing from Islamic scriptural texts and traditions is, however, left begging in Oloyede's papers and presentations. For example, in his paper— "In Search of a Peaceful Society" presented at the reunion luncheon of the University of Lagos Muslim Alumni Association on June 25, 2000, Oloyede's attention focuses solely on the dimension of justice in society as a prerequisite for peace. His conclusion is that

> Peace... could not be attained unless there is justice and control. Islam encourages man to long for peace through the observance of justice and it considers any appropriate step, be it peaceful or military, towards peace as justifiable unless injustice is uprooted from the surface of the earth... To Muslims, justice to Allah requires that His expressed wish (the Shariah) be non-negotiable... We therefore conclude by calling on the government of the Federal Republic of Nigeria to accept the reality of legal pluralism as the only applicable system of justice in Nigeria...[108]

From Oloyede's conclusion above, we highlight two issues. First, "Islam encourages man to long for peace through the observance of justice

---

104. Paden, *Muslim Civic Cultures and Conflict Resolution*, 183.

105. Paden, *Muslim Civic Cultures and Conflict Resolution*, 183–88.

106. As at the time of writing this volume.

107. Oloyede "That All May Be One," 37–44; and Oloyede, "In Search of a Peaceful Society"; Oloyede, "Secularism and Religion."

108. Oloyede, "In Search of a Peaceful Society," 18–19.

and it considers any appropriate step, be it peaceful or military, towards peace as justifiable . . ."[109] The issue is this: can resort to military means ever engender a peaceful society? On our part, we doubt it, for I maintain that physical or military war, which unavoidably always leads to human bloodshed, hardly ever produces authentic and enduring peace. War can only continue to breed war, not peace. Secondly, Oloyede believes that the Islamic law must be a "non-negotiable" in Nigeria but he fails to engage the practicality of its outworking in a country where demographically non-Muslims (Christians, ethno-religionists, and people of other faiths in Nigeria together) outnumber Nigerian Muslims.

Yet, in another paper published in *Islam and the Modern Age*, Oloyede attempts to discuss Muslim engagement with non-Muslims around the theme of 'Secularism and Religion.'[110] But his argument is at best selective. He engages Quranic verses such as Q. 9:6: "And if any one of the polytheists seeks your protection, then grant him protection so that he may hear the words of Allah. Then deliver him to his place of safety. That is because they are a people who do not know" but he makes no mention of the preceding verse: "And when the sacred months have passed, then kill the polytheists wherever you find them and capture them and besiege them and sit in wait for them at every place of ambush. But if they should repent, establish prayer, and give *zakah*, let them [go] on their way. Indeed, Allah is Forgiving and Merciful."[111] Such ambivalence in Oloyede's voice—at one time insisting on non-negotiability of the Shari'a, and at another presenting an unbalanced view of Muslim tolerance of "the other"—leaves one with nothing but doubt if he can be counted as a scholar with a peacebuilding voice insofar as non-Muslims are concerned.

That said, it does not imply that there are no Nigerian Muslims who are engaging in peacebuilding efforts. One example, which we consider to be a positive deviance, is the case of Imam Muhammad Ashafa, who has been working together with Pastor James Wuye to build peace in local communities. We will come back this in the next section on artisans of peace. But before we turn to that, we maintain that Nigerian Muslim scholars of the caliber of Farid Esack of South Africa and *Ustadh* Mahmoud Taha and his protégé, Abdullahi Ahmed An-Naʿim both of Sudan, are needed today within the Nigerian context.

---

109. Oloyede, "In Search of a Peaceful Society," 18.
110. Oloyede, "Secularism and Religion," 31–34.
111. Sahih International, *Al-Qurʾan al-Kareem*, 9:5–6.

4.3 ARTISANS OF PEACE WITHIN THE MUSLIM *UMMA*: PEACEBUILDING INSIGHTS FROM NON-AFRICAN AND AFRICAN CONTEXTS

We outlined in chapter 2 some of the historical elements that need be considered for conceptualizing a peacebuilding-contextual theological paradigm for Nigeria's context of Islamist acute violence. We explore now some insights from both non-African and African contexts that will be helpful to conceptualize a peacebuilding-contextual theology germane for a context of acute violence. The rationale undergirding this is tied to the idea that we can glean and apply knowledge from those who precede us. Obviously, ignoring to learn from people who have trodden the same road, one is bound to repeat the same mistakes and slide into the same pitfalls in which those who have gone before had made and fallen into respectively. In her contribution to *The Oxford Handbook of Religion, Conflict, and Peacebuilding*, S. Ayse Kadayifci-Orellana "argues that effective peacebuilding strategies in Muslim contexts should engage Islamic conceptions of peace and justice, and work together with credible agents of peace, including religious leaders."[112] There are "credible agents of peace" from the Muslim *umma*, who have been engaging in peacebuilding either in their capacity as leaders in their community of faith or as leaders of organizations or movements. In view of this, our goal here is to survey a few Muslim religious leaders or organizations who have been engaging in peacemaking and peacebuilding employing the tools and resources resident in their Islamic faith and tradition.

But before we begin discussion on these key artisans of peacebuilding, one needs to answer the question: Who can be considered an artisan of peace? The answer to this question provides the criteria for distinguishing between peacebuilders and those involved in other activities we might not strictly classify as peacebuilding such as relief, community development, women rights' advocacy etc. In a report compiled by Salam: Institute for Peace and Justice for Clingendael: Netherlands Institute of International Relations, the following criteria were established to determine who could be counted as peacebuilding actors: "They were considered peacebuilding actors if their objectives and activities included peacebuilding activities of advocacy, education, observation, transnational justice and intra/inter-faith dialogue . . . with the aim of resolving conflicts and establishing peace."[113] The distinguishing marks, therefore, include advocacy, mediating between parties in conflict, observation, education, transitional justice and inter-faith, intra-faith and intercultural dialogues. With these criteria in mind we

---

112. Kadayifci-Orellana, "Peacebuilding in the Muslim World," 430.
113. Abu-Nimer and Kadayifci-Orellana, "Muslim Peacebuilding Actors," 11.

first survey a couple of non-African Muslim artisans of peace, followed by a survey of another couple within the African continent.

4.3.1 Muslim Artisans of Peace in non-African Contexts

In contexts of violence involving adherents of two or more religious faiths, peacebuilding requires artisans of peace from the different religious communities or camps affected by the violence. Even when violence is within the confines of a given religious faith (that is: intra-religious), peacebuilding still requires artisans of peace from the different camps involved. Although our discussion here is on 'Muslim Artisans of Peace', in the examples that follow some non-Muslim artisans of peace are mentioned alongside the Muslim artisans of peace with whom they were involved in building peace. The purpose of mentioning the non-Muslim artisans is to provide essential context for our discussion. Our goal here is to put in relief the argument that there are Muslims who subscribe to building peace in contexts of violence. But we need to, however, bear in mind that they do so with other artisans of peace from non-Muslim religious communities since peacebuilding in contexts of violence always involves artisans of peace from the affected camps.

With the above note in mind, our first non-African example of peacebuilding artisans comes from Bosnia-Herzegovina (BiH). Without delving into the historical background of the conflict,[114] on June 9, 1997, two years after the end of the Bosnia war, religious leaders consisting of a Muslim leader (Reisu-l-ulema, Dr. Mustafa Cerić), the Serbian Orthodox church leader (the Metropolitan of Dabar-Bosna Nikolaj), the Roman Catholic church leader (the Archbishop of Verhbosan-Sarajevo), and the President of the Jewish community of Bosnia-Herzegovina signed and issued a public statement they called "Statement of Shared Moral Commitment."[115] With the issuance of this Statement the Inter-Religious Council of Bosnia-Herzegovina (IRC-BiH) was created. In that statement they avouched that though the various faith communities "differ from each other, and that each of them feels called to live true to its own faith, [yet they acknowledged that their] religious and spiritual traditions hold many values in common, and that these shared values can provide an authentic basis for mutual esteem, cooperation and free common living in Bosnia-Herzegovina."[116] The Inter-Religious Council of Bosnia-Herzegovina worked together to see to the enacting of the

---

114. For a short background on the conflict in Bosnia and Herzegovina, see the entry in *Encyclopedia Britannica*, "John R. Lampe," https://www.britannica.com/event/Bosnian-conflict and at http://www.history.com/topics/bosnian-genocide.

115. Fischer, *Peacebuilding and Civil Society in Bosnia-Herzegovina*, 199.

116. Fischer, *Peacebuilding and Civil Society in Bosnia-Herzegovina*, 199.

"Law on Freedom of Religion and Legal Position of Churches and Religious communities in Bosnia and Herzegovina"—a law that was passed by the Parliamentary Assembly of Bosnia and Herzegovina in January 2004, and published on March 9 the same year in Bosnia and Herzegovina's Official Gazette No. 5/04 at Sarajevo. In that law, clauses that sue for peacebuilding are evident. Article 4, clause 1 reads in part:

> Everyone has the right to freedom of religion or belief, including the freedom to publicly profess or not a religion. Also, everyone has right to adopt or change his or her religion, and the freedom—individually or in community with others, in public or private—to manifest his religion or belief in any manner in worship, practice and observance, maintenance of customs and other religious activities ....[117]

Honoring the right of "everyone . . . to adopt or change his or her religion, and the freedom . . . to manifest his [or her] religion or belief in any manner in worship, practice and observance . . ." is what constitutes true religious freedom. This freedom articulated in this law is essential for constructing peacebuilding pathways. The matter of conversion or the decision to change one's religion or faith is what must be left to the realms of the divine. We posit that humans must let God be God. The boundary line for people of every faith, in my conception, must be to bear bold but humble witness of their faith in deed and words (where possible), but with respect and trust towards "the other." As per the decision for persons to submit to that witness lies beyond the acts of humans. Such must be considered as dimensions of the divine—acts of God alone. Thus, each one should be persuaded of his or her convictions and be ready to bear the responsibilities ensuing from such persuasion and subsequent decisions, for each will be answerable to the divine at the time of judgment.

On the matter of religious freedom, here is what a former British Prime Minister, David Cameron, had to say during a visit to Egypt and Kuwait in February 2011: "Freedom and democracy are the best way to bring peace and prosperity to the Middle East . . . Greater openness can lead to greater stability."[118] It is, therefore, a major contribution to peacebuilding in Bosnia-Herzegovina for the Muslim religious leader, Dr. Mustafa Cerić (Reis-il-Ulema of the Islamic Community of BiH) to sanction the terms of religious freedom stipulated both in the "Statement of Shared Moral Commitment"

---

117. Parliamentary Assembly of Bosnia-Herzegovina, "Law on Freedom of Religion and Legal Position of Churches and Religious Communities in Bosnia and Herzegovina."

118. Kirkup, "Democracy Is Route to Peace in Middle East."

and the in the "Law on Freedom of Religion and Legal Position of Churches and Religious communities in Bosnia and Herzegovina." It must be reckoned that this law was indeed a brainchild of the Inter-Religious Council of Bosnia-Herzegovina. The organization's Assembly (made up of high religious leaders of the Islamic community, the Serbian-Orthodox Church, the Roman Catholic Church and the Jewish community) selected a group of legal experts in 1999 representing each of the religious communities involved to work together and to draft a new law in regard to freedom of religion.[119] In 2002, the draft was sent to the country's President for review and later presented to the Ministry of Human Rights who worked together with the IRC-BiH legal experts and finally sent the law to the Parliament for ratification. The involvement of Muslim leaders and Muslim legal experts in the articulation, drafting, and ratification of such a law, in my judgment, will remain an eloquent testimony to Bosnia-Herzegovina Muslims making significant contribution to peacebuilding. Their examples should be emulated by many other Muslim leaders and legal experts in other contexts.

The second clause of Article 4 of this law is worthy of attention: "Churches and religious communities shall not, when teaching religion or in other actions, disseminate hatred and prejudices against any other Churches and religious communities or its members, or against the citizens of no religious affiliation, or prevent their freedom to manifest in public their religion or belief."[120] The underlying reason why this clause is worthy of note is because it evokes what Bahraini intellectual and author, Dhiyaa Al-Musawi called (as we have already alluded to) the "language of hate and culture of death"[121] An example of such indoctrination, for example, is found in elementary and secondary school texts books used in some Muslim countries. Children are taught that Jews are apes and Christians are swine—whom Muslims must extricate from the earth in order to establish *al-hikimiyyat* Allah (what I call *Allahcracy*). Such teaching still remains in the educational and religious curriculum of certain Muslim countries, either officially or traditionally. In her testimony to the United States Congress, Nina Shea, who directs the Center for Religious Freedom at the Hudson Institute's Center for Religious

---

119. See slides 16–20 in IRC-BiH Presentation posted on their website, which gives the development and historical background of the organization: http://www.mrv.ba/upload/attachments/irc_bih_OVt.pdf.

120. Parliamentary Assembly of Bosnia–Herzegovina, "Law on Freedom of Religion and Legal Position of Churches and Religious Communities in Bosnia and Herzegovina."

121. Abu Dhabi TV, *Bahraini Liberal Author Dhiyaa Al-Musawi*.

Freedom, presented her findings from her "study of Saudi textbooks for grades 1 through 12 in the religious curriculum"[122] She expressed

> fears that the Saudi government was indoctrinating its young people in violent and belligerent teachings ... [because she discovered that Saudi] textbooks teach an ideology of hatred and violence against Jews, Christians, Shiites, Sufis and Ahmadis, Hindus, Bahais, Yizidis, animists, sorcerers, and "infidels" of all stripes, as well as other groups with different beliefs ... Christians, Hindus and those "practicing witchcraft" are to be fought and killed," according to the texts. Each year, these textbooks directing religious hatred, violence and war indoctrinate six million Saudi students and reach untold millions of others as they are spread far and wide in the Muslim world by a state that claims moral authority as the custodian of Islam's holiest sites.[123]

Nina Shea's testimony does not stand alone, and it is not only in Saudi Arabia that such indoctrination is practiced in the Muslim world. In 2006, a non-partisan American research group, Freedom House, smuggled textbooks out of Saudi Arabia and examined them. The group "found that despite promises of change from leading Saudi officials, including Saud al-Faisal, the foreign minister, and Turki al-Faisal, the ambassador to America, schoolbooks in the kingdom still promote hatred of those who do not practise its strict form of Wahhabi Islam"[124] *The Telegraph*'s Middle East Correspondent, Harry de Quetteville, affirmed that the report issued by the Freedom House "also alleged that some of the textbooks are used in official Saudi schools around the world."[125]

Imam Shaikh M. Tawhidi, also known as "Imam of Peace" and a leading Muslim critic of Islamists' acts of violence, makes a similar case in his YouTube video response to Islamists' killing of Coptic Christians in Egypt in May 2017. Tawhidi critiques the Grand Mufti of Australia, Dr. Ibrahim Abu Hamid, whom he asserts was trained at Al-Azhar University in Cairo Egypt—the Ivy league theological university of the Muslim world. Tawhidi, alleges that in Al-Azhar University

> they teach the students that it's okay to wipe yourselves in the toilets with the pages of the Bible and the pages of the Torah and you can insult Christianity and insult Judaism... because it's not real Islam and that it's not the religion of God, therefore,

122. Believers Portal, "Jews Are Apes, Christians Are Swine."
123. Believers Portal, "Jews Are Apes, Christians Are Swine."
124. de Quetteville, "Christians Still 'Swine' and Jews 'Apes' in Saudi Schools."
125. de Quetteville, "Christians Still 'Swine' and Jews 'Apes' in Saudi Schools."

wipe yourself in the toilet with the pages of their Book. But if someone draws a cartoon about the Prophet Muhammad (peace be upon him) and his family you want to go and behead him. But it's okay for you to go and do that to other people's religious and Holy Books.[126]

With such teachings, it will be a draconian task to pursue pathways to peacebuilding without a reconsideration and reintegration of those tenets in Islam that advocate for peace with "the other." In the light of these, Clause 2 Article 4 of the Bosnia-Herzegovina Law on Religious Freedom (to which Muslim leaders and Muslim legal experts in Bosnia-Herzegovina fully assented) remains revolutionary and an example Muslims of all countries and contexts should emulate. It goes further to support this chapter's thesis that, indeed, *there exist unmined concepts, resources and tools in Islam that can be harnessed and creatively employed toward peacemaking and peacebuilding in contexts of Islamists-orchestrated acute violence.*

The second example of Muslim artisans of peacebuilding in non-African context comes from Turkey. It is the Gülen Movement (Hizmet in Turkish)—a movement named after Turkish Muslim scholar, Fethullah Gülen. The "movement is a worldwide civic initiative rooted in the spiritual and humanistic tradition of Islam and inspired by the ideas and activism of Mr. Fethullah Gülen."[127] It is a faith-based movement that draws from Islamic "values such as love of the creation, sympathy of the follow human, compassion and altruism . . . "[128] In Turkey, the Gülen Movement—reckoned to be "the largest civic apolitical movement"[129]—underpins its activities on spiritual values such as love for neighbor, tolerance of the other, human rights, integrity, as well as material and social values such as democracy, science and education, creation care and the arts. For brevity, we dwell here only on Gülen's theology of peace which undergirds this peacebuilding community-based movement.

Whereas, Samuel P. Huntington saw in the ensuing challenges orchestrated by globalization and pluralism a "clash of civilizations", Fethullah Gülen, *par contre*, foresees a "collaboration of civilizations" in a globalized world.[130] Gülen believes such a collaboration could be realized through interfaith dialogue and education. Gülen's pursuit for peacebuilding is grounded

---

126. Imam Tawhidi, "Persecution of Christians in Egypt," Counter 12:41—13:15, Counter 12:41 to 15:15, at https://www.youtube.com/watch?v=bec7tpBqR-U.

127. Gülen Movement, "What Is the Gülen Movement."

128. Gülen Movement, "What Is the Gülen Movement."

129. Esposito and Yilmaz, *Islam and Peacebuilding*, 9–10.

130. Bozkurt and Yildirim, "Fethullah Gülen's Vision for Peace," 47.

upon his Islamic faith conviction on love. He couples his faith conviction on love with hard work, which together provides the framework for activism—of which the Gülen Movement has been characterized. Gülen's theology of peace, grounded on love, is not limited to his fellow Muslims alone. In accordance with Quranic verses such, Q. 5:32, Gülen firmly holds to "the integrity of the individual regardless of ethnic or religious background."[131] Through Gülen's teachings and writings, his movement has been serving as a model for collaboration with others "to overcome the problems of humankind, regardless of religious, ethnic or cultural differences. The movement sets a precedent, not only with its activities, but also through its ways of generating financial support, thanks to its revivification of the Islamic values of giving and hospitality."[132]

Sociologist and scholar, Helen Rose Ebaugh, analyzes the movement in her volume, *The Gülen Movement: A Sociological Analysis of a Civic Movement Rooted in Moderate Islam*, and maintains that the Gülen Movement is a civic movement anchored in moderate Islam and "advocates quality, modern education for all youth, interfaith and intercultural dialog, and mutual cooperation among cultural and religious groups."[133] In addition to these elements, the movement assists the needy in society as well as contributing to global peace. Ebaugh based her analysis on interview data she collected during her visits to institutions with Gülen roots in Turkey and the United States.

Mohammed Abu-Nimer and Ihsan Onur Yilmaz in their joint contribution to the volume *Islam and Peacebuilding: Gülen Movement Initiatives* reiterates the point we have previously made in this chapter—that "Muslim values of peace include concepts such as *ihsan* (perfect goodness, healing, reconciliation), *samah* (forgiveness), *sabr* (patience), *adl* (justice), *taqwa* (piety), *aml al-khayr* (good deed), and collective sense of communal peacemaking and human solidarity (*ummah*)."[134] Abu-Nimer and Yilmaz posit that these concepts form a solid theoretical framework upon which peacebuilding from Islamic perspective can be pursued.

From the two non-African examples of Muslims' involvement in peacebuilding it is evident that Muslims are employing concepts, resources and tools in Islam to engage in peacemaking and peacebuilding initiatives in their communities and in contexts characterized by violence. Are there any African Muslim examples employing these concepts, resources,

---

131. Esposito and Yilmaz, *Islam and Peacebuilding*, 12.
132. Gülen Movement, "What Is the Gülen Movement."
133. Ebaugh, *Gülen Movement*, 107.
134. Abu-Nimer and Yilmaz, "Islamic Resources for Peacebuilding," 41.

and tools for peacebuilding in African contexts? This is the focus of the next subsection.

4.3.2 Muslim Artisans of Peace within the African Context

The first example in Africa comes from Kenya, East Africa. It is a movement that was started by a woman—who unfortunately died in a ghastly vehicle accident on July 14, 2011, Mrs. Dekha Ibrahim Abdi (1964–2011). Dekha founded the Wajir Peace and Development Committee and was also involved in founding the Coalition for Peace in Africa, and Action for Conflict Transformation. Dekha said she "acquired her deep insights into conflict dynamics not as an academic but through her grassroots activism as a young woman in Northern Kenya who simply could not accept the violence between the different ethnic communities. She later used her own experience to help and train others."[135] In an interview she granted to Katherine Marshall of the Berkley Center for Religion, Peace and World Affairs at Georgetown University in May 2010, Dekha recounts how she began to work for peace in northern Kenya and how that peacebuilding efforts evolved. Mrs. Ibrahim Abdi was a teacher and an educator and she focused her work on bringing education to nomadic people—who were always on the move. In regard to the sort of conflicts in which Wajir Peace and Development Committee was involved in building peace she said

> The community was ethnic Somalis and Kenyan nationals. There were factions within the community, and they were one against the other. But about three years down the line, this mutated and changed. At first, there was not a religious dimension, but this did arise, because there was a Christian minority that was being attacked. The tensions did not arise because of historic religious problems within the community, but were sparked by a problem in a different part of the country. Again, we used the same kind of shuttle diplomacy. And we created through that process interfaith groups that took root and have lasted.[136]

Mrs. Ibrahim Abdi pointed out that the conflict was initially political but it later took on regional dynamics because of the influx of refugees and arms from Ethiopia and Somalia. Dekha and her collaborators became more and more aware of the "international dimensions of conflicts... [and of the role that] national and international politics played... in [their]

---

135. http://www.independent.co.uk/news/obituaries/dekha-ibrahim-abdi-2315364.html/.

136. Ibrahim Abdi, "Discussion with Dekha Ibrahim."

community. Religious tensions were not at all obvious or pronounced in the early years, but they did emerge, within the Muslim community and beyond, as the broader world intruded more and more into [their] lives."[137] Conflicts, therefore, may be traced to a specific cause (political, ethnic, religious etc.), but they might morph into complex dynamics which englobe other dimensions that were not part of the initial cause.

On the specific peacebuilding initiatives of Wajir Peace and Development Committee, Dekha said they involved both traditional and religious leaders in their communities. Muslim and non-Muslim religious leaders were invited to become involved in the peacebuilding process. They sought to analyze the specific contexts and did so with the parties affected by the violence. In order for their peacebuilding initiative to remain relevant and effective, the actors were flexible vis-à-vis the constantly changing dynamics of the contexts of violence. Creativity and innovation were encouraged in their peacebuilding process. With these elements, the peacebuilding actors were able to achieve peace and reduce violence in northern Kenya.

The point needs to be underscored that Dekha Ibrahim was a Muslim woman and according to an obituary written by Scilla Elworthy and published in *The Guardian*, "Dekha's spiritual identity as a Muslim formed a strong foundation for her peace work. She explored the Qur'an's teaching on understanding the soul in terms of bringing about durable peace. Indeed, she encouraged individuals and communities in conflict to examine themselves using verses from the Qur'an."[138] Thus, Dekha's peacebuilding initiatives were strongly grounded upon her Islamic faith—an observation that further supports our argument that *within Islam there abound concepts, resources and tools that can be employed for peacebuilding in the contexts of violence.*

Our second African example of Muslim artisans of peacebuilding comes from Nigeria—an example we previously alluded to. Imam Muhammad Ashafa has been working together with Pastor James Wuye to build peace in a number of communities in northern Nigeria. They co-authored the book, *The Pastor and the Imam: Responding to Conflict*, which documents their efforts toward peacemaking and peacebuilding. Ashafa and Wuye assert that:

> Religion today, instead of serving as a source of healing sickness, hunger, and poverty, and stimulating tranquility and peaceful co-existence among human beings, is used to cause sadness. It is bringing pain instead of relief, hatred instead of love, division

137. Ibrahim Abdi, "Discussion with Dekha Ibrahim."
138. Elworthy, "Dekha Ibrahim Obituary."

instead of unity, sadness instead of joy, discrimination and destruction instead of accommodation and development. This is especially true between some adherents of Islam and Christianity. Nigeria has its own share of this negative phenomenon. Its ethnic-religious conflict has become a matter so serious and devastating that it can now be seen as a harbinger of the danger of a crisis such as those that have engulfed the former Yugoslavia, Rwanda and Liberia.[139]

Ashafa and Wuye's story has been documented in the volume *Peacemakers in Action: Profiles of Religion in Conflict Resolution*,[140] and in *Religious Contributions to Peacemaking*.[141] On November 6, 2009, the Fondation Chirac awarded its first Conflict Prevention Prize to Imam Muhammad Ashafa and to Pastor James Wuye for their peacebuilding efforts in Nigeria. During the award ceremony, former French President, who owns the foundation, described these Nigerian artisans of peace as among those who "blaze new paths, ignoring the lazy logic of fatality . . . embody hope . . . fight against evil . . . give hope a chance . . . [and] prove that the best is possible."[142] In his own speech at that same ceremony held at the Amphitheater in Sorbonne, the then French President, Nicolas Sarkozy, said: "Our two Nigerian laureates have demonstrated—in a country that sorely needs such proof—that people of different religions can live together in peace. There are, frankly, so few of you who believe in these ideas and strive to put them into practice that it behoves us to pay tribute to the courage and the spirit of peace that underpin your work."[143]

Indeed, "there are so few. . . who believed in these ideas and strive to put them to practice . . ." It is possible to garner the resources of peace that exist in different religious traditions and employ them pragmatically to build peace. That said, we must, however, acknowledge that the path Imam Ashafa and Pastor Wuye have trodden did not begin with ease, and we should not expect that those who would travel such roads of peacebuilding

---

139. Ashafa and Wuye, *Pastor and The Imam*, 1.

140. Little and Tanenbaum Center for Interreligious Understanding, *Peacemakers in Action*, 247–77.

141. Smock, *Religious Contributions to Peacemaking*, 17–28; see also: Tongeren et al., *People Building Peace II: Successful Stories of Civil Society*, 226–32. For an update on Ashafa and Wuye's story, see Dubensky and Tanenbaum Center for Interreligious Understanding, *Peacemakers in Action*, 2:427–37.

142. http://www.fondationchirac.eu/wp-content/uploads/2009/11/discours-jc-anglais-charte.pdf. See also: Dubensky and Tanenbaum Center for Interreligious Understanding, *Peacemakers in Action*, 2:429.

143. http://www.fondationchirac.eu/wp-content/uploads/2009/11/0611-fondation-jacques-chirac-version-anglaise.pdf.

would have it otherwise. Ashafa and Wuye were rivals at the onset but they have become brothers in peacebuilding. Both were involved and affected by acute religious violence involving Christians and Muslims in their communities in the early 1990s. Pastor Wuye lost his right arm and close relations, while Imam Ashafa lost his mentor and teacher. However, events unfolded that galvanized into their founding of "Muslim-Christian Dialogue Forum (MCDF), a religious grassroots organization that has been active in mediation and reconciliation efforts between Muslim and Christian communities in [northern] Nigeria since 1995."[144] Their testimonies, captured in an audio-video documentary,[145] reveal that working together toward peacemaking, given their divergent religious beliefs, has not in any way been without challenges—both from each other and from the communities they have sought to mediate and enact peacemaking. Some of the fruit that their efforts have yielded include the encouragement of dialogue and community engagement "involving people from all sides of conflicts."[146] Besides, they continue to take their peacebuilding initiatives beyond the borders of Nigeria—to Khartoum and Baghdad.[147] The case of Pastor Wuye and Imam Ashafa, in my opinion, is an illustration that, indeed, Muslims can work together with non-Muslims for constructing peacebuilding pathways in their communities and contexts of violence. A multiplication of such efforts or initiatives is needed, not only in Nigeria but also in other regions where inter-faith conflicts exist and continue to engender violence. And who are those who must champion such a course if not those invited to participate with the triune God in his mission in world—that is: followers of Jesus?

We have highlighted a few Muslim artisans of peacebuilding from both non-African and African contexts. The logical conclusion we draw from these trailblazers—to borrow Jacques Chirac's expression of those who blaze new paths—is that *there exist within Islam concepts, resources, and tools that can be harnessed and employed in constructing pathways to peace.* Given that there are concepts, resources, and tools in Islam that can be harnessed and employed in constructing peacebuilding pathways, what are the possible points of commonality between Muslims and Christians' peacebuilding perspectives? This is the question we attempt now to engage.

---

144. Little and Tanenbaum Center for Interreligious Understanding, *Peacemakers in Action*, 247.

145. Channing, *Imam and The Pastor*.

146. Dubensky and Tanenbaum Center for Interreligious Understanding, *Peacemakers in Action*, 2:430.

147. http://www.fondationchirac.eu/en/2010/02/from-kaduna-to-baghdad-and-khartoum/.

4.4 CHRISTIAN-MUSLIM CARREFOUR FOR PEACEBUILDING

In our concluding section in chapter 2, I defined a *carrefour* as an intersection or crossroads. We noted that roads may merge at a carrefour, and that a carrefour may equally refer to a marketplace with the sense of a place where, not only sellers and buyers converge but also different merchandise and commodities are brought to converge. For the purpose of consistency, we retain that language here to portray the "Christian-Muslim *Carrefour* for Peacebuilding", which depicts the emerging crossroad from Muslims' perspectives of peacebuilding (as we have seen from the preceding sections of this chapter) and similar concepts from the Christian tradition. Our purpose for pointing our attention to this carrefour is double pronged. First, it is to delineate those principles, concepts, resources, and tools that are common to both faith traditions. Second, it is to gather the materials required for a constructive peacebuilding-contextual theology grounded upon a *staurocentric* theoretical framework—a task we undertake in the last chapter. We noted that a carrefour of knowledge can become a market place of ideas. Thus, just as the Turkish Muslim teacher and scholar, Fethullah Gülen, has opined, instead of seeing the challenges existing between different civilizations and religious traditions as a clash, one can, in fact, perceive them as opportunities for collaboration. Such perception places value on difference and diversity, echoing Adiele Afigbo's model of inter-group relationship highlighted in chapter 3. In such a model, Afigbo maintains that " . . . exchange implies that one gives what one has in plenty and receives what one lacks. In short, people involved in inter-group relationship along the lines of this model do for, or give to, one another what each cannot either do for, or give to himself."[148]

Thus, we begin outlining the carrefour by pointing first to Khaled Abou El Fadl's writing on the theme of *iḥsan*—a theme we surveyed above. Abou El Fadl asserts that *iḥsan* is a term in the Qur'ān, which besides its literal meaning of kindness, also implies "to beautify and improve upon." He maintains that such action of "beautification or improving upon can have meaning only in the context of a certain sociological understanding and practice."[149] He supports his assertion by citing Qur'ān 4:135:

> O you who have believed, be persistently standing firm in justice, witnesses for Allah, even if it be against yourselves or parents and relatives. Whether one is rich or poor, Allah is more

---

148. Afigbo, "Age of Innocence."
149. Abou El Fadl, *Place of Tolerance in Islam*, 14.

worthy of both. So follow not [personal] inclination, lest you not be just. And if you distort [your testimony] or refuse [to give it], then indeed Allah is ever, with what you do, Acquainted.[150]

On this El Fadl writes: "The idea that Muslims must stand up for justice even against their own self-interests is predicated on the notion that human beings are capable of achieving a high level of moral agency."[151] The element of standing up for justices even against one's own self-interest finds a point of intersection in Christian Scriptures. I refer to this as a *staurocentric* element.

In Phil 2:4 each follower of Jesus is admonished to "look not only to his [or her] own interests, but also to the interests of others" and to have the mind that is in Christ Jesus. The "mind which is in Christ Jesus" is elaborated in the Christ Hymn, Phil 2:6–11—where the *kenosis* principle is found in verse 7 (ἀλλ' ἑαυτὸν ἐκένωσεν *all' heauton ekenōsen*)—but himself, he emptied.[152] The Lord Jesus Christ poured out (emptied) his own life on the cross (σταυρός—*stauros*), and he left this principle as a model for those who would follow him. The Apostle Peter, writing to followers of Jesus in the dispersion (diaspora) said: "For to this you have been called, because Christ also suffered for you, leaving you an example, so that you might follow in his steps" (1 Pet 2:21). In the penultimate chapter of this volume, we will engage in a broader exegetical investigation around this theme of *staurocentric* pathway. It suffices to note at this juncture that there exists a mystery in Jesus's death produced at his Calvary event. The cross has many implications of death and life for the follower of Jesus. It entails dying to the propensity to hold on to one's man-made security on the one hand, but entrusting one's entire life and being to Jesus and then awaiting the resurrection, which without failure engenders a multiplied life, on the other hand.

We argue that this element of the cross is reflected in Islamic scriptures but may have been apparently denied and ignored by many Muslims over the centuries of Islamic history. Abou El Fadl brings it to the fore in his assertion that Q. 4:135 enjoins Muslims to stand up for justice even when such action would be against their own interest. He buttresses his assertion while honing on the true meaning of *jihad*—"to strive hard or struggle in pursuit of a just cause,"[153] he adds: "according to the Prophet of Islam, the highest form of jihad is the struggle waged to cleanse oneself from the

---

150. Sahih International, *Al-Qur'an al-Kareem*, Q. 4:135.
151. Abou El Fadl, *Place of Tolerance in Islam*, 14.
152. This is my translation.
153. Abou El Fadl, *Place of Tolerance in Islam*, 19.

vices of the heart."[154] What could be more true? The evil and violence in the heart of individual humans, if mastered and overcome, would lead to overcoming the multiplied evil and violence in the structures of community and society. Eminent Islamic Studies scholar, J. Dudley Woodberry asserts: "The primary problem is not the war on the ground but the war in the human hearts that then spills out on the ground."[155] It is unfortunate that any religious tradition would be fighting the physical 'war on the ground' which was only there because it spilled out from the hearts of those fighting that war. The Roman Catholic Church committed this error when Popes and people sanctioned the Crusades. Islamists Muslims continue to commit the same error when they sanction a 'war on the ground' when it is indeed some sort of war spilling out from their own human hearts.

If anything must be said loud and clear it is this: 'War on the ground' breeds blood; and blood that is poured, *not* in the war of self-giving for the good of "the other", can only breed more blood, more evil and more violence. Physical war that entails human bloodshed will hardly ever engender peace. Such may birth a temporary, but false peace. Put metaphorically, a thorn-bush never bears apples or grapes. Thorn-bushes will always produce thorns—spikes that prick, stab, and wound. The realm of war must, instead, be in the spiritual—first against our human fallen nature and the evil and violence that exist in our human hearts, and second against the unseen powers of darkness, whether they are perceived as systemic societal structures or as unseen demonic principalities and powers. When individual humans triumph over the evil in their respective human hearts there would be little or no evil or violence on the ground to combat, because the roots of the evil and violence in the society would have been rooted out. The way to such victory, I maintain, is the cross—a concept that we are now arguing exists as resource both in the Christian and Muslim traditions. I am very aware that the cross in Islam is an objectionable symbol. Its shadow is, nevertheless, cast in Islam by the element of seeking justice even against one's own self-interest (Q. 4:135). Should this concept be emphasized (though it doesn't have to be called "the cross" by Muslims) among both communities of faith, what great highways to peacemaking and peacebuilding we would be constructing, not only in the arenas of Islamist violence, but worldwide!

Another carrefour we find in both traditions is the theme of "neighbor" or the response to the question: "Who is my brother/sister?" In our survey of the witness to peace in the Qur'ān, we made reference to the Qur'ān's account

---

154. Abou El Fadl, *Place of Tolerance in Islam*, 19.

155. Woodberry and Basselin, *Resources for Peacemaking in Muslim-Christian Relations*, viii.

of Adam's two sons (Cain and Abel) found in Q. 5:27–29; and also to a couple of commentaries on that pericope. In addition, we drew attention to Q. 5:32 and to Ibn Kathir's commentary who asserts that the verse "states that whoever kills a soul without justification—such as in retaliation for murder or for causing mischief on earth—will be as if he has killed all mankind, because there is no difference between one life and another."[156]

From the Christians' perspective, Jesus taught on this theme in Luke's account recorded in Luke 10: 25–37. The narrative of the Good Samaritan in this account loudly asserts that one's neighbor is not necessarily his or her ethnic/religious neighbor, but anyone in need of one's help, support and assistance irrespective of ethnicity or religious affiliation. As the ease of travel, the preponderance of migration (people on the move) and of globalization in the twenty-first century bring humans from the four cardinal points of the earth closer and closer, we are bound to recognize that the boundaries of who is our neighbor have expanded from the limited ethnic and religious boundaries within which we were born and raised. My neighbor today may be a Chinese fellow student who sits in the same seminar class with me in Pasadena, California, even though I come from one small village, Umuduruejeme in Umudim, Imo State, Nigeria. Your neighbor today, may be a Saudi Muslim woman attending a conference on Islam with you in one of the ivy leagues in the east coast of the United States, or a student from Myanmar sitting in the class where you teach, or an Indian machine learning engineer working with you in an Artificial Intelligence outfit nestled in Silicon Valley in the Bay Area of northern California. Thus, in both the Christian and Muslim communities of faith, we argue that the theme or concept of "neighbor" is a common ground and it is an element, a resource, and a tool that can be employed to advance the construction of peacebuilding pathways in the context of violence.

Furthermore, we surveyed three basic principles found in the *aḥadith* namely justice (*'adl*), beneficence or goodness (*iḥsan*), and compassion (*raḥma*). Following the argument of some Muslim scholars (Mohammed Abu-Nimer and Majid Khadduri for example), we posited that *there exists an unmined wealth of concepts and tools that can be explored, harnessed and employed in the challenge of peacemaking and peacebuilding in the context of Islamist violence.* Here, we simply highlight the carrefour where these principles in the Islamic tradition intersect with the Christian tradition. What the LORD [YHWH] requires of followers of Jesus include to do justice, to love kindness and to walk humbly with God (Mic 6:8). The Lord Jesus called these principles the "weightier matters of the law" while

---

156. Ibn Kathir, *Tafsīr Ibn Kathir*, 2:113.

chiding Jewish scribes and Pharisees who placed more value on other matters (Matt 23:23). Besides, the fruit that the Holy Spirit produces in the lives of those who submit to Jesus include "love, joy, peace, patience, kindness, goodness, faithfulness, gentleness, [and] self-control; [and] against such things there is no law" (Gal 5:22–23). Justice, beneficence, and compassion are undeniable Christian virtues that become manifest through the outworking of the Holy Spirit in the lives of people who follow Jesus without hypocrisy and dissimulation. The charge to love "the other" is made very explicit in various ways in the New Testament. Jesus set the bar very high for those who would follow him. He said:

> Love your enemies and pray for those who persecute you, so that you may be sons of your Father who is in heaven. For he makes his sun rise on the evil and on the good, and sends rain on the just and on the unjust. For if you love those who love you, what reward do you have? Do not even the tax collectors do the same? And if you greet only your brothers, what more are you doing than others? Do not even the Gentiles do the same? You therefore must be perfect, as your heavenly Father is perfect. (Matt 5:44–48)

These words of Jesus are affirmed by the Apostles in their letters to all followers of Jesus. John the Apostle, for example, wrote: "If anyone says, "I love God," and hates his brother, he is a liar; for he who does not love his brother whom he has seen cannot love God whom he has not seen. And this commandment we have from him: whoever loves God must also love his brother" (1 John 4:20–21). As we have earlier argued, one's "brother/sister" or "neighbor" must *not* be understood as restricted to one's ethnicity or religious affiliation. From these Christian positions, we posit that there exists, indeed, a carrefour where both the Christian and Muslim traditions meet on matters concerning justice, beneficence and compassion, and that this carrefour should serve as a common ground toward constructing pathways for peacemaking and peacebuilding, not only in the context of violence, but also in community building.

Before we conclude this chapter, it necessary to make a brief observation on "A Common Word Between Us and You" and how it could serve peacemaking and peacebuilding initiatives. It can be considered as a landmark 'carrefour' document. Hence, we focus on what is relevant to peacebuilding therein. "A Common Word Between Us and You" is an open letter that was signed by 138 leading Muslim scholars and clerics, addressed to Christian leaders and denominations worldwide on October 13, 2007.[157] The initiative attracted multiple responses and a number of works have been published around the theme of interfaith dialogue generated by the open letter. Insofar as I am aware, at least two graduate theses have been written around this theme.[158] The Yale Center *for* Faith & Culture at Yale Divinity School issued a response to that letter barely a month after the release of "A Common Word" (ACW) and the said response was published in the *New York Times* on November 18, 2007. In the preamble of the Yale Response, the responders wrote: "We receive the open letter as a Muslim hand of conviviality and cooperation extended to Christians worldwide. In this response we extend our own Christian hand in return, *so that together with all other human beings we may live in peace and justice as we seek to love God and our neighbors* (emphasis is mine)."[159]

The authors of and signatories to "A Common Word" (ACW) noted that the adherents of the two world religions—Christianity and Islam—constitute more than half of the world's population. In view of this fact, they asserted that lack of peace and justice between these two communities of faith will deny the world "meaningful peace."[160] Furthermore, whereas ACW cited a *ḥadith* which we have already mentioned in our survey in this chapter (Sunnan Ibn Majah, Book 1, Hadith 69) wherein the Messenger of Islam said *"None of you has faith until you love for your neighbour what you love for yourself* (emphasis in the cited source)"; the Yale Response on its part makes reference to 1 John 4:8 "whoever does not love [the neighbor] does not know God" and "whoever does not love his brother who he has seen cannot love God who he has not seen" 1 John 4:20.[161] The point made in these interfaith dialogical documents are, in my opinion, a carrefour that must be made the most of for building peace in the context of Islamist violence.

One of the pragmatic steps toward the construction of pathways to peacebuilding will entail (as was noted in the Yale Response) leaders of

---

157. The Royal Aal Al-Bayt Institute for Islamic Thought, *Common Word Between Us and You*, v; The Royal Aal Al-Bayt Institute for Islamic Thought, *Common Word*, 7.

158. Joseph Victor Edwin, "A Common Word Between Us and You: A New Departure in Muslim Attitude Towards Christianity" being a dissertation submitted to the University of Birmingham for the degree of Master of Philosophy (MPhil) in March 2010; and Laura Elizabeth Provencher, "A Critical Analysis of the Islamic Discourse of Interfaith Dialogue" being a thesis submitted to the Graduate College of the University of Arizona, for the degree of Master of Arts, Department of Near Eastern Studies, 2010.

159. Volf et al., *Common Word*, 51.

160. The Royal Aal Al-Bayt Institute for Islamic Thought, *Common Word Between Us and You*, 7; Volf et al., *Common Word*, 53.

161. Volf et al., *Common Word*, 54.

the two communities of faith "at every level to meet together and begin the earnest work of determining how God would have [them] fulfill the requirement that we love God and one another."[162] On my part as a follower of Jesus, authentic truth-telling must be the bastion of collaboration. As we have already highlighted, a number of Muslim scholars have opined a reformation of Islamic thought.[163] Among the thoughts that will require such reform or re-reading include the Muslims' resort to *taqiyya* (which we have mentioned in a previous subsection) employed to honor the commitments they may make for a dialogical peacebuilding. Similarly, Christians on their part must jettison aggressive and unhospitable approaches in their encounter with Muslims, speaking the truth from the heart and employing Martin Accad's *kerygmatic* approach, which requires trust and respect for the other. Some of the ground work that this will require include expunging of hateful teachings—such as the one we have mentioned wherein Muslim children are taught that Jews are apes and Christians swine; and that it is permissible to Muslims to use the pages of the Bible as toilet paper. The same applies also to those Christians who think that by burning the Qur'ān they are gaining a spiritual ground. This sort of work must be done from the grassroots, supported with structures in which religious leaders affirm and sanction the teaching of love for "the neighbor." It is upon such speaking of truth to one another from the heart with trust and respect that a true common ground can be set for peacebuilding.

Lastly, though not the least, both Christianity and Islam are "missionary" religions. In other words, adherents of both faiths see it as their duty and responsibility to woo and win non-followers of their way to adhere to their faith. My position is that, indeed, the matter of conversion lies beyond the act of humans. Conversion—a heart-felt conviction and decision to forsake a faith one has been groomed in to follow another faith—can only be an act of God, not of humans. In my opinion, where people are coerced to follow a faith, they remain slaves and hardly experience the liberty of their spirits. Followers of every faith should be allowed to have the liberty and be given the freedom to share their faith while respecting the other. There should neither be coercion nor enticing to win anyone to one's side. The act to win someone over to one's faith lies in the spiritual. So let Muslims live out and be witnesses to Islam by word and acts of kindness to non–Muslims. And let Christians do the same. Both Christians and Muslims must exercise the

---

162. Volf et al., *Common Word*, 56.

163. Examples include the Bahraini scholar Dhiyaa Al-Musawi who posits that "We [Muslims] need to reform and to reshape religious thinking . . . " Abu Dhabi TV, *Bahraini Liberal Author Dhiyaa Al-Musawi*; Abū Zayd et al., *Reformation of Islamic Thought*; and An-Na'im, *Toward an Islamic Reformation*.

liberty to bear witness to their respective faiths to others (through actions of kindness and by words), but the action of conviction and conversion of people to any faith must be left to the realms of the divine. If any must do anything to change "the other" by fighting, let the fighting be only between him or her and the God to whom he/she wishes to win over the other. We put it differently in the words of Gideon's father, Joash, "Will you contend for Baal? Or will you save him? Whoever contends for him shall be put to death by morning. If he [Baal] is a god, let him contend for himself, because his altar has been broken down" (Judg 6:31). Let men and women stop contending for the God whom they serve. If YHWH be God, let Him contend for Himself! And if Allah be Allah, let Him contend for Himself!

It may be considered an insult on and an affront to God for mere humans to fight for Him. Who can arrogate to himself or herself such a power to fight on God's behalf? Is God so weak and incapacitated that He cannot fight for Himself? Peacebuilding will be within reach when, as humans, we love the neighbor and bear witness to the other of our faith, but leave God to do what makes Him God—convicting and converting people and nations to Himself in whichever way and methods He chooses, which (I believe) is devoid of violence. Thus, both Christians and Muslims should position themselves for peacebuilding while bearing witness of their faith, speaking the truth in love, and respectful toward the other, but leaving the matter of wooing and winning into the hands of the divine.

Our focus in this chapter has been on peacebuilding concepts from Islamic and Muslim perspectives. We have argued that *there exist within Islam concepts, resources, and tools that can be harnessed and employed in constructing pathways to peace*. We proceed in the next chapter to explore more concepts of peacebuilding but from African ethno-linguistic cultures.

5

African Concepts for Peacebuilding-Contextual Theology

THE CONDENSED PARKOUR OF Islamic texts and of some Muslim artisans of peace (in African and non-African contexts) undertaken in the previous chapter led to the tangible conclusion that there exist within Islam concepts, resources, and tools that can be harnessed and employed for peacebuilding-contextual theology. In this chapter, we turn our reflection toward indigenous African concepts that can be constructively and critically incorporated in peacebuilding-contextual theology. We recall that in chapter 3 we put forth the idea that peacebuilding-contextual theology be admitted into the house of contextual theologies, not only for African contexts but also in our globalizing world. Thus, it is rational then that we now reflect on the African concepts that lend themselves to peacebuilding. The question this chapter attempts to answer is: What concepts of peacebuilding are embedded within African cultures that may be employed and integrated in developing peacebuilding-contextual theology?

We first cast a bird's eye view on a few sub-Saharan African peacebuilding concepts—as found in contemporary literature, and in the next chapter, we will zoom our reflection-flashlight on Nigeria's ethnolinguistic cultures—drawing sparsely from literature and principally from the narrative data of our research interviews conducted in northeastern Nigeria where the context is marked by the *Islamist-acute-violence* orchestrated by Boko Haram. At the end of chapter 6, we will then highlight the intersection these African concepts for peacebuilding share with peacebuilding-contextual theology. The common argument of chapters 5 and 6 is simply that African concepts of peacebuilding are models that must be studied and understood, and then constructively and critically integrated into peacebuilding-contextual theology, not only in African contexts of violence but also in other non-African contexts of violence. The follow-up question regarding "the how" of critical and constructive integration will be taken up in our last chapter.

Given that in sub-Saharan Africa there are a little over three thousand and four hundred ethnolinguistic peoples,[1] we can only undertake a panoramic view of peacebuilding concepts resident within some of them. That is the reason our review here is only 'a bird's eye view'. We engage in exploring concepts that have been identified in some scholarly works, whether they were identified by African scholars themselves or by non-African scholars who study Africa. A few concepts from Eastern, Southern, and Western Africa are hereby highlighted. Concepts are defined and named as they are perceived by the people among whom those concepts are autochthonous. For each concept identified, our overarching goal is to respond to the two questions: What is the connection between the concept and peacebuilding? And how can it be employed in peacebuilding in the context of violence?

Before we begin, there is need to underscore a caveat. There are several concepts in several cultures (not only in Africa) that may be employed for peacebuilding and yet we continue to see so much bloodshed and wars. The caveat is this: The fact that there are peacebuilding concepts or resources in our human cultures and contexts does not imply that peace will automatically exist. In fact, most of the concepts and resources emerged because of the conflict humans experience—which proceeds from the brokenness in our world and which J. Dudley Woodberry calls "war in the human hearts that then spills out on the ground."[2] We study the concepts and resources in order to find ways to cultivate peace, not that the existence of the concepts in themselves will produce peace by themselves. With that caveat in mind, we now turn to the discussion.

---

1. Ethnolinguistic people is defined as a grouping of individuals who are demographically and significantly large in population and who are tied by the same language or dialect, the same ancestry, the same culture, and land. They also share affinity in worldview—having the same perception of reality. For statistical information on the various regional ethnolinguistic peoples grouping, see https://joshuaproject.net/regions and https://joshuaproject.net/regions/8. About 1,298 ethnolinguistic groups are found in East and Southern Africa, and 2,223 are found in West and Central Africa. These do not include those in North Africa, which are often grouped with the Middle East.

2. Woodberry and Basselin, *Resources for Peacemaking in Muslim-Christian Relations*, viii.

5.1 *UBUNTU*: "I AM BECAUSE WE ARE; AND SINCE WE ARE, THEREFORE I AM"

Undoubtedly, René Descartes' epistemological concept contributed greatly in shaping the Euro-American Enlightenment thought. The Cartesian epistemology is grounded on Descartes' dictum: '*Je pense, donc, je suis*' — I think; therefore, I am. If we imagine an epistemological spectrum, Descartes' concept is at one end of that spectrum putting emphasis on the individuality of a person. But at the other end of our imaginary epistemological spectrum sits the African philosophical dictum: "I am because we are; and since we are, therefore I am." This African worldview of the individual vis-à-vis community is generally referred to as *ubuntu*. Kenyan theologian, John S. Mbiti in his seminal work, *African Religions and Philosophy*, presents this Africa concept in his description of an African's concept of a person. Mbiti writes:

> Only in terms of other people does the individual become conscious of his own being, his own duties, his privileges and responsibilities towards himself and towards other people. When he suffers, he does not suffer alone but with the corporate group; when he rejoices, he rejoices not alone but with his kinsmen, his neighbours and his relatives whether dead or living. When he gets married, he is not alone, neither does the wife "belong"[3] to him alone. So also the children belong to the corporate body of kinsmen, even if they bear only their father's name. Whatever happens to the individual happens to the whole group;—and whatever happens to the whole group happens to the individual. The individual can only say: "I am, because we are; and since we are, therefore, I am." This is a cardinal point in the understanding of the African view of man.[4]

Similarly, Nigerian theologian, Justin Ukpong highlights the same African epistemology. Ukpong maintains that "Africans define themselves not in egoistic terms but rather in terms of their community and thus find their identity there."[5] Comparing the African philosophy and understanding of the individual with the Euro-American epistemology based on René Descartes' dictum, Ukpong asserts that "the Cartesian *cogito ergo sum* (I

---

3. Mbiti puts the word "belongs" in quotation marks to indicate that only a husband of a wife possesses conjugal rights towards his wife. It is an abomination in Africa for a wife to share her marriage bed with any other person, other than her husband. Thus, "belongs" must not be understood to mean that an African wife belongs to everyone in her husband's kindred in respect to conjugal rights.

4. Mbiti, *African Religions and Philosophy*, 141.

5. Ukpong, *African Theologies Now*, 60.

think therefore I exist) expressed in the African context becomes *cognatus ergo sum* (I exist because I belong to a family)."[6] *Ubuntu*, as an African epistemological concept, is grounded on this philosophy. Elina Hankela—whose doctoral research at the University of Helsinki focused on the study of *ubuntu*—describes it as "an ethic . . . that treasures a set of relational qualities or virtues that contribute to certain kinds of human relationships that reflect interdependence in community; openness to others, affirming others. . . , sharing, hospitality, compassion, care . . ., and so on."[7]

Etymologically, the word, *ubuntu*, "is an Nguni[8] term, [and] terms with similar meanings are found in African languages all over sub-Saharan Africa."[9] Archbishop Desmond Tutu, who chaired the South African Truth and Reconciliation Commission (TRC) employed *ubuntu* as a theological framework for enacting reconciliation in South Africa. Following the collapse of the apartheid regime and during the negotiations for the South African 1993 Interim Constitution, the same concept was used for reconciliation in South Africa.[10] Albeit, the term *ubuntu* has gained global currency through its use in South Africa's context of reconciliation vis-à-vis apartheid, yet it is a concept ubiquitous in sub-Saharan African cultures, though with different linguistic appellations and modifications.

Christian B. N. Gabe, whose research focuses on peacebuilding, transitional justice, restorative justice and victim-offender mediation, in his excellent article gives various cognate equivalents of the term *ubuntu* in various Eastern and Southern African languages. Some of the equivalent terms include: *umuntu, umundu, bumuntu, vumuntu, bomoto*, and *gimuntu*. Gabe maintains that "the basic idea of *ubuntu* is shared by many indigenous peoples in sub-Saharan Africa under different names."[11] Birgit Brock-Utne also underscores the same, pointing out that "*ubuntu* is found in diverse

---

6. Ukpong, *African Theologies Now*, 60.

7. Hankela, *Ubuntu, Migration, and Ministry*, 5.

8. Nguni is a group of languages spoken in Southern African sub-region. There are three major language clusters within the Nguni group namely: (1). Zulu (comprising of Zulu of Zululand, Zulu of Natal, Lala, Qwabe, Ndebele of Transvaal, Ndebele of Zimbabwe, Ngoni of Nyasaland and Ngoni of Tanganyika); (2). Xhosa (comprising of Gcaleka, Ndlmbe, Gaika, Thembu, Bomvana, Mpondomse, Mpondo, and Xesibe); and Tekeza of Swaziland (comprising of Old Mfengu, Swazi or Swati, Baca, Hlubi and Phuthi). Doke, *Southern Bantu Languages: Handbook of African Languages*, 23–24, 91. See also https://www.revolvy.com/page/Nguni-languages.

9. Gade, "What Is Ubuntu?," 486; See also: Schoeman, "African Concept of Ubuntu and Restorative Justice," 293.

10. Gade, "What Is Ubuntu?," 485.

11. Gade, "What Is Ubuntu?," 486.

forms in many societies throughout Africa, most especially among the Bantu languages of East Central and Southern Africa."[12]

The meaning of *ubuntu* is deep and varied. In Gabe's research, the analysis of data from the narratives given by those to whom the question "What is *ubuntu*?" was posed revealed two major categories, namely: responses that define it as a moral virtue of a person, and those that define it as a "phenomenon according to which persons are interconnected."[13] Desmond Tutu provides a quintessential African philosophical understanding of *ubuntu*. Tutu writes:

> *Ubuntu* is very difficult to render into a Western language. It speaks of the very essence of being human. When we want to give high praise to someone we say, "*Yu, u nobuntu*"; "Hey, so-and-so has *ubuntu*." Then you are generous, you are hospitable, you are friendly and caring and compassionate. You share what you have. It is to say, "My humanity is caught up, is inextricably bound up, in yours." We belong in a bundle of life. We say, "A person is a person through other persons." It is not, "I think therefore I am." It says rather: "I am human because I belong. I participate, I share." A person with *ubuntu* is open and available to others, affirming of others, does not feel threatened that others are able and good, for he or she has a proper self-assurance that comes from knowing that he or she belongs in a greater whole and is diminished when others are humiliated or diminished, when others are tortured or oppressed, or treated as if they were less than who they are.[14]

Ubuntu, where practiced, reflects the virtue and values that Africans attach to others. It also reinforces the concept for people to be humane to one another because the welfare of one individual is intrinsically connected to the good of the other. The corollary proposition also holds true: the misfortune, pain or suffering of one also affects the other because we form one family of humans. Birgit Brock-Utne highlights the same meaning of *ubuntu*, in her contribution to the *International Journal of Peace Studies*, wherein she asserts that the "concept . . . denotes a cultural world-view that tries to capture the essence of what it means to be human."[15]

Furthermore, *Ubuntu* reflects the imprint of *imago Dei* in humans, and highly values the common good of the community rather than on

---

12. Brock-Utne, "Peace Research with a Diversity Perspective," 114.
13. Gade, "What Is Ubuntu?," 487.
14. Gade, "What Is Ubuntu?," 487.
15. Brock-Utne, "Peace Research with a Diversity Perspective," 114.

the individual. Desmond Tutu's theology of *ubuntu* is based on his understanding of *imago Dei*, argues Michael Battle. "Tutu's understanding of the *imago dei* [sic] as human interdependence develops into his theology of Ubuntu . . . [his] theological interpretation of [*ubuntu*] counters the theological narrative of apartheid [and it has] to do with how the *imago dei* [sic] is made intelligible in South Africa."[16] This connection between *ubuntu* and humans made in the image of God translates into human relationships that seek the good of all.

With all the above said, we turn now to the question: What is the connection between the concept of *ubuntu* and peacebuilding? In chapter 4, we pointed out J. Dudley Woodberry's assertion that "[t]he primary problem is not the war on the ground but the war in the human hearts that then spills out on the ground."[17] We also cited the position of a Muslim scholar who attests that "according to the Prophet of Islam, the highest form of jihad is the struggle waged to cleanse oneself from the vices of the heart."[18] Both Woodberry's "war in the human heart" and Abou El Fadl's "the vices of the heart" point to the fact that if the violence that breeds and grows in the hearts of people are defeated, then the chances of "war on the ground", of jihad with weapons that cause bloodshed, of قِتَال—*qitāl*[19] and other forms of violence will be very negligible, to say the least. Should the principle of *ubuntu* be lived out in a community, people within that community will seek the well-being of others because their own wellbeing is intrinsically dependent on that of the others. *Ubuntu* becomes a peacebuilding resource because where it is upheld as the people's perception of reality and lived out, it weakens the propensity of violence and war. No one will engage in a harmful action against someone else when the perpetrator knows that whatever that action may be, it will (in some way) turn around to impact him or her harmfully. *Ubuntu* tends to instill the understanding that we, as humans, are connected to one another just as the different organs of the human body are connected. Some harm or pain that happens to a part affects the entire body. Being cognizant of this creates in the minds of people the propensity to seek good for others instead of seeking to outdo or outshine them. Such a relational

---

16. Battle, *Ubuntu*, 29,30.

17. Woodberry and Basselin, *Resources for Peacemaking in Muslim-Christian Relations*, viii.

18. Abou El Fadl, *Place of Tolerance in Islam*, 19.

19. In Arabic, قِتَال—*qitāl* has a wide range of meanings but the primary sense is: battle, fight, combat, and hostilities that lead to the death of people and to destruction. It is used 13 times as a verbal noun in the Qur'ān http://corpus.quran.com/qurandictionary.jsp?q=qtl.

connectivity between *ubuntu* and *imago Dei* gives credence to its integration and application in peacebuilding.

And how can *ubuntu* be employed in peacebuilding in the context of violence? Peacebuilding comprises peace research, peace education and peace action. Thus, in the domain of peace education, the concept should be taught, not only in citadels of learning, but from the cradle. It will need become a culture that is valued and incorporated in societies in order for the result to be tangible. To whatever dimension the concept is employed, to that same degree it will yield peacebuilding results.

The practical application of the concept of *ubuntu* can be viewed as stratified. In other words, *ubuntu* can be applied at different strata of human community. The micro-stratum of applying *ubuntu* relates to interpersonal relationships in different dimensions. The first dimension is within the smallest unity of community—the family. In African cosmology, the family is not just the unit family consisting of a couple and their children, but also the extended family. Within that smallest unit of community, *ubuntu*'s goal is that persons in the community understand that actions intended to harm the other will certainly boomerang to inflict some form of harm as well on the perpetrator. The properties of *ubuntu* that Desmond Tutu highlights apply beginning from this layer. Persons in the community do not "feel threatened that others are able and good . . . [because they have] a proper self-assurance that comes from knowing that [they are part of] a greater whole . . . "[20] When any member of the community fails, others in the same community fail. When someone in the community is honored, that honor is shared and bestowed upon all the other community members. And as Tutu put it "when others are tortured or oppressed, or treated as if they were less than who they are"[21] all the others share in that torture, oppression or ill treatment.

Beyond the first stratum comes the larger community of which the family is part of. This larger community can be the clan, the village (in the African sense of the word— the geographical space where people of different clans who share the same ancestors dwell), or neighborhoods (in the sense of modern towns and cities where people reside even though they are of diverse origins). At this layer, geographical locus is a major determinant. *Ubuntu*, when applied at this layer, implies that people who share geographical space understand that whatever harm planned and perpetrated against people within that space, will somehow turn around to impact them as well. This layer is usually more forceful in local African

---

20. Tutu, *No Future Without Forgiveness*, 31.
21. Tutu, *No Future Without Forgiveness*, 31.

settings than in neighborhoods in modern cities and towns. But the point is that people living within the same geographical space can see themselves as neighbors and seek common good for all.

Yet, another stratum of applying *ubuntu* is at the level of relationships between two or more ethnic communities, towns or cities. The case of Tutsis and Hutus of Rwanda fits into this stratum. The neglect of *ubuntu* between the two people groups resulted to the Rwandan genocide. At this layer, it might not necessarily be on a national political level, but could entail problems involving two local communities, ethnic groups, cities, or towns.

On a macro-stratum, relationships between nation-states or groups of nation-states require applying *ubuntu*. Nigeria as a country is a nation-state in the West African sub-region. Whatever ill befalls Nigeria will somehow boil over to touch the neighboring states—Cameroun, Niger Republic, The Chad, Benin Republic and even some other nation-states that do not share boundaries with Nigeria. Conflicts, economic or political oppression amongst nation-states in regional proximity boils over to impact other states not directly involved in those conflicts or oppression. We have already alluded to the impact the Boko Haram orchestrated-violence has had on some of Nigeria's neighbors. The conflict in Syria presents another glaring example. Many European countries have been impacted by it because of the massive flight of refugees inundating Europe. The current Russian war on Ukraine is another glaring example. Neighboring nation-states to Ukraine have been inundated with Ukrainian refugees and soaring global inflation has impacted many countries not involved at all in the Putin war. Our position is that humans from all geographical spaces on our planet need to understand that whatever harm we do to the other will certainly turn around to impact the perpetrators. United States of America may engineer a war with its allies in the Middle East and think that the geographical space we call 'the United States of America' is far-flung away from Middle Eastern countries, and therefore, that they will not be impacted beyond the economic strain of war expenditures. Lessons from the Iraqi war (for example) have, however, shown that globalization with its attendant elements does not spare the United States from receiving a share of refugees from the countries wherein they engage in war. Refugees from lands where the United States is not involved in war are also flocking into it, even though the United States is not involved. And what is more? The influx of refugees into a given country implies that the refugee-receiving country will have to draw from its economic and human resources to care for those refugees.

This argument holds true for any other country. Russian leaders, for example, may conceive and approve military operations in Ukraine thinking that it will only bring good to Russia. The *ubuntu* philosophy will counsel

Russian leaders otherwise, because whatever human oppression and pain Russia may bring upon Ukraine or any other nation-state (whether geographically far or near to Russia) will in some way return to impinge upon and impact Russia and Russians negatively.

Thus, at such a macro-stratum, the foreign policies of nation-states ought to consider integrating the philosophy of *ubuntu*, because policies aimed to benefit one's nation-state but at the expense of harming another—whether the harm is economic, political, or territorial—will turn out in some way to become a harm on the country that made and implemented that policy. All nation-states need to see themselves as a community of nations. *Ubuntu* can serve as an epistemological framework to undergird such worldview among nation-states.

Where offence, oppression, and injustice have already been perpetrated, *ubuntu*'s aim is restorative as opposed to retributive. In South Africa, where *ubuntu* was employed to undergird the reconciliation after apartheid, it shaped the approach of restorative justice (as opposed to retributive justice) to deal with the wounds inflicted by apartheid. Marelize Schoeman has shown that "there is a significant correlation between traditional justice practices as found in the ubuntu philosophy and restorative justice theory and practice."[22]

I have pointed out elsewhere that peacebuilding does more than seek restoration or resolving already existing conflicts. Instead, it "is the proactive, conscious and structured efforts geared toward establishing the parameters that create a peace ("שָׁלוֹם"—*shalom*) culture and prevent conflict, acute violence, or war. It is preventive, intentional, and is not a reaction or response to crisis that has already begun, ... Peacebuilding does not wait for a context of conflict before it begins."[23] If we understand peacebuilding in this manner, then at all the layers of possible application of *ubuntu* identified above, people will be called to live the *ubuntu* principle (where no crisis or conflict already exists) in order to undercut the chances of any form of inflicting injustice or oppression and thereby preventing possible war or conflict. In other words, where people responsibly apply *ubuntu* in life and community, there will exist a keen awareness that fomenting evil against someone else, another community, against a people group, or against another nation-state will ultimately have a boomerang effect thereby returning the evil perpetrated (at least to some degree) upon its initiators, instigators, and perpetrators.

---

22. Schoeman, "African Concept of Ubuntu and Restorative Justice," 292.
23. Anyanwu, "Pneumatological Considerations," 337.

With the above submissions, we argue, therefore that *ubuntu* can be applied for peacebuilding, not just in contexts of existing conflict and oppression, but more importantly in no-conflict contexts. Peace education will be the part to take for instilling such understanding at various levels of human relationships (interpersonal, inter-community, inter-ethnic, inter-people groups, inter-national, and inter-regional). If that is done, the propensity to cultivate the culture of peace will rise, undercutting potential wars and conflicts. Such approach will also provide basis for sustainable development because in the context of war or conflict, communities and governments redirect resources and energy required for development toward resolution of those conflicts. Onyebuchi Echekwube, in an annual Nigerian Academy of Letters' lecture, argued the same point positing that employing the *ubuntu* principle, which Echekwube calls "communalist system[24] . . . engenders peace, tranquility and of necessity, the much needed development of the various communities."[25]

5.2 *NABADRAADIN* AND *GUURTI*: "LET US TALK" AND "COUNCIL OF ELDERS"

Our guiding question for the concepts we are assessing remains: What is the connection between the concept and peacebuilding, and how can it be employed in peacebuilding in the context of violence? The discussion that follows directly answers this two-part question insofar as the *nabadraadin–guurti* concept is concerned. But what is this *nabadraadin–guurti* concept?

Nabadraadin (let us talk) and *Guurti* (council of elders) are two-interrelated concepts autochthonous to Somalia, a country in the Horn of Africa where war wasted many lives. John P. Lederach and Angela Lederach in a joint contribution to the volume, *Building Peace from Within*, present four case studies of some African grassroots peacebuilding initiatives. One of the case studies had its locus in Hargeisa in northwestern Somalia. The Lederachs call the concept "the wandering elders" which draws from the Somaliland council of elders called *guurti*. In Somaliland, however, locals refer to the concept as *nabadraadin* which means 'let us talk.'[26]

---

24. In Echekwube's lecture, "Communalist System" is not understood as "communalism" but rather as *ubuntu*. He cites the *ubuntu* African adage "I am because we are" in John S. Mbiti's *African Philosophy and Religion*, and further buttresses his argument with other African proverbs (Igbo and Yoruba) that express the same *ubuntu* epistemological worldview. Echekwube, *African Philosophy*, 25.

25. Echekwube, *African Philosophy*, 26.

26. Lederach and Lederach, "Let Us Talk," 37.

Nabadraadin is a grassroots peacebuilding concept in Somaliland that consists of local elders, sheiks, and a ruling religious leader (sultan) travelling from one sub-clan to another among waring communities to engage in discussions and talks aimed at reconciliation.[27] These elders, sheiks and sultan from the sub-clans are usually highly respected and opinion leaders. In the Lederachs' case study, there were three elders, two sheiks and one sultan. The three elders "formed an *ergada*, a travelling group of elders that would venture out to meet the other warring sub-clan elders in an effort to persuade them to participate in a *guurti*, a gathering of elders, poets, spokespersons and chosen representatives of the various sub-clans."[28] But prior to the travels of the *ergada* (traveling group of elders) from clan to clan, women married across clans go ahead as forerunners. Cross-clan wars imply that fathers-in-law, husbands and sons of cross-clan-married women engage in war with their wives' fathers, brothers, nephews, and other relations. Thus, the cross-clan-married women become heralds going ahead of the *ergada* to assure that the elders are not attacked.[29]

As the *ergada* travels, the elders invite the elders of the other clans with whom they have been at war to join in the gathering of elders (*guurti*) for talks (*nabadraadin*). They "create a region-wide consultation culminating in a grand *guurti*" —that is: a large gathering of elders, poets, spokespersons and chosen representatives of the various sub-clans. These elders then engage in several talks that ultimately lead to "the formation of a parliament, space for traditional leaders, and local peace initiatives between the sub-clans that were still fighting."[30] Ahmed Yusuf Farah, who was one of the leading anthropologists on Somalia, followed this process in Somaliland and refers to the case as "roots of reconciliation" as reflected in the title of his work—*Somalia: The Roots of Reconciliation: Peacemaking Endeavours of Contemporary Lineage Leaders: A Survey of Grassroots Peace Conferences in "Somaliland."*[31] The *nabadraadin–guurti* concept of Somaliland "stands as perhaps one of the most extraordinary and least documented processes of its kind."[32] Marleen Renders' doctoral research in Somaliland and Nairobi (Kenya)[33] provides

---

27. Renders, *Consider Somaliland*, 81.
28. Lederach and Lederach, "Let Us Talk," 37.
29. Lederach and Lederach, "Let Us Talk," 38.
30. Lederach and Lederach, "Let Us Talk," 38.
31. Farah and Lewis, *Somalia*.
32. Lederach and Lederach, "Let Us Talk," 39.
33. Renders, *Consider Somaliland*, xv. *Consider Somaliland* is the published volume of Marleen Render's research.

some historical and anthropological support for presenting this concept as one of Africa's concepts for peacebuilding.

A few insights emerge from the *nabadraadin–guurti* concept. The role of community leaders and elders in traditional African societies is critical for peacebuilding. This theme was flagged as one of the emerging categories from the narrative data of research interviews conducted in northeastern Nigeria for the purpose of this study, which we discuss in the next chapter on "Peacebuilding Concepts from Nigeria's Ethnolinguistic Cultures." In African communities, elders are men and women who are held in honor and who have proven character. They lay aside their personal interests and labor for the interest of their entire communities because they hold that their welfare and that of their families are tied to the welfare of the community—a principle that has its root in *ubuntu*, discussed in the preceding subsection. In the Somaliland case, the Somaliland northern elders refer to themselves "as *dab damin*, which literally means 'extinguishing fire' [an expression that aptly describes their role as those saddled with the responsibility of] restricting the explosion of social upheaval."[34] It is important not to confuse African community elders with political leaders—who on the contrary are products of a Western political process.[35]

A second insight for peacebuilding from the *nabadraadin– guurti* concept emerges from the role women play in African societies. Women serve as peace-bearers. In the Lederachs' case study, women went ahead of the elders as heralds. Cross-clan marriage ties become a tool Africans harness for peacebuilding in times of inter-clan conflicts. Marleen Renders points to the contribution of "Hargeysa[36] businesswomen [who] published an open letter in the newspaper in the name of what they called the Hargeysa Women Community, requesting the conflicting parties to 'avoid all steps that endanger the peace of the country and give a chance to Somaliland enemies'"[37] In a focus group interview conducted during the research fieldwork for this study, this element emerged in one of the discussions. In some ethnic groups in Nigeria, when two clans are at war, the elders of the

---

34. Farah and Lewis, *Somalia*; Farah, "Roots of Reconciliation," 21. See also Lederach and Lederach, *When Blood and Bones Cry Out*, 25; Lederach and Lederach, "Let Us Talk," 37.

35. The difference between African traditional elders in their traditional African contexts and modern-day African political leaders (who are products of Western political models) requires further study and investigation. The scope of the current study restricts my discussion and exploration on this theme.

36. Authors use different autographs for the name of this Somali city. Whereas the Lederachs use "Hargeisa," Marleen Renders uses "Hargeysa."

37. Renders, *Consider Somaliland*, 210.

warring clans in consultation encourage their sons and daughters to intermarry. The premise is that when such cross-clan marriages occur, then the clans will hardly go to war given that if they do, they will only be fighting their own daughters' husbands and children.

In the Somaliland case, a third insight that emerges relates to the long talks of the *guurti* which evolved into the creation of an official organization that made significant political contribution towards resolving the conflict in their land.[38] Although, a traditional and unofficial council of local elders (in the sense of having political legitimacy before governments), yet the *guurti*'s role in bringing the elders of warring clans to the reconciliation table later became harnessed for peacebuilding and for community development. For about three months in 1993, enlarged meetings of the Somaliland *guurti* were held in Boroma—a gathering that came to be known as "the Boroma Conference."[39] For several months of talks, poetry and songs, the grand *guurti* finally proposed that the northeast and northwest region of Somali be "declared independent as the Republic of Somaliland. The road to the declaration was built on hundreds of discussions; initiated, failed and re-initiated negotiations; small and larger subclan agreements; compensations and more talk."[40]

Although Somaliland has not received international recognition as an independent country, the truth, however, remains that "the northwest and northeast of what was Somalia have had far less fighting than other regions to the south,"[41] and the reconciliation and less fighting so far witnessed in the northeast and northwest are products of the of labors of the *guurti* and their *nabadraadin*. The role of the council of elders (*guurti*) in tandem with locally initiated talks (*nabadraadin*)—both being the local concepts imbedded in the culture—were key elements that helped to install peace in northern region of Somalia.

The *nabadraadin–guurti* peacebuilding concept is genuinely African and can be employed in African contexts. Just as the *ubuntu* concept is found in many parts of Africa although expressed in different forms, similarly the *nabadraadin–guurti* concept is also present among many African peoples. Cameroonian philosopher, Jean-Godefroy Bidima, in his volume, *La Palabre: Une Juridiction de la Parole*,[42] points to this concept although he identifies it using a French word '*palabre*'—exchange of speech, discourse

38. Renders, *Consider Somaliland*, 81.
39. Lederach and Lederach, *When Blood and Bones Cry Out*, 27.
40. Lederach and Lederach, *When Blood and Bones Cry Out*, 27.
41. Lederach and Lederach, *When Blood and Bones Cry Out*, 27.
42. Bidima, *La Palabre*.

or talks for the purpose of resolving conflict. Birgit Brock-Utne, similarly, identifies the concept as an African peacebuilding method, albeit with a Portuguese word, *Palaver*.[43] Thus, there is no disputing the pervasive spread of the concept in sub-Saharan Africa.

Before we leave the discussion from Somalia, an important historical factor that contributes to the shaping of Somalia's context of conflict requires to be highlighted. As we pointed out in our historical review (chapter 2), European colonization of African lands exacerbates conflicts in Africa. In Somalia's case, the wider northern region (that is: Somaliland) was colonized by the British, whereas the southern regions were under the control of the Italians. The two regions merged on July 1, 1960.[44] Conflicts which the two regions in the Horn of Africa experience cannot be divorced from the European colonial injustice.[45] The Europeans' partition of African lands (to satisfy their economic and political avarice without consideration of the peace of the African people and of the cultural boundaries that existed between the various African ethnolinguistic groups) remains one of the major elements that breed conflict, violence, and war in many African regions. Thus, in every effort to build peace in African contexts, the indigenous concepts of peacebuilding among the peoples need be studied and constructively employed while exploring how best to undo (or at the least, minimize) the evils introduced by colonization. The effort to undo or minimize the evils of the colonization factor is proving to yield peace in Rwanda's context where the genocide sought to decimate its people in the early 1990s. To this case we now turn to cast a bird's eye-view.

5.3 *GACACHA* COURT SYSTEM AND THE *ABANYARWANDA* CONCEPT

Our closing remarks on the Somaliland *nabadraadin* concept discussed in the preceding subsection highlighted again the colonization factor that constitutes one of the elements breeding conflict in African sub-regions. Rwanda is not exempt from such colonialization factor. Today's Republic of Rwanda was originally "under German control as German East Africa in the late 1800s, and following the defeat of Germany in World War I, it was placed under Belgian administration."[46] Thus, the cultural intrusion of the Europeans negatively impacted some African concepts of living,

---

43. Brock-Utne, "Peace Research with a Diversity Perspective," 115.

44. Renders, *Consider Somaliland*, 15.

45. For a more elaborate discussion on how the colonization factor shaped the formation of the Somali State, see chapter 2 in: Renders, *Consider Somaliland*, 33–58.

46. Levinson, *Ethnic Groups Worldwide*, 159.

marginalized, and sought to erode certain ancient landmarks and values which bound Africa's peoples to dwell together despite their differences and diversity. Some African scholars[47] have argued along this line to buttress the stance that ethnic demarcations "of Rwandan peoples is a product of the colonialists who deliberately manipulated small differences between the groups for their selfish ends."[48]

Where ethnic domination of one ethnolinguistic people over the others within a given political entity created by Europeans has created conflict, we maintain that the European partition and scramble for African lands constitute factors that have largely continued to exacerbate conflict in the continent. The reason being that African political states and boundaries created by European colonists without consideration for the cultural differences and diversities turned out to serve as manipulation machines that create inequalities in many African political states[49]—a situation that was practically inexistent prior to the colonial era.

In view of the foregoing, the colonialization factor ought not be ignored in peacebuilding initiatives in conflict areas within Africa. The task of peacebuilding in contexts of conflict in Africa must therefore encompass the retrieval of African concepts and values, which the colonialists' impingement buried in corrosive and erosive political riverbeds. In Rwanda's case, that retrieval implies the 'resurrection' of the *Gacacha*[50] court system—a concept we now succinctly discuss.

During the first half of the 1990s Rwanda witnessed a horrific genocide.[51] Three major people groups (Hutu, Tutsi, and Twa) constitute today's

---

47. See for example: Mbanda and Wamberg, *Committed to Conflict*; Mbembe, *On the Postcolony*; Mamdani, *When Victims Become Killers: Colonialism, Nativism, and the Genocide in Rwanda*. These African scholars maintain that some African concepts existed before the intrusion of European colonialists and that these concepts are not novel innovations.

48. Maphosa et al., *Building Peace from Within*, 123.

49. Mbembe, *On the Postcolony*, 44.

50. There exists variant autography of this word. Some authors use "*gacaca*": Clark, *Gacaca Courts, Post-Genocide Justice and Reconciliation in Rwanda*; Check, "Politics of Alternative Justice in Post-Genocide Rwanda," 137; "*gaçaça*": Moyo and Yoichi, *What Colonialism Ignored*, 10; and others "*gacacha*." Where I cite the work of any author, I retain the author's own spelling, but I defer to Bishop John Rucyahana's spelling "gacacha" on the grounds that he is a Rwandan indigene. Rucyahana and Riordan, *Bishop of Rwanda*, 202. Philip Clark's excellent volume provides a down-to-earth and scholarly exploration of "gacaca as an institution, . . . its objectives . . . its effectiveness in responding to the legacies of the [Rwandan] genocide" Clark, *Gacaca Courts, Post-Genocide Justice and Reconciliation in Rwanda*, 3–4.

51. The Hutus were instigated, organized and supported by a major world power to kill the Tutsis. See Wallis, *Silent Accomplice*; Rucyahana and Riordan, *Bishop of Rwanda*, 3–7.

Republic of Rwanda.[52] Demographically, the Hutus are the majority (about 84 percent of Rwanda's population), followed by the Tutsis (15 percent), and the Twas (1 percent). The demographically majority group, the Hutus were instigated, organized and supported by a major world power to kill the Tutsis.[53] The Rt. Reverend John Rucyahana, formerly the Anglican Bishop of Rwanda who chaired Rwanda's National Unity and Reconciliation Commission, opened his book, *The Bishop of Rwanda*, with these words: "In 1994, at least, 1,117,000 innocent people were massacred in a horrible genocide in Rwanda, my homeland in central Africa . . ."[54] Rucyahana's goal in the volume was not necessarily to detail the horrific events. He rather opted to "tell an amazing, uplifting story. . . the story of the new Rwanda . . . [which he asserts] has turned to God, and which God is blessing."[55] What peacebuilding concept(s) undergirded the reconciliation initiatives post-Rwandan genocide? Succinctly put, the *Gacacha* court system is one of Rwanda's precolonial concepts that Rwandans employed to undergird post-genocide reconciliation, forgiveness and peacebuilding in their land.

As the news of the Rwandan genocide hit international media, the United Nations (UN) intervened and established an international tribunal for prosecuting the genocide perpetrators. The courts were located in Arusha in Tanzania, and have come to be known as Arusha Courts.[56] Whereas the Arusha Courts employed the Western model of retributive justice which only led to chains of reprisals and counter-reprisals, the Rwandans themselves later turned to their local restorative justice concept called *Gacacha* courts, and it yielded fruits of reconciliation. Bishop Rucyahana gives us a succinct account of the origins of this concept. "*Gacacha* is the name of the grass that grows in the community compounds. Historically, Rwandans sat on gacacha to testify and work out their problems. When there was a grudge between people, they came together and sat on the grass around the compound to discuss it."[57] South African research specialist, Nicasius Achu Check, elaborates this further:

---

52. Mutisi, "Addressing Ethno-Political Conflicts," 120; Levinson, *Ethnic Groups Worldwide*, 159; Mandryk, *Operation World*, 719; Murray, *Cultural Atlas of Africa*, 187–88.

53. Wallis, *Silent Accomplice*; Rucyahana and Riordan, *Bishop of Rwanda*, 3–7.

54. Rucyahana and Riordan, *Bishop of Rwanda*, xv.

55. Rucyahana and Riordan, *Bishop of Rwanda*, xv.

56. Check, "Politics of Alternative Justice in Post-Genocide Rwanda," 138; Rucyahana and Riordan, *Bishop of Rwanda*, 161, 202.

57. Rucyahana and Riordan, *Bishop of Rwanda*, 202.

> The *gacaca* courts are community-based dispute-resolution tribunals, which were employed in pre-colonial Rwanda to deal with minor infractions such as inheritance, civil liability, theft and conjugal matters... Unwritten indigenous Rwandan law guided its organisation, composition and sentencing methods. One thing that became apparent after the arrival of the Germans in the territory in 1884 was that *gacaca* was headed by a reputed sage who commanded respect and esteem in his neighbourhood.[58]

Rwandans resorted to employing this precolonial concept to address the pain, anger, bitterness, and guilt that both victims and perpetrators of the genocide were undergoing. It "began in a few villages on an experimental basis" Rucyahana attests, "but [it] proved so successful that it was soon expanded to one village in each province, and now it is in every district in the country."[59] The *Gacacha* court system has its root in the participation of the entire community. Everyone in the village can ask questions and the courts are presided over by a group of people chosen by the people themselves based on their testimony of faithfulness to truth and who have earned respect in their communities by their lives[60]—a criteria similar to the Somaliland *guurti* (council of elders) discussed previously. Those chosen were then trained by the government to do their work. The fruit of the *Gacacha* court system has been attested and lauded, because it was not only effective, but additionally provided the opportunity for perpetrators to repent of the evils they perpetrated on others, on the one hand; and on the other hand, it provided the safe place for victims to declare and pronounce forgiveness.

The *Gacacha* concept is authentically Rwandan and is being integrated into the peacebuilding process in Rwanda's post-genocide context. The argument outlined here buttresses the thesis in this chapter that African concepts of peacebuilding are potential models that must be studied, understood, constructively, and critically integrated into peacebuilding initiatives within African contexts of conflict and for establishing peace cultures within contextual African landscapes.

Alongside the *Gacacha* court system, is another concept being encouraged and employed in Rwanda to dispel the hatred created along ethnic lines. In her balanced contribution to the volume *Building Peace from Within*, Martha Mutisi (whose doctoral research focused on conflict analysis and resolution at the School of Conflict Analysis and Resolution

---

58. Check, "Politics of Alternative Justice in Post-Genocide Rwanda," 137.
59. Rucyahana and Riordan, *Bishop of Rwanda*, 202.
60. Check, "Politics of Alternative Justice in Post-Genocide Rwanda," 119, 138.

at George Mason University), presents this other Rwandan concept called *Abanyarwanda* as a case of 'ethnic amnesia'.[61] Mutisi's contribution outlines how the Rwandan government and people are "evoking notions of unity as a well [sic][62] of confronting ethno-political conflict"[63] The Rwandan concept of *Abanyarwanda* concept is "a strategy that is being used by the Rwandan government to address its ethno-political conflict in the aftermath of" the Rwandan genocide.[64] But what exactly is the *Abanyarwanda* concept?

Mutisi defines *Abanyarwanda* simply as (Rwandan-ness) "which essentially means that Rwandans have a shared past, and that they are not disaggregated groups such as Hutu, Tutsi or Twa."[65] In other words, Rwandans are becoming more and more culturally inclined to view themselves as one people—Rwandans—not as Hutus, Tutsis or Twas. The Rwanda Patriotic Front (RPF) revived this Rwandan concept post-genocide and adopted it in order "to reject all forms of ethnic divisionism of the past,"[66] and the goal has been to nurture national unity and reinforce reconciliation. Mutisi attests,

> Reconciliation has emerged as a strong narrative for the Rwandans from the government to civil society and ultimately to grassroots communities . . . The argument is that an ethnically unified Rwanda is the key to sustaining present and future peace and is the vehicle towards sustainable peace, reconciliation, development and democracy. This is where the *Abanyarwanda* notion comes in, with its emphasis on bridging the identity fissures and promoting one-ness.[67]

Bishop Rucyahana points out that "identification cards and passports for Rwandan citizens just say "Rwanda" now, without any reference to whether the person is Hutu or Tutsi, because that type of classification was applied for evil and destruction."[68] The purpose of such a national policy is to create unity and belongingness which deemphasizes ethnicity.

One question that arises, though, is whether or not the *Abanyarwanda* concept existed prior to the colonial era. Or, is it a recent formulation introduced to heal the wounds and brokenness of the genocide? Some scholars

---

61. Mutisi, "Addressing Ethno-Political Conflicts," 119–36.
62. Read: ". . . as a way of. . . " not "as a well of. . . "
63. Mutisi, "Addressing Ethno-Political Conflicts," 119.
64. Mutisi, "Addressing Ethno-Political Conflicts," 119.
65. Mutisi, "Addressing Ethno-Political Conflicts," 119.
66. Mutisi, "Addressing Ethno-Political Conflicts," 121.
67. Mutisi, "Addressing Ethno-Political Conflicts," 121.
68. Rucyahana and Riordan, *Bishop of Rwanda*, 173.

who argue that the "concept, ... existed before colonialism ... [maintain that] prior to the colonial era, Rwanda comprised a harmonious and egalitarian society where the difference between Hutus, Tutsis and Twas was not ethnic-based ... The concept of *Abanyarwanda* is [therefore] used to glorify Rwanda's past where various groups lived in peace and intermarried."[69] Such claims cannot be dismissed given the manner the colonialization factor already alluded to impacted the people and created corrosive and erosive riverbeds for many African traditional concepts. Thus, it should be held that the *Abanyarwanda* concept is not a new invention, but rather one that had existed before the corrosive and erosive currents of colonialization bludgeoned upon it. Whereas the *Abanyarwanda* concept is now helping Rwandans to cultivate a culture of togetherness and unity, which is consequently placing the country to gain grounds in nation-building and development; the *Gacacha* court system, is fortifying the former to provide grounds for repentance and forgiveness—an element of *staurocentric*[70] pathways.

This *staurocentric* element of forgiveness interlaced with the retrieval of the *Gacacha* court system and the *Abanyarwanda* concept now contribute to the grounds gained in reconciliation and peacebuilding in Rwanda. Rwandans did not just 'move on' after the genocide sweeping their pain and guilt under the carpet. Instead, they identified the role that forgiveness must play in their context and that such grace required a divine intervention. Bishop John Rucyahana called it "the miracle of forgiveness."[71] On his part, Nobel Peace Prize laureate, Archbishop Desmond Tutu, while addressing Rwandans in a rally in Kigali a year after the genocide told them that "the cycle of reprisal and counterreprisal that had characterized [the Rwandan] national history had to be broken and that the only way to do this was to go beyond retributive justice to restorative justice, to move on to forgiveness, because without it [forgiveness] there was no future."[72]

Retributive justice was the path taken by the Arusha Courts established by the United Nations to serve as an international tribunal for prosecuting the genocide perpetrators. But Rwandans found a better model in what is arguably their God-given concept embedded in their culture—the *Gacacha* court system that predates the intrusion of Western models, and that emphasizes restorative over retributive justice. Restorative justice invites the perpetrator to acknowledge his or her participation in evil and to repentance, on the one hand; and the victim to gracious forgiveness, on

---

69. Mutisi, "Addressing Ethno-Political Conflicts," 122.
70. *Staurocentric* pathways form the crux of our discussion in chapter 7.
71. Rucyahana and Riordan, *Bishop of Rwanda*, 158–59.
72. Tutu, *No Future Without Forgiveness*, 260.

African Concepts for Peacebuilding-Contextual Theology 163

the other hand. Thus, the part that forgiveness has played and continue to play in reconciliation and peacebuilding in Rwanda's post-genocide cannot be denied.[73] This element, which we refer to as a *staurocentric* pathway, gave impetus to the new Rwandan policies that encouraged Rwandan-ness (*Abanyarwanda*).

These concepts (*Gacacha* and *Abanyarwanda*) we have identified above have contributed to the transformation which Rwanda is currently experiencing in peacebuilding, reconciliation, and consequently, development. Other African peoples can emulate the Rwandan example by critically retrieving their own equivalent local concepts that can be constructively integrated into peacebuilding. Turning to West Africa, we cast another bird's eye view on one more grassroots initiative, this time eliciting women's role to broker peace in a Liberian context of conflict.

5.4 AFRICAN WOMEN IN PEACEBUILDING: AN EXAMPLE FROM LIBERIA

On Christmas eve of 1989 Liberia plunged into civil conflict "when Charles Taylor's National Patriotic Front (NPFL) forces invaded Liberia through Nimba County from the neighbouring Côte d'Ivoire,"[74] and the war continued for over a decade. Liberian-born scholar—George Klay Kieh Jr.—who has published extensively on political and conflict issues relating to Africa, highlights some of the causes of the war, its protagonists and players, their underlying motivations, its impact on the country and the West African sub-region, and some efforts that were made to broker peace.[75] He also proffers reasons why the international community, particularly the Western powers, ignored the Liberian conflict and did not intervene when it erupted. I do not intend to discuss these elements here.[76] Our interest, instead, is in the role Liberian women played in the peacebuilding process that ended the war.

One of the Liberian women who played a prominent role in peacebuilding in the context of the conflict in Liberia, Leymah Gbowee, has

---

73. More examples of the role of forgiveness are highlighted in chapter 7.
74. Afolabi, *Politics of Peacemaking in Africa*, 73.
75. Kieh, "Combatants, Patrons, Peacemakers, and the Liberian Civil Conflict."
76. More than 400 volumes and about a thousand articles and book chapters have been published in the last 25 years on the subject of the Liberian conflict. Among them are the works of George Klay Kieh Jr.: *First Liberian Civil War; Ending the Liberian Civil War; Zones of Conflict in Africa*; and of Babatunde Tolu Afolabi, *Politics of Peacemaking in Africa*.

published her memoir[77] describing the process. Gbowee spearheaded the movement and in 2011 she was named a Nobel Peace laureate. Furthermore, a video documentary, *Pray the Devil Back to Hell* produced by Abigail Disney and directed by Gini Reticker, traces the peacebuilding pathways the Liberian women (at home and in dispersion) treaded in their action for peace. From these resources, *inter alia*, we underscore the importance and place of women as an African potential for peacebuilding—a resource that must not be ignored or neglected in peacebuilding initiatives in African contexts.

Leymah Gbowee recapitulates a historical precedence to the Liberian women action for peace. She attests that the Aba women's riot which began during the last quarter of 1929 in southeastern Nigeria remains "alive in West Africa, as women's groups continue to use their numerical strength, sisterhood and shared experiences to effect change."[78] Whereas southeastern Nigerian women in 1929 employed the African traditional women's force to demand for low taxes imposed by the colonial tax-masters,[79] the Liberian women, about sixty years later, employed the same force to push for peace and end the Liberian civil war in 2003. Margery Perham shows that a review of the character of the women's riots in southeastern Nigeria—widely known in literature as the 'Aba riots' (a misnomer[80]), reveals "the overwhelming impression. . . of the vigour and solidarity of the women."[81] It was the same spirit of solidarity and sisterhood that Liberian women employed in order to enforce peace in Liberia's context of war. But how did the Liberian women do that? The following account provides the response to this question.

After more than a decade of war in Liberia, the Economic Community of West African States (ECOWAS), together with the International community, mounted pressure on Charles Taylor and the warring parties in the conflict to convene in Accra, Ghana for peace talks. Prior to the talks which started on June 4, 2003, Liberian women had begun organizing themselves under different peace organizations to demand the end of the war. Women in Monrovia, the capital city of Liberia, mobilized themselves

77. Gbowee and Mithers, *Mighty Be Our Powers*.
78. Gbowee, "Effecting Change through Women's Activism," 50.
79. Perham, *Native Administration in Nigeria*, 206–20.
80. The name we find in literature—"Aba Women Riots"—gives the impression that the riots occurred in Aba in present day Abia State, Nigeria. Aba was and remains a principal hub of commerce in southeastern Nigeria. However, the riots brewed first in Owerri Province—the Igbo heartland, and then spread to Aba, Calabar in today's Cross River State, and ultimately to Opobo in today's Rivers State, Nigeria.
81. Perham, *Native Administration in Nigeria*, 211.

across religious lines. Their religious barriers were set aside to unite and use their sisterhood as African women to mount pressure on the warring parties to make peace. Where some objected to a joint Christian-Muslim women movement working together for peace, Vaiba Flomo, who was the Secretary of the Women Peace Building Network (WIPNET) attests: "Some Christians said, being a follower of Christ, and going to walk along with the Muslims means we are diluting their faith. But the message we [the women organizers] took on was: Can a bullet pick and choose? Does a bullet know Christian from Muslim?"[82]

While the women were organizing for peace, Charles Taylor and the warlords who were denied positions in Taylor's government and who united themselves under the Liberians United for Reconciliation and Democracy (LURD) were all bent on more bloodbath. The women creatively organized sit-ins along the roads through which Charles Taylor and his men ply. For over one week, they just sat on the roadsides under blazing sun and rain, chanting 'We want peace!' As days passed, desperation led the women to adopt sex-strike—denying their male partners of sex and telling them to do whatever they, as men, must to do to end the war. The sex-strike stirred most men to make moves toward peace. The women continued their sit-in in the parliament building area in Monrovia whatever the weather, until Charles Taylor could no longer ignore them. On April 23, 2003 Taylor granted audience to the women. Many of the women of the Women in Peacebuilding Network went to the presidential mansion, where Leymah Gbowee, their coordinator, was called upon to present their case to President Taylor.[83] The women coupled their actions with prayers whatever their religious affiliation.

The Liberian women's local peacebuilding action, and pressure from ECOWAS and the International community finally pressured Charles Taylor and the warlords to convene in Accra Ghana for peace talks. Leymah Gbowee, in an article attests:

> The women of Liberia under the banner of the Women in Peacebuilding Network (WIPNET) had earlier initiated advocacy and non-violent protests to pressure both sides to cease fire unconditionally. Seven women representing various organisations within the network went to Ghana (where the negotiations were being held) to mobilise Liberian refugee women to join the campaign. The women began protesting on the day that the peace talks officially commenced. It was

82. Reticker, *Pray the Devil Back to Hell*, Counter 10:12–10:39.
83. Reticker, *Pray the Devil Back to Hell*.

anticipated that the talks would last three weeks, but in reality, they lasted for three months.[84]

The sit-in action that began in Monrovia, Liberia, was also started in Accra at the venue of the peace talks. Gbowee further adds:

> During the sit-in, the women also demanded that no Liberian delegate would be allowed to leave the conference room for any reason until the agreement was signed. The women said their actions were intended to show to the world that they had finally had enough of the war in Liberia and were taking a stand to safeguard what was left of their society and communities."[85]

As the talks dragged on, the women barricaded the doors of the meeting place insisting that the warring parties must come to an agreement. Their insistence finally yielded fruit when the parties signed the Comprehensive Peace Agreement (CPA) in August 2003. Scholars unquestionably consider the women's peace action to be the motivating force that led to the agreement. Babatunde Tolu Afolabi, in his volume affirms that truly "women's groups played a key role in ending the Liberian conflict."[86] It was largely so because the different Liberian women peace organizations such as the Liberian Women Initiative (LWI), the Mano River Women Peace and Security Network (MARWOPNET), and the Women in Peacebuilding Network (WIPNET) "were instrumental in encouraging the participation of belligerents in peace negotiations, as well as putting an end to violence against women and children."[87] Signed agreements are, however, only promises. Promise-keeping of such agreements demands a greater moral obligation and virtue. Liberian women continued their labor for peace by pushing the parties to keep the promises they made in the Comprehensive Peace Agreement. The women's involvement "in the Disarmament, Demobilisation and Reintegration (DDR) process"[88] was one of the very pragmatic ways they continued their action for peace. They provided the authorities with information from their communities on what was working and what was not.

What are the lessons we can learn from the account of the Liberian Women Mass Action for Peace? Can the Liberian women action for peace be considered an African concept? The traditional role and force of women in

---

84. Gbowee, "Effecting Change through Women's Activism," 51.

85. Gbowee, "Effecting Change through Women's Activism," 51.

86. Afolabi, *Politics of Peacemaking in Africa*, 5; see also Fuest, "Liberia's Women Acting for Peace"; Gbowee, "Effecting Change through Women's Activism," 51.

87. Afolabi, *Politics of Peacemaking in Africa*, 5.

88. Gbowee, "Effecting Change through Women's Activism," 51.

Africa is indeed a concept to be reckoned with. There are other African examples to support this claim. One of them is the 'Aba Women's Riot' of 1929 of which Gbowee made mention.[89] One may argue that the case of the Aba Women's Riot was not geared toward peacebuilding. Yes, it was not. Nevertheless, it was the same ingrained role of African traditional women's role and force that was employed to check the colonialists' draconian tax laws. Thus, we can assert that the force of African women can indeed be employed for peacebuilding, socio-political development, and nation-building. The Liberian women's peace action amply exemplifies this assertion.[90]

From the Liberian example, we find a more internal argument to support our claim that the Liberian women action for peace is an African concept. That argument lies in the grassroots' composition of the Liberian women who initiated and coordinated the peace movement. Historically and broadly-speaking, the Liberian civil society is composed of two main strands—the indigenous Liberians and Americo-Liberians whose origins are tied to emancipated ex-slaves repatriated to Africa from America.[91] There exists, therefore, the indigene-settler dichotomy which runs in the veins of the Liberian civil "society since its creation in 1821—though admittedly much less pronounced in recent times."[92] Although there were two major streams of the Liberian women peace movements (the Liberian Women Initiative, LWI, and the Mass Action for Peace. MAP), it was indeed the grassroots indigenous group (MAP)—led by Leymah Gbowee and Vaiba Flomo—that did the dirty and lowly aspects of the peacebuilding actions, such as sit-ins on the roads despite the weather, sit-ins by the floors and doors at the venue of the Accra peace talks.

On the other hand, women of the Americo-Liberian stream who belong majorly to the elite echelon of the Liberian society were the ones invited to attend and had seat at the negotiating table of the talks in Accra.[93] We do not imply that women of the Americo-Liberian stream did not contribute towards the Liberian women peace actions. Rather, we emphasize that it was the involvement, methods, and principles employed by the indigenous strand of Liberian women that served as the peacebuilding capital which produced the ultimate peace results. On the one hand, the Americo-Liberian

---

89. Gbowee, "Effecting Change through Women's Activism," 50.

90. There is yet another example to support our argument, but because it comes from Nigeria, it is more fitting to discuss it in the next chapter. It is the "Egbo-o Ho Ho" concept which women in southeastern Nigeria employ to arbitrate conflict in their societies.

91. Afolabi, *Politics of Peacemaking in Africa*, 51–52.
92. Afolabi, *Politics of Peacemaking in Africa*, 135.
93. Afolabi, *Politics of Peacemaking in Africa*, 135–36.

women, who are mostly the educated elites used the means and methods informed by their Western education and which defines their culture. And on the other hand, the indigenous Liberian women resorted to the methods and means they have learned from their African ancestors.

Furthermore, women become exposed to large-scale sexual violence and abuse during wartimes. This was exactly the case during the Liberian war. The same situation is true, as we briefly pointed out in chapter 2, in Nigeria's context of Islamist violence, wherein Islamists abduct school girls and keep them as their sex slaves. In regard to the dangers that women in Africa face during wartimes, Gbowee attests that "women in Liberia were . . . the main targets of rape and other forms of sexual violence. . . The use of rape as a weapon of war indicated the unique type of battle that women face during wartime; that is, they are the violated during the violation, the victims of the victimisation, and the captured of the captors."[94] When such social injustice is blatant and widespread, African women rise to protest seeking justice, not just for themselves, but much more for their children. Thus, African women's desire for social justice stirs grassroots engagement in peace actions, as Gbowee affirms that "[t]he rationale behind women's peace activism is to promote social justice in West Africa."[95]

Before we end the discussion on the Liberian women's action for peace, it needs be added that the women's peacebuilding actions did not only lead to the end of the Liberian conflict, but also to the election of Ellen Johnson Sirleaf as President of Liberia (2006–2018). Ms Ellen Johnson Sirleaf became the first African woman to be ever elected President of her country.[96] In a speech delivered after her election she said: "I want to here now gratefully acknowledge the powerful voice of women from all walks of life, whose votes brought us to victory. They defended me, they worked with me, they prayed for me. It is the women who labored and advocated for peace throughout our region."[97] Leymah Gbowee attests that "there is no way that the history of Madam Sirleaf will be written without the history of the women's peace work."[98] German anthropologist, Veronika Fuest, affirms the same, maintaining that "[t]he first-ever election of a

---

94. Gbowee, "Effecting Change through Women's Activism," 50.
95. Gbowee, "Effecting Change through Women's Activism," 50.
96. Fuest, "Liberia's Women Acting for Peace," 114. See also https://www.britannica.com/biography/Ellen-Johnson-Sirleaf.
97. Reticker, *Pray the Devil Back to Hell*, Counter 1:06:19sec–1:06:45.
98. Reticker, *Pray the Devil Back to Hell*, Counter 1:06:49.

female head of state in Africa can be seen as a sign of a wider social movement associated with peace."[99]

Thus, with the above submissions, we reiterate that the concept employed to broker peace in Liberia's context was typically African, and therefore, restate the driving argument in this chapter that Africans have African means and methods and when they are employed in addressing African problems, we obtain God-given African solutions. Given that this study has its locus in Nigeria, we proceed in the next chapter to outline the major peacebuilding concepts that emerged from our ethnographic research in Nigeria.

---

99. Fuest, "Liberia's Women Acting for Peace," 114.

6

Peacebuilding Concepts from Nigeria's Ethnolinguistic Cultures

IN THE PRECEDING CHAPTER, the trajectory of our discussion was on the African concepts that lend themselves to peacebuilding. Therein we sought to respond to the question: What concepts of peacebuilding are embedded within African cultures that may be employed and integrated in developing peacebuilding-contextual theology? In this chapter, we take up the same question but specifically within Nigeria's ethnolinguistic cultures. Within Nigeria's context of Islamist violence, we, therefore, pose the question: What are the potential concepts for peacebuilding-contextual theology autochthonous to Nigeria's ethnolinguistic peoples that we may employ for integration into conceptualizing *staurocentric* pathways for peacebuilding?

6.1 PEACEBUILDING CONCEPTS FROM THE ETHNOGRAPHIC RESEARCH IN NIGERIA

The peacebuilding concepts we identify here emerged from the analysis of narrative data obtained during my fieldwork. Data were obtained from the transcribed research interviews (individuals and focus groups) conducted between September and November 2018 in Nigeria. Themes for peacebuilding concepts emerging from both individual and focus group interviews are identified according to their conceptual proximity. From our analysis, it was not surprising to observe that concepts overlap across different ethnolinguistic peoples of Nigeria, similar to what we already highlighted in chapter 5 in our assertion that many African concepts are ubiquitous in sub-Saharan Africa, albeit they have different linguistic expressions according to different people groups. The concepts are discussed according to their rubrics, not according to the specific ethnolinguistic groups among which they are autochthonous. Where a concept is unique to an ethnic group, we indicate that uniqueness. Nevertheless, that does not necessarily imply an absolute peculiarity because if further research is to be conducted with a wider sample of participants from many more ethnolinguistic groups, there will be a high probability of finding a similar concept expressed differently among other ethnolinguistic groups within Nigeria and across sub-Saharan Africa. As in the preceding chapter, the argument here remains that African concepts of peacebuilding are models that must be studied and understood, and then constructively and critically integrated into peacebuilding-contextual theology, not only in African contexts of violence but also in other non-African contexts of violence.

With the above notes in mind, we discuss the following concepts: (1) the *nzu* concept, (2) hospitality, (3) the *gammo* and *gaya* concepts—the power of community, (4) agency of community festivals and rituals, (5) the *egbo-ho-ho* concept, and (6) cross-clan marriages as a tool for peacebuilding. As we have already annotated in chapter 1, citations from transcribed research interviews follow the pattern: Tyriaka, D1#4 n–z.[1]

6.1.1 The Nzu Concept: An African Universal Ethics of the Stranger

African traditional ethics of the stranger is one of the concepts that emerged from our research. One individual interview participant, referred to it as "universal ethics", which he defined as "an ethic beyond boundaries, regional boundaries, sectional boundaries."[2]

From the African traditional perspective, this universal ethics of the stranger is manifest in various forms. Among the Igbos, for example, it is the concept of painting *nzu* (local white chalk or white clay) on the hand of the stranger who comes into their community. In regard to this Tyriaka, who himself is not Igbo, affirms: "A stranger comes to your village, he is vulnerable because he is a stranger. So how do you secure this stranger? They [the Igbos] give the white chalk. The host will now get the white chalk and put it

---

1. Tyriaka stands for a pseudonym used for Participant Number 4 from Denomination 1, "n–z" stands for the line numbers of words or expressions extracted from the transcribed interview. Pseudonyms are adopted for participants alongside the code name for either the denomination or focus group. Subsequent citations from a particular participant will only mention the Participant's pseudonym and the line numbers of the transcribed interview, say Tyriaka n–z.

2. Tyriaka, D1#4:293–294.

on your arms.³ Now you can move anywhere in the community because you are part of it. This is called, *nzu* in Igbo culture".⁴

Another participant of Igbo origin who has been studying the concept—elaborated on the Igbos' *nzu* concept. He said: "When you go to an Igbo man's house, the first thing he will give you is *nzu*. And what does *nzu* translate to in Igbo cosmology? . . . To an Igbo, *nzu* is peace, hospitality, love. *Nzu* is an acceptance that I have received you. *Nzu* means that when you come to my land, you have come to my land with peace and I will be willing to share peace with you".⁵ The Igbos recognize that people migrate for serval reasons such as famine, inter-tribal wars or in search of safety. The Igbos themselves believe they were migrants who settled in present day southeastern Nigeria. Thus, in cognizance of this fact, they extend a universal ethics to a stranger who may migrate into their communities. Participant Nzeka, D4#2, affirmed that if you are a stranger entering a traditional Igbo community, the first thing you must do is to "go to the elders of the land and . . . present yourself. And the first thing they [the elders] will give you is *nzu*. And what does it entail? We give you peace."⁶

The *nzu* concept does not stand alone among *Ndi* Igbo (Igbo People). To further affirm that they have received the stranger, the Igbos offer *oji*—kola nut. Participant Nzeka, attests that after someone has offered *nzu* to the stranger, he "will now present kola nut to you—which is life, sharing life with him [the stranger]. Somebody who is sharing life with you, I don't think he will mean evil to you. He has accepted you."⁷ When kola nut is presented to the stranger, the Igbos pronounce words of blessings and prayer alongside that presentation. Typical among such words is the Igbo maxim: *Onye wetara oji, wetara ndu*—The one who brings kola, brings life. Chinua Achebe in his signature fact-based novel, *Things Fall Apart*, portrays the significance of presentation of kola nut in Igbo culture.⁸

Participant Nzeka goes further to elaborate on where *nzu* can be marked and its dual and conceptual significance to peacebuilding and hospitality.

---

3. The Igbos take *nzu* (local white chalk, or white clay), grind it to powder, form a paste with water and then paint or smear it on the back of the stranger's hand or on his or her lower arm.

4. Tyriaka, 342–345.

5. Nzeka, D4#2:10–215.

6. Nzeka, 19–21.

7. Nzeka, 24–26.

8. Achebe, *Things Fall Apart*, 5.

Peacebuilding Concepts from Nigeria's Ethnolinguistic Cultures 173

You can mark the *nzu* at the back of your palm. If you are woman, it can be marked on the upper part of the breast . . . It can also be marked on any other part of your body that can be visible, such that if I see you, I know that the community has accepted you. That is love, it's a pure love. And because the community has accepted you, they know that you will not go to live in the sky. They will show you where the farm is. Go there and farm. As long as you do what is within the concept of farming in the community, because there are other laws that bind the farming system in the land. So those laws that could violate the relationship between man and the earth goddess. So you should be able to know that. So that aspect is where an Igbo man is unique in his own life—sharing out. So and once one shares out he is willing to share whatever he has with somebody else. He means peace, until and only when you want to assert ownership. Then there we have a problem with you. You are now transgressing and then there will be no peace. But for you to come and live and farm and raise your children and become whatever you want, the society is going to give you that.[9]

Furthermore, the *nzu* concept relates in some respect to the '*nabadraadin*—let us talk' concept which the Somaliland *guurti* (council of elders) employ in peacebuilding (as discussed in section 5.2 of chapter 5). Our research participant added that "the *nzu* sharing provides a relational condition whereby two people are now talking. And when two people are talking they are sharing their minds. You are knowing my pain and I am understanding your pain and we are able to resolve. But while we are not talking, all whatever peace conference you are building is not going to work."[10] Thus, the *nzu* concept does not only serve as a demonstration of acceptance and hospitality, but also as an invitation to the host and the stranger to relate and talk. In such interaction, they share each other's pains and joys, and consequently empathy and sympathy.

The narrative around the *nzu* concept affirms the African universal ethics of the stranger among the Igbos of Nigeria, of which Participant Tyriaka maintained that this genre of universal ethics can be likened to Jesus's ethic. He said "Christ has now created a new humanity that is not based on blood boundaries or communal boundaries, or tribal boundaries."[11] The participant avows, however, that due to the reoccurring violent attacks people have been experiencing, this African traditional universal ethics of the stranger is

9. Nzeka, 32–45.
10. Nzeka, 63–67.
11. Tyriaka, D1#4: 300–301.

eroding in practice. He underscores that Nigerian "Christians under attack and suffering violence... now create boundaries—denominational and religious boundaries to help each other."[12] Nevertheless, he insists that "those who practice ethics beyond your boundaries are only exceptional people who subscribe to Jesus's ethics. So, those who subscribe to Jesus's ethnics now believe that what people do to you is not a barrier to what you can do for them, ... because Jesus's love has no boundaries, [and] the love of God is not bounded by any boundaries. It is universal."[13]

Drawing from this argument, we posit then that the African universal ethics of the stranger—demonstrated in the Igbo *nzu* concept can be retrieved and contextually employed in peacebuilding in Nigeria's context of Islamist violence. Admittedly, this sounds simplistic. Nevertheless, we maintain that the *nzu* concept is a concept standing out there in the horizons of peacebuilding-contextual theological discourse, which should be studied and constructively and critically integrated into peacebuilding initiatives. Dissecting the complexity that will be involved in praxis and application of *nzu* concept in Nigeria's context of Islamist violence will evidently require further study. It should suffice us to know, to say the least, that this concept exists and can be studied and integrated into peacebuilding initiatives in Nigeria's context. Its equivalent among other ethnolinguistic groups in Nigeria can be unearthed and studied as well. Before we leave our discussion on the *nzu* concept, we note that the Igbos also use *nzu* (as a natural material) for other purposes, besides its use as a symbol of acceptance, hospitality and its significance for peacebuilding.

6.1.2 Hospitality: An African Means for Peacebuilding

Hospitality is another theme that emerged from our research interviews as one of African ethos that must be retrieved and employed for peacebuilding in Nigeria's context of violence. Interestingly enough, one of the participants (Ahmed) who spoke on hospitality as an African concept for peacebuilding happens to come from a royal Muslim background in northeastern Nigeria and holds two master's degrees in Islamic studies, as well as a doctoral degree in Islamic law. He was formerly an associate professor of Islamic law in Saudi Arabia, where he had an encounter with Jesus in a vision, which led him to embrace faith as a follower of Jesus Christ.

To give context to Ahmed's response, we first posed the question that elicited his answer: Are there any possible African cultural processes, practices, or proclamations, that you think the church in Nigeria can adopt

12. Tyriaka, 302–303.
13. Tyriaka, 304–308.

in order to develop peacebuilding? Ahmed responded: "I really think the answer is yes. One of the greatest African cultures that is very common, I don't want to say the practice is common to everyone, but the majority of African cultures have what we call hospitality. Hospitality would go a long way in helping us building bridges."[14] He went further to insist: "I mean we have to come back to our African roots. In northern Nigeria, for example, we ended up . . . having this mentality of 'us versus them'. And that stopped our . . . [practice of] hospitality . . . "[15]

Speaking on how Nigerian followers of Jesus in northern Nigeria can retrieve hospitality as a means for peacebuilding, Ahmed asked rhetorically: "How can we be able to invite a Muslim into our houses and make effort to come to their houses as well?" He responded to his self-posed question.

> We need to figure out how to bring back hospitality into the equation, because if we [Nigerian followers of Jesus] treat them as enemies; if I were Satan, that is exactly what I would do. [Satan] wants you to help them so much to send them to hell, . . . [he, Satan] wants them to go to hell, and he wants to keep you there. But at some point we [Jesus's followers] have to say: No! That is not our identity. That is supposed to be theirs [the enemy's identity]. So when you feel like you are hating somebody, you want to kill them, just be convinced; allow the Holy Spirit to tell you 'That is not you, that is not what you are called to be.' So we need to go over [overcome] our hatred and bring back our culture of hospitality. And doing hospitality will really take us a long way.[16]

Ahmed admits that with the coming of Islam into northern Nigeria, some northern Nigeria cultures have been distorted and replaced with Islamic forms. In view of this, he opines that some of the indigenous hospitality rituals in today's northern Nigerian Muslim communities have probably eroded, because those practices are no longer tolerated if one openly practices them.[17]

Nevertheless, despite such apparent erosion of the African hospitality culture among some of the cultures, there remains a 'remnant'[18] among

---

14. Ahmed, D4#1:423–426.
15. Ahmed, 428–430.
16. Ahmed, 432–441.
17. Ahmed, 448–451.
18. "A remnant" here implies a deviant few, who refuse to conform to the predominant societal norms, but prefer to stick to giving hospitality to 'the other' even when it implies risking their own lives and that of their families.

northern Nigerian Muslims who have not jettisoned the God-given ethos of hospitality engrained in them and in their culture. In this regard, in his 2008 volume—*Hospitality and the Other*, accomplished and renowned pentecostal theologian, Amos Yong, weaved "three strands" into that work, namely: (a) the nexus between the theology of hospitality and of religions; (b) the central virtue attached to "a correlative set practices" of hospitality; and (c) "the pneumatological framework" tying the first two strands together.[19] Yong, in weaving his "three strands" of the volume first showed from three case studies (among which Nigeria is one), that there exists "glimmers of hope in various acts of interreligious hospitality" in our "postmodern and pluralistic world of interreligious war and violence."[20] In Yong's Nigerian case study, he cites an example from David L. Windibiziri's article, showing that

> there have also been some signs of hope in Muslim neighbors protecting and saving Christians and vice versa. One Christian testified, "An old Muslim man took me into his house where I stayed until 6.30 p.m." while two elderly Christian men said they 'managed to escape and were saved by a Muslim acquaintance who hid them, along with eight women and two young men, in his house close to the church premises."[21]

There are similar examples to corroborate this position that the African traditional concept of hospitality still persists among some northern Nigerian Muslims, and that Nigerian followers of Jesus must revive it and employ it for peacebuilding. Nigerian-born scholar whose research focuses on Christian-Muslim relations, African studies and intercultural studies, Akintunde E. Akinade, drawing from Amos Yong's example cited above maintains that "[i]n spite of the constant contestation for power, resources, and symbolic relevance that exists between Nigerian Christians and Muslims, there are still many instances and stories of fraternal fellowship between them in different parts of the country."[22] Paul Hedges refers to this as "the dialogue of life" or "human dialogue" whereby "people are seen as central and it is the interaction between them on a personal level that is seen as important. It tends to dominate at grassroots levels being concerned with day-to-day

---

19. Yong, *Hospitality and the Other*, xiii.
20. Yong, *Hospitality and the Other*, xiv.
21. Yong, *Hospitality and the Other*, 19, and n68: "David L. Windibiziri, "Neighborology, Mutuality and Friendship," in *Dialogue and Beyond: Christians and Muslims Together on the Way*, ed. Sigvard von Sicard and Ingo Wulfhorst (Geneva: Lutheran World Federation, 2003), 89–95, esp. 92–93."
22. Akinade, *Christian Responses to Islam in Nigeria*, 66.

meeting and encountering . . . "[23] Dooshima Abu, who reports for BBC News in northern Nigeria, points to another example of this 'dialogue of life' or 'human dialogue'. Abu wrote on July 1, 2018:

> When an imam in Nigeria saw hundreds of desperate, frightened families running into his village last Saturday [that is: June 30, 2018], he decided to risk his life to save theirs. They were fleeing from a neighbouring village—a mainly Christian community. They say they came under attack at about 15:00 (14:00 GMT) from about 300 well-armed men—suspected cattle herders, who are mostly Muslims—who started shooting sporadically and burning down their homes. Some of those who managed to escape ran towards the mainly Muslim neighbourhood nearby where the imam lived, arriving over the next hour. The cleric immediately came to their aid, hiding in total 262 men, women and children in his home and mosque.[24]

The example cited above is not an isolated case. A northern Nigerian Church leader and scholar, Dauda,[25] whom we interviewed testifies to his own experience. He maintained that in the midst of Islamist violence in Nigeria ". . . there are instances of grace happening in the sense that during crises situations some Muslims would protect Christians who they happen to know in their neighborhood and vice-versa."[26] Dauda further elaborates:

> I know of a theological school that decided to take in a Muslim man who was hurt by the surrounding people in order to hide him, and they eventually smuggled the young man out in the trunk of a car to a place where he can get medical treatment. After about a month, the family of the young man called back to this seminary to thank them. My wife and I took up a Muslim woman and her daughter because they were caught in a crisis. We kept them in our home and my pastor took them to a place where they could find a car to return home. My church paid their transportation back to where they were coming from, so there are instances like that . . .[27]

---

23. Hedges, *Controversies in Interreligious Dialogue*, 60–61; see also Akinade, *Christian Responses to Islam in Nigeria*, 66n67.

24. Abu, "Imam Who Saved Christians from Muslim Gunmen."

25. Participant D1#1, Dauda, earned two MA degrees and a PhD from universities in the United States and has served in various leadership roles both in higher education and in pastoral ministry in his denomination in northern Nigeria.

26. Dauda, D1#1:137–139.

27. Dauda, 139–142.

Dauda used the expression "grace happening" to underscore that it takes God's grace for someone to risk his or her life in order to protect the "other" whose religious identity is the same as that of the violent perpetrator. He noted: "I know it sometimes happens in Muslim context whereby a Christian is protected but I know . . . it only takes the grace of God."[28]

Another participant, Zuruaga—a pastor, responding to the same question on African cultural processes, practices, or proclamations, that the church in Nigeria can adopt in order to develop peacebuilding, said: "African's have always been hospitable people, and I can tell you this is one of the key reasons why many . . . non-indigenes of our local communities were able to be settled" in communities other than those belonging to their ethnic group.[29] Zuruaga buttresses this with an Hausa adage: "*Karban baki kan sa ka marabchi mala'ika*, meaning: in hosting someone that is coming to your place (maybe a visitor, a passerby) you are able to host an angel. So it may be an angel coming through that individual and when you accept that person, and give him [or her] some kind of hospitality treatment that person might be an angel."[30] This adage resonates with the New Testament injunction ". . . not to neglect to show hospitality to strangers, for thereby some have entertained angels unawares" (Heb 13:2).[31]

Hospitality is also demonstrated by sharing a meal. Amadu, a Pastor from Borno State, in northeastern Nigeria, attests in his response to the question on African processes, practices, or proclamations for peacebuilding, maintaining that among his own Bura people "somebody with whom you eat together will not have the mind of harming you."[32] Among Bura people of Borno State, sharing a meal together signifies that a bond of relationship has been created—a bond that can be considered as strong as a covenantal commitment not to harm the one with whom you share that meal.

One other participant highlighted another form of the expression of hospitality in his ethnolinguistic group. Participant Andraus from the Nga people of Plateau State stated that among his own people a stranger is viewed as "graceful and have blessings accompanying him . . ." In other words, the Nga people hold that "when you have a stranger and you treat him [or her] well, God would bless you for doing that."[33] In one of the

---

28. Dauda, 158–160.
29. Zuruaga D1#3:247–249.
30. Zuruaga, 250–253.
31. I am unable to verify whether or not this adage in Hausa language predates the arrival of the New Testament Scriptures where the same idea is found.
32. Amadu, D2#2:297–298.
33. Andraus, D2#1:340–342.

focus groups, a participant drew attention to how sharing of food between Christians and Muslims used to be the practice while he was young. He attests that while growing up, during "Christmas, we had Muslim neighbors and we . . . share food with them, and they also brought food to us, during their own celebrations."[34]

There is a caveat that must not, however, be ignored in sharing of meals and giving hospitality to Muslims. Whoever will become a host to Muslims must not ignore Muslim food restrictions because not all foods are *halāl* (permitted) for Muslims. Thus, sacrifice and love must be factored-in on the part of the Christian giver of hospitality. When a Christian offers food to a Muslim, the latter may receive it with gratitude but may not eat it for fear of transgressing his or her religious and ritual restrictions on food. Another participant in Focus Group #1 highlighted this important element, insisting that

> the truth is that some of our Muslim friends, when you give them food they, throw it away, they don't eat. They would receive it with gratitude, but behind you they throw it away, because they do not trust what it is, especially, when it is chicken, because they believe you are the one that slaughtered the chicken, and to them it is an abomination to eat anything slaughtered by a Christian.[35]

The focus group participant also pointed out how such barriers can be overcome by an intentional and creative demonstration of love to Muslims. He describes his own mother's creativity to overcame the barrier. His mother, who in her deliberate and creative effort to demonstrate hospitality to her Muslim neighbors, organizes dinner for them.

> [She invited a well-respected] Muslim in the community, someone that she was fully aware that this man would not keep quiet, so he will tell his friends that this woman called him to come and slaughter a goat for them. . . , When she called them for dinner, they ate the dinner because the man told them that he was the one who slaughtered the goat. . . So we can be deliberate about eating together . . .[36]

---

34. Participant, Focus Group #1:440–442. References to focus group interviews follow the same pattern as individual interviews. Focus Group #1 denotes the focus group with participants in Denomination #1, Focus Group #2 with Denomination #2, and Focus Group #3 with Denomination #3.

35. Focus Group #1:467–471.

36. Focus Group #1:472–478.

Thus, it is not only what is offered as food to a Muslim that must be carefully weighed in hospitality, but also, who slaughters what is prepared where the food contains any form of animal meat. Giving hospitality will serve as an avenue for peacebuilding in view of the opportunities of ordinary human encounters and attachment[37] it creates in the hearts of both the host and the guest. Evelyne A. Reisacher's contribution on this theme with particular application to "Muslim-Christian Attachment" in her award-winning volume *Joyful Witness in the Muslim World*, corroborates the idea that ordinary human encounters can become platforms for creating human attachment.[38]

The concept of hospitality is not limited to the ethnolinguistic cultures in Nigeria so far mentioned above. The Yoruba people constitute, alongside the Hausa/Fulani and the Igbos, one of the major ethnolinguistic blocks in Nigeria. Thus, it is fitting to highlight as well the Yoruba concept of hospitality, although not garnered from my research interviews but from literature. 'Wande Abimbola, in his contribution to the volume, *Attitudes of Religions and Ideologies Toward the Outsider*, examines some of the attitudes of the Yoruba traditional religion to people of other faiths.[39] He notes that "examples [exist] in Yoruba mythology where a stranger is honored and given valuable things even as soon as he enters the town . . ."[40] a practice that is not just a myth but also praxis among Yoruba people in typical traditional settings. This Yoruba practice of hospitality is attested to in their welcome of both Islam and Christianity to dwell alongside Yoruba traditional religion without violence. Abimbola underscores this point observing that the rejection of "brute force in communal living"[41] is reckoned as very essential in the Yoruba traditional upbringing.

Closely related to the Yoruba concept and practice of hospitality is the Yoruba notion of àlàáfíà, which is the Yoruba's conception of peace, harmony and wholeness. The notion of àlàáfíà resonates with both the Judeo-Christian concept of *shalom* and the Islamic notion of *salām*. Adeshina

---

37. We can look closely into the theme of "attachment" through the lens of Attachment Theory, but I do not consider the present work the forum to delve into that discussion. Some introductory texts to the theory include: Green and Marc, *Attachment and Human Survival*; Cassidy and Shaver, *Handbook of Attachment*. John Bowlby is regarded to have originated Attachment Theory. Bowlby's trilogy is an asset to understanding this theory Bowlby, *Attachment and Loss*; Bowlby, *Fifty Years of Attachment Theory*; Holmes, *John Bowlby and Attachment Theory*. See also Reisacher, "Process of Attachment Between the Algerians and French."

38. Reisacher, *Joyful Witness in the Muslim World*, 21–42.

39. Abimbola, "Attitude of Yoruba Religion Toward Non-Yoruba Religion," 135–45.

40. Abimbola, "Attitude of Yoruba Religion Toward Non-Yoruba Religion," 138.

41. Abimbola, "Attitude of Yoruba Religion Toward Non-Yoruba Religion," 141.

Ekanola, presents this Yoruba conception of peace in his contribution to the volume, *The Plagrave Handbook of African Philosophy*,[42] wherein he maintains that *àlàáfíà* "incorporates the notions of *ìrẹ́pọ̀* (harmony) and *ìṣọ̀kan* (unity) among humans in society and also between humans and other supernatural entities."[43]

6.1.3 Gammo *and* Gaya *Concepts: Community Power in Peacebuilding*

Community power in peacebuilding is another theme that emerged from the interviews. A female Margi[44] participant, in her response to the question on African cultural concepts and processes of peacebuilding said:

> Margi people are generally brave people, but they are peaceful people as well. There is a saying in Margi language that says: "*Titi tuku 'a rumbwa mai*" that means, "one hand cannot hold a roof". So, Margi man by all means tries to live in peace with his brothers or his neighbors. So there are certain festivals, there are also cultural activities that we do in my tribe that promote peace because everybody can come, it's a cultural festival that brings people together, such as the festival of the rain which holds at the beginning of the raining season.[45]

There are two concepts that we can draw from this. The first is in regard to the power of community, and the second, the agency of community festivals or similar cultural activities. We treat these two as different concepts—community power in peacebuilding and festivals and rituals as means for peacebuilding.

First, the power of community in peacebuilding is expressed in the Margi adage: "'*Titi tuku 'a rumbwa mai*'" —which implies that only one person cannot hold or raise a roof. To understand this concept, we must first explain the context. In many rural African villages, houses are made of mud mixed with hay, and in most places they are constructed in spherical shapes. After the walls are built-up, the roof is then assembled on the ground with rafters made of bamboo and carefully weaved thatch as the covering. After the rafters and thatch have been assembled to form the

---

42. Ekanola, "Yorùbá Conception of Peace," 671–80.

43. Ekanola, "Yorùbá Conception of Peace," 671.

44. The Margi is a people group found in today's Adamawa and Borno States of northeastern Nigeria. See http://www.oxfordreference.com.fuller.idm.oclc.org/view/10.1093/acref/9780195337709.001.0001/acref-9780195337709-e-2523 or the "Margi" entry in Gates and Kwame, *Encyclopedia of Africa*.

45. Salamatu, D3#2:199–205.

single roof unit, it must then be carried up and fixed upon the built-up wall. Thus, the Margi saying to which Salamatu (D3#2) referred implies that only one person cannot raise the assembled roof unit and fix it upon the built-up wall. The philosophical undertone is that in our African communities, the hands of people in the community are required to work together in order to mount a roof that provides shelter and protection. Such a work cannot be done by only one person.

Another participant, Jibreel, also made an allusion to this concept of peacebuilding, noting that when the roof-unit is ready to be fixed upon the walls, "you mobilize the whole community."[46] People come and put their hands together to raise up the unit. This roof unit is referred to as *gammo* in Hausa language. Jibreel's argument in his explanation of the *gammo* concept is that the entire community must be involved in raising the means that secures community protection, which also undercuts the chances of violence. Jibreel pointed out another community concept called *gaya* in Hausa.

Most rural communities in northeastern Nigeria are peasants. Traditional local methods prevail as the primary method of farming and means of subsistence. Jibreel pointed that many communities engage in *gaya* which "means we come and farm in your farm today, and tomorrow we will go and farm in mine . . . We say: Look! It will be faster for you to finish your farm. If you're going to farm alone, you won't be able to finish it. So let us organize *gaya*. So we organize like 10, 15, or 20 families today, we go to your farm, and tomorrow we come to mine. The next day we go to Mr. B; another day we go to Mr. C."[47]

In a focus group discussion, a participant gave another Hausa proverb to depict the power of community participation in peacebuilding. The focus group participant draws his own image, not from raising a *gammo* or organizing a *gaya*, but from raising children in the community. The image is drawn from a saying in their community, in Hausa language: "*Yaron da ke cikin maman shi yaronta ne. Amma in an haife shi yaron anguwa ne*" which he interpreted to mean: "When a child is in his mother's womb, the child is the mother's child. But when he/she is born, the child belongs to the community . . . The idea is that, the community is responsible for training a child, so that when a child grows up, whatever he does, anyone from the community can discipline him, anyone from the community can correct him."[48] We may then pose the question: What is the co-relation between community involvement in child upbringing and peacebuilding?

46. Jibreel, D4#4:172–178.
47. Jibreel, 206–210.
48. Focus Group #1:484–488.

Some human elements foment violence. There exists a relationship between people's propensity to violence and their upbringing. Studies in psychological and behavioral sciences have shown that such relationship exists.[49] If concepts and values of peace and well-being of the community are instilled in a child's upbringing, then in adulthood, the child's likelihood to participate in violence will be reduced. On the other hand, if those concepts and values were absent in a child's upbringing, the child's proclivity toward becoming an agent of violence will be high. This underscores the reasons why the onus of raising a child in most African communities does not rest single-handedly upon a child's biological parents, but upon the community into which he or she is born.

In chapter 2, we highlighted the challenges and contribution of the *al-majiri* (plural: *al-majirai*) phenomenon to Islamist violence in northern Nigeria, what Virginia Comolli refers to as "the *almajiri* syndrome."[50] We noted that these *al-mjirai* are not only children at risk to their own lives, but also to the entire society where they are left at the mercy of living off the streets. Furthermore, we pointed out that the psychological and societal repercussions of the *al-majiri* phenomenon in Muslim youths in northern Nigeria have been identified, and that there exists a complexity and complication it introduces—not only in regard to the upbringing of Muslim children, but also in respect to the framework of Islamists- and politically-motivated violence in the country. A participant in one of our focus groups pointed to this phenomenon as a factor that exacerbates violence in northern Nigeria.

> Let me also include the *al-majiri* school because I remember in 2011 during the post-election violence in Gombe, they [the *al-majirai*] are the ones that were mostly used to go and attack and kill people. So they use the small boys, they give them small ammunitions [such as] . . . cutlasses, sticks and all of that. They chase people and kill, then and when the military caught them, they interrogated them, they said [it was] the *al-majiri* boys. Their masters or teachers gave them one thousand Naira[51] [each] to go and do this thing. So the *al-majiri* school is also key because that is where they are being indoctrinated. That's where

---

49. See for example: Bergman and Andershed, "Predictors and Outcomes of Persistent or Age-Limited Registered Criminal Behavior," 164–78; Christoffersen et al., "Upbringing to Violence?" 367; Christoffersen et al., "Violent Life Events and Social Disadvantage," 157–84; Zaikman et al., "Influence of Early Experiences and Adult Attachment on the Exhibition of the Sexual Double Standard," 425–45.

50. Comolli, *Boko Haram*, 25.

51. In 2011 when the event the focus group participant referred to occurred, one thousand Naira in Nigeria was worth about 6.5 US dollars, at the most.

they are being brainwashed. So they use them, they easily use these ones, and even the Boko Haram attack—if you look at [it] the people they mostly use are young, young children [the *al-majirai*, who are] just teenagers who could hardly decide. Once you just ask them [to] go and do this thing, they will just go and do it without thinking. So these are the people that they mostly use . . . for carrying out all of these attacks.[52]

The menace which the *al-majirai* pose in times of crisis and violence gives weight to the argument that upbringing is a factor that may determine an adolescent or adult's proclivity toward the perpetation of and/or participation in violent acts.

Thus, if a community ignores its children, demonstrates hate toward them, and does not provide communal care to them in their childhood years, the chances of those children becoming candidates for inciting violence, or "a ready-army that can be recruited to perpetrate violence"[53] will be high during their adolescent and young adult years. The implication then is that the values a child imbibes from his or her childhood years reflect on his or her propensity to either ensure the well-being of his or her community or become a party to those who disrupt the community's peace. Thus, a community's involvement in raising up a child in African communities can be co-related to the child's contribution to the community's future peace and flourishing.[54]

Besides community participation in the upbringing of children, interview participant, Jibreel, notes the importance of the influence of community opinion leaders in peacebuilding initiatives in African contexts—a theme similar to the Somaliland concept of employing *guurti* (council of elders). In such initiatives, it is essential to first mobilize community opinion leaders—those "who incite [the people in the community] to do what they do . . . [and] when they say stop, people will stop."[55] An opinion leader may be the village head, a chief, the African traditional priest, or even a youth whose influence in the community commands respect. When such

---

52. Participant, Focus Group #1:130–141.

53. Danjibo, "Islamic Fundamentalism and Sectarian Violence," 8.

54. I avow that this argument requires longitudinal studies in African contexts. Some studies that have been done by Psychologists and Behavioral Scientists focus mainly on the relationship of upbringing to crime, sexual behaviors, domestic violence etc. As at the time of this writing, I am yet to come across any work written on this relationship as it pertains to peace in a community. Nevertheless, where relationships between crime and upbringing has been established, it can be inferred that similar relationship exists in regard to community peace.

55. Jibreel, D4#4:219–221.

community opinion leaders see reason for peacebuilding they will be in a position to summon the rest of their respective communities to engage in peacebuilding with one another.

The theme of community power in peacebuilding as a concept was preponderant in all our interviews. One more example comes from a focus group participant in Focus Group #2. The name of the participant's ethnolinguistic group is what reflects the concept. He said: "I am Mwughavul. And the meaning of the word . . . is *Mun ki mwan a vul* meaning: 'we walk two by each other's side. No one person should be walking [alone]. And . . . the English meaning is: 'Two are better than one', or 'Two is wealth'. . . that is the traditional concept of the Mwughavul man, we will [need] to make the Muslims understand that you cannot exist alone."[56]

All these examples around the theme of community power resonate with the Nguni concept of *ubuntu*, which we discussed in chapter 5. It supports the argument that *ubuntu* is expressed in different ways in many sub-Saharan African cultures. Thus, community power in peacebuilding—whether it is from the *gammo* (raising the roof) concept, the *gaya* (community participation in farming), community responsibility in raising children, the winning over of the heart of community opinion leaders, or *Mun ki mwan a vul* (we walk two by each other's side)—entails concepts resident in cultures in northeastern Nigerian that can be further studied, understood, and constructively employed for the purpose of peacebuilding.

6.1.4 The Agency of Community Festivals and Rituals for Peacebuilding

So far, we have discussed three concepts for peacebuilding from ethnolinguistic groups in Nigeria—the *nzu* concept, hospitality, and the *gammo-gaya* concepts imbedded in community power. Three other concepts (festivals and rituals, *egbo-o ho-ho*, and cross-clan marriages) compel our attention, and each of them has some sort of link to community as well.

Community festivals is an idea that emerged from Salamatu's response to our question on African concepts of peacebuilding. The Margi people summon the festival of the rain—called *Yawal* in Margi language. They "call for it [*Yawal*] at the beginning of the raining season to give thanks to the gods and to ask them to bestow their blessings on the lands because the rain is now coming. We [the Margi people] will be planning to go back to the farm so they [the gods] should smile on us again, and give

---

56. Focus Group #2:410–415.

us bountiful harvest, and give us good health, and bless us."[57] The missiological and contextual question that arises from this is: Should Margi followers of Jesus identify with *Yawal* or not, since it involves giving thanks "to the gods"? Briefly, it suffices us to know that Margi followers of Jesus direct their thanksgiving and entreaties toward the Supreme God, whom they refer to as *Ijumthlagu* [literally, the Almighty God] and whom they identify as the Creator. Formerly, the Margi Christian community discouraged *Yawal* festival, but it's coming back again as parents want to introduce their children back to the culture. So Christians participate in the festival but reject the aspect involving animal sacrifice. Margi Christians may be on the path to redeeming the *Yawal* festival—stripping it of those cultural aspects inconsistent with Christian teaching and applying Christian hermeneutical understanding to other aspects to redirect entreaty, praise and glory to *Ijumthlagu*, the Almighty God.[58]

The festival, as a means for peacebuilding, brings people together across cultural boundaries. It is also a time of celebration when women groups come to dance. Such celebration across Margi cultural boundaries helps to weave threads of peace among Margi and neighboring non-Margi communities.

In relation to Muslims, the Margi people who follow Jesus exchange gifts with their Muslim neighbors during religious festivals. Salamatu explains that: "during Christmas we [Margi] Christians also send our gifts and food to Muslims around in the community and during *Salah* [Muslim religious festivals, *Eid*] there is still sharing... [i.e.] exchange of gifts."[59] Similar to religious festivals and celebrations is wedding ceremonies. Focus group participants underscore that "during [Christian] weddings, . . . Muslims also want to attend our weddings, although they do not like going to the church, they are comfortable with the reception."[60] In some cases, "you find a situation that in a family you have Christians and Muslims in the same family, so we attend our weddings. If it is a Muslim wedding, we go and support them . . . During the Christian wedding, we notify them also and they come."[61]

Other focus groups discussions highlighted the use of sports and games—local wrestling matches, soccer and moonlight games—as means for peacebuilding engagement with Muslims. The argument is that as

57. Salamatu, D3#2:210–213.

58. WhatsApp communication with Participant (Salamatu, D3#2) on February 4, 2019.

59. Salamatu, 235–239.

60. Focus Group#1:535–534, and Focus Group #2:493–499.

61. Focus Group#1:538–541.

relationships are built through festivals, religious celebrations, sports, games and rituals, strands for attachment between communities are weaved which consequently serve as a means for peacebuilding engagement.

6.1.5 Egbo-o Ho-Ho *Concept: African Women's Power in Peacebuilding*

Another concept for peacebuilding with links to community power in peacebuilding is one where women are the principal actors. It's the *egbo-o ho –ho* concept. The *egbo-o ho ho* concept is autochthonous to my hometown, Umudim, in Ikeduru local government of Imo State—an example we briefly connected to our discussion on African women in peacebuilding (section 5.1.4). Fittingly, a participant observer has written a short article about it and we draw from that published article.

Whereas I am Igbo, my spouse, Dolapo (at the time of my writing, a PhD candidate at Tufts University's Friedman School of Nutrition and Food Policy in Boston, Massachusetts), is Yoruba. As a participant observer, she was moved to see the method women in my home village—Umuduruejeme in Umudim—employ to resolve conflicts and install a peace culture. Her observation led to an article now published in *The Community Psychologist*. She writes,

> In rural Eastern Nigeria, a cry, "Egbo-o Ho Ho!" sets in motion the process of conflict resolution. Egbo-o- Ho Ho is an onomatopoeic expression that someone makes when in a fight or in any social conflict considered a great injustice. At the shout, "Egbo-o Ho Ho," all the women in the community drop whatever it is they are doing and rush to the scene of the incident. All the women are committed to coming out to help any member of the community in distress. Upon arrival, they will inquire from the person who gave the shout what it is all about. They will then seize some valuable items from the homes of both parties involved in the case and set a date to arbitrate the matter. On the day of the case, the people involved in the conflict appear before the women. Then, each one states his or her case, and the women will decide who is at fault and whether the shouting of Egbo-o Ho Ho was justifiable in that instance. They will then place a fine on the offender. Since it is a rural community, the fine is not usually monetary. It could be a goat, or gallons of palm oil, or clothing materials. Where the offender is not able to pay, the women have the liberty to sell the goods belonging to the

offender that they had earlier seized. The funds from the sales will then be used to fund social projects for the community.[62]

Anyanwu affirms that "Egbo-o Ho Ho provides [the] social mechanism for the rural communities in which it is practiced" to effectively deal with conflict in their communities.[63] The use of *Egbo-o Ho Ho* concept in Umudim adds value to the role women play in their community, and provides them the platform for "adjudication and peace building, in addition to raising children and being domestic hands."[64] *Egbo-o Ho Ho* also serves as a social deterrent for those who are plotting to foment conflict or disrupt social justice, consequently instilling a culture of peace. No one dares cry "*Egbo-o Ho Ho*" when there is no cause for it. Anyone who dares cry wolf with *Egbo-o Ho Ho* faces dire penalties which the village women determine. With that concept in place, Umudim communities enjoy peace without any local police or vigilante groups. Character and values of respect for the other are unconsciously instilled in people as they grow up in the village.

For the reader to grasp the weight of the power of women in this case, some insight into the context is necessary. All the women who undertake arbitration using the *Egbo-o Ho Ho* concept are women married into the village from outside. None of the women is an indigene of the village because no one can marry a woman from his own village. It is an abomination to do so. (There are even some villages that cannot inter-marry between themselves because of proximity of their ancestral clans). So it is important to note that all married women in any given village where *Egbo-o Ho Ho* concept is employed were married from another town or village (provided inter-village marriage is permitted between the woman's ancestral village/clan and that of her husband). Women in every village consider their husbands' village as theirs and for their children. So, as the saying goes: As you make your bed, you lie on it, these women are committed to creating a culture of peace in their villages, so that they and their children can live and lie down therein peaceably. No man, irrespective of his position or possession, is exempt from the power the women can exercise over him should that man commit an offence or injustice that warrants an *Egbo-o Ho Ho* cry. These women's purpose is solely to create a society and culture where peace prevails for they are keenly aware that such a society is expedient for them and their children to live and thrive.

A question that arises from this, however, is: Can such a village-localized concept contribute to meaningful peacebuilding in contexts

62. Anyanwu, "Egbo-o Ho Ho! A Cry for Crisis Intervention," 31.
63. Anyanwu, "Egbo-o Ho Ho! A Cry for Crisis Intervention," 31.
64. Anyanwu, "Egbo-o Ho Ho! A Cry for Crisis Intervention," 32.

involving outsiders? In other words, how may the *egbo-o ho ho* concept be applicable outward? We underscore in response that this concept is not village-bounded because neighboring villages and towns uphold the same practice. The respective councils of elders hold themselves accountable, such that people from neighboring villages or towns cannot transverse into another village to commit an unjust act with the mindset that they may be speared of the consequences because the act was not committed in their own village. Simply put, similar concepts and mechanisms are indeed put in place to achieve the same goal vis-à-vis outsiders—just as we highlighted in the discussion on the *nzu* concept.

Another insight is worthy of explication in regard to the *egbo-o ho ho* concept. The expression comes from an Igbo word for a bird of prey, the hawk—*egbe*. In Igbo villages, hens raise their brood of chicks by taking them around the village to find food. Often, hawks (*egbe*) hover in the atmosphere searching to prey on little and helpless chicks. When a hawk sees one positioned for capture, the hawk swings fast down to pick up its prey. But the villagers do something amazing. When they see a hawk trying to swing down, they raise some shout *o-Ho-Ho* to scare away the hawk (*egbe*). And it works—scaring away the predator and saving the prey when the shout is raised promptly. So the women formed the expression "*Egbo-o Ho Ho*" by combining the word for hawk (*egbe*) with the shout that is often raised to scare away predating hawks (*o-Ho-Ho*) to form *Egbo-o*[65]*-Ho-Ho*. The idea behind the *Egbo-o Ho Ho* concept is linked to this practice of scaring away the hawk (*egbe*) that wants to come and prey upon little and helpless chicks. It is apt because it translates a community practice used to protect prey from predator into a one that is being used for protecting the weak from the strong, the helpless from the unjust, and thereby creating peace.

That said, we must also highlight alongside the above argument that rural-urban migration has, nonetheless, introduced certain dynamics that rob people of the traditional values and virtues which mold them to conform to the culture of peace. The fact remains, however, that African women in their traditional habitats possess cultural contextual concepts they employ for local peacebuilding. The facts we have advanced above amply demonstrate that African women are, not only a force for peacebuilding, but also a force to be reckoned with for socio-political emancipation, reconciliation and nation-building.

---

65. The final "e" in *egbe* contracts and is assimilated by "o" to give "*Egbo-o*." If it were to be written out fully, the shout will be "*Egbe o Ho-Ho*."

6.1.6 Cross-clan Marriages as Means for Peacebuilding

The final concept, still connected to women, is cross-clan marriages. There exist numerous African concepts for peacebuilding as there are numerous ethnolinguistic groups in Africa. Various groups employ means and methods passed down to them by their forefathers. One other concept emerging from our research is the use of inter-clan or cross-clan marriages as a means for peacebuilding.

In Focus Group #3, a participant from Glavda people group in Gwoza Local Government Area of Borno State brought this concept up in response to the question on African concepts for peacebuilding. In the participant's own words, he describes the concept as follows:

> ... in Glavda which is a dialect in Gwoza Local Government, there is a kind of concept with which peace can be sustained in a community. Anytime war broke out, ... the elders will come back to their senses and say: 'No, we cannot continue to fight that war. Anytime we go for this war from both sides we record casualties.' So, what they [the elders] would do is [to] send a message. The elders will send a message from the other community and say: 'No, if we continue in this war, we can destroy ourselves; so what we need to do is: we have to establish a treaty we have to end this war. What was it that caused this war? How can we correct it?' Then to cement that kind of treaty the youth will be encouraged to marry from villages that they are fighting with. What is going on there is [this], ... if a youth from this community marries from the other community, give it ten to twenty years, if war breaks out you would be killing your niece and nephew yourselves. Invariably the idea there is that if you should have intermarriage relationship with them that peace is going to last more than just to end it at a treaty.[66]

This concept among the Glavda people of Borno State in northeastern Nigeria reflects part of the Somaliland *nabadraadin–guurti* concept where cross-clan-married women in a community serve as heralds or peace-bearers. In the Lederachs' Somaliland case study[67] to which we alluded in the previous chapter, we pointed out that cross-clan marriages position women to play an important role in peacebuilding. The same is true among the Glavda people of Borno State. Besides the role of women in galvanizing peace between waring communities, the Glavda marriage ties established through such cross-clan marriages produce children who serve as living

---

66. Focus Group #3:531–543.
67. Lederach and Lederach, "Let Us Talk."

signposts to the clans and communities that they cannot engage in war. Thus, in matters that will normally led to war, the Glavda elders (like the Somaliland *gurrti*) will enter into talks to find ways to resolve their differences instead of resorting to conflicts that engender bloodshed.

Having pointed to the Somaliland example where cross-clan-married women serve as peace-bearers and to the same concept mined from our research in northeastern Nigeria, one sociological question that may arise then is: Are women, therefore, used as pawns in sub-Saharan African societies given that most of those societies are patriarchal? From one perspective it might be viewed as such. In practice, however, the women see themselves as vital members of their societies who must do all they could to create a peaceful society where they and their children could live and thrive without molestation. Women are often the most vulnerable in contexts of conflict and violence. We alluded to the dangers Liberian women experienced during the Liberian war, which was one of the motivating factors that led to the rise of Liberian women peace actions that made a huge contribution toward a definite end of the Liberian conflict. Sub-Saharan African women are well aware that they have a vital role to play in ensuring peace in their communities. The *Egbo-o Ho Ho* concept we described and the Liberian Women's peace actions are testimonies to this fact. Thus, cross-clan marriages as a means of peacebuilding is not to say that women become peacebuilding pawns. Instead, it bestows honor on African women because without them their fathers, husbands, brothers, and other male relations stand the danger of completely destroying themselves in contexts of war.

Furthermore, cross-clan marriage does not imply that women are forcefully given away in marriages to men from a warring clan. Instead, they are encouraged without coercion. If cross-clan marriages were to be coercive, then women in cross-clan marriages will be considered as victims or peacebuilding pawns. But that is not the case. In view of this, African men must highly honor and value their women because the latter serve, not only as mothers, sisters, and wives, but also vital artisans of peace in African societies where conflicts and violence erupt. Many African women, through their peace actions, have risked their personal comfort and some even their very lives in order to install peace in their societies because their motherly instincts push them to seek the wellbeing and flourishing of their children, fathers, husbands, and other relations.

6.2 CARREFOUR OF AFRICAN CONCEPTS WITH PEACEBUILDING-CONTEXTUAL THEOLOGY

Taking up again our carrefour metaphor put forth in chapters 2 and 4, we outline now the intersections of African concepts with peacebuilding-contextual theology. In our introductory paragraph in this (and in the preceding) chapter we posed the question: What concepts of peacebuilding are embedded within African cultures that may be employed and integrated in developing peacebuilding-contextual theology? Put differently in relation to Nigeria's context of Islamist violence: What are the potential concepts for peacebuilding-contextual theology autochthonous to Nigeria's ethnolinguistic peoples that we may employ for integration into conceptualizing *staurocentric* pathways for peacebuilding?

In an attempt to respond to these questions, we first cast a bird's eye view in chapter 5 on some African concepts that have been unearthed and that have been employed in some African contexts to build peace. Among them is the Nguni concept of *ubuntu* which became the philosophy for reconciliation and forgiveness in the South African context of apartheid, and extended to Rwanda in the context following the 1994 genocide. When the UN-sponsored model of the Arusha Courts failed to ensure peace in Rwanda, Rwandans themselves resorted to their local *Gacacha* court system while integrating the concept of forgiveness imbedded in *ubuntu* as well as their Rwandan concept of *Abanyarwanda*. The Somaliland *Nabadraadin* (let us talk) concept connected with their *gurrti* (council of elders) were employed by their *ergada* (travelling elders) to galvanize peacebuilding between waring communities in Somaliland. In our survey of some African concepts, it was important to include an example of women's action for peace—an initiative that did not only lead to peacebuilding in war-torn Liberia but also earned the Liberian peace activist, Leymah Gbowee, a Nobel Peace Prize, and produced the first-ever female president of a country in the African continent. All the examples we outlined are evidence showing how these African concepts intersect with peacebuilding-contextual theology because the concepts are local and are applied in contexts of conflict and violence to install peace.

Furthermore, from the narrative data of our research in Nigeria as outlined in this chapter, we extracted concepts autochthonous to some ethnolinguistic groups to which interviewed participants belong. The preponderant emerging themes included: the universal ethics of the stranger (the *nzu* concept), hospitality, community power (expressed in the *gammo-gaya* concepts), agency of festivals, and the role of women in peacebuilding (the *Egbo-o Ho-Ho* concept and cross-clan marriages). The fact that interviewed participants did not consult with one another, belong to varying ethnolinguistic people groups, are members of different church denominations, and includes men and women who come from different geographical locations, makes it remarkable. Having surveyed these concepts, we conclude this chapter (as we did in chapter 5) asserting that, indeed, African concepts of peacebuilding are models that need be studied and understood, and then constructively and critically integrated into peacebuilding-contextual theology, not only in African contexts of violence but also in other non-African contexts. The question on how these African concepts discussed in these two chapters (5 and 6) can be integrated into conceptualizing *staurocentric* pathways for peacebuilding will be taken up in the concluding chapter—after we must have discussed *staurocentric* model (our theoretical framework for this study), which is the task we undertake in the next chapter.

7

Staurocentric Pathways to Peacebuilding-Contextual Theology

THE PURPOSE OF THIS chapter is to lay the foundation for the last—chapter 8. Methodologically, we first engage in a brief investigation on the meaning of the cross (σταυρός–*stauros*) beyond the definition we provided in the introductory chapter. Such an investigation enables one to, first, grasp the theological understanding of the concept in Greco-Roman times, and second, shows how Jesus ultimately overturned its meaning. Drawing from Jesus's example and the first Christian martyr (Stephen), we outline the principal elements that are characteristic of *staurocentric* pathways. The second section highlights the trajectories of departure from the *staurocentric* motif beginning from the time of Emperor Constantine and later crystallizing into the Roman Catholic Church's adoption of the Crusades. We explore also what the model might look like in contexts where the demographics of Jesus's followers may be either in the majority or in the minority. In the third segment, we point to contemporary examples of *staurocentric* forgiveness employed in contexts of violence. And lastly, section four makes a case for the intersection of the *staurocentric* approach and peacebuilding. The pivotal argument in this chapter is that the *staurocentric* model is God's instrument for triumphing over violence, and thus, should be espoused by Jesus's followers in every era and context for responding to their respective contexts of violence, and therein lies the core thesis of this monograph.

7.1 *STAUROS* IN GRECO-ROMAN TIMES AND HOW JESUS OVERTURNED ITS MEANING

The use of the cross (Greek: σταυρός—*stauros*[1]) as an instrument of crucifixion was restricted to slaves in ancient Greece. Crucifixion was undeniably the most horrendous, ruthless and intensified method of inflicting penalty on people. Mark T. Finney notes that under the Romans, it was

> among the most aggravated methods of execution known collectively as the *summum supplicium*, which were employed for the most serious penalties by offenders of low status. These covered several forms of the death penalty, and included, in order of increasing severity: decapitation (*decollatio*), burning (*vivus uri* or *crematio*), and crucifixion (*crux*).[2]

The Romans used it as "one of the strongest means of maintaining order and security"[3] to deter prospective revolutionists fighting for freedom from Roman domination. Jewish historian, Flavius Josephus, gives accounts of some mass crucifixion of such freedom fighters in Judea. Josephus attests that "Varus using a detail from his army, sent out around the countryside after those responsible for the commotion; and of the many who were rounded up, those who showed themselves less disturbance-prone he placed under guard, whereas those who were most responsible—about 2,000—he crucified."[4] Steve Mason and Honora Chapman, who translated and edited the works of Josephus comment that

> The first crucifixions in War ... [were] conducted by Alexander Ianneus against his own subjects ... This is the first instance of Roman crucifixion —"the most pitiable of deaths," as Josephus remarks ... Crucifixion, which seems often to have followed a severe beating, was both a painful and a humiliating way to die. Although not invented by the Romans, it was widely used by them, especially for slaves, bandits, rebels, and provincial criminals.[5]

Evidently, dying by crucifixion was stigmatic. Finney argues that besides "the many humiliating aspects that this form of punishment employed, the primary reason for this would appear to be the immeasurable

---

1. Hereafter, I only retain the transliteration of the Greek word into Latin letters—*stauros*.
2. Finney, "Servile Supplicium," 125.
3. Kittel and Friedrich, *Theological Dictionary of the NT*, 7:573.
4. Josephus, *Flavius Josephus*, 1b:52. See also Josephus, *Antiquities of the Jews*, 946.
5. Josephus, 1b:52.

dishonor which lay in its association with that of a slave and of the utter shame that such an association would bring . . . [and] as early as the writing of the Greek historian Polybius . . . it is the humiliation of crucifixion that comes to the fore."[6] The cross was a public execution method that, in an honor and shame culture, brought the uttermost shame to its victim and also leaves a stigma on the victims' family and friends.

The stigmatic characteristic of the cross is paradoxical when viewed in the light of the triune God's choice of it as a method to overcome the power of death, evil, sin and violence. God, in the Old Testament, had often employed what appears foolish to humans to overturn the wise.[7] It seems that the triune God, in dealing with evil and violence, chooses to use the most unlikely means. "The death on the cross was the lowest stage of humiliation but also the completing of obedience . . . to God's will [through which Jesus Christ] accomplished the work of redemption."[8] Out of an instrument of humiliation and horrendous death a pathway to divine eternal life was created. Out of what was abhorred (and is still loathed) emerges an instrument that defeats death, evil and violence.

Paul brings his theology of the cross to the fore, asserting that the "word of the cross[9] is folly to those who are perishing, but to us who are being saved it is the power of God."(1 Cor 1:18). The cross during the Greco-Roman world remained a symbol of disgrace, dishonor, humiliation and offense. But that was from a human perspective. From God's own viewpoint, it became an instrument for overcoming the power of death, evil, sin and violence. "For many the cross may well have been offensive. To mention the cross regularly, as. . . the apostle Paul does, and to envisage it as the instrument of God's glory would perhaps have sounded monstrous and detestable", Finney states.[10] This statement remains true in contemporary times because to suggest that through the application of the cross we can overcome violence that ravages our world would appear outrageous and repugnant. Martin Hengel summarizes this in the following words: "The heart of the Christian message, which Paul described as 'the word of the cross' (λόγος τοῦ σταυροῦ), ran counter not only to Roman political thinking, but to the whole ethos of religion in ancient times and in

---

6. Finney, "Servile Supplicium," 126.

7. One example in the OT is Joseph (Jacob's son) telling his brothers who demonstrated hate and were devoid of compassion toward him, "you meant evil against me, but God meant it for good, to bring it about that many people should be kept alive, as they are today" (Gen 50:20).

8. Kittel and Friedrich, *Theological Dictionary of the NT*, 7:575.

9. ὁ λόγος . . . ὁ τοῦ σταυροῦ —*ho logos ho tou staurou*

10. Finney, "Servile Supplicium," 133.

particular to the ideas of God held by educated people."[11] In the ancient world, therefore, the idea that "the pre-existent Son of the one true God . . . died the death of a common criminal on the cross, could only be regarded as a sign of madness."[12] The idea is even more outrageous to Muslims, who cannot fathom the Christian claim of God coming in human form, submitting to the limitations of human flesh and (to make it more grievous) die a horrendous death on the cross. This remains one of the grounds underlying the Muslims' out-right dismissal of the Christian Scriptures as corrupted, because the New Testament affirms and attests to the death of Jesus Christ. Muslims, instead, hold that Jesus did not die but was taken up to heaven alive according to the testimony of the Qur'ān that states:

> And [for] their saying, "Indeed, we have killed the Messiah, Jesus, the son of Mary, the messenger of Allah." And they did not kill him, nor did they crucify him; but [another] was made to resemble him to them. And indeed, those who differ over it are in doubt about it. They have no knowledge of it except the following of assumption. And they did not kill him, for certain.[13]

All things considered, to the Jews, the Greeks, the Romans, the barbarians, the Muslims, and to all peoples, the cross remains an unimaginable offense, scandal, and ignominy.

7.1.1 Jesus Overturns the Meaning of Stauros

We can then ask the question: But how did Jesus's death on the cross and his resurrection overturn the significance of the cross? Josef Blinzler's words are apt to begin an attempt to respond to this question. He writes:

> There is no event of either ancient or modern times which has affected humanity more deeply and more enduringly, occupied the thoughts of succeeding generations more intensively, touched hearts more deeply, captivated humanity's religious and artistic imagination more completely, or given stronger impetus to human strivings that the drama of which the final scene took place one Friday more than nineteen-hundred years ago–it was

---

11. Hengel, *Crucifixion in the Ancient World*, 5.

12. Hengel, *Crucifixion in the Ancient World*, 6–7. "Justin [Martyr]. . . describes the offense caused by the Christian message to the ancient world as madness (μανία) and sees the basis of this objection in Christian belief in the divine status of the crucified Jesus and his significance for salvation" (1).

13. Sahih International, *Al-Qur'an al-Kareem*, 4:157.

actually the seventh of April of the year 30 A.D.-on a hill outside the wall of Jerusalem.[14]

The event Blinzler refers to is no other but the event of Jesus's death on the cross. Whereas Blinzler's study is around the question that has been "hotly contested for centuries and which even today exercises and disturbs the minds of men"[15] (that is the question: who was responsible for pronouncing Jesus guilty and for his execution?); the question we attempt to respond to here is rather, how has that event of Jesus's death on the cross overturned the meaning of the cross both in human history and life?

In attempting to respond to the foregoing question, we first look at Jesus and the cross as a way of life. We base our argument on the grounds that Jesus is God's Word "through whom [God] created the world" (Heb 1:2); Jesus is the Word who "was with God in the beginning" (John 1:1–2) and whom God foreordained to drink the cup of the cross. At the event of Jesus's arrest, he hinted he could appeal to the "Father and he will at once send . . . more than twelve legions of angels" (Matt 26:53). This hint conveys an idea of military power. If it was a need for military might, Jesus was not bereft of the power of convocation. But he did not choose that path. He chose to drink the cup of the cross in obedience to the Father's will (Matt 26:39, 42; Luke 22:42; Phil 2:8). The hymn of Christ in Paul's letter to the Philippians is helpful to respond to the question we are posing. Paul wrote: "And [Jesus] being found in human form, he humbled himself by becoming obedient to the point of death, even death on a cross [θανάτου σταυροῦ—*thanatou staurou*]" (Phil 2:8).

Obedience to the Father is a capital asset that Jesus cherished and held tenaciously to, even when obedience meant suffering. Obedience coupled the cross of Jesus with his suffering. Differently put, the cross of Jesus is a carrefour of suffering and obedience. There, obedience and suffering crossed paths. Suffering here must be understood as suffering, not for wrong-doing, but for righteousness sake or suffering necessitated by obedience. Jesus's humility and obedience to the point of death on the cross are elements of emptying himself (*kenosis*). Gordon Fee highlights that the verb (ἐκένωσεν—*ekenōsen*) in Phil 2:7 "means to become powerless, or to be emptied of significance."[16] Jesus Christ, though he had the privileges of being divine as the Son of God, yet he became poor (2 Cor 8:9), he relinquished those divine privileges and status to become a slave/servant (δούλου)—the

---

14. Blinzler, *Trial of Jesus*, 5–6.
15. Blinzler, *Trial of Jesus*, 6, 21.
16. Fee, *Paul's Letter to the Philippians*, 211.

lowest status attributable to any human.[17] It is this downward mobility of Jesus—from his position as the Word of God by whom all things were created, to his incarnation (becoming human), to humbling himself in becoming a slave/servant, to accepting unjust judgment by humans he created, to accepting to die the most horrendous, ignominious, and detestable death any human could ever die (death on the cross)—it is this downward mobility that we refer to as the cross (*stauros*) of Jesus. Demetrius K. Williams argues that in the context of the hymn of Christ

> the cross is the climax to the narrative about Jesus Christ's privilege and loss (or voluntary abdication) of status. The reference to the cross also serves to contrast those who are not willing to adopt a similar attitude of obedience and self-sacrifice. Thus the attitude of Christ that characterized his journey to the cross consisted of humility (ἐταπείνωσεν) and obedience (ὑπήκοος). All who do not operate in this fashion are 'enemies of the cross'.[18]

We argue, therefore, that Jesus overturned the meaning of *stauros* by his suffering on the cross and his obedience to the Father's will. Now, let us turn to certain elements that characterize the new *stauros* which Jesus established.

7.1.2 Some Elements Characteristic of Staurocentric Pathways

There are certain elements that characterize *staurocentric* pathways. These elements are the pathways to the *staurocentric* model. The first is what I refer to as *staurocentric* forgiveness. It was displayed at the event of Jesus's death on the cross. While hanging on the cross, Jesus prayed: "Father forgive them, for they know not what they do" (Luke 23:34). It was also displayed at the event of Stephen's lapidation. From Luke's account, the first of Jesus's disciples to drink the cup of the cross (*stauros*) was Stephen, who was lapidated (Acts 6:8—8:1). Although Stephen was not crucified on the cross as Jesus, but the event of his lapidation possesses characteristics similar to the cross. He was stoned "outside the city" (Acts 7:58) just as his Master, Jesus, was crucified outside the city (Matt 27:31–33; Mark 15:20b–22; John 19:17–20; Heb 13:12).

Furthermore, in step with his Master, Stephen prayed for his malefactors. Whereas Jesus prayed: "Father forgive them, for they know not what they do" (Luke 23:34), Stephen on his part implored: "Lord, do not hold this sin against them" (Acts 7:60b). Thus, we count forgiveness as a

---

17. Williams, *Enemies of the Cross of Christ*, 131–32.
18. Williams, *Enemies of the Cross of Christ*, 133.

major element that characterize the *staurocentric* life. Hans Conzelmann's commentary on Acts 7:59 affirms that "Stephen's death is reminiscent of the death of Jesus,"[19] and F. F. Bruce underscores the point further affirming that "the request made by our Lord to the Father should soon be repeated to the Lord himself by Stephen is evidence for the rapid emergence of a high christology."[20] Thus, we do not limit the *staurocentric* motif to crucifixion. Rather, other forms of suffering, injustice and violence experienced as a result of following Jesus and characterized by Jesus's model of humility and voluntary self-giving can be reckoned as *staurocentric*. It is *staurocentric*, therefore, to be praying for (not against) one's malefactors, asking God not to lay to their charge the pain, injustice, and retribution for the evil and violence they perpetrate.

The second element of *staurocentric* pathways is the act of entrusting oneself to God. While Jesus was hanging on the cross he cried out: "Father into your hands I commit my spirit" (Luke 23:46). Peter makes an allusion to this element when he writes concerning Jesus, who: "When he was reviled, he did not revile in return; when he suffered, he did not threaten, but continued entrusting himself to him [God] who judges justly" (1 Pet 2:23). Similarly, Stephen cried out: "Lord Jesus, receive my spirit" (Acts 7:59). Stephen's cry and prayer for (not against) his malefactors were both similar to his Master's cry and prayer on the cross. The act of entrusting oneself to God in the face of violence demonstrates the eschatological hope to life—a hope that does not see the end of one's physical life as the end of life, but looks forward to the resurrection life—the life beyond the cross.

Yet another element of *staurocentric* pathways pertains to the results of such life. One of the results of Jesus's death on the cross and his resurrection is that through the cross Jesus destroyed the power of death (Heb 2:14 cf. 1 Cor 15:54–56). He overturned the meaning of the cross and by it overcame death and its violence. Therefore, submitting to the lowliest and the most ignoble position in life reflects what the cross is all about. And opting for the lowliest and most humiliating state is an element and a reflection of *stauros* (the cross), and that is the path Jesus trod. I maintain, therefore, that Jesus has left this pathway as a model *par excellence* for those who follow him to emulate (Luke 9:23). By employing the pathway of the cross, Jesus's followers can overturn evil and violence in their world. This model, as it appears, is the heavenly model Jesus saw in the heavenly courts before his incarnation. And he came and built according to it, just as Moses erected the Tabernacle according to the pattern shown to him on the mount

---

19. Conzelmann, *Acts of the Apostles*, 60.
20. Bruce, *Acts of the Apostles*, 212.

(Exod 25:40, 26:30; Acts 7:44, Heb 8:5). In this model depicted in the hymn of Christ, Jesus is presented as the model *par excellence* for Christians. He is "the supreme example of the humble self-sacrificing, self-giving service that Paul... [urged] the Philippians to practice in their relations one toward another,"[21] and also a supreme example of obedience.

Another element characteristic of *staurocentric* pathways is the results that accrue from it, which further supports our earlier argument that Jesus overturned the meaning of *stauros*. What was the aftermath of his death and resurrection? This is brought to the fore in Phil 2:9–11, which points to exaltation resulting from Jesus's humility, obedience, and voluntary self-giving. The subject of the first half of the hymn of Christ (Phil 2:6–8) is Jesus. In its second half (Phil 2:9–11) the subject moves to the Father (διὸ καὶ ὁ θεὸς Therefore, God...). The emphasis moves from Jesus's humility, obedience and voluntary self-giving to "the Father [who] is now presented as decisively intervening and acting on his Son's behalf. Jesus's self-humbling reached the absolute depths in his most shameful death, a death on the cross (θανάτου δὲ σταυροῦ, v.8)."[22] Two verbs denote the action of God the Father, namely: ὑπερυψόω (to highly exalt), and χαρίζομαι (to bestow upon).

Jesus, who in the first half of the hymn, is the subject of the verbs and participles, now becomes the object of the Father's exaltation and bestowing of a name that is above every name. The connection between this second half of the hymn to the first is the conjunction 'διὸ καὶ... '—and therefore. The implication is that what follows the conjunction (the exaltation and bestowing of a name) would not have occurred if the first part (vv. 6–8) did not happen. In other words, the Father's exaltation of the Son and his bestowing of a name upon Jesus were both contingent upon Jesus's humility, obedience, and voluntarily self-giving to die on the cross. We can assume that had Jesus not followed through with the cross, there would not have been an exaltation and a bestowing of the name.

We affirm, then, that Jesus, through his embrace of the cross (*stauros*), has obtained a name that is above every name and implicitly overturned the meaning of the cross. New Testament scholar, Donald Senior, affirms this position asserting that "the death of Jesus on the cross forever changed the meaning of crucifixion from the perspective of Christian faith."[23] Jesus did not only destroy the power of death, evil, sin and violence through the cross, but much more, he obtained a name that is above every name in addition to

---

21. O'Brien, *Epistle to the Philippians*, 205.
22. O'Brien, *Epistle to the Philippians*, 232–33.
23. Senior, *Why the Cross?*, 11.

"making peace by the blood of his cross" (Col 1:21). This is a characteristic element of Jesus's cross (the *staurocentric* life).

We can also argue from Stephen's *staurocentric* life, how the same element yielded a similar result. "And the witnesses [to Stephen's lapidation] laid down their garments at the feet of a young man named Saul... And Saul approved of his [Stephen's] execution... But Saul was ravaging the church, and entering house after house, he dragged off men and women and committed them to prison." (Acts 7:58b; 8:1, 3). It was this same "young man named Saul" whom Jesus encountered on the road to Damascus (Acts 9), and who became the preacher of the same Jesus and the gospel he persecuted. The Saul mentioned in this text is the same as Paul the apostle. He testified to how he approved Stephen's death (Acts 22:20) and persecuted the church (Acts 22:4; 26:10; 1 Cor 15:9; Gal 1:13; Phil 3:6; 1 Tim 1:13). The same Saul who approved of Stephen's execution and ravaged (λυμαίνομαι—*lumainomai*)[24] the church, turned out to become an instrument for proclaiming the message he persecuted.

Could it be that Stephen's prayer: "Lord, do not hold this sin against them" (Acts 7:60b) was heard in such an ironic manner, that Stephen's baton was passed on to Saul? The inference we can make is that as Jesus's model of the cross (*stauros*) leads to resurrection life, so also do the *staurocentric* pathways of his followers produce Jesus's life in others. Such life is often produced in those who oppose Jesus, because they overcome "by the blood of the Lamb and by the word of their testimony, for they loved not their lives even unto death" (Rev 12:11).

Jesus's death on the cross produced resurrection. Assuredly, followers of Jesus who die according to the pattern of Jesus's cross are not raised from the dead on the third day as Jesus was. Nevertheless, they live on with Jesus in eternity and will be raised at Jesus's Second Advent. But before then, their death produces life in those who ravage them and their message. Stephen's *staurocentric* death produced life in the young man named Saul. Paul, himself, makes an allusion similar to this argument. He wrote: "For we who live are always being given over to death for Jesus's sake, so that the life of Jesus also may be manifested in our mortal flesh. So death is at work in us, but life in you" (2 Cor 4:11–12).

---

24. This word (λυμαίνομαι *lumainomai*), is a *hapax legomenon* in the Greek New Testament. It is used only in Acts 8:3 in the entire Greek NT. F. F. Bruce notes that it is "a classical verb... an appropriate verb for the ravaging of a body by a wild beast. Paul uses an equally strong verb when he says [he] made havoc of" [the church]" (Gal. 1:13" Bruce, *Acts of the Apostles*, 215. Such description highlights another form of the cross. Followers of Jesus who are ravaged or upon whom havoc is done are implicitly drinking the cup of the cross from the hands of those who ravage them and do them havoc.

Our argument is that *staurocentric* life, which often entails suffering injustice as Jesus did, produces Jesus's life in the other. This is not to say that the *staurocentric* life implies passive endurance at the hands of perpetrators of injustice and evil. On the contrary, *staurocentric* life entails active demonstration of love and proclamation of blessing to the wrong-doer—actions diametrically opposed to the actions of injustice and evil. In Paul's (Saul's) case, although he approved the execution of Stephen and ravaged the church (actions of injustice) yet the prayer of the Jesus's followers he ravaged (an action opposed to Paul's) turned around to produce life in him. Indeed, not only in Paul was life produced, because following Stephen's death many disciples of Jesus in Jerusalem were dispersed and they proclaimed the gospel wherever they went leading to the multiplication of their numbers. Luke's record affirms that "those who were scattered [following Stephen's death and the persecution] went about preaching the word" (Acts 8:4). Philip went to Samaria and proclaimed the message, and then went on to lead (most probably) the first African—the Ethiopian eunuch—to faith in Christ. In one of Eusebius's work translated with an introduction by Christian F. Crusé, Eusebius noted that "a great number of Greeks at Antioch, to whom the gospel had been preached by those who were scattered by the persecution of Stephen" believed in Jesus.[25] This is a *staurocentric* element. In the *staurocentric* model, even though death (the cross) may initially appear to prevail over the body of those who follow Jesus's model, yet the resurrection life of Jesus gets produced in many.

Grounded on the forgoing, I argue that in the same manner, if followers of Jesus must obtain victory over violence in the world, then, we have to walk the path that Jesus modeled through his *staurocentric* life. This was the path trodden by Jesus's followers during the early Christian centuries until the Constantinian era—an era to which we now turn briefly.

7.2. CONSTANTINE, THE CRUSADES AND THE CROSS (*STAUROS*) IN CONTEXTS

Here, we outline the trajectories that led to the Church's departure from Jesus's *staurocentric* model—a departure I consider an antithesis which has militated against the Church's ability to triumph over violence in our modern world. To follow the path of "the Constantinian mistake"[26] and the Crusades will not produce victory over violence. And if it cannot, then the model must be abandoned by those who follow Jesus. Drawing from church history we attempt unpacking the progressive impact the church had in

25. Eusebius, *Ecclesiastical History of Eusebius*, 53.
26. Yoder, *War of the Lamb*, 51.

the early Christian centuries and how the model that propelled the impact weakened following the Constantinian mistake.

Interspersed sporadic persecution and martyrdom of Jesus's followers continued through the first three centuries after the event of the cross—that is: after Jesus's death and resurrection. The 'grain of wheat' (Jesus's life) had fallen into the ground and died (John 12:24). But it germinated and was reproducing life in many people around the then Mediterranean world despite the various replicas of the cross—the display of Jesus's *staurocentric* life in his followers. The more Jesus's followers were being unjustly threated and hewed down by imperial Roman powers and local authorities, the more their number multiplied. Distinguished church historians, Dale T. Irvin and Scott W. Sunquist affirm that irrespective of "the encumbrance of imperial opposition marked by short but intense bouts of persecution, the political and cultural influence of churches . . . increased. Significant numbers of converts were beginning to join from the upper classes."[27] Distinguished scholar, Robert Wilken, attests that by

> the end of the first century there were fewer than ten thousand Christians in the Roman Empire [of which its] population at the time numbered some sixty million. . . By the year 250, however, the number had risen to more than a million, almost two percent of the population. . . By the year 300 Christians made up to 10 percent of the population, approximately six million.[28]

Renowned American sociologist of religion, Rodney Stark, affirms the same, attesting that several "historians have proposed an estimate of the size of the Christian population for the year 300, and all are in close accord at about 6 million."[29]

What does this demographic estimates of Jesus's followers during those early centuries have to say to us in relation to the cross? Elementary botany teaches that when a seed is sown in the ground, it first undergoes a certain process under certain conditions before it brings forth its shoot above the ground. The planted seed first imbibes water in the soil (a process called imbibition in elementary biology), then it swells. This process of swelling is often forceful, and owing to the force the seed coats are ruptured (a kind of death) in order for the radicle to be let loose. Before bringing its shoot above the ground, the seed first sends out root down into the soil to enable absorption of water. These steps must occur within favorable limits of temperature range for germination and growth to be

---

27. Irvin and Sunquist, *History of the World Christian Movement*, 1:155.
28. Wilken, *First Thousand Years*, 65–66.
29. Stark, *Triumph of Christianity*, 156.

achieved. The environment within which the seed is planted is essential. The presence of water and heat are essential for germination.

Taking a cue from this natural process of seed germination, we infer from Jesus's metaphor in John 12:24 that his life in human form is analogous to a grain of wheat. His death on the cross and burial is analogous to a grain of wheat falling to the ground and dying. His resurrection parallels a seed bringing forth its shoot. The shoot brought forth that goes on to bear much fruit is a metaphor alluding to the reproduction of Jesus's resurrection life in others. Similarly, the baptism of persecution that included injustice and acute violence in the form of execution, which Jesus's followers experience can be likened to the cross—suffering injustice for doing good. We must note that 'dying' in this context is not limited to physical death resulting from execution or persecution because of one's identity with Jesus. The cross also encompasses postures and actions that replicate Jesus's love to the one perpetrating evil and injustice. Certainly, it may ultimately entail being killed, and in such a case the *staurocentric* life continues to proclaim blessing even while dying in the hands of his or her killer.

The point is this: if we avoid Jesus's cross, we will also avoid resurrection. Stop the cross, and you constrain, at least to a certain measure, the multiplication of Jesus's life or the quality of faithfulness. Is this what may have happened when the church began to lose her *staurocentric* privilege and gain imperial privilege instead? We peer into that now.

7.2.1 From Constantine's Cross to the Crusades: A Gross Misrepresentation of Stauros

Here, we discuss the trend leading to the Church's diminishing hold to the *staurocentric* life beginning from Constantine's era, and then demonstrate how Constantine's cross and the Crusades together have etched a gross misrepresentation of what Jesus's cross truly stands for.

The dawn of the fourth century AD ushered in dramatic changes for the Christian Church. Eminent Church historians affirm that the conversion of Constantine, a Roman Emperor, was pivotal to those changes. Nevertheless, I rather contend that the cross was the pivot of whatever changes that occurs in the Church catholic—whether the changes may be considered beneficial or detrimental. Robert Wilken attests that with Constantine's conversion "to the new religion early in the [fourth] century, the Church began to assume a prominent role in society. Latter in the century, under Emperor Theodosius, Christianity was declared the official religion of the Roman Empire."[30] This

---

30. Wilken, *First Thousand Years*, 75.

change gave the church an imperial status. But how did it happen? Without going into historical details,[31] we simply and succinctly present what pertains to our discussion on the cross (*stauros*).

While Constantine was marching to war in 312 AD against "his first formidable opponent, Maxentius,"[32] Eusebius recounts that Constantine knew "well that he would need more powerful aid than an army can supply because of the mischievous magical devices practised by the tyrant [Maxentius] . . . "[33] Constantine turned to pray to the God who transcends the universe and while in prayer he received what Eusebius, Constantine's historiographer, called "a divine sign:"

> About the time of the midday sun, when day was just turning, he [Constantine] said he saw with his own eyes, up in the sky and resting over the sun, a *cross*[34]-shaped [emphasis in italics is mine] trophy formed from light, and a text attached to it which said, 'By this conquer'. Amazement at the spectacle seized both him and the whole company of soldiers which was then accompanying him on a campaign he was conducting somewhere, and witnessed the miracle. He was, he said, wondering to himself what the manifestation might mean; then, while he meditated, and thought long and hard, night overtook him. Thereupon, as he slept, the Christ of God appeared to him with the sign which had appeared in the sky, and urged him to make himself a copy of the sign which had appeared in the sky, and to use this as protection against the attacks of the enemy.[35]

According to Eusebius, the sign Constantine saw was a superimposition of two Greek letters, *chi* (χ) and *rho* (ρ)—the first two letters in the Greek word for Christ (Χριστός—*Christos*). Constantine wasted no time in obeying the vision and adopting the sign as his emblem before engaging in the war against his first formidable enemy, Maxentius, and also in subsequent wars.

---

31. Church History scholars have engaged in providing the historical details from primary sources. One major primary source is the writings of Emperor Constantine's historiographer, Eusebius, who was Bishop of Caesarea. See for example: Eusebius, *Life of Constantine*; Eusebius, *History of the Church from Christ to Constantine*; Eusebius, *Eusebius—The Church History*. Modern church history scholars, drawing from primary sources, have critically and chronologically laid down the historical details. See for example: Latourette, *History of Christianity*, 91–108; Wilken, *First Thousand Years*, 75–87; Frend, *Rise of Christianity*, 473–517; and Irvin, *History of the World Christian Movement*, 155–65.

32. Latourette, *History of Christianity*, 1:91.

33. Eusebius, *Life of Constantine*, 79–80.

34. This emphasis in italics highlights the connection to our discussion here.

35. Eusebius, *Life of Constantine*, 81.

The sign, called *labarum*, became Constantine's imperial emblem and in 314 AD the symbol of the *cross* "first appeared on his coins."³⁶

Constantine's vision and emblem of the cross (interpreted in relation to Jesus Christ and the victory it ostensibly ensured for him) made him to be increasingly and favorably inclined toward Christianity. Hence, death by means of the cross "was . . . banned by Constantine I (after 314 CE), and replaced by the 'fork' (*furca*), whereby the criminal was hung by the neck from a horizontal wooden shaft until dead."³⁷ During his reign as emperor, freedom of religion was installed.³⁸ Erudite and distinguished church historian, Kenneth Scott Latourette, avows that with passing time "Constantine came out more and more pronouncedly in favour of Christianity . . . [and] he granted to members of the Christian clergy the freedom from all contributions to the state which had been the privilege of the priests of other religions which were accorded official recognition."³⁹ Irvin and Sunquist affirm the same, noting that

> Constantine extended legal recognition and then imperial support to the religion. . . To many who were living in the Roman empire in the first quarter of the fourth century, however, the course of events appeared to be nothing short of miraculous. Little in their experience had prepared the churches for the rapid institutional transformations that took place as clergy began to receive funds from the imperial treasury . . . ⁴⁰

Before Constantine, however, persecution of Jesus's followers served as a sort of purifying fire for the Jesus movement. Jesus's followers were greatly marginalized and called atheists because they resolutely refused to sacrifice to the Roman gods or worship emperors as gods.⁴¹ And despite all the injustice meted toward them, they continued demonstrating care, compassion, forgiveness and love toward the society wherein they lived.

---

36. Latourette, *History of Christianity*, I:92.

37. Finney, "Servile Supplicium," 125; see also: Kittel and Friedrich, *Theological Dictionary of the NT*, 7:574.

38. The document installing freedom of religion has been called the "Edict of Milan" but Robert Wilken maintains that "the term is a misnomer. It was not an edict, but a letter posted by Licinius from several cities in the East . . . Like other official correspondence, however, it was written in the name of both emperors [Constantine and Licinius] and its content reflects the hand of Constantine" Wilken, *First Thousand Years*, 85.

39. Latourette, *History of Christianity*, 1:92.

40. Irvin and Sunquist, *History of the World Christian Movement*, 1:155.

41. Irvin and Sunquist, *History of the World Christian Movement*, 1:34.

Pre-Constantinian era, the church was viewed as a sect and considered as the scum of the society. Only those genuinely persuaded by the Holy Spirit of the truth of the gospel joined their ranks. But with the granting of imperial privileges there occurred an influx of mixed rabble—those who sought to join the Christian flock for the purpose of obtaining imperial privileges, not necessarily for the sake of following in the path of Jesus's cross. The mixed rabble joined the ranks of the Church oblivious of the Jesus's *staurocentric* life—seeking for what they can gain. I posit that it was from this point that the *staurocentric* life of the church began to wane. In the words of John Howard Yoder, it is "*the Constantinian mistake.*" This mistake is a deviation of locus from the cross as a symbol of death that yields resurrection life to a symbol employed for violence and human bloodshed. (Again, by death here we do not restrict it to only physical death, but inclusive of actions of dying to oneself in order to reflect Jesus's life).

Yoder asserts "that it is possible to overcome the Constantinian mistake only by a basic renewal of the entire Christian movement. Conversely, it is possible to renew the entire Christian gospel by overcoming the Constantinian mistake."[42] Insofar as how this mistake led to institutionalization and diversity of the Church, erudite Church historians, Irvin and Sunquist maintain that

> Constantine's embrace of Christianity . . . was the first step toward a great synthesis of religion, state. and culture in the Roman world. At the same time, it set in motion forces that led to even greater institutional diversity in the churches of the world. By the end of the sixth century, the Christian movement had fractured into several diverging theological traditions, despite the best efforts of bishops and emperors alike to achieve unity among the churches.[43]

Certainly, it is praiseworthy that Constantine became favorably inclined towards Christianity, lending support to the movement. In our evaluation from Church history, the grounds gained by Christianity was the product of the grains of the "wheat' that had previously fallen to the ground, died, sprouted, and yielding Jesus's life in people. Thus, it must be maintained that when the cross of Jesus no longer remains the locus of the church, when the church shelves away her *staurocentric* living, the focus shifts to other things (such as institutionalization according to the standards of the world).

---

42. Yoder, *War of the Lamb*, 51. Emphasis in italics is Yoder's.
43. Irvin and Sunquist, *History of the World Christian Movement*, 1:155.

Should one retort that the Constantinian development produced institutionalization leading to the expansion of the Church, then we must point out that on the contrary it (the Constantinian development) did not help multiply the number of Jesus's disciples. Instead, it opened the flood gates to many who ostensibly identified with the Church (for the purpose of gain) but knew neither the Head of the Church—Jesus—nor of his *staurocentric* life. That paradigmatic shift weakened the power of the Church's witness. If the Church's testimony in the world must remain credible in any context, those who identify themselves as her members must be prepared to walk the path of the cross that Jesus walked. The pragmatic ways of doing so will evidently vary in differing contexts and time.

For those who lived in the context of early Christian centuries, their witness resounded to the pagan world that sought to eradicate them through their demonstration of love, forgiveness, and care for the poor and the sick. Despite the love and care they demonstrated, yet many of them were martyred. Rodney Stark, in his evaluation of the credibility of martyrdom says that pagans respected the Christian "faith from having observed, or even having taken part in, the torture of martyrs. The pagan onlookers knew full well that they would not endure such tribulations for their religion. Why would so many Christians do so? . . . This sort of unease and wonderment often paved way for new conversions" to Christianity.[44] The cross of Jesus, when lifted up in the lives of his followers draws people to faith in Jesus, for in the cross the world beholds a *jamais vu*—what they have never ever seen. This buttresses our thesis that a *staurocentric* theological model is God's instrument for triumphing over evil, sin, and violence. If the church in any context and space is seeking to build peace, then she must consider the cross, explore, and find appropriate contextual pathways to model *staurocentric* living among those who attack and oppose her message. Circumventing the cross will most assuredly drive the church farther away from *shalom*.

Just as we have not delved into the historical details of Constantine's impact on the Church limiting our survey to what is pertinent vis-à-vis the cross, we now do the same in our survey of the Crusades knowing that volumes have been written on the subject.[45]

It was Winter 1095 in Clermont, France, at a church council. Pope Urban II preached a sermon "in which he called on Frankish knights to vow to march to the East with the twin aims of freeing Christians from the yoke of Islamic rule and liberating the tomb of Christ, . . . from Muslim control.

---

44. Stark, *Triumph of Christianity*, 151–52.

45. Runciman, *History of the Crusades*; Riley-Smith, *Oxford Illustrated History of the Crusades*; Tyerman, *God's War*; Riley-Smith, *Crusades*; and also the eloquent six-volume work of Setton, *History of the Crusades*.

As soon as he had finished Adhhémar of Monteil, the bishop of Le Puy . . . came forward and was the first to take *the cross*, while the crowd called out 'God wills it!'"[46] It is essential to note how early *the cross* was put on the fore to stir people to war. From this point onward, Pope Urban II "urged various churchmen to preach the cross in France, and, . . . he himself took the lead by proclaiming the crusade at a number of centres that he visited . . . He also dispatched letters and embassies beyond France . . . [and], as the news of what he had proclaimed at Clermont spread through the West, so men and women of all social classes and occupations *took the cross*.[47] Some questions can be posed from Pope Urban II's rhetoric. Can Christians be freed from 'the yoke of Islamic rule' through war? Does liberating the tomb of Jesus, of whom the angels declared "He is not here but has risen" (Luke 24:6) worth shedding the blood of people for whose sake the same Jesus died and rose in order to liberate from the captivity of the true enemy—the devil, sin and death? Would the risen Christ care about the relics of his empty tomb at the expense of lives of people he died to redeem? I truly wonder if anyone posed these or similar questions to Pope Urban II.

Pope Urban II's arousing call insisted that taking up the cross to fight in order to liberate Jerusalem "was no ordinary act of temporal warfare but a task enjoined on the faithful by God Himself . . . Urban instituted the ceremonial granting of crosses to those who had sworn to undertake the Jerusalem journey. Thus they became 'signed with the cross', *crucesignati*."[48] The words of Jesus concerning taking up the cross daily and following him (Matt 10:38; 16:24, Mark 8:34; Luke 9:23, 14:27) were twisted and misappropriated. The cross became a "badge, banner and talisman"[49] and then a business.[50] The First Crusade (1096–1102) culminated in the recapture of Jerusalem on July 15, 1099. But the ostensible victory was short-lived, for two years later (in 1101) the Turks in Asia Minor defeated the last wave of the First Crusaders. In all the wars ensuing from the arousing call to the Crusades, human blood flowed. Several other Crusades followed the First, and some became lumped and numbered as the Second (1147–1149), Third (1189–1192), Fourth (1202–1204) and Fifth (1217–1229) Crusades according their times. Many other Crusades not numbered among these five Crusades followed. Christopher Tyerman observes that "[b]etween 1095 and, say, 1500 there were scores of military operations that attracted the privileges

---

46. Riley-Smith, *Oxford History of the Crusades*, 1. Emphasis in italics is mine.
47. Lloyd, "Crusading Movement," 35. Emphasis in italics is mine.
48. Tyerman, *Fighting for Christendom*, 28.
49. Tyerman, *Fighting for Christendom*, 29.
50. Tyerman, *Fighting for Christendom*, 125–54.

associated with the wars of the cross. Yet only a few later became known by a number, all of them aimed at Muslim targets in and around Syria and Palestine in the eastern Mediterranean."[51] Certainly, neither Pope Urban II nor his early crusaders may have imagined that what they embarked upon was going to set a precedence for many other wars spanning from their time (end of the eleventh century) up to the seventeenth century.[52]

Modern scholarly appraisal of the Crusades points out the disastrous and destructive consequences and legacy which the Crusades left behind, not only as it relates to Christian-Muslim witness, but also in relation to Jews and the Greek Church. Norman Housley asserts that "there is no point in disguising the fact that the effect of the crusades on Christian-Muslim relations was profoundly destructive."[53] Jonathan Riley-Smith also affirms that "leading Christian churchmen in the Western tradition—Catholic and Protestant—are not only ashamed by the fact of the Crusades but are also in a state of denial. Embarrassed by this aspect of their past, they have underplayed its importance in their history, while maintaining that it really had very little to do with their religion."[54] In a lecture delivered at the International Islamic University in Islamabad, Pakistan in 2005, the then Archbishop of Canterbury, Dr. Rowan Williams, asserted,

> Jesus in the gospels opposes violence, even in self-defence, for any individual . . . Most Christians would now say that the history of the Crusades, for example, or the religious wars in Europe in the sixteenth and seventeenth centuries, were serious betrayals of many of the central beliefs of Christian faith. Any modern attempt to revive a crusading ideal is not likely to be supported by most Christian believers.[55]

Thus, we maintain that the Crusades were destructive to Christians and Muslims alike and have become a watershed marring, to a great degree, modern Christian witness to Muslims. In addition to theological barriers between Christianity and Islam, the fact of the Crusades also becomes another blockage to cross-cultural Christian workers seeking to love Muslims today and to reflect the life of Jesus among them. Such workers are more often than not regarded as 'Crusaders' of some sort. It is an uphill task to persuade Muslim minds (especially those from North Africa and

---

51. Tyerman, *Fighting for Christendom*, 32.

52. For a chronology of the Crusades and many other military campaigns classified as the Crusades, see Riley-Smith, *Oxford History of the Crusades*, 390–401.

53. Housley, "Crusades and Islam," 190.

54. Riley-Smith, *Crusades, Christianity, and Islam*, 4.

55. Williams, "What Is Christianity?"

the Middle East) that the Crusades are not in accordance with the Christian faith. Prior to Jesus's death and resurrection by which he overturned the meaning of the cross, the cross was viewed with contempt. Although it was despised and was an instrument of cruel and most ignominious death, yet it became God's instrument of forgiveness, redemption and reconciliation. But the Crusades, unknowingly to its authors, promoters, and participants, ironically sought to overturn what Jesus had already done—that is: overturning the meaning and view of the cross back to a symbol of destructive death as opposed to redemptive death.

As a symbol, the cross remains abhorrent to Muslims till today. I recall an incident in Rabat, Morocco in early 2001. I asked a local furniture maker to engrave a symbol of the cross, an open book, and a dove[56] on the wood of the Moroccan salon I had purchased for our sitting room. The man blatantly refused and when I asked him why, he asserted that Muslims do not associate themselves in any way with the cross. I insisted asserting I will pay him for his labor, but he adamantly refused, saying, it is for him a religious devotion to hate the cross and have nothing to do with it. It took me a few years of interactions with Moroccan Muslims to come to grasp the depth of the negative legacy that the Crusades left behind and which continues to hang over Christian-Muslim encounters and witness, even after several centuries.

To further buttress Muslims hatred of the cross as a symbol I give two other examples. The first is the Red Cross Society's logo, which is simply a red cross. In Muslim lands (at least those that I have lived in or visited), where the Red Cross in present, they swap the red cross logo with a red crescent. Most Ambulances in many parts of the world have the symbol of the cross on them. In medicine, the symbol used to portray healing is that of a serpent entwined around a cross or pole—an allusion to the pole Moses raised up in the wilderness, which is a prophetic symbol of the cross (Num 21:9 cf. John 3:14). In Muslim lands, however, these symbols are categorically replaced with the crescent, because of the aversion etched on Muslims minds by the Christian cross and the Crusades. It is on this grounds that I assert that the Crusades were a gross misrepresentation of *stauros*—Jesus's cross that implies and connotes redemptive death.

Jesus's view of his followers taking up the cross is definitely and diametrically opposed to taking up the cross and the sword proclaimed by the pioneers, preachers, and participants of the Crusades. On the day of Jesus's arrest, his disciples "who were around him saw what would follow, they said, 'Lord, shall we strike with the sword?' And one of them struck

---

56. The cross was to represent the death and resurrection of Jesus, the open book the Scriptures and the dove the Holy Spirit.

the servant of the high priest and cut off his right ear. But Jesus said, 'No more of this!' And he touched his ear and healed him" (Luke 22:49–51). In Matthew's own account Jesus said: "Put your sword back into its place. For all who take the sword will perish by the sword. Do you think that I cannot appeal to my Father, and he will at once send me more than twelve legions of angels?" (Matt 26:52–53).

Followers of Jesus must take Jesus's words seriously—these words: 'No more of this!' No more of physical swords to fight for God's cause. Insofar as Jesus is concerned, the cross must supplant the sword. The theology of the cross must trump the theology of glory that avoids the cross. The path to glory and triumph is by passing through the cross. Therefore, the method and means of war must morph from a human physical means to a spiritual means, because although "we walk in the flesh, we are not waging war according to the flesh. For the weapons of our warfare are not of the flesh but have divine power to destroy strongholds" (2 Cor 10:3–4). For those who identify with God's Kingdom, the event of Jesus's death on the cross and of his resurrection changed the arena of warfare from the physical to the spiritual.

I assert that no human authority or council (whether ecclesiastical or secular) will ever be wiser than the triune God, who in his divine wisdom, chose to let the incarnate Word of God be crucified on the cross in order to employ it as a divine instrument of redemption and reconciliation. To turn the cross into a symbol and sign synonymous with the sword and bloodshed is a gross aberration of what Jesus meant it to be. The way of the cross (which we refer to as the *staurocentric* path), is God's instrument for triumphing over death, evil, sin and violence. This is our pivotal argument.

7.2.2 *The Cross in Contexts*

In our twenty-first century world, we are still confronted with various forms of violence—religious, political, ethnic, economic, or a hybrid of any of these. We argued above that Jesus overturned the meaning of *stauros* through his death on the cross and his resurrection from the dead. In addition, his followers during the early Christian centuries held to the worldview that suffering for righteousness sake was a path to triumph. The argument resonates with Judith Perkins's argument in her volume, *The Suffering Self*, wherein she contends "that the discursive focus in the second century on the suffering body contributed to Christianity's attainment of social power by helping to construct a subject that would be present for its call."[57] Perkins maintains that the "triumph of Christianity was, at least in part, a triumph

57. Perkins, *Suffering Self*, 3.

of representation."⁵⁸ We must, however, acknowledge that followers of Jesus during the early Christian centuries lived in contexts where they were the demographic minority. As we know, times and contexts change. In different contexts where Jesus's followers form either the demographic majority or are equal in demographics with people of other faiths, how should they (Christ's followers) respond to violence? Resort and revive the Crusades? Or take the *staurocentric* pathway? The contextual realities might not be as simple as posing such a binary question.

In the context of Jesus's followers of the early Christian centuries, they were in the minority. Church historians and sociologists are in accord that it was not until the third Christian century that the population of Jesus's followers reached about 10 percent of the population of the then Roman Empire. As we have already pointed out, Robert Wilken, maintains that by "the end of the first century there were fewer than ten thousand Christians in the Roman Empire [of which its] population at the time numbered some sixty million . . . "⁵⁹ which was a negligible 0.17 percent of the population of the empire at that time. Thus, Jesus's followers in that context were evidently demographically in the minority. The question we may then pose is: How should Jesus's followers living in a context of demographic and democratic majority apply the *staurocentric* motif? Put differently, what place might the *staurocentric* motif have in contexts where Jesus's followers are in a demographic majority as opposed to being in the minority? Let us unpack this question.

A query in the *World Christian Database* showed that for 2015, Christians in the United States make up 74.86 percent of the entire United States' population as against 1.38 percent for Muslims.⁶⁰ The demographic data of all those who identify as Christians are far above the same for other religious faiths in the United States. A similar query ran for Nigeria shows that for the year 2015, Christians constitute 46.18 percent, whereas Muslims are 45.19 percent of Nigeria's population. Editors of the *World Christian Database* and the *World Christian Encyclopedia: Third Edition*,⁶¹ estimate that by the year 2025, the population of Nigeria will hit 233.3 million out of which about 46.18 percent identify as Christians and 45.85 percent as Muslims,⁶² thus, making Christians and Muslims to share almost equally Nigeria's population. In such contexts of demographic superiority

---

58. Perkins, *Suffering Self*, 3.
59. Wilken, *First Thousand Years*, 65; Stark, *Triumph of Christianity*, 156.
60. Johnson and Zurlo, "World Christian Database."
61. Johnson and Zurlo, *World Christian Encyclopedia*.
62. Johnson and Zurlo, "World Christian Database."

or equality, the question is not whether Christians should jettison our thesis of Jesus's *staurocentric* motif and employ political, demographic, and democratic power to respond to violence. Instead, we ask (as already posed above): How should Jesus's followers living in a context of demographic and democratic majority apply the *staurocentric* motif?

We will attempt a robust response to this question in chapter 8 where we constructively and critically explore the contextual dimensions it should entail using the Nigerian context as locus. But before we get there some points need to be underscored. It is expedient to emphasize that the thesis of Jesus's *staurocentric* motif must not be restricted to contexts of inferior demographic contexts as it was the case in the early Christian centuries. I am strongly inclined (as a follower of Jesus) to the notion of following Jesus's patterns and pathways. As we have already argued, the model depicted in the hymn of Christ depicts Jesus as the model *par excellence* for his followers. In the words of Australian New Testament scholar, Peter T. O'Brien, Jesus is "the supreme example of the humble self-sacrificing, self-giving service that Paul . . . [urged] the Philippians to practice in their relations one toward another."[63] Another reason buttressing my expressed inclination is drawn from the hint we briefly alluded to regarding Jesus's power of convocation. He could have summoned "twelve legions of angels" (Matt 26:53) to defend him at the event of his arrest, yet he refrained. I maintain that Jesus's model ought to remain the model that his followers should replicate and reflect to the world in every context until Jesus's Second Advent and until he returns to point to a different paradigm.

With that said, twenty-first century followers of Jesus (in whatever context we may imagine) ought not dare walk a different path vis-à-vis the path that Jesus walked. Walking the *staurocentric* path in the twenty-first century will lead to a no less triumph over evil and violence as Jesus obtained through the cross and his resurrection, and to a no less triumph as the early followers of Jesus during the first Christian centuries. Thus, the example that Jesus set, and followed by his early followers, must not be regarded as obsolete, out of mode, and ineffectual. I maintain that the cross remains God's instrument for defeating evil and violence. Furthermore, I reiterate a fact we have already mentioned—that the *staurocentric* life is not just the posture and readiness to die literally for the sake of following Jesus, rather it encompasses a self-giving life that serves, cares, forgives, and loves "the other" even when "the other" is the perpetrator of evil or injustice.

The manner Christians in any context understand themselves in terms of the cross is essential if they must demolish and tear off the veneers

---

63. O'Brien, *Epistle to the Philippians*, 205.

of misconceptions and legacy which the Crusades have left behind, especially in Muslim minds. Jonathan Riley-Smith, in the conclusion of one of his volumes, *The Crusades, Christianity, and Islam*, underscores that the Crusades "were not thoughtless explosions of barbarism. The theory of force that undelay them was relatively sophisticated and was considered to be theologically justifiable by a society that felt itself threatened."[64] He further posits that it is difficult to comprehend "the intensity of the attachment felt for the holy places in Jerusalem, the concern aroused by heresy and physical assaults on the church and the fear the Westerners had of Muslim invaders . . ."[65] Again to the question: How should Jesus's followers living in a context of demographic and democratic majority apply the *staurocentric* motif? Or what should twenty-first century followers of Jesus do when our lives and community are threatened, whether we are in a context of demographic and democratic majority or not? Here, we advance a preliminary response. As already stated above, we will attempt a more robust response in chapter 8 using Africa's context as locus.

First for Jesus's followers who dwell in contexts of demographic and democratic minority, we suggest the examples of the early followers of Jesus, who themselves dwelt in similar context, be adopted. The Jerusalem those first century Christians knew was destroyed barely forty years after Jesus's ascension. They neither took up a physical symbol of the cross nor the sword to fight in order to reclaim the relics of Jesus's cross, of Jesus's tomb, and keep the sacred places. In the three subsequent centuries, Christians suffered brutal deaths. Their properties were confiscated. They considered it an honor to suffer injustice (or even die if it came to that) for the name of Jesus.

Second, for Jesus's followers dwelling in contexts of demographic and democratic majority, we similarly suggest keeping with the *staurocentric* model. The *staurocentric* model must not be understood to be restrictive to contexts of minority. It is an empowering model that points "the other" to Jesus when fleshed out by Jesus's followers. So in a demographic majority context, followers of Jesus can respond to violence by doing exactly the opposite. Some examples we will highlight below will buttress this point. But before highlighting them, we recall Miroslav Volf's *End of Memory* (cited in chapter 2), where he maintains that for evil to fully triumph it requires "two victories . . . not one. The first victory happens when an evil deed is perpetrated; the second victory, when evil is returned. After the first victory, evil would die if the second victory did not infuse it with new life."[66] Violence and injustice

---

64. Riley-Smith, *Crusades, Christianity, and Islam*, 79.

65. Riley-Smith, *Crusades, Christianity, and Islam*, 79.

66. Volf, *End of Memory*, 9.

are forms of manifestation of evil. To deliver the second victory to evil when violence and/or injustice are/is perpetrated (that is when evil has gained its first victory) is synonymous to revenge, retaliation, or repaying evil for evil (Prov 20:22; Rom 12:17; 1 Thess 5:15; 1 Pet 3:9). In this regard, Gregory Boyd maintains that "[t]it for tat, eye for an eye, tooth for a tooth—this is what makes the bloody kingdom of the world go around."[67]

Jesus's followers, whether they form a demographic majority or minority in their context, are certainly not called to be party to those who make "the bloody kingdom of the world go around."[68] Rather, they are called to be agents of peace. Thus, being in a demographic majority context insofar as Jesus is concerned does not give his followers the latitude to resort to the model and metaphor of the Crusades, which (I argue) was a metaphor for delivering to evil the second victory it requires to triumph in various medieval contexts. It is a great responsibility, therefore, upon Jesus's followers to replicate and reflect Jesus, who although possessed the power of convocation that he could have availed himself of to involve "more than twelve legions of angels" (Matt 26:53) for his defense, did not appeal to that power.

So to the question: How should Christ's followers respond to various forms of violence aimed against them? The response remains: We need return to the *staurocentric* model, because it is God's instrument for triumphing over violence irrespective of its context, source, and magnitude. For those who may insist that a different approach be employed, especially in a demographic majority context, we have need to be reminded of John Wesley's 1760 sermon, "The Use of Money" wherein he called on his hearers:

> *Gain all you can*, without hurting either yourself or your neighbor, in soul or body, . . . *Save all you can*, by cutting off every expenses which serves only to indulge foolish desire, to gratify either the desire of the flesh, the desire of the eye, or the pride of life, Waste nothing . . . on sin or folly. . . . And then, *Give all you can*, or in other words give all you have to God.[69]

Wesley's call to Methodists of the mid-eighteenth century to "*Gain all* [they] *can*. . . *Save all* [they] *can*. . . and *Give all* [they] *can*. . ." is a call all Jesus's followers in every era ought to also heed, and that not only in regard to the use of money, but also in regard to socioeconomic, political and military power. Heeding to the first two of Wesley's exhortation (gaining all and saving all) without taking heed to the third (giving all) leads to increasing one's socioeconomic and political power. Holding on the first and the second,

67. Boyd, *Myth of a Christian Nation*, 24.
68. Boyd, *Myth of a Christian Nation*, 24.
69. Collins and Vickers, *Sermons of John Wesley*, 29: The Use of Money.

not only on the matters of money, but also in matters concerning political power leads the Church to despise the power of the cross of Jesus. Certainly, another question arises from this.

Should followers of Jesus completely relinquish political power where they are in demographic majority context? My answer is simply no. Rather, in such contexts, followers of Jesus must demonstrate humility and self-giving that characterize Jesus's *staurocentric* life. Their political and socioeconomic power must instead translate into means of serving the other and not into military power to demonstrate superiority and to physically subdue. Consequently, we maintain that should followers of Jesus in all time and contexts hold on to the a *staurocentric* theological model epitomized by Jesus's example, it will become for us an instrument to vanquish violence. Where Jesus's followers jettison the *staurocentric* model and hold on to using socioeconomic, political, and military power to physically harm the other, then we will be exposed to the same results that ensued following the Crusades.

We turn our attention now to a few contemporary examples of *staurocentric* life demonstrated in forgiveness wherein certain believers in Jesus Christ have trodden the *staurocentric* path. These examples are neither from the early followers of Jesus nor from the early Christian centuries. These are examples of *staurocentric* forgiveness from within the last quarter of a century.

7.3 CONTEMPORARY APPROPRIATION OF *STAUROCENTRIC* FORGIVENESS

Two precursors are essential here. First: Why the focus on *staurocentric* forgiveness above all the other elements of *staurocentric* pathways previously outlined? And second: Should the tenability of *staurocentric* forgiveness be limited to contexts where those who embrace it are the demographic minority as against the demographic majority of the wrong-doers in contexts of violence?

Regarding the first precursor, we maintain that forgiveness is a very important element characteristic of the *staurocentric* model. The basic reason is that where *staurocentric* forgiveness is absent unforgiveness, rancor, hatred, thirst for revenge and retaliation prevail. Implicitly where these prevail, all the other *staurocentric* elements can hardly ever be realized. Thus, *staurocentric* forgiveness paves the pathway for all other *staurocentric* elements. Without forgiveness the wronged cannot pray for and bless the wrong-doer who perpetrates violence and injustice. Some contemporary examples of *staurocentric* forgiveness demonstrate how this element of the *staurocentric* model breaks down the power of violence and denies evil the triumph it seeks to obtain.[70] They also illustrate that following the way of the cross remains valid and possible, not only in our time, but in all ages until the eschaton when peoples "shall beat their swords into plowshares, and their spears into pruning hooks; [and] nation shall not lift up sword against nation, neither shall they learn war anymore" (Isa 2:4; Mic 4:4).

The second precursor pertains to demographic disparity that may exist between the wronged and the wrong-doer(s) in contexts of violence. Should *staurocentric* forgiveness be only tenable and applicable where and when Jesus's followers are the demographic minority? In what follows, we draw two examples from Africa (Rwanda and Egypt) and one from the United States of America. We could point to more examples, but we survey only these few by reason of space constraint and believe those surveyed suffice to support our thesis. In Rwanda's context, the Hutus make up about 84 percent of Rwanda's population as against the Tutsis' 15 percent. This is essential to underscore given our earlier discussion on demographic majority or minority contexts. In Rwanda's context of violence, the Hutus were the demographic majority and the Tutsis the minority. Many Hutus and Tutsis, however, all identify themselves as Christians. Thus the context of violence was not necessarily interreligious but ethno-political not to mention the role of an external superpower—France. Furthermore, Tutsis were not the only victims of the genocidal violence. Some Hutus were also victims.

In the case of Egyptian Copts, they are the Christian majority in Egypt in comparison with other streams of Christians. Nevertheless, all Christians including the Copts are the minority in Egypt compared to the majority Muslim population. Similarly, the Amish (as we will elucidate later) are a demographic minority group within a context of Christian demographic majority in the United States. Given these complex elements, one may erroneously conclude that *staurocentric* pathways are only tenable where Jesus's followers find themselves in demographic minority contexts. But I contest such a conclusion based on Jesus's power of convocation (already alluded to)—where he could have summoned legions of angels to fight on his behalf. My contention is that *staurocentric* posture is not to be limited to contexts of demographic minority but in every context in order to reflect the model we see in Jesus. In other words, in whatever context followers of Jesus find themselves, Jesus still invites his followers to walk the road of the cross.

With that said, we turn to the three examples of *staurocentric* forgiveness demonstrated by Jesus's followers in different contexts of violence. The oppressed or the wronged demonstrate to their oppressor(s) or

---

70. Volf, *End of Memory*, 9.

wrong-doer(s), through the grace of forgiveness, the *staurocentric* pathway thereby triumphing over violence through the cross. The grace of forgiveness is like a silver thread running through all the examples.

7.3.1 From the Rwandan Genocide

In chapter 5 we pointed to the fact that the *staurocentric* element of forgiveness was interlaced with the Rwandan grassroots *Gacacha* court system and the *Abanyarwanda* concept in order to install reconciliation and peacebuilding in post-Rwandan genocide context. Here, we zoom into a few examples of the *staurocentric* element of forgiveness to which we made mention in chapter 5. It is unnecessary to repeat the background historical information we weaved into chapter 5 regarding the Rwandan genocide.

Often, many ask the question: Where was God when millions of people were being killed in Rwanda? The same question is often asked of the Jewish holocaust undertaken by Nazi Germany. Why didn't God do anything? Tom Townsend, a CNN journalist and writer, during his visit to sites of the Rwandan genocide, asked that question to Steven Gahigi, a genocide survivor, and Gahigi's response was: "Asking where God was in all this is the wrong question. The right question is, 'Where was man?'"[71] Bishop John Rucyahana (whom we cited in chapter 5) maintains that to ask such a question "is like saying God forgot Jesus when He was on the cross."[72] Although Jesus cried out on the cross, "My God, my God, why have you forsaken me?" (Matt 27:46); yet God did not forsake him, for God accomplished his purpose of redemption and reconciliation through Jesus's death on the cross and did not allow Jesus to see corruption (Ps 16:10 cf. Acts 2:27; 13:34–35). In the Rwandan case, even though the world watched and the world super-powers pretended as though they were unaware (just as the world watched the Son of God hang on the cross), yet from a posture of faith, God is turning the evil and violence which Rwanda experienced into stories of forgiveness and blessing.

Having mentioned Steven Gahigi, we begin with his example of *staurocentric* forgiveness. Gahigi escaped to Burundi when the genocide began. On his return, fifty-two members of his family had been murdered. He found himself homeless, without a family. Later he enrolled in a Seminary, and in 1999 began visiting the prison in Rilima, Bugeser district, where many genocide perpetrators were serving prison terms. Gahigi got involved with the Rwanda Prison Fellowship, and in the Rilima Prison he met those

---

71. Townsend, "Forgiving the Unforgivable."
72. Rucyahana and Riordan, *Bishop of Rwanda*, xv.

who had killed members of his family. Rucyahana recounts Gahigi's testimony of healing and forgiveness in his volume. Gahigi said

> I returned to Rwanda, but all I thought about was revenge . . . I just wanted to punish those who had killed. I had been a preacher, and I spent many hours asking God how He could have allowed such a thing. Then God showed me that people who killed in the genocide did so because they didn't know God. And now God was asking me to help them know Him. . . It was not easy . . . Then came a day I saw one of the people who killed my family and God told me to forgive him. I didn't think I could do it, but when the man saw me and asked for my forgiveness, God gave me the grace to do it. And then I began to heal inside."[73]

The path to Gahigi's healing and forgiveness cannot, indeed, be easy. Yet, for those who find their reference in Jesus who overturned the meaning of the cross, it is made feasible and possible. Gahigi recounted a dream he had in a conversation with Tom Townsend, which helped him to eventually see his survival as a vocation and motivated him to proclaim the gospel to genocide perpetrators in prison. In his dream, Gahigi saw "a mob beating Jesus as he hung on the cross. A voice told Gahigi, 'Those people beating Jesus are the ones Jesus helped. They killed your countrymen and your family, but you can help them.'"[74] Waking up from his sleep and dream, Gahigi began weeping. He then trusted "that he had the power to forgive and to help others forgive. He began preaching reconciliation, and he sought out the prisoners who killed his family."[75] Gahigi became a Pastor to those who had killed his family asserting that Jesus's mission was to forgive the sins of all people—for whose sake he came and who killed him. In the same manner, Gahigi, forgave and served those who had murdered his own family. This is a clear contemporary example of the *staurocentric* forgiveness.

A former General Vice-President of the General Conference of Seventh-Day Adventists, Mark Finely, recounts two amazing testimonies in a TV Production with Shawn Boonstra. The first is that of Pastor Amon Rugelinyange—a Tutsi leader of the Seventh-Day Adventist Church in an area of Rwanda. Rugelinyange survived the genocide because he was away preaching during the genocide and was hidden by a Hutu church elder. Pastor Rugelinyange narrates that after the genocide, he was brought to a prison. In his own words: ". . . behind the jail there were five men . . . the ones who murdered my wife, my children and my grandchildren . . . and

---

73. Rucyahana and Riordan, 193.
74. Townsend, "Forgiving the Unforgivable."
75. Townsend, "Forgiving the Unforgivable."

the police handed me a gun and said, 'You have every right to put a bullet in every one of their heads. They brutally murdered your wife and your children.'"[76] Pastor Rugelinyange's response to the police and the response he received to a question he posed to those men who had massacred his family is stunning. He said and asked: "I cannot shoot them; I have already forgiven them. But I have a question to ask? What were my wife's last moments like? What were my children's last moments like? What were my grandchildren's last moments like?" And the murderers responded, "We were so stunned. They were praying for us. They were singing hymns."[77]

Praying for one's murderer and singing hymns? Where could that possibly be ever heard? Only at the cross of Jesus. And what could spur a person in the face of violence to pray for (not against) the one unjustly killing him or her if not the cross of Jesus Christ?

The second narrative from Mark Finley[78] regards Mrs. Adele Selfu, whose husband was hacked to death before her eyes alongside forty-five others in the basement of a Catholic Church building, and herself left almost dead there for three days. Adele's husband was a Pastor. The Rwandan genocide militia flayed him with a machete, struck him severally and finally slit open his throat. While blood "was spurting from his body and he was breathing his last, [he was] praying for those who killed him . . ."[79] The one being killed was the one praying for (not against) his killer—an approach that certainly resonates with Jesus's method while hanging on the cross.

Adele's body was still among the corpses lying in the site of the massacre. Those who came to bury the dead three days later, found that she still had pulse. She was taken to a hospital and her recovery lasted three years. With scars on her back, skull, shoulder and with a wrist that was partially cut off, Adele surmounted the anger and resentment and then gave herself to serving in prisons established for inmates of the genocide perpetrators. In one of the prisons in close proximity to where Adele lived, she narrates to Mark Finley:

> Pastor Mark, one day a young man named Luis fell at my feet and he was weeping and kissing my feet. And as I looked down at his face, I saw that he was the young man who rushed in with the machete and killed my husband. He was the young man who put this scar on my head. And he looked up at me and said,

---

76. Finley, "New Life for a Dying Nation: Forgiveness, Baptism."
77. Finley, "New Life for a Dying Nation: Forgiveness, Baptism."
78. Pastor Mark Finley also narrates this second testimony in a YouTube video: https://www.youtube.com/watch?v=8nAfIne_jUM.
79. Finley, "New Life for a Dying Nation: Forgiveness, Baptism."

'Adele, would you forgive me?' I pulled him up and I embraced him and said, 'In the name of Jesus, I will forgive you.' ... Pastor Mark, my heart was racing, but I knew that Christ had forgiven me and that I could forgive this murderer. I began studying the Bible with prisoners, and Luis came to the Bible studies. He made a decision that he would follow Jesus and be baptized. But he said: 'Before I'm baptized, I want to stand before the prison publicly and ask you, Adele, for your forgiveness.'

On the day of his baptism, he stood ... and said, 'Adele, I brutally murdered your husband. I put a knife mark, a machete scar, on your head, will you forgive me?' Before those prisoners, before he was baptized, I forgave him. My son took his father's death so hard. And Luis said, 'I want to talk to your son.' And my son went to his cell. And Luis said, 'I want you to forgive me.'

Luis became a model prisoner. The grace of Christ was flowing through his life. He was a new young man. After three years, the government let him out of prison for good behavior. But he had no place to live because Luis had his father and mother murdered in the genocide. And I said, 'Luis, you come and I'll adopt you as my son.' And for the last couple of years, he has been living in my home. Pastor Mark, 'Would you like to meet Luis?'[80]

Adele's story seems to epitomize a contemporary example of *staurocentric* forgiveness, since it reflects Jesus's model demonstrated on the cross. The same humans who killed him on the cross, he now grants the Spirit of adoption for them to become children of God. For a woman to adopt a young man who killed her husband before her very eyes is a portrait of the *staurocentric* pathway that we are making a case for in this study. Such love is unfathomable, too wonderful, and unsearchable for the human mind, yet it is God's model. It is to such path the triune God invites Jesus's followers, the church, to travel on in our world of violence.

There are other stories of forgiveness that serve as examples from the Rwandan genocide, but space constrains us. Some have been highlighted through the work of Pieter Hugo, who visited Rwandan in 2014—two decades after the genocide—and captured inconceivable pictures of perpetrator/survivor pairs. In each pair was a forgiven Hutu perpetrator and the forgiving Tutsi survivor. A few of the pair pictures captured by Hugo and published in *The New York Times* were only part of a larger body of work that was displayed under the auspices of Creative Court—an art organization based in The Hague–at the occasion of remembrance of the two

---

80. Finley, "New Life for a Dying Nation: Forgiveness, Baptism."

decades of the Rwandan Genocide.[81] In all of those portraits, the theme of forgiveness is central and common to each story.

We previously pointed to Desmond Tutu's statement made at a rally in Kigali in 1995. After Tutu had visited sites of the genocide in the suburbs of Kigali, the capital, and within the capital itself, he also visited the prisons where majority of the perpetrators where held. Then at the rally in Kigali, Tutu made the case for forgiveness, maintaining that "the cycle of reprisal and counterreprisal that had characterized [the Rwandan] national history had to be broken and that the only way to do this was to go beyond retributive justice to restorative justice, to move on to forgiveness, because without it [forgiveness] there was no future."[82] The way to overcoming evil is by treading the path of beneficence, not by repaying evil with evil. Humility is the path to demolishing pride. Triumph over violence cannot be achieved by riposting violence, but by a self-giving and voluntary sacrifice to love the perpetrator and oppressor. This is the *staurocentric* pathway. It is unfathomable, not only to the natural human mind, but also to the devil. It is, nonetheless, the triune God's instrument for triumphing over death, the devil, evil, sin and violence. Two other contemporary examples are worth mentioning.

7.3.2 From Coptic Christians in Egypt

Coptic Christians in Egypt have witnessed several attacks by Muslim Islamists since the wake of the Arab Spring. It was Sunday, February 15, 2015. The world stood in awe as the Islamic State in Syria and Iraq (ISIS) released a video[83] of twenty-one Egyptian Christians whom they slaughtered by the banks of the Mediterranean Sea in Libya. What was the response of some Egyptian Christians? We may not know so much. Nevertheless, two days later, the Bible Society of Egypt released a tract in the press entitled *Two Rows by the Sea*. The words of the tract were then sub-titled with the video of the execution, wherein the executioners were all wearing black with veils over their faces as opposed to their victims whom they dressed in orange with open faces. The entire words of that poem[84] is worth quoting.

> Two rows of men walked the shore of the sea,
> On a day when the world's tears would run free.

---

81. Hugo and Dominus, "Portraits of Reconciliation."
82. Tutu, *No Future Without Forgiveness*, 260.
83. The video can be accessed here: https://vimeo.com/127460692.
84. The poem was written in Arabic but has been translated into Dutch, English, French, German, Spanish and Turkish.

One a row of assassins, who thought they did right,
The other of innocents, true sons of the light.
One holding knives in hands held high,
The other with hands empty, defenseless and tied.
One row of slits to conceal glaring-dead eyes,
The other with living eyes raised to the skies.
One row stood steady, pall-bearers of death,
The other knelt ready, welcoming heaven's breath.
One row spewed wretched, contemptible threats,
The other spread God-given peace and rest.
A Question... Who fears the other?
The row in orange, watching paradise open?
Or the row in black, with minds evil and broken?[85]

Bibles4Egypt.com points out that as the twenty-one men "were being executed [by the Islamists] cries of 'O Jesus' could be heard in the background."[86] Ramez Attalah, General Secretary of the Bible Society of Egypt, reports the comment of his female coworker at the Bible Society of Egypt's office. The young woman said the faith of the executed Christians had left her "very encouraged. [She further added:] What has happened has shown me that there are Christians today who are brave enough to face death rather than deny their Lord . . . It has shown me that the Gospel message can still help us to hold onto the promises of God, even when facing death."[87] This young woman's response reflects what often was the response of Christians during the early Christian centuries. As believers in Jesus are unjustly killed for their faith, the oppressors envisage instilling terror to deter others from following Jesus. On the contrary, such martyrdom only fires up the faith of surviving followers of Jesus, helping them to devote themselves more and more to Jesus.

A second example from Egypt must not elude our attention. It happened on Palm Sunday, April 9, 2017. It was a double attack, one in the city of Alexandria at the Copts St. Mark's Cathedral by the coast of the Mediterranean and the second at Mar Girgis Cathedral, Tanta in the Nile delta. Death toll of the duo attack rose to forty-nine and scores were injured. Naseem Faheem was the guard at St. Mark's Cathedral. An Islamist

---

85. Atallah, "Two Rows By the Sea"; Bible Society of Egypt, *Two Rows by the Sea*. Used with permission from the Bible Society of Egypt.

86. Bible Society of Egypt, "Special Scripture Distributions: Bibles4Egypt."

87. Atallah, "Two Rows By the Sea."

suicide bomber had approached the Cathedral and Mr. Faheem sought to redirect the former to go through the metal detector, and it was there that the bomber detonated his apparatus. Jayson Casper—a writer at *Christianity Today*, observes: "Faheem saved the lives of dozens inside the church,"[88] for there would surely have been more casualties in Alexandria, where "18 civilians and 4 police officers were killed."[89]

A reported *staurocentric* response that stunned Muslims in Egypt was the declaration of forgiveness by Faheem's widow. Over a national talk show aired all over Egypt, she said (with her children beside her): "I'm not angry at the one who did this. I'm telling him, 'May God forgive you, and we also forgive you. Believe me, we forgive you. You put my husband in a place I couldn't have dreamed of.'"[90] The renown Egyptian Muslim host of the talk show, Amr Adeeb, was mesmerized as he watched Mrs. Faheem declare those words. After "[t]welve seconds of silence . . . an awkward eternity on television" writes, Casper, Adeeb said: "The Copts of Egypt . . . are made of . . . steel!"[91] Adeeb was so dumbfounded, that he began to stammer pointing to how Egyptian Copts have borne several atrocities over centuries, and yet they remain faithful to their faith. Adeeb added: "How great is this forgiveness you have? . . . If it were my father, I could never say this. But this is their faith and religious conviction."[92] Millions—Muslims and Christians alike—were astounded like Adeeb across the Egyptian airwaves.

Pope Tawadros II—the 118th Pope of Alexandria and Patriarch of the See of St. Mark—made reference to the events of bombings and killings in the two churches in his Easter Sunday Papal encyclical that year. He spoke of four features present in Paul's words in Phil 3:10 namely: the knowledge of Christ, the power of his resurrection, the fellowship of his sufferings, and being conformed to his death. The Pope declared in his encyclical:

> We remember the martyrs of the Palm Sunday. With their blood, they recorded a new page in the history of our Egyptian Coptic Orthodox Church. . . The fellowship of His sufferings that is described by St. Paul means that resurrection comes after suffering. The fellowship of sufferings happens when man shares it. There is no glory without pain. There is no crown of life without the crown of thorns. The crown of thorns gave us the crown of life. There is no resurrection without the cross. That is why

---

88. Casper, "Forgiveness."
89. CNN, "Death Toll Rises to 49 in Palm Sunday Bombings."
90. Casper, "Forgiveness."
91. Casper, "Forgiveness."
92. Casper, "Forgiveness."

> we go through the fellowship of suffering as human beings and as a church. We describe many of these accounts in the narratives and events of the martyrs. Our Egyptian Coptic Orthodox Church became the 'Church of Martyrs' and is renowned by this name worldwide. That is why we say: 'The Mother of the Martyrs is so beautiful' meaning the church . . . [93]

We have earlier noted that the reason Jesus embraced the cross, besides his obedience, is that beyond the cross there is resurrection. It is this same reason that floods the hearts of Jesus's followers in the face of death. Pope Tawadros II put it in other words in his encyclical: "There is no glory without pain. There is no crown of life without the crown of thorns. The crown of thorns gave us the crown of life. There is no resurrection without the cross."[94] This is the grounds that can motivate Christians to choose *staurocentric* pathways in living and in response to violence. In order for the death of a Christian not to be in vain and for the death of the martyrs to reproduce life as a grain of wheat that first falls to the ground, the grace of forgiveness must flow like streams from Christians to those who hate and persecute them. The cross is the Christians' indomitable weapon for triumphing over violence.

Lastly, we turn to another contemporary example—forgiveness in the context of gun violence in the United States.

7.3.3 From the Old Order Amish

It was October 2, 2006 in a small Amish settlement, Nickel Mines, in Lancaster, Pennsylvania. One Mr. Charles Carl Roberts IV has done the unimaginable to students of West Nickel Mines School—shooting and killing five school children and leaving another five seriously injured. Authors of *Amish Grace*, who are scholars of Amish life, attest that Mr. Roberts turned "a tranquil schoolhouse into a house of horror, [and] shattered a reassuring American myth–that the Old Order Amish remain isolated from the problems of the larger world."[95] The details of Roberts IV's horrific action are not our focus here.[96] Instead, our interest is in the *staurocentric* response of the Amish community which followed the Nickel Mines schoolhouse shooting. A preamble about the Amish may be

---

93. Tawadros II, "2017 Papal Message of the Glorious Feast of the Resurrection."
94. Tawadros II, "2017 Papal Message of the Glorious Feast of the Resurrection."
95. Kraybill et al., *Amish Grace*, xi.
96. For the details of the shooting and its aftermath, see Kraybill et al., *Amish Grace*.

fitting to give context to the discussion on their response to the incident of gun violence which they experienced.

The 2017 population estimates of the Amish in the United States, according to Amish Studies, was 313,215. The states of Pennsylvania and Ohio take the largest of that figure—74,250 and 73,780 respectively—about 47 percent of the total Amish population in the United States. A few Amish are also found in Canada (5,175) and South America (Bolivia–50, and Argentina–35).[97] The basic fact about the Amish is that they live socially- and technologically-separated lives in their settlements, away from modernity, but at the same time negotiating and "interact[ing] with the wider world by bargaining with modernity."[98] Common practices among the Amish include: "rural residence, German-based dialect, eight-grade education, church services in homes, small local churches, lay ministers, church-regulated dress, selective use of technology, horse-and-buggy transportation and nonparticipation in the military."[99]

Speaking of roots, a majority of Amish families own a copy of *Martyrs Mirror*—a big volume that "focuses on the persecution of religious dissenters, faithful minorities who suffered at the hands of the powerful, and those who were scorned by 'the world' as they sought to follow the humble and nonviolent example of Jesus."[100] The tome, *Martyrs Mirror*, often read in Amish homes reminds them that suffering for the sake of following Jesus is something to be expected from the world and that faithfulness to Jesus could mean death. Historically, the Amish themselves tie their root to "a small group of radical dissenters who questioned the whole premise of the medieval state-church system in which the government mandated correct belief and the church blessed civil and military activity."[101] (This we briefly highlighted in chapter 3—section 3.3.1). Thus, those who were weary of the system "insisted that a true church would be composed only of those who separated themselves from the corrupting influence of the world and obediently followed the teachings of Jesus, including his commands to live humbly and to reject violence even in self-defense."[102] They rejected infant baptism, insisting that baptism should be voluntary and only for those who grasp the implications of following Jesus as disciples. They were called Anabaptist because they re-baptized adults who had been

---

97. http://groups.etown.edu/amishstudies/statistics/population-2017/.
98. Nolt, *Amish*, 2.
99. Nolt, *Amish*, 8.
100. Nolt, *Amish*, 12.
101. Nolt, *Amish*, 13.
102. Nolt, *Amish*, 13.

baptized as infants and have made commitment to live as Jesus's disciples. As we noted in chapter 3, some were later called Mennonites, after Menno Simons (1496–1561)—an influential Dutch theologian.[103]

The nexus of this brief review of the Amish root and life to our discussion relates to their ethic of non-violence (discussed in chapter 3), but also their embrace of suffering and of forgiveness to those who wrong them. So how did the Amish community in Nickel Mines respond to Charles Carl Roberts IV's shooting, killing, and wounding of their children at West Nickel Mines School on October 2, 2006? Their response was two directional—towards Amish families whose children were killed or wounded and toward the shooter's own family. To the affected Amish families, they provided support. But what shocked the world was their response to reach out and proclaim forgiveness to the shooter (although Roberts IV killed himself in the shooting) and to his family. While the world outside the Amish society were responding with compassion, providing therapy and seeking to help, "the Amish themselves were doing another kind of work. Softly, subtly, and quietly, they were beginning the difficult task of forgiveness."[104] Roberts IV, after shooting the ten children at the Amish schoolhouse also shot himself and died, living a widow and children. The Amish realized they were not the only victims, but that Roberts IV's widow and children were also victims.

One of the Amish ministers in a proximate church district, called Amos, with three other Amish went to find the shooter's widow (Amy) and her children. They found them at Amy's father's house with her parents, and they spent some time commiserating with the family. Amos said "we just talked with them for ten minutes to express our sorrow and told them that we [the Amish] didn't hold anything against them."[105] While Amos and his three Amish colleagues were with Roberts IV's widow (Amy), their children and in-laws, another Amish man at another end had gone to visit the shooter's father, Mr. Roberts III, and after standing with the man for about an hour he took Mr. Roberts III "in his arms and said, 'We forgive you.' [And the following day], Roberts' parents received many visits and calls from other Amish people who also expressed forgiveness and gracious concern."[106] The stories and expressions of forgiveness flowed like streams from the Amish in Nickel Mines and other nearby Amish settlements toward the gunman's

---

103. Further details on Amish life, roots and history can be gleaned from the volumes cited above Nolt, *Amish*; Kraybill et al., *Amish Grace*, as well as from: Dyck, *Introduction to Mennonite History*.

104. Kraybill et al., *Amish Grace*, 43.

105. Kraybill et al., *Amish Grace*, 44.

106. Kraybill et al., *Amish Grace*, 44.

family. The Amish people attended the burial of the shooter and invited the shooter's family to attend the burial of their own children.

The flow of forgiveness from the Amish did not just end in words and visits. Three Amish scholars (Donald B. Kraybill, Steven M. Nolt, and David L. Weaver-Zercher) write:

> Forgiveness also flowed in the form of dollars. When the Nickel Mines Accountability Committee formed two days after the shooting, committee members discussed their desire to help the Roberts family... [A member of the committee said:] 'It's not right if we get $1,000 and they [Roberts' family] get only $5. After contacting the Roberts family, the committee designated some [of] its funds for the killer's widow.[107]

Besides the assistance the Accountability Committee had committed to providing for Roberts IV's family, many individuals from the Amish community went further to contribute money and made "donations to the Roberts Family Fund established by the Coatesville Savings Bank."[108] With such an Amish outpour of forgiveness and practical demonstration of Jesus's *staurocentric* life, Amy, Roberts' widow, testified saying "the kindness of the Amish has helped us tremendously... It helps us to know that they forgave us."[109] Ten days after the shooting, the Roberts family released a public statement thanking the Amish community. In that statement they said: "Your [Amish] compassion has reached beyond our family, beyond our community, and is changing our world, and for that we sincerely thank you."[110]

The world was stunned at the demonstration of Amish grace and forgiveness. But what eluded the attention of news reporters and the media was the roots of such grace and forgiveness. What was the underlying power that spurred the Amish at Nickel Mines and their nearby Amish settlements to so respond to such a tragedy in the often unheard of manner they did? It is their attachment to Jesus and understanding of the implications of the cross. As has been pointed out, in most Amish homes, are copies of *Martyrs Mirror*, besides their Bible. From that volume they read the stories of those who have gone before them following on the path of the cross. Furthermore, the Amish roots to the Anabaptist[111] movement must not be forgotten. They

---

107. Kraybill et al., *Amish Grace*, 47.
108. Kraybill et al., *Amish Grace*, 47.
109. Kraybill et al., *Amish Grace*, 47.
110. Kraybill et al., *Amish Grace*, 47.
111. The Amish became separated from the Anabaptists and Mennonites towards the end of the seventeenth century, when Jakob Ammann felt that the Anabaptists were becoming eager to be socially accepted. So Ammann formed churches determined to distinguish themselves from the corruption of society. For concise details and the history of their migration to North America see chapter two "Amish Roots" in Nolt, *Amish*.

Staurocentric *Pathways to Peacebuilding-Contextual Theology* 231

were imprisoned and martyred in Europe by Roman Catholic church-state authorities during the sixteenth century AD. They remained committed to nonviolence response toward their persecutors.

Nonviolence does not imply inaction and passivity. It is rather an active show of Christ's kindness, grace and forgiveness to those who revile and persecute. The response of the Amish in Nickel Mines following the gun violence in their schoolhouse in October 2006, I posit, has its roots in their belief and attachment to the cross. It is a demonstration of *staurocentric* forgiveness. And that forgiveness spurred the Amish of Nickel Mines to flesh out other elements of *staurocentric* pathways buttressing our thesis that God uses the cross to triumph over death, evil, sin and violence. The Church in our contemporary era can espouse this model in responding to violence wherever the latter rears its head—whether it is in an ethno-political, Islamists or gun-violence context. Now, before turning to tie the knots between *staurocentric* contextual theology and peacebuilding praxis in our last chapter, we outline below the intersection of *staurocentric* pathways to peacebuilding.

7.4 *STAUROCENTRIC* CARREFOUR WITH PEACEBUILDING

From Isa 53:5 (cited in 1 Pet 2:24), we make a case for the intersection of *staurocentric* pathways with peacebuilding. The pericope in which the Isaiah passage is situated (Isa 52:13—53:12) refers to the exaltation of the Suffering Servant. It is one of four Servant poems in Second Isaiah (Isa 42:1-9; 49:1-13; 50:4-9; and 52:13—53:12). Old Testament scholars have advanced ideas[112] as to the identity of the Servant. Gary V. Smith affirms that an examination of the various Servant poems leads to the conclusion that the Servant's identity is "a messianic royal figure."[113] John Goldingay and David Payne underscore the point that from a traditional Christian perspective "some irony attaches to the fact that the one entity which is outside the purview of 52.13—53.12 is an individual future redeemer, a 'Messiah.'"[114] In my own understanding, this "messianic figure" is ultimately Jesus Christ.

In Isa 53:5, two passive verbal forms מְחֹלָל-*mᵉḥōlāl*-was pierced, and מְדֻכָּא-*mᵉḏukkā*-was crushed, and two nouns מוּסָר-*mūsar*-chastisement, חַבּוּרָה-*ḥabbūrā*-wounds are used. We can make a connection employing the Old Testament Hebrew feature of parallelism prevalent in OT poetic genre. The first level of Hebrew parallelism lies in the first two lines of the verse as follows:

---

112. For a summary of various scholarly positions regarding the identity of the Suffering Servant see: Smith, *New American Commentary*, Isa 52:13—53:12.

113. Smith, *New American Commentary* 318.

114. Goldingay and Payne, *Critical and Exegetical Commentary*, 2:286.

> But he was pierced for our transgression //
>
> He was crushed for our iniquities

The verbal form, מְחֹלָל–*mᵉḥōlāl*—pierced, (Polal participle, masculine singular absolute) is parallel to the verbal form, מְדֻכָּא–*mᵉdukkā*—crushed, (Pual participle, masculine singular absolute), the noun 'transgression' is parallel to 'iniquities'. Similarly, from the last two lines of the verse we observe that the two nouns (מוּסַר–chastisement and חֲבֻרָה–wounds) are also in parallelism, thus, we have the following:

> Upon him was the chastisement that brought us peace //
>
> And with His wounds we are healed.

Placing the first part of the verse in parallelism with the second part we have the following:

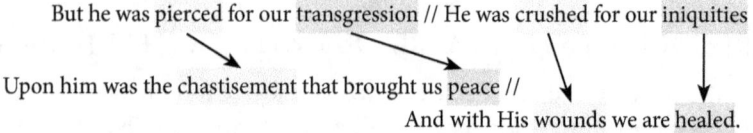

The Suffering Servant, upon whom the actions of piercing, crushing, chastisement, and wounding were directed, paradoxically produced peace and healing. In addition, 'our transgression' was exchanged for peace, and 'our iniquities' for healing all because of the Suffering Servant taking upon himself those violent actions of piercing, crushing, chastisement, and wounding. This is *staurocentric* in character. For the first two lines, the first passive verb 'was pierced' parallels the second, 'was crushed'. Furthermore, the verbal action of piercing the Servant parallels the noun 'chastisement'; whereas the verbal action of crushing the Servant parallels the noun 'wounds'. The result is that the beneficiaries of the Suffering Servant's vicarious suffering received, in place of their transgression, peace; and, in place of their iniquities, healing. What may this indicate in regard to the *staurocentric* carrefour with peacebuilding?

The problems that required solution are the transgression and iniquities. Transgression and iniquities are elements that introduce broken relationships. Wherever there is wrongdoing (transgression) there also will the need for peace and healing exist. The Suffering Servant met these needs—providing peace and healing by receiving the paradoxically opposite actions of piercing, crushing, and nouns of chastisement and wounds. From the model set by the Suffering Servant, we can, therefore, maintain that there exists a meeting point between his *staurocentric* path and the peace (and implicitly the reconciliation) he makes possible through his cross. This meeting point is the carrefour of *staurocentric* path and peacebuilding. It is at such a carrefour that reconciliation is made possible. In addition, at such carrefour forgiveness is conceivable and made possible.

Christian tradition and exegetes are convinced that this poem of the Suffering Servant (Isa 52:13—53:12) are fulfilled in Jesus Christ, and we concord with this stance. Goldingay and Payne caution, however, not to limit its fulfilment to only Jesus Christ, lest such limitation robs "the passage of much of its power. . ."[115] They posit that "the point about this exposition is to urge the Christian community to be like Jesus in its handling of attack. . ."[116] Goldingay and Payne also connect the poem to the hymn of Christ in Phil 2:4–11, the hymn from which we have argued that Jesus overturned the meaning of *stauros* by his voluntary self-giving to die on it and by his obedience to the Father's will to drink its cup. In the hymn of Christ, Paul invites Jesus's followers to have the same mind among themselves. We must always remember that this mind of Christ, which we are exhorted to have, is the mind that Jesus had in order to make the cross a carrefour where peace, healing and forgiveness can meet and triumph violence. That kind of 'mind' was the underlying secret to Jesus's self-giving, his obedience, and ultimately his triumph and exaltation. Thus, we can assert that at Jesus's cross (*stauros*), suffering and obedience cross paths, but also at that cross (*stauros*), peace and healing of broken relationships happen. At the cross judgment and mercy meet, and at the cross violence is vanquished by the peace Jesus engenders. It is important to underscore that the peace Jesus's *staurocentric* life engenders is not one-dimensional Instead, it is holistic to ensure restoration of broken relationships.

There is no disputing the fact that we live in a broken world. This brokenness can be depicted as three–dimensional (see Figure 1 below). The first axis is vertical—which is the brokenness of the relationship and communion between the human spirit and his/her Creator, God. This vertical brokenness forms the y-axis and it is foundational. The second is horizontal, but with two axes—the x-axis and the z-axis. The x-axis of brokenness is the axis of broken relationship and fellowship between humans and their fellow humans. The x-axis is often multifaceted. It can be relationships along racial, gender, ethnic, political, economic, regional, national, professional,

---

115. Goldingay and Payne, *Critical and Exegetical Commentary*, 2:286.
116. Goldingay and Payne, *Critical and Exegetical Commentary*, 2:286.

religious and even along theological lines. And thirdly, the z-axis of brokenness, which can be viewed as ecological brokenness. It is the brokenness of the relationship and care that ought to exist between humans and other created things—the environment, the earth, plants, animals, et cetera.

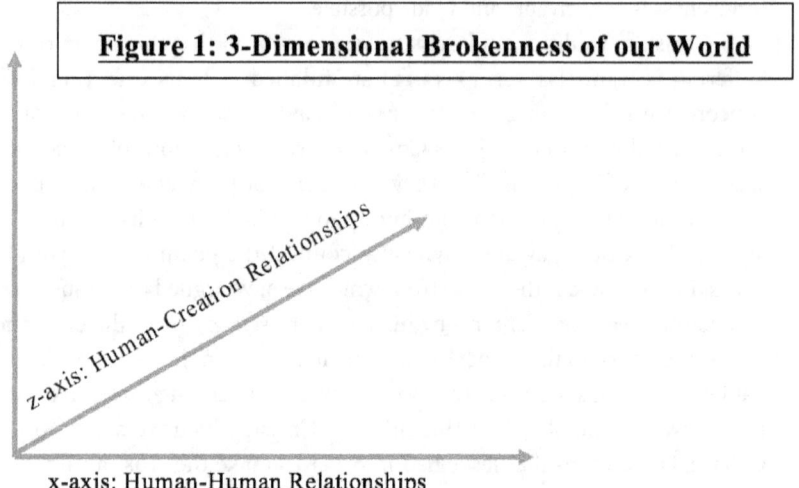

Figure 1: 3-Dimensional Brokenness of our World

Basically, wherever the y-axis relationship is not restored and healed, it is often difficult to heal and restore the other two axes. True and enduring peacebuilding, in my judgment, ought to begin from the vertical axis but not exclusively limited to it, for the Holy Spirit in the world engaging in *missio Dei* can begin from anywhere he wills to restore and heal. The late Australian missiologist, Ross Langmead, writing on conversion as reconciliation posits a similar schema, though differently conceived. He writes: "Christian conversion can be seen as reconciliation in at least three dimensions: being reconciled to God, ourselves and others."[117] Langmead, elsewhere,[118] later includes the dimension of reconciliation with the creation—ecological, environmental and creation care. I include the z-axis as a dimension that also requires peace. Thus, peacebuilding is essential for cultivating culture of peace in our broken world while we wait for the "not yet" or the consummation when the Prince of Peace will install true and everlasting peace. For "[o]f the increase of his government and of peace there will be no end, on the throne of David and over his kingdom, to establish it and to uphold

---

117. Langmead, "Transformed Relationships," 10.

118. See Langmead, "Reconciliation at the Heart of God and Mission," 5. Langmead argues that: "The setting right of relationships which is at the heart of God's mission includes our relationship to the environment."

it with justice and with righteousness from this time forth and forevermore. . . " (Isa 9:7) and "[i]n his days may the righteous flourish, and peace abound, till the moon be no more! (Ps 72:7). We should not presume that whatever degree of peacebuilding we may engage in in this broken world would restore all things. Participation with the Holy Spirit in peacebuilding through the *staurocentric* pathway will certainly attenuate conflicts and restore broken relationships, but not until the triune God brings about the consummation of all things at the eschaton, human labors for peace would only be a reflection of the "not yet", not its fullness.

From the three-dimensionality of brokenness, we observe that the first dimension of peace is spiritual. It involves reconciliation in the God-human axis. The second is peacebuilding in the human-human relationship axis and the third entails a human-creation relationship. The necessity for peacebuilding in any context of violence is obvious because of human propensities toward violence and toward breaking relationships—whether it be God-human relationship, human-human relationship or human-creation relationship. The existence of broken relationships, (which often may boil over and manifest in various forms of violence, hostility and sometimes wars) makes peacebuilding an ever-growing need. Since violence and broken relationships happen, the need for peacebuilding, which I have defined as "a proactive, conscious and structured efforts directed toward establishing the parameters that create peace"[119]—must not be ignored by the church in every context and space. And in this regard, I argue that the *staurocentric* path remains the most viable model for Jesus's followers to adopt because with it Jesus made peace and healing possible. For Jesus's followers in Nigeria who live in contexts of violence involving the religious other, one may then ask: Where lies the *staurocentric* carrefour with peacebuilding in a context marked by Islamist/Muslim and African contexts? Drawing from the resources for peacebuilding resident in Islam outlined in chapter 4 and from African concepts extracted from both literature and narrative data of our research outlined in chapters 5 and 6, we turn now to our concluding chapter to attempt a response to this question.

---

119. Anyanwu, "Pneumatological Considerations," 337.

8

Peacebuilding Carrefour

Staurocentric Contextual Theology and Praxis for African Contexts of Acute Violence

PEACEBUILDING CONCEPTS FROM ISLAMIC and Muslims' perspectives formed the focus of discussion in chapter 4. And in chapters 5 and 6 we turned to the African ethnolinguistic landscapes to mine some peacebuilding concepts autochthonous to Africa. Chapter 6 focused particularly on those concepts extracted from our ethnographic research in Nigeria. In chapter 7, we outlined the historical and theological trajectories surrounding our theoretical framework (the *staurocentric* model), arguing that the event of Jesus's death and resurrection overturned the meaning of the cross as it was known in the then Greco-Roman world. We highlighted a few examples where Jesus's followers employed an element of the *staurocentric* model to respond in a context of violence.

The overarching task of this last chapter is to tie the trajectories of the previous five chapters together, mapping out the contours of the carrefour formed by the intersection of the triadic motifs—the *staurocentric* framework, Islamic/Muslims' perspectives, and African concepts for peacebuilding. Put differently, we discuss here the peacebuilding-contextual theology and praxis emerging from the intersection of the *staurocentric* model, the peacebuilding concepts from Islamic/Muslims' perspectives, and from African concepts for peacebuilding. We attempt to respond to the question: How can Christians by employing the *staurocentric* approach pattern their response to violence after Jesus's model demonstrated in his triumph over death, evil, sin, and violence? Can Jesus's followers in the twenty-first century adopt the path of Jesus's cross to overcome violence that pervades our world? More pertinent to our research on peacebuilding-contextual theology in Nigeria's context of Islamist acute violence, we respond to the question: How can the church in Nigeria employ the same model in a manner that constructively and critically integrates African concepts for peacebuilding-contextual theology and the peacebuilding resources found in Islam in order to, at the least, build peace? Finally, we will also present our encompassing concluding reflections in this chapter.

8.1 *STAUROCENTRIC* CARREFOUR AND PROPOSALS: TOWARD A CONSTRUCTIVE AND CRITICAL INTEGRATION FOR PEACEBUILDING-CONTEXTUAL THEOLOGY

Two questions guide our discussion in this section. The first is: Where is the *staurocentric* carrefour with peacebuilding in a context marked by Islamic/Muslim and African contexts? And the second: How can African concepts be constructively and critically integrated for peacebuilding-contextual theology in contexts of acute violence? The first subsection here (8.1.1) seeks to respond to the first, and in the second (8.1.2), we will point to how the concepts may be applied constructively and critically for peacebuilding-contextual theology.

8.1.1 *Islamic and African Cultural Concepts at the Staurocentric Carrefour*

The concluding section of chapter 4 outlined the emerging contours of Christian-Muslim carrefour for peacebuilding. We sought to point out the emerging intersections of Muslims' perspectives of peacebuilding with certain Christian concepts. Similarly, in chapters 5 and 6 we mapped out the emerging concepts for peacebuilding from some ethnolinguistic cultures in sub-Saharan Africa, identifying some from literature and some from the narrative data of our research. Here, we identify the ways these concepts form a carrefour with *staurocentric* characteristics, where they do. We limit our emphasis to those elements that may be considered as *staurocentric* in principle.

First, we take up Khaled Abou El Fadl's observation based on Qur'ān 4:135 where Muslims are admonished to stand firm in justice even if it is against themselves, or against their family relatives. Abou El Fadl maintains that such a concept in Islam shows that humans can attain a high level of moral virtue.[1] The notion of Muslims standing up for justice even against their own self-interest possesses a *staurocentric* characteristic as we noted

---

1. Abou El Fadl, *Place of Tolerance in Islam*, 14.

in chapter 4. It is *staurocentric* because it entails certain form of death to oneself in order to act for justice even when such action does not yield an instant benefit to the actor. The fact that this notion is present in Islamic thought creates a carrefour for *staurocentric* peacebuilding-contextual theology that can be constructively employed in peace education and action in contexts of Islamist violence. In chapter 6, we highlighted a couple of examples in Nigeria where some Muslims have displayed this characteristic by practicing the African concept of hospitality and thus protecting some religious others in contexts of violence.

The *staurocentric* element therein lies in the danger that could attain the Muslim who takes in a non-Muslim to protect from imminent attack or acute violence being perpetrated by Muslims. If the Muslim attackers were to learn that a Muslim was protecting a non-Muslim being targeted for acute violence, then that 'Muslim Samaritan' will be considered a traitor (to say the least) or as a *kafr*—an infidel who merits the same lot as the targeted-religious-other. It is, therefore, fitting to maintain that there exists a *staurocentric* characteristic imbedded in such an Islamic notion to sacrifice one's interest in order to stand or act for justice for the other. We also recall Mohammed Abu-Nimer's argument that peacebuilding in Islam is grounded on principles such as "*'adl* (justice), *iḥsan* (beneficence), *raḥma* (compassion), and *hikmah* (wisdom)."[2] Acting for justice is an element that contributes to peacebuilding, and standing up for justice even when such an action may entail danger for the Muslim actor is *staurocentric*.

Second, adjoined to the theme of *'adl* (justice), are *iḥsan* (beneficence) and *raḥma* (compassion). Muslim scholars, Reza Shah-Kazemi and Mohammad Hashim Kamali, agree that these themes are related and they form essential elements that Muslim communities must adopt to ensure a flourishing community. Both Shah-Kazemi and Kamali maintain that Muslims' demonstration of *raḥma* (compassion) must not be limited toward Muslims, but toward non-Muslims as well, in cadence with the traditions of the prophet.[3] The *staurocentric* element lies in the genre of self-giving it entails for someone to demonstrate justice, compassion and goodness to a religious or ethnic other. Human-brokenness along religious, ethnic, cultural and political lines limits peoples' display of justice and compassion toward the other. But when those limiting boundary lines are crossed to extend justice, compassion, hospitality et cetera to the other, it can be considered *staurocentric*.

---

2. Abu-Nimer, *Nonviolence and Peace Building in Islam*, 49.
3. Shah-Kazemi, *Spirit of Tolerance in Islam*, 12; Kamali, *Dignity of Man*, 1–8, 70.

A third genre of the cross forming a *staurocentric* carrefour for peacebuilding in contexts of Islamist violence can be drawn from the Sudanese cleric's (*Ustadh* Mahmoud Mohammed Taha) Second Message of Islam. According to Taha, the 'First Message of Islam' (which captures the Quranic injunctions of *jihad* against the other) was deficient in ensuring economic equality, democracy, and social well-being.[4] Taha classifies the Sword verse of the Qur'ān (Q. 9:5) as one of the verses that represent the 'First Message of Islam' and which became "the basis for the Shari'a of *jihad*, while the verse of Shura [consultation] provided the Shari'a of government, in accordance with the principle of guardianship of the mature individual [the Prophet] over the community."[5]

In my estimation, it will take a genre of *staurocentric* self-giving for Muslim artisans of peace to align with Mahmoud Mohammed Taha's novel and revolutionary thought, rejecting physical aggression against the other in order to build peace. The present study is not, however, focused on the Muslims' peacebuilding action(s), but rather on the Christians' peacebuilding-contextual theology. Hence, it is outside our scope to wade into those waters. Nonetheless, Taha's position presents the Christian artisans of peace with concepts that can be harnessed in dialogical peacebuilding initiatives with their Muslim counterparts. Taha's 'Second Message of Islam' consisting of people moving "away from base animal drives and develop[ing] a superior moral character."[6] creates a *staurocentric* carrefour that can be employed in dialogical peacebuilding endeavors. As we noted in chapter 4, Taha refers to violence as "[t]he law of the jungle—the law of violence and oppressive force—[that should] be replaced by the law of justice, truth and compassion—thereby improving the equality of human relations."[7] I argue that this is the model Nigeria's Imam Muhammad Ashafa has adopted in his dialogical peacebuilding initiative with Pastor James Wuye (discussed in chapter 4). Imam Ashafa and Pastor Wuye's peacebuilding endeavor showcases, in the Nigerian context, the *staurocentric* carrefour for peacebuilding which I posit. Furthermore, the peacebuilding ideas of Imam Shaikh M. Tawhidi, who has earned for himself the epithet 'Imam of Peace' stands as another example of a *staurocentric* crossroad because Tawhidi, as a cleric, opposes resort to violence against the non-Muslim other. Fethullah Gülen's pursuit for peacebuilding grounded upon his Islamic theology of peace and love not limited to his fellow Muslims belongs to the same *staurocentric* carrefour,

4. Ṭāhā, *Second Message of Islam*, 166.
5. Ṭāhā, *Second Message of Islam*, 166.
6. Ṭāhā, *Second Message of Islam*, 161.
7. Ṭāhā, *Second Message of Islam*, 161–62.

for in rhythm with Qur'ān 5:32, Gülen firmly holds to "the integrity of the individual regardless of ethnic or religious background."[8]

Our last example of *staurocentric* intersection with Islamic/Muslims' perspectives (though not the least) relates to the self-giving approaches of Muslim clerics and legal experts in Bosnia-Herzegovina, who fully consented to Article 4, clauses 1 and 2 of the Bosnia-Herzegovina Law on Religious Freedom (cited in chapter 4). For fluidity, we recall these articles here:

> Everyone has the right to freedom of religion or belief, including the freedom to publicly profess or not a religion. Also, everyone has right to adopt or change his or her religion, and the freedom—individually or in community with others, in public or private—to manifest his religion or belief in any manner in worship, practice and observance, maintenance of customs and other religious activities . . .
>
> Churches and religious communities shall not, when teaching religion or in other actions, disseminate hatred and prejudices against any other Churches and religious communities or its members, or against the citizens of no religious affiliation, or prevent their freedom to manifest in public their religion or belief.[9]

It is evidently novel and revolutionary for a Muslim to acquiesce to a legal article passed in his or her country's parliament for "everyone . . . to adopt or change his or her religion, and [have] the freedom. . . to manifest his [or her] religion or belief in any manner in worship, practice and observance . . ."[10] As we opined in chapter 4, it is very significant that Muslim leaders and Muslim legal experts were involved in the articulation, drafting, and ratification of such a law. It is an eloquent witness to Bosnia-Herzegovina Muslims making significant contribution to peacebuilding. In my judgment, there exists an element of self-giving involved therein, in that those who were involved in the articulation, drafting, and ratification of such law laid aside the language and culture of death and violence that largely dominates the narratives around Muslim encounters with the non-Muslim other. I maintain, therefore, that there exists a *staurocentric* carrefour for peacebuilding formed with certain Islamic notions and the perspectives of some

---

8. Esposito and Yilmaz, *Islam and Peacebuilding*, 12.

9. Parliamentary Assembly of Bosnia–Herzegovina, "Law on Freedom of Religion and Legal Position of Churches and Religious Communities in Bosnia and Herzegovina," Article 4, clauses 1 & 2.

10. Parliamentary Assembly of Bosnia–Herzegovina, "Law on Freedom of Religion and Legal Position of Churches and Religious Communities in Bosnia and Herzegovina."

Muslim artisans of peace. And if from the Islamic and Muslim perspectives such *staurocentric* carrefour exists for peacebuilding, how much more ought we to expect from the perspective of those who follow Jesus, who himself epitomizes the *staurocentric* life?

Turning to the African concepts, we highlight now their *staurocentric* carrefour.

* * *

The bird's eye view of African concepts for peacebuilding cast in chapter 5 uncovered the Nguni concept or philosophy of *ubuntu*; the Rwandan concepts of the *Gacacha* court system and *Abanyarwanda*; the Somaliland concepts of *Nabadraadin* (let us talk), the *gurrti* (council of elders), and their *ergada* (travelling elders); and the example of Liberian women's action for peace. From the narrative data of our research in Nigeria, we extracted some indigenous ethnolinguistic concepts, the emerging preponderant themes being: the *nzu* concept (the universal ethics of the stranger), hospitality as an African means for peacebuilding, the *gammo* and *gaya* concepts (community power in peacebuilding), agency of festivals and rituals, and the role of women in peacebuilding evidenced through the *Egbo-o Ho-Ho* concept and cross-clan marriages. So, where does the *staurocentric* carrefour lie with peacebuilding insofar as African concepts are concerned?[11]

The concept of *ubuntu* is grounded on the principle of "I am, because we are; and since we are, therefore, I am."[12] In a community where the concept of *ubuntu* is translated from mere orthodoxy to orthopraxy, people within that community seek the wellbeing of others first because their own wellbeing is intrinsically dependent on that of others. Furthermore, the relational connectivity between *ubuntu* and *imago Dei* (as we pointed out in chapter 5) creates in the minds of people in an *ubuntu*-practiced community the propensity to seek good for others instead of seeking to outdo, outshine, or outstrip them. Such propensity to first seek the good of the other suggests a *staurocentric* carrefour because it entails self-giving, a denying of self to some degree in order to make the other obtain the intended good. Every seeking of good for the other will to some measure entail self-giving, which is characteristic of the *staurocentric* life. In view of this I argue that there exists a *staurocentric* carrefour with *ubuntu*.

---

11. My response to this question follows no specific order of the African concepts mentioned. I discuss closely related ideas sharing proximity of coherence to *staurocentric* carrefour.

12. Mbiti, *African Religions and Philosophy*, 141.

The same principle applies to concepts of hospitality, the African ethics of the stranger (the *nzu* concept), the *gammo* and *gaya* concepts, as well as the *nabadraadin* (let us talk), the *gurrti* (council of elders), and the *ergada* (travelling elders) concepts. In each of these, the subjects of the actions which the concepts imply must necessarily give up something in order that the result of those actions might yield peace and wellbeing for the other. To practice hospitality, especially in the case of protecting someone who is a target of acute violence, exposes the host to different forms of danger. In our discussion on hospitality as an African means for peacebuilding (chapters 5 and 6), we pointed out a few examples from both literature and from our narrative data—examples of people who risked their lives to host and protect the religious other in a context of violence. I argue that such self-giving that puts the host in danger in order to protect his/her guest has a *staurocentric* connotation, and, therefore, creates a carrefour. Similarly, in discussing the *nzu* concept, which portrays the African universal ethics of the stranger, the intrinsic self-giving ethos is evident from the fact that the one who offers *nzu* (local white chalk or white clay) to the stranger, welcomes the latter, gives up some of his or her comfort in order to create a flourishing space for the stranger. To go as far as giving the stranger a portion of land to both dwell and farm without demanding monetary compensation, which is part of the praxis in the Igbo *nzu* concept for strangers, is *staurocentric* in essence.

It is also *staurocentric* for Somaliland *gurrti* (council of elders) and their *ergada* (traveling elders) to have to transverse boundaries of waring communities, despite the evident dangers on the roads, in order to engage in talks with the *gurrti* of the other side and to enact peace. In regard to the Rwandan concept of the *Gacacha* court system where confessions and forgiveness of the offender are paramount, we underscore the fact that forgiveness is costly. It is costly, first for the one who received the hurt and who does not demand retributive justice upon the offender, but instead waves his or her legal rights and releases the offender to go free. Secondly, it is also costly on the part of the offender who receives forgiveness because such forgiveness places a great responsibility upon the one forgiven to go and do the same. *Staurocentric* forgiveness does not demand reparations in terms of monetary payment of damages done. Indeed, the wrongs done in most cases cannot be undone. Thus, *staurocentric* forgiveness releases the wrong doer and invites him or her to also release those who may have wronged him or her or will someday do so.

In addition, for the forgiven one, a retrospective reflection over the act of violence he/she perpetrated and the subsequent pain inflicted on the forgiver kindles a sense of grief and pain that he or she was party to such an act. Certain forgiven ones may even find it hard to forgive themselves, thereby requiring psycho-therapeutic interventions. So forgiveness is not cheap. Even though forgiveness is costly to both the forgiver and the forgiven, yet it is also restorative and life-giving. Thus, it can be characterized as *staurocentric*. Without diving into a theological discourse, we simply point to Jesus's forgiveness offered to all humans on the cross and the subsequent efficacy of life that such *staurocentric* forgiveness engenders in the lives of those who receive it.

Lastly, in our discourse on the part African women play in peacebuilding, we highlighted their indispensable role—whether it is through their local organization to adjudicate and install peace (the *Egbo-o Ho-Ho* concept being an example) or through the practice of cross-clan marriages. In chapter 6, we argued that it is not a question of women being used as pawns for peace, rather it bestows honor on African women because without them their fathers, husbands, brothers, and other male relations stand the danger of destroying themselves in contexts of war. We maintained that African women have often risked their personal comfort and some, even their very lives, in order to install peace in their communities. Often, their motherly instincts motivate them to seek the wellbeing and flourishing of their children, fathers, husbands, and other relations. The Liberian women in their peacebuilding actions defiled rain and sweltering sunshine, fasted, prayed, denied themselves and their spouses sex, and went to every length that was humanly imaginable in order to bring about peace in Liberia. Cross-clan married women, whether in Somaliland or in northeastern Nigeria (as our research revealed) pay some form of price to serve as 'cross-bridges' that oust violence and war between their natal and marital communities. Such self-giving and sacrifice which women bring to the table of peacebuilding creates, in my judgment, a *staurocentric* carrefour. Therein, a form of sacrifice is found that births life and peace.

8.1.2. Constructive and Critical Integration for Peacebuilding-Contextual Theology

Before we forge ahead to face the crucial question of how the concepts can be constructively and critically integrated for peacebuilding-contextual theology in contexts of acute violence, we first explicate what we mean by "constructive" and "critical" integration. The peacebuilding-contextual model I am proposing is intrinsically tied to Jesus's *staurocentric* model. It is, therefore, essential to evaluate the concepts in the light of the cross (σταυρός–*stauros*).

Firstly, peacebuilding-contextual theology will be deemed "constructive" where we do not resort to only biblical studies, church history, and historical theology as our only resources for theological inquiry and integration. Veli-Matti Kärkkäinen, a leading and distinguished constructive systematic theologian and my primary interlocutor on this matter, maintains that constructive theology is by

> nature . . . an integrative discipline . . . [and] to practice well constructive theology, one has to utilize the results, insights, and materials of all other theological disciplines, that is: biblical studies, church history and historical theology, philosophical theology, as well as ministerial studies. [He further adds that] to do constructive theology well, one has to engage also non-theological and nonreligious fields, such as natural sciences, cultural studies, and. . . the study of living faiths . . .[13]

Based on Kärkkäinen's broad view of constructive theology, we use the term "constructive" here in a quasi-manner because we do not utilize insights from a wide range of disciplines. In addition to the bedrock of Christian theology upon which we base our thesis (that is: *staurocentric* model), we seek to integrate into our peacebuilding-contextual theology resources from two non-Christian theological resources namely, the resources we have extracted from Islam (one of the living faiths Kärkkäinen mentions), and ethnolinguistic concepts autochthonous to Africa, which fall within the boundaries of Kärkkäinen's "cultural studies." The attempt to integrate these notions and concepts that are outside the house of Christian theology is what makes my integrative endeavor "constructive." A complete constructive integration will entail including resources and insights from other disciplines beyond the areas we have navigated in this study—which, indeed, opens a door for further research where one may seek to integrate peacebuilding resources from Judaism, Buddhism, Hinduism, natural sciences, as well as other Christian theological disciplines which we did not draw from in this study.

Secondly, critical evaluation entails the search for elements that cohere with Jesus's *staurocentric* model. But how can we critically assess African concepts to ascertain if they are fitting to be proposed for integration as a *staurocentric* pathway? In other words, what should serve as our measuring tool? Max Stackhouse suggests that "since we can have some prospect of knowing something reliable about God, truth, and justice in sufficient degree to recognize it in views and practices of others, we should judge every context [and here I include concept] by establishing what is and what is not divine, true, and just in that context [concept]."[14] Thus, by judging every concept garnered from our research (on African concepts

---

13. Kärkkäinen, *Christ and Reconciliation*, 1:13.
14. Stackhouse, *Apologia*, 26.

for peacebuilding) in the light of what we know about God, truth and justice we can establish if a concept or perspective has any form of coherence with Jesus's *staurocentric* model. In chapter 7, we employed this principle to measure the actions of Jesus's followers to ascertain if their responses to violence and persecution can be adjudged *staurocentric*. We employ the same measurement for African concepts and resources from Islamic theology and Muslims' perspective for peacebuilding. In addition to coherence, our critical evaluation also points out foreseeable caveats that may encumber pragmatic application.

With the above understanding on what we mean by "constructive" and "critical", we now dive into responding to the question: How can Christians by employing the *staurocentric* approach pattern their practices in response to violence after Jesus's model demonstrated in his triumph over death, evil, sin, and violence?

* * *

UBUNTU—THE POWER OF COMMUNITY: A CONSTRUCTIVE AND CRITICAL INTEGRATION

First, the *ubuntu* concept comprises of both the elements of *staurocentric* forgiveness and value placed on humans as a reflection of *imago Dei*.[15] It is a concept that seeks restorative (not retributive) justice. There are several Nigerian parallels to it—some of which include: the *gammo, gaya, Mun ki mwan a vul* concepts highlighted from our research data (chapter 6). We simply call it 'the power of community' because of the many ethnolinguistic terms identified in Nigeria. The coherence of the *ubuntu* concept with the *staurocentric* pathway resides in three elements. First, Jesus's cross meant giving up himself in order that others may enter into peace with God, with other humans and also with creation. Secondly, the *staurocentric* pathway entails forgiveness declared toward the offender and perpetrator of violence and injustice. Thirdly, it seeks to redeem the *imago Dei* in humans.

Evidently, no human self-giving can ever compare with or equate Jesus's self giving on the cross. Nevertheless, flickering reflections of Jesus's *kenotic* sacrifice can be identified in some God-given concepts in some cultures.[16] These *staurocentric* elements identified are intrinsic in the *ubuntu* concept. Speaking of the forgiveness part, Archbishop Desmond Tutu insisted that without it (forgiveness), there will be no future for our

---

15. Battle, *Ubuntu*, 29–30.

16. Abraham's willingness to offer up his son (Isaac) as a burnt offering in obedience to God's word is an example. A contemporary example can be found in Don Richardson's *Peace Child*, which points out the redemptive analogy in the peace child example among the Sawi people of Irian Jaya.

conflict-ridden African lands.[17] The concept also entails giving up one's own individual comfort and well-being for the good of the community because for the African, the former's safety and well-being is tied to the latter's. One of our research participants highlighted this notion maintaining that "as far as Africa is concerned . . ., individuals do not make community, [rather] it is community that makes individuals."[18]

In chapter 7 we reviewed the *staurocentric* example demonstrated in Mrs. Adele Selfu of Rwanda—a widow who adopted the young man (Luis) who killed her husband and inflicted machete wounds on her head and shoulder believing to have left her dead. Rescue operatives found that Adele still had pulse three days after the genocidal attack, while she was still lying in the pool of blood in the midst of about 45 corpses including her husband's. After Adele's recovery, she engaged in ministry helping genocide perpetrators in prison. It was there she met Luis. When Luis was released and had no place to return to, Adele adopted him.[19] We also pointed to the example of a Muslim Imam who risked his own life to hide Christians in his home and mosque from other Muslims seeking to kill the Christians. One of our interview participants spoke of another example concerning a theological seminary that took risks to protect Muslims.[20] These examples display coherent flickering reflections of the *staurocentric* pathway and demonstrate ways Christians can pattern their practices after Jesus's *staurocentric* model in response to violence.

Furthermore, the examples we point to from African contexts cohere, as well, with nuggets of the Anabaptist nonviolence ethics, which we reviewed in chapter 3 wherein we pointed to John Howard Yoder's mention of the "messianic community." Yoder's position (grounded in the Anabaptist tradition) subscribes to and practices the power of community found in African contexts long before the gospel was proclaimed in Africa. In regard to the "messianic community", Yoder writes: "The messianic community's experience . . . is not a life for heroic personalities. Instead, it is a life for a society. It is communal in that it is lived by a covenanting group of men and women who instruct one another, forgive one another, bear one another's burden, and reinforce one another's witness."[21]

In regard to praxis, we noted in chapter 3 the five emphases which Glen H. Stassen's Just Peacemaking theory entail. Lisa S. Cahill pointed that

17. Tutu, *No Future Without Forgiveness*, 260.
18. Tyriaka, D1#4:433–434.
19. Finley, "New Life for a Dying Nation: Forgiveness, Baptism."
20. Dauda, D1#1:139–142.
21. Yoder, *Nevertheless*, 135.

the first of those emphases is that it "is not only about ideas, theories, or principles."²² It entails proactive participation of people in building their community. This is exactly what we found from the African contextual concepts of *ubuntu, gammo, gaya,* and *Mun ki mwan a vul.*

A critical dimension that we must consider in a constructive integration of the *ubuntu, gammo, gaya,* and *Mun ki mwan a vul* concepts in Nigeria's context of Islamist violence relates to undercutting the Islamists' opposing ideology which reckons everyone who refutes and refuses to subscribe to their own agenda (including Muslims) as enemies. We must highlight that these Islamists are, nevertheless, in a minority. We maintain that for enduring peacebuilding, the *ubuntu* concept promises some fruit if the Muslim majority are engaged via their community opinion leaders, who themselves see the futility of the Islamists' actions. A greater optimism for the constructive integration of *ubuntu* concept outweighs the pessimism therein in view of the evident peacebuilding fruit it has borne in South Africa and Rwanda where the concept has been employed to drive reconciliation and nation-building.

Further critical dimension for the Nigerian context concerns the ongoing erosion of the power of African traditional community in the face of rural-urban migration, globalization, and impact of Western values. The power of community-bonding has weakened in urban settings between people of differing ethno-religious groups living within the same urban neighborhood compared to what is traditionally obtainable in rural settings. In addition, the quest for greener economic pastures pushes the power of community to the margins. One of our interview participants, Tyriaka, pointed to this unfortunate trend. He noted:

> The unfortunate thing today in Nigeria [is that] anywhere you go we do not have communities. We have individuals living in segregated tribal groups, . . . I had always told them if we have communities in northeast Boko Haram cannot breakthrough no matter what, because the role and function of a community is exactly the same with the role and function of government. Community protects the lives of individuals.²³

Monthly tribal or hometown meetings of urban residents who hail from the same town or tribe appear to be the best trending in urban settings and such meetings do not equate with the strong power of community upon which *ubuntu, gammo, gaya,* and *Mun ki mwan a vul* concepts can be constructed or developed. Given this trend, it requires an uphill

22. Cahill, "Just Peacemaking," 196.
23. Tyriaka, 451–456.

task and creativity to achieve the integration of these eroding African concepts in the contemporary context of Islamist violence in Nigeria. We point this out, in order, to demonstrate the critical work that must be undertaken in order for the constructive integration of these concepts to yield sustainable and tangible peacebuilding results. With that said, work toward it can, however, begin from the rural communities where the power of community remains strong.

* * *

Hospitality: Toward a Constructive and Critical Integration and Praxis

Pope Paul VI was the first Pope to ever visit Africa. In his homily on July 31, 1969 in Kampala, Uganda, he amazed his audience declaring that Africans "[i]nded possess human values and characteristic forms of culture which can rise up to perfection such as to find in Christianity, and for Christianity, a true superior fullness, and prove to be capable of a richness of expression all its own, and genuinely African."[24] Hospitality is the second concept we tender for critical integration. It is, undoubtedly, one of Africa's values which we tie to Pope Paul VI's African "human values and characteristic" which he asserted contains "forms of culture . . . capable of a richness of expression all its own, and genuinely African."[25]

Hospitality is imbedded in the power of community. Christine D. Pohl, in her volume, *Living into Community*, posits that "[c]ommunities in which hospitality is a vibrant practice tap into deep human longings to belong, find a place to share one's gifts, and be valued."[26] Nonagenarian Canadian Catholic philosopher who founded l'Arche community for people with developmental and intellectual disabilities, Jean Vanier, on his part maintains that hospitality "is one of the signs that a community is alive. To invite others to live with us is a sign that we aren't afraid, that we have a treasure of truth and of peace to share."[27]

We cannot overstate the importance for followers of Jesus to demonstrate hospitality toward our Muslim neighbors despite the odds. The odds are those shadows that hospitality may cast and may discourage its practice in the context of violence. One of these include the fear of being betrayed or exposed to attack. We must echo Veli-Matti Kärkkäinen's

---

24. Paul VI, "Eucharistic Celebration at the Conclusion of the Symposium."
25. Paul VI, "Eucharistic Celebration at the Conclusion of the Symposium."
26. Pohl, *Living into Community*, 379.
27. Vanier, *Community and Growth*, 266.

position in respect to "Christian theology of creation [that] is based on the goodness of creation and cultivates graceful hospitality . . . refuses to ontologize violence, war, and conflict."[28] Based on such vision of "graceful hospitality", Jesus's followers can give themselves to welcoming and hosting Muslims despite the odds. The odds may include a double-pronged danger that welcoming and hosting a Muslim may elicit.

First, the host may never ascertain the trustworthiness of the guest, for the latter may be playing the role of a spy or an informant to those who seek to harm the former. In order to counter this fear, Jesus's followers must remember the *staurocentric* pathway because the one "who ate [Jesus's] bread lifted his heel against [him—Jesus]" (John 13:18b; cf. Ps 49:9). Jesus was well aware of his friend's betrayal and yet he did not evade loving and eating with him. In fact, the same betrayer was Jesus's ministry treasurer and "he used to help himself to what was put into [the moneybag]" (John 12:6). I posit that Jesus knew that his treasurer "was a thief"(John 12:6), and yet did not transfer the treasury role to another among the Twelve. In the same manner, I posit that Jesus's followers can look to his model and extend heads, hearts, hands and homes of hospitality despite the odds.

The second odd that welcoming and hosting a Muslim may produce relates to exposure to attack not connected to the guest transmitting information. If an Islamist gets to know that Mr. C (a Christian) is hosting and protecting Mr. M (a Muslim) or vice-versa, then both Messieurs C and M may become objects of attack. In regard to this danger, we still maintain that a *staurocentric* mindset will keep the Christian undeterred to offer and receive hospitality.

The other critical point we observe in regard to hospitality as an African concept, which followers of Jesus must employ, surrounds the issue of *halāl* and *harām*.[29] A Christian hosting a Muslim must be aware that the dynamics of what can be prepared and presented as food in the Christian's home must take into consideration foods that Muslims consider as *halāl* (permitted). If (for example) in Mr. C's home eating pork was never an issue, when Mr. C opts to extend hospitality to Mr. M, the former (Mr. C) must assure the latter (Mr. M) that there will be no preparation and eating of pork while the latter is in that home. It will entail becoming all things for all people. Like Paul, we can say: To the Muslims I became a Muslim, in order to win Muslims . . . "To the weak I became weak, that I might win the weak. I have become all things to all people, that by all means I might

---

28. Kärkkäinen, *Hope and Community*, 5:180.

29. In Islamic culture, *halāl* foods are ritually permitted for consumption, whereas, *harām* foods are prohibited. According to Muslim ethics, eating *harām* foods in Islam defiles a Muslim.

save some. I do it all for the sake of the gospel, that I may share with them in its blessings" (1 Cor 9:20–23). It is *staurocentric* to give up one's right in order to display Jesus's life to people to whom that life remains blurred or hidden. If this principle is not taught in our churches, we may not see it play out in our culture. Those who are intentional about it are conceiving constructive ways for extending their hands, heads, hearts, and homes to welcome and receive Muslims. In chapter 6, we pointed to an example of a focus group participant's mother, who devised ways to invite Muslims to eat at her home with the assurance that the food was both *halāl* and prepared according Muslim religious prescriptions. We posit that Nigerian Christians need to multiply similar means. Prominent pentecostal theologian, Amos Yong, rightly posits that

> the many tongues and many practices of the Spirit of God [must serve as] the means through which divine hospitality is extended through the church to the world, including the worlds of the religions, and that it is precisely through such hospitable interactions that the church in turn experiences the redemptive work of God in anticipation of the coming kingdom.[30]

Drawing from Yong's thesis in his volume, *Hospitality and the Other*, we maintain that Jesus's followers ought not employ pentecostal blessings only for the acquisition of our material and ephemeral pursuits. Instead, we must employ pentecostal blessings for extending "divine hospitality" to the religious and ethnic other so that both the former and the latter may ". . . experience the redemptive work of God in anticipation of the coming kingdom."[31] Yong, drawing from the Luke-Acts narrative, paints "Jesus as the paradigm of hospitality because [Jesus] represents and embodies the hospitality of God."[32] Thus, the *imago Dei* that followers of Jesus embody must, therefore, shine through *staurocentric* hospitality among others.

Speaking of hospitality from the African perspective, Julius Gathogo defines African hospitality "as that extension of generosity, giving freely without strings attached."[33] Gathogo's definition draws from Austin Echema's, who describes "it as an unconditional readiness to share"[34]— a definition we connect to the *nzu* concept of universal ethics of the stranger, in regard of which we have already pointed out that for a community to go as far as giving the stranger a portion of land for settlement and for subsistence

---

30. Yong, *Hospitality and the Other*, 100.
31. Yong, *Hospitality and the Other*, 100.
32. Yong, *Hospitality and the Other*, 101.
33. Gathogo, *Christ's Hospitality from an African Theological Perspective*, 72.
34. Echema, *Corporate Personality in Traditional Igbo Society*, 35.

farming without demanding monetary compensation except to commit to dwelling in peace with the hosts is *staurocentric* in essence.

Constructively, the praxis of African hospitality surpasses theory. In other words, it is not just talked about in African communities, rather, it is lived out. Zuruaga, one of our interview participants highlighted this, pointing us to a Hausa saying: "*Karban baki kan sa ka marabchi mala'ika*, meaning: in hosting someone that is coming to your place (maybe a visitor, a passerby) you are able to host an angel."[35] Along the same optic, John Mbiti, drawing from Nigerian Methodist scholar Bolaji Idowu's *Olodumare: God in Yoruba Belief*, maintains that

> [g]ood character shows itself in . . . chastity before marriage and faithfulness during marriage; hospitality; generosity, the opposite of selfishness; kindness; justice; truth and rectitude as essential virtues; avoiding stealing; keeping a covenant and avoiding falsehood; protecting the poor and weak. especially women; giving honour and respect to older people; and avoiding hypocrisy."[36]

All the virtues, which Mbiti enumerates, encapsulate Pope Paul VI's African "human values and characteristic" that he asserted contains "forms of culture . . . capable of a richness of expression all its own, and genuinely African."[37] Besides, the African concept of hospitality, African women's role in peacebuilding merits our constructive and critical attention as well.

* * *

Gender Perspectives: Constructive and Critical Integration in Peacebuilding

Women's role in peacebuilding has been evidenced through local grassroots movements and recognized by the international community. We pointed to the Liberian women's action for peace and to the *Egbo-o ho ho* concept in southeastern Nigeria, as examples of local grassroots participation. The United Nations Security Council, on October 31, 2000 "adopted resolution (S/RES/1325) on women and peace and security,"[38] wherein peacebuilding actors are urged to increase women's participation in peace and security

---

35. Zuruaga D1#3: 250.

36. Mbiti, *African Religions and Philosophy*, 277; cf: Moila, *Challenging Issues in African Christianity*, 1; Gathogo, *Christ's Hospitality from an African Theological Perspective*, 72.

37. Paul VI, "Eucharistic Celebration at the Conclusion of the Symposium."

38. OSAGI, "Landmark Resolution on Women, Peace and Security."

initiatives. Irrespective of the contribution and positive impact women can make in peacebuilding, there exist, however, some challenges that must be overcome for their contribution to yield peacebuilding fruits, particularly in Nigeria's context of Islamist violence. We point out here a couple of major challenges, which are socioeconomic in nature.

Given the dynamics of change in many rural communities caused by rural-urban migration, many young women migrate to urban cities in search of education—considered a ticket to a better economic earning. This trend depopulates the traditional rural areas of women who can serve as agents of change. While in urban areas, people (not only women) gravitate toward individualistic tendencies rather than the power of community entrenched in their local rural landscapes. The power of community tends to lose its grip on people because people become preoccupied with their respective educational or economic pursuits. At best, they may only attend their tribal or hometown meetings in the cities or urban centers where they have settled. People living in the same neighborhood hardly connect except for issues regarding neighborhood utility services. Therefore, there exist no bonds to promote women action for peace which would have naturally been the case had they remained in their natural rural habitat.

In the Liberian women's case, women peace actors were pushed to the wall because they and their young female children became victims of rape and other forms of atrocities. Such pain and suffering galvanized grassroots mobilization of women that transcended ethnic and religious boundaries. In regard to the *staurocentricity* of African women's role in peacebuilding, we have already pointed to the self-giving characteristics of the Liberian women peace actors. They defiled rain and scorching sunshine. They fasted and prayed. They also denied themselves and their spouses sex and went to every length that was within their human power in order to bring about peace in Liberia. The action of self-giving to seek the good of the community, as we have already pointed out, is, in essence, *staurocentric*. It is not unique to Africa. David Augsburger, in his volume *Dissident Discipleship*, narrates the story of seventy women who engaged in a procession in the heat of gang violence that erupted in the early 1990s in Boyle Heights in Eastern part of Los Angeles, California. While people were

> hiding behind locked doors, . . . [these women] brought food, guitars, and love. As they ate chips and salsa and drank Cokes with gang members, they began to sing the old songs of Jalisco, Chiapas, and Michoacán. The gang members were disoriented, baffled; the war zones were silent . . . By nonviolently intruding and intervening they "broke the rules of war". The old script

of retaliation and escalating violence was challenged and changed . . . the women christened their nighttime journeys "love walks."[39]

The Boyle Heights women's idea to engage in the procession was born while they gathered for prayer and reading the Matt 14:22–23. They were challenged to step out and walk with Jesus on the waters of the gang violence happening in their city.[40] It is, in my opinion, spot-on that these women nicknamed their action "love walks."

Another gender element extracted from our research pertains to cross-clan marriages. Can this concept be constructively and critically integrated into *staurocentric* peacebuilding? We posit upfront that cross-clan marriages may not be an option for Christ's followers as a *staurocentric* means for peacebuilding. We discuss it, nonetheless, as a matter of critical assessment because our research data flagged it. The critical question we ask regarding cross-clan marriage between (Christians and Muslims) as one of the concepts extracted from our research interviews is: Should Jesus's followers in Nigeria inter-marry with Muslims for the purpose of peacebuilding? From the Muslims' perspective cross-religious marriage is encouraged as a means of winning the non-Muslim spouse to Islam, especially if it involves a Muslim man espousing a non-Muslim woman. Muslim men are permitted by Islamic law to marry chaste women from "the People of the Book" (that is: Jews and Christians). This Islamic ethic is grounded on Qur'ān 5:5 ". . . And [lawful in marriage are] chaste women from among the believers and chaste women from among those who were given the Scripture before you, when you have given them their due compensation, . . ."[41]

On the contrary, Christians are discouraged from espousing non-Christians—an exhortation grounded on the teaching on "unequal yoke."

> [14]Do not be unequally yoked with unbelievers. For what partnership has righteousness with lawlessness? Or what fellowship has light with darkness? [15]What accord has Christ with Belial? Or what portion does a believer share with an unbeliever? [16]What agreement has the temple of God with idols? For we are the

---

39. Augsburger, *Dissident Discipleship*, 126.
40. Augsburger, *Dissident Discipleship*, 125.
41. Sahih International, *Al-Qur'an al-Kareem*, 5:5. See also Esposito and DeLong-Bas, *Shariah*, 113. Another verse of the Qur'ān (2:221) interdicts Muslims from marrying non-believers until the latter believe. The Arabic term in that verse referring to non-believers (الْمُشْرِكَاتِ—*al-mushrikāt*) may be interpreted in various ways by Muslims, and have been translated into English as "polytheistic women" (Dr. Mustafa Khattab—*The Clear Quran*); "idolatresses" (Picthall); "female associates (Those who associate others with Allah)" (Da. Ghali).

temple of the living God; as God said, "I will make my dwelling among them and walk among them, and I will be their God, and they shall be my people (2 Cor 6:14–16 cf. 1 Cor 7:39).

In view of this and in many Nigerian contexts, Nigerian Christians display a high degree of reluctance toward marrying Muslims. In simple terms, the implication is that the African concept of cross-clan marriages applies only to a Christian-Christian marriage across ethnic-cultural boundaries. In other words, Christians in Nigeria (and it can also be said of other African countries) marry cross-culturally and cross-ethnically provided the spouses are followers of Jesus. Followers of Jesus frown at and disapprove of marriage union between a Jesus's follower and someone who has not made a commitment to follow Jesus even if the latter comes from the same cultural or ethnic group. Thus, cross-clan marriage may not be considered a viable means for enacting peace between inter-religious communities in conflict in Nigeria's context of Islamist violence. Where a conflict is between clans, then this concept will surely be a tool to employ. But where the conflict has a religious (Christian-Muslim) element, it poses a challenge from the Christians' perspective. Furthermore, the fact that Islamists in northeastern Nigeria engage in abducting young Christian women—particularly from boarding high schools— and forcefully taking them as their sex slaves complicates the matter.[42] Thus, we suggest that cross-religious marriage for the purpose of peacebuilding may not be an option for followers of Jesus.

With the arguments put forth in the preceding subsections, we maintain that African concepts of peacebuilding be constructively and critically studied, understood, and then integrated into peacebuilding-contextual theology within African contexts of conflict and for establishing peace cultures within African landscapes. We recognize, nonetheless, that the confluence of Western culture and encroachment of Western methods introduce societal disruptions that are now becoming powerful currents eroding local African values and methods. But the trend of this genre of erosion can be checked by conscious and community efforts to retrieve and integrate these African "human values and characteristic [possessing] forms of culture . . . capable of a richness of expression all its own, and genuinely African."[43] That said, I do not imply that constructive and critical integration of African peacebuilding methods in African contexts of violence should jettison the non-African concepts. Rather, we must find creative ways of integrating proven non-African methods that can add value to the African concepts for

---

42. The abduction of the Chibok and Dapchi school girls are widely-known examples.

43. Paul VI, "Eucharistic Celebration at the Conclusion of the Symposium."

peacebuilding. African means and methods must first be revived through critical peace studies, education and constructive integration and action. And the Nigerian church has need to stand up to this task.

8.2 TOWARD *STAUROCENTRIC* PRACTICES FOR THE CHURCH IN NIGERIA

From all the above, we can ask: How then can the church in Nigeria espouse Jesus's model of the cross in order to overcome Islamist acute violence and open doors of all *staurocentric* practices to the other? How can followers of Jesus imitate Jesus in the context of Islamist violence in Nigeria by employing Jesus's model of the cross as a means for overturning evil and violence in their context? To these question, we respond that the church in Nigeria will need to embrace *staurocentric* pathways. We argue that if the church in Nigeria must obtain a decisive victory over violence, then, we cannot eschew following after Jesus's *staurocentric* model.

In the Nigerian context, a saying has become commonplace among Christians: Jesus told us to turn the other cheek, we have turned the other cheek, and we have no other (that is: no third) cheek left to turn. By this it is implied that we have been slapped on both cheeks and since we don't have a third cheek to turn, it is now time to arise and physically fight back the 'enemy' and self-defend ourselves. (And the 'enemy' is often synonymous in the Nigerian context to Muslims or the non-Christian other). But contrary to this position, I have tried to posit in this study an alternative model—a model that calls the Church to return to the life of the cross according to Jesus's model. In chapter 7, I raised the question about the tenability of *staurocentric* pathways in demographic minority contexts. A brief survey drawn from the *World Christian Database* and the *World Christian Encyclopedia: Third Edition* shows the Nigerian Christian-Muslim population is shared almost equally between the two religious faiths.[44] We maintained in chapter 7 that in whatever context followers of Jesus find themselves, Jesus still invites his followers to walk the road of the cross. Thus, in Nigeria's context of violence which we may refer to as a demographic equal context, *staurocentric* pathways are as tenable as they are in either a demographic minority or majority context.

Again, I reiterate my contention based on Jesus's power of convocation—where he could have summoned legions of angels to fight on his behalf—that *staurocentric* pathways are not to be limited to contexts of demographic minority but are applicable in every context in order to reflect the model we see in Jesus. It is by the *staurocentric* model that triumph over

---

44. Johnson and Zurlo, "World Christian Database."

violence can be assured because violence becomes turned to peace and healing in the face of the cross. I do not posit for a passive fatalistic posture. Rather, I am calling for a *staurocentric* mindset that positions followers of Jesus to give themselves to love and serve the other, including those who perpetrate violence and injustice against them. In what follows, I elucidate some of the pragmatic ways that the *staurocentric* mindset can be fleshed out drawing from both the resources we have outlined in the preceding chapters and sections of the present one. It must be said upfront, that pragmatic ways through which the church in Nigeria can embody *staurocentric* pathways will certainly entail a lot of work both at micro and macro structural levels. I outline, here some of these pathways and briefly discuss them.

8.2.1 *Kerygma of* Staurocentric *Pathways*

Kerygma, in simple terms, is public proclamation by a herald. The place to start, therefore, is from the pulpit ministries[45] of the church. The meaning that Jesus's death and resurrection has given to the cross (*stauros*) must be proclaimed from the church's pulpit ministries. In the *kerygmatic* ministries of the church, Jesus's cross must be distinguished from the marred understanding that "the Constantinian mistake" and the Crusades sought to paint it. The *kerygma* of *staurocentric* pathways must, therefore, begin at this micro level, elucidating the message of the cross—its meaning, its implications, and the narratives of those who have lived it in past and contemporary eras. Through the *kerygma* of Jesus's *staurocentric* pathways and of his followers (both historic and contemporary), the correct *staurocentric* worldview will be formed. This is essential in order to elicit action. The statement of a participant in one of our focus groups buttresses this position. Asked about how the church in northern Nigeria could respond to acute violence, the participant first spoke of Jesus's way of responding to issues and then added "I think for the church to do it . . . we must first of all teach our members to understand how Jesus and what Jesus is expecting of us to do; how he wants us to relate with these people [Muslims]. Then, when we know the word, then we can now take action."[46]

As the understanding of Jesus's *staurocentric* life permeates into the hearts of Jesus's followers through its *kerygma*, we can expect to see pragmatic efforts that will begin to emerge in local small groups in the

---

45. By pulpit ministries of the church I mean all avenues through which the church proclaims the gospel and instructs the faithful: sermons, teachings, Bible studies, educational ministries of the church, theological training for ministers of the church et cetera.

46. Focus Group #1:412–414.

churches, which can serve as grassroots support groups to demonstrate Jesus's *staurocentric* life in their communities. At such a micro level, we can trust the Holy Spirit working in the hearts of Jesus's followers to flesh out the life of Jesus's cross in those communities.

8.2.2 Restorative and Public Declaration of Forgiveness

The carrefour formed by the African concept of *nabadraadin-guurti* (discussed in chapter 5) and *staurocentric* forgiveness (discussed in chapter 7) can be harnessed and fleshed out as a practice. Public events of declaration of forgiveness should be organized within communities that have experienced violence and attacks. Followers of Jesus whose loved ones were killed or hurt, or who themselves were hurt, and who have forgiven the perpetrators of such acute violence should be asked to publicly declare their forgiveness for the community to hear it. Such public declaration should be done with the community elders and opinion leaders present—whether they are followers of Jesus or not.

In discussing Muslims' perspectives and African concepts at a *staurocentric carrefour*, we pointed out that forgiveness is costly, and yet restorative. The praxis being proposed here is not undoable or unrealistic. Our research revealed a few people who have demonstrated forgiveness towards those who killed their loved ones. Zuruaga, one of our interview participants said:

> My own father was killed in a religious crisis . . . Many people came out to share their experiences . . . how God enabled them to pass through [it and] to move on. Most of the ministry engagement I had was to the Muslim community, because I grew up in the North . . . I did a lot of ministry in the North and I have shared Christ to Muslims and this is after my own father was killed by Muslims just to talk about how a lot of us don't harbor hatred towards them because I know my father is with Jesus . . .[47]

We also pointed to the example of Mrs. Adele Selfu of Rwanda as a contemporary demonstration of *staurocentric* forgiveness. Thus, despite the costliness of forgiveness, Jesus's followers can receive grace and walk Jesus's path who, while hanging on the cross, publicly pleaded with the Father to forgive his malefactors. Hence, I posit that the church creates and adopts rituals and liturgies of public declaration of forgiveness. It goes without saying that such public declaration must be accompanied with

---

47. Zuruaga, D1#3:258–264.

prayers over and for the communities, and for (not against) the agents of acute violence and injustice.

8.2.3 Loving and Blessing Muslim Communities: Schools, Healthcare, Tree-planting, and Boreholes

In our research interviews, we asked participants how Jesus's followers in Nigeria can contribute to peacebuilding. The theme of loving Muslims was ubiquitous in their responses to that question. To avoid encumbering our discussion, we quote only a few participants: In one of the individual interviews, a participant said: "We are called to love. . . we are called to love our enemies, which is not easy by the way . . ."[48] In a focus group discussion, a participant reminded us:

> The Bible remains our absolute standard for measuring every truth and the truth of the Bible says: Love your enemies. No true Christian can run away from that. At the end of the day, we can only but love, and love and just keep loving, whichever way we can, wherever we find ourselves. It doesn't matter the pain, we can allow the Holy Spirit to help us look past the pain and just keep loving our enemies.[49]

In chapter 4 we mentioned Bosnia-Herzegovina. Daniela Augustine tells the story of how the Church in Croatia under the leadership of Peter Kuzmič defiled danger in their context of war to bring aid and support to Muslim communities. Evangelical (Pentecostal) Church in Croatia having been persuaded by their leader, Kuzmič, formed a humanitarian relief organization called Agape. The organization "delivered daily food and medicine to tens of thousands of people throughout the territories devastated by destruction and outbreaks of starvation across Croatia and Bosnia/Herzegovina."[50] Two of Agape's "young workers risked their lives to bring medicine to Bosnia city of Bihać (where artillery fire, which did not cease for three years, dissuaded all others from going."[51] In an interview which Kuzmič granted to Augustine, he poignantly emphasized that "[p]roclamation alone could become counterproductive in such a context [of war]. People need to *see* love."[52]

---

48. Ahmed D4#1:233, 240–241.
49. Focus Group #1:584–588.
50. Augustine, *Spirit and the Common Good*, 214.
51. Augustine, *Spirit and the Common Good*, 215.
52. Augustine, *Spirit and the Common Good*, 214. (Emphasis in italics is Augustine's).

I came across a similar narrative from Angola's context of war. At a conference of mission leaders and networks, I met António Mussaqui, Pastor of Victory Presbyterian Church, in Luanda, Angola, who shared a similar story. During the second phase of the Angola war (1993–2002)[53] a group of four young people from Victory Presbyterian Church risked their lives, leaving Luanda that was considered safe and went to Caxito taking food supplies and clothes to people in Caxito, which was under fire. Residents of Caxito marveled at the daring demonstration of love from these young people who brought aid to them at the risk of their own lives. Ultimately, a church sprung up in Caxito following the end of the war on April 4th, 2002, for many residents of Caxito were deeply moved by the love demonstrated toward them.

Thus, in regard to the theme of love, I posit that the church in Nigeria must employ pragmatic ways to demonstrate the love of Jesus to Muslim communities and neighborhoods, becoming a blessing inspired by Jesus's *staurocentric* life. Churches in Nigerian urban centers will need to extend the message of the gospel they proclaim to move their faithful toward creative actions aimed at community-building, for in so doing, the seed for peacebuilding actions will be sown. Church activities must go beyond those tailored toward spiritual edification and include those aimed at creating positive impact in urban communities. Our research interview participants identified four principal pragmatic actions that churches in Nigeria can engage in among Muslim communities to demonstrate the *staurocentric* peacebuilding model by loving and blessing Muslim communities. These are: (a) establishing schools (particularly to undercut the challenges and contribution of the *al-majiri* phenomenon in northern Nigeria), (b) providing healthcare facilities, (c) tree-planting to check desertification, and (d) providing boreholes in Muslim communities. What follows succinctly elaborates each of these pragmatic actions, all emerging from our ethnographic research data.

Establishing schools for the *al-majirai* in northern Nigeria—a phenomenon we pointed out in chapters 2 and 5—is one pragmatic actions identified. An organization—to which one of our research participants belongs—undertakes in such projects in view of peacebuilding. Jibreel, responding to the question on if there are ways their organization has been engaging in peacebuilding said:

---

53. The first phase of the war in Angola occurred between 1975 and 1991 after which there was peace agreement. But the war resumed in January 1993 and finally ended on April 4, 2002.

> for instance, in some places in one of the villages in Adamawa state where the Muslims and the Christians (the non-Muslims) were putting this kind of thing we were able to *build a school*. And then, *we sank two boreholes. We sank one borehole for the Muslims and another borehole for the other non-Muslim community* [emphasis is mine]. And then, since they knew we are Christians, they said: Look these people don't have anything against us, so that [brought] peace. Peace began to reign again . . . We have done that severally. . . . And then, we go to IDP [camps] where the IDPs are mostly Muslims (90% Muslims and sometimes 100%) because there are a lot of IDPs [camps] in the northeast . . . [54]

Another participant pointed to the different actions his denomination has undertaken to love and bless Muslim communities in northern Nigeria. He said:

> ECWA also has an arm called the POD (People Oriented Development) of ECWA and this arm of ECWA goes into neighborhoods and tries to see whatever is needed, which could be to *dig wells*, to improve *agriculture* and the likes. POD does not discriminate on whether it's a Muslim or Christian community, we also have the ECWA *rural development, hospitals, clinics, primary and secondary schools* [emphasis is mine] which ECWA has tried to use to reach people in the communities and build bridges with the Muslims in an attempt to share the gospel . . . [55]

Actions of loving and blessing identified by the two participants cited above include: sinking of boreholes, agricultural, educational, healthcare, and rural development projects. (We focus on the educational part for now, and will return to the others in the later paragraphs). Many Muslim communities in northern Nigeria remain the most educationally disadvantaged in the country. The church in Nigeria can undertake the task of establishing educational structures to educate and increase social integration and formation in matters of hygiene and value of human life.

Such projects must not be embarked upon without involving local Muslim community leaders, and must not repeat the mistakes of colonial mission schools that marginalized freedom of religion for non-adherent students of their institutions.[56] Doing so will in the long-run undercut the menace that the

---

54. Jibreel D4#4:97–105.

55. Dauda D1#1:69–75.

56. See for example Chetty and Govindjee, "Freedom of Religion of Children in Private Schools."

al-majiri phenomenon presents in Nigeria's contexts of violence. The concept of power of community imbedded in the African concepts of *ubuntu, gammo, gaya,* and *Mun ki mwan a vul* can serve as the peacebuilding-contextual and constructive philosophy driven by Jesus's *staurocentric* model for undergirding the engagement praxis enunciated here.

Followers of Jesus in Nigeria must not leave matters concerning the *al-majirai* to the Muslim communities and the political governing authorities. In this study, I am positing that the church in Nigeria integrate love and care for *al-majirai* as part of Jesus's call to them to love the religious other. In order to avoid the pitfalls of repeating the mistakes of colonial mission schools, churches can undertake projects in consultation with Muslim opinion leaders in Muslim communities and neighborhoods to establish schools and care homes for *al-majirai*, and to do so with sincere motives—not thinking that their goal will be to 'convert' the *al-majirai* to become Christians. I have already pointed out in chapter 4 that both Christians and Muslims must position themselves for peacebuilding while bearing witness of their faith, speaking the truth in love with respect toward the other, but leaving the matter of wooing and winning into the hands of the divine.

Here, I maintain that Jesus's followers should not wait for Muslims to do this. Nigerian churches establishing schools and care homes for *al-majirai* will be a witness in itself when it is done with the understanding that the dimension of faith in Jesus Christ is not ultimately a human-orchestrated act, but the work of the Holy Spirit. For the follower of Jesus who seeks to participate with Jesus in his redemptive mission in the world, two pragmatic actions are required namely: first and foremost, prayer and intercession for (not against) "the other" and the practical actions of witness through the demonstration of self-giving love and service. We recall here our assertion in chapter 4 that if anyone must do anything to change "the other", let it be only a spiritual tussle between him or her and the God to whom he/she wishes to win over the other. The actions of loving and blessing Muslim communities must be done by Jesus's followers not as baits to capture targets, but as a reflection of the love of God the Father who "makes his sun rise on the evil and on the good, and sends rain on the just and on the unjust" (Matt 5:45).

Further dimensions on establishing schools in Muslim communities that must be explored and studied include: church-state relations and the possible impediments that might be encountered. Whatever the case may be, I propose that churches or Christian organizations seeking to undertake such actions of loving and blessing Muslim communities must do so with dialogical involvement of the local Muslim and opinion leaders.

Turning to the idea of establishing healthcare facilities, it is a well-known fact that Muslim young girls are given away in marriage at very young age (sometimes at age 12 or in their early teens). This practice is rampant in northern Nigeria and consequently, there have been several Vesicovaginal Fistula (VVF) cases reported in northern Nigeria. Experts who have studied VVF cases in Nigeria attest that "studies revealed that primiparous women[57] were the most vulnerable group."[58] Studies in different northern Nigerian cities reveal that the mean age range of VVF patients fall between 13 and 16.[59]

In regard to providing healthcare for VVF patients, Dauda, our research participant said "there is a special ward that is dedicated to treating women suffering from VVF which is caused by early childbirth. And the ECWA Hospital in Jos is one of the best places to receive treatment for that. Most of the women in this wing are Muslims."[60] Similar to the People Oriented Development of ECWA, the *Ekklesiyar Yan'uwa a* Nigeria (EYN) has a department they call Disaster Relief Ministry. One of our interview participants narrated some of the activities of this department in EYN, which includes providing trauma workshops for victims. The participant, Ayuba, narrated stories of Muslims who marveled at the generosity of Christians despite being the objects of Muslims' acute violence.[61]

The third action of loving and blessing Muslim communities in northern Nigeria, which the church in Nigeria can undertake is the action of tree-planting. Desert encroachment is a reality in northern Nigeria. Fulani herdsmen, who have become a source of violence and attacks on Nigerian villages in the middle belt and the southern parts of Nigeria, are people on the move. Desertification is one of the factors forcing them to move southward in search of green pastures for their herds. In one of our focus groups, a participant opined:

> Israel had turned a desert into a forest, can we do something as a church in Nigeria, for those people? We can go to the north and plant economic trees. We can do [tree]-planting [as] mission work. So we can go planting trees because in the far north [of Nigeria], you don't see economic trees. The trees you see are just those that grow on their own. So can the church be deliberate in planting trees? Can we go there [and do tree-planting] as a

57. Women giving birth for the first time.
58. Ijaiya et al., "Vesicovaginal Fistula," 293–98.
59. Ahmed et al., "Obstetrics Fistula Repairs in Kano, Northern Nigeria," 545.
60. Dauda D1#1:90–93.
61. Ayuba D3#1:240–246, 250–259.

mission work, to plant trees for free? . . . we just tell them that we are here just to plant these trees for you for free.[62]

The thought put forth by the focus group participant cited above obviously evokes ideas elucidated in Marthinus L Daneel's *African Earthkeepers* volumes.[63] The church in Nigeria can learn from the examples in Zimbabwe where Daneel's work involved the mobilization of churches to enact "earth healing" ceremonies and tree-planting liturgies. Should the church in Nigeria go all the way to engage in tree-planting exercises in Muslim communities in northern Nigeria without seeking support from the Nigerian government, such action will be a *staurocentric* praxis. It entails self-giving, blessing, and doing good for "the other" often considered as an "enemy." Such actions will speak of Jesus's life of loving the ones who were bent on hurting and cutting him off. Can the church in Nigeria do this (a question posed by our focus group participant)? We respond to the affirmative if it is brought to the awareness of the church as a *staurocentric* peacebuilding pathway through the *kerygmatic* ministries of the church.

In addition to schools, healthcare facilities, and tree-planting, another action identified is sinking boreholes to provide portable water. One of our interview participants includes sinking boreholes and food distribution in communities touched by Boko Haram attacks and in camps for Internally Displaced Persons (IDPs) as part of their denomination's actions of loving and blessing Muslim communities.[64] Two other research participants (Dauda and Jibreel) pointed to these actions as well. Whereas Dauda mentions that "POD (People Oriented Development) of ECWA . . . goes into neighborhoods and tries to see whatever is needed, which could be to *dig wells* . . .[65] Jibreel said "we sank two boreholes. We sank one borehole for the Muslims and another borehole for the other non-Muslim community."[66] We posed the question to Jebreel: What is it that informs you people going to a community that has fought against you and sinking a borehole for them, building a health center for them? The participant's response was:

> It's the Christian love . . . We are Christians and we are missionaries and we suppose to preach peace. We suppose to bring people together. That's the purpose [of] Christ's coming to earth. We go out to preach peace to let people live together. Apart from

62. Participant, Focus Group #1:648–654.

63. Daneel, *African Earthkeepers: Interfaith*; Daneel, *African Earthkeepers: Environmental*; Daneel, *African Earthkeepers: Wholistic*.

64. Ayuba D3#1:240–246, 250–259.

65. Dauda D1#1:69–71.

66. Jibreel D4#4:99–100.

the issue of eternity, at least we are here on earth first before we talk about anything after death. So while we are here we ought to live in peace with one another and so Christ is our center and then Christ is our inspiration.[67]

The mention of "Christ is our center and . . . our inspiration" reminds us of the Anabaptist principle of Jesus as focus and the cross as locus (discussed in chapter 3). Thus, love is a *staurocentric* pathway for peacebuilding. We maintain that its demonstration must not be limited to microcosmic individual stratum, but also taken to the level of the "messianic community" (to use John Yoder's words) toward the world around it. What we have sought to emphasis from the examples drawn from both literature and our research data are the pragmatic pathways the church in Nigeria can adopt to demonstrate the power of Jesus's love in Muslim communities.

Besides the fact that such actions of love demonstrate Jesus's *staurocentric* life, they are also affirmed in the African *ubuntu, gammo, gaya*, and *Mun ki mwan a vul* concepts. The existence of these concepts within African cosmologies reinforces, for African followers of Jesus, the possibility of the *staurocentric* pathways. I hold, therefore, that the church in Nigeria must multiply the application of the concept of the power of community integrated with Jesus's *staurocentric* model. The *kerygmatic* ministries of churches can be a tool to employ for motivating Nigerian followers of Jesus to flesh out Jesus's *staurocentric* life through pragmatic social actions. My argument is that the church in Nigeria can multiply such practices in communities where needs are waiting to see the love of Jesus fleshed out. Jesus's followers necessarily require a *staurocentric* posture to be positioned to love those who have been the agents of acute violence against them. Thus, I reiterate that the *staurocentric* path of loving the other with respect and leaving the rest to God who judges justly must remain praxis in the church in Nigeria where it is already being done, and be expanded and introduced where it is yet to become praxis.

8.2.4 Community and Civil Societal Actions

Besides direct actions of compassion and love from Jesus's followers toward Muslim communities in Nigeria, there exist other approaches that should also be constructively integrated for peacebuilding in Nigeria's context of violence. Constructive approaches must critically incorporate resources for peacebuilding from the religious other—Muslims, in Nigeria's case and context. In our discussion on Muslim artisans of peace within the African

---

67. Jibreel D4#4:122–127.

context (subsection 4.3.2), we highlighted Imam Muhammad Ashafa and Pastor James Wuye among those who have been working together through community and societal actions toward peacebuilding in the context of violence. The duo co-founded the Muslim-Christian Dialogue Forum (MCDF), and through the community actions of the Forum have been involved in mediation and reconciliation efforts between Muslim and Christian communities in some parts of northern Nigeria. I posit that similar community and civil societal actions can be multiplied in various cities, towns, and communities in Nigeria. Such actions do not need to wait for incidents of violence to provoke praxis. The practice of such actions should be undertaken even where there are yet no incidents of attack or acute violence in communities. Again, followers of Jesus's must be in the frontline, initiating them with extended hands, hearts, and homes of hospitality to Muslim artisans of peace in their communities.

One participant pointed to the actions of his church's Non-Governmental Organization (NGO) in Yola, Adamawa State called Horn of Hope Vision for Peace Community Development of Nigeria (HOHVIPAD), which is primarily involved in peacebuilding. The organization is involved with the American University of Nigeria (AUN) in Yola, in the Adamawa Peacemakers Initiative (API). The Adamawa Peacemakers Initiative is composed of some members of the "AUN faculty, the key religious members from both sides—Muslims and Christians, [and] we are there to build peace and we have done so much in the community."[68] At the height of insurgent Islamists attacks in Adamawa State, API did not only intervene to bring relief to victims, but also continues to work towards establishing peace and rebuilding trust "cutting across various religious lines, because the suspicion we have here in time past was that the Christians always challenged and suspected the Muslims to be involved and the Muslims also suspected and challenged the Christians."[69]

Activities which API has employed include: peacebuilding through sports (which we have more to say shortly), providing Information Technology (IT) training for students at risk and basic entrepreneurship training.[70] The efforts of community and societal action of the API involving Christian and Muslim leaders working with faculty members of AUN have been recognized in Nigeria, having elicited visits from the Swedish and Swiss Ambassadors in Nigeria; and internationally, having received an international

68. Hope D4#3:12–16.

69. Hope, 21–24.

70. Weybrecht, "Adamawa Peacemakers Initiative and the American University of Nigeria."

award in recognition of its peace work.[71] According to our interview participant, the Bishop and the Imam involved in API were invited to the United Nations Commission for Refugees, Geneva, in 2015, where their contribution to peacebuilding in Adamawa State through their collaboration in API was applauded by the international community.[72]

In view of such existing examples, churches in Nigeria can, therefore, initiate and multiply similar community and civil societal actions, which may include the creation of local arts and crafts centers, skill-acquisition structures aimed at creating employment for the youth, and sports activities. A participant in one of our focus groups had the following to say in regard to what his own local church is doing.

> Two or three weeks ago we had General Youth Week. Our focus of the week was Love Therapy. This was teaching us to love Muslims. The idea was that we will come with a Muslim friend to church, . . . we played a football [soccer] match in the morning, and in the evening you will come with a Muslim friend from the team we played with (a Muslim team). So when they came around, we ate together and we told them we love them in spite what has been happening between Christians and Muslims."[73]

Another participant in the same focus group elaborated on "Love Therapy Week":

> my church, taught us to bring Muslims to the church [premises]; . . . and tell them we love them and . . . to eat from the same plate. We played soccer together, and we did that with love. We played in such a way that we did not hurt anyone, when someone falls we walk up to him and tell him sorry, and we help him up; it is a deliberate thing . . . I had someone I loved so much, who was killed by a Muslim, it pained me so much that I never wanted to see a Muslim close to me, I never wanted a Muslim as my friend. But I can tell you that after the Love Therapy Week . . . , I was able to make friends with Muslims, the ones we played football [soccer] together with . . .[74]

Yet another participant pointed out what a Pentecostal church in northern Nigeria is doing—employing the common interests that youths have in sports as a means for peacebuilding. The church shows

---

71. Barry, "American University of Nigeria-Led Adamawa Peacemakers Initiative."
72. Hope, D4#3:26–27.
73. Focus Group #1:281–287.
74. Focus Group #1:590–597.

football [soccer] matches where Muslims and Christians come to the same church auditorium to watch the match together. They interact, and because they support the same clubs, you find that Christians and Muslims are supporting a particular club. They do whatever they can to, interact with their colleagues from other churches. Churches are doing that, especially in the Pentecostal settings; they are doing that a lot.[75]

Such societal actions involving the youth in the community gradually builds degrees of attachment that they become protective of one another. Similar civil societal actions involving traditional African plays was also flagged in our research data. Interestingly, the participant making allusion to John S. Mbiti's "I am because we are," maintained that going to the stream to fetch water and bath together and participating in moonlight plays are among the things that bring their community together. He stated: "During moonlight, young people come out to dance and do what we call *langa*[76]. . . a game that brings young people together."[77]

The idea of bringing the community together falls back to the creation of attachment between playmates. Attachment created in their hearts serves as a tool for peace because in contexts of violence, they are committed to protecting their friends even when they do not share the same religious faith. Furthermore, through sports and play, youths are being educated on the dangers of bowing to pressure to join Islamist groups such as Boko Haram. The activities of the Adamawa Peacemakers Initiative (API) have included such approaches to deter young people from joining insurgent groups.[78] In order for the followers of Jesus to continue and multiply in the directions elucidated here, churches must look beyond its own comfort and seek ways to use resources (human, economic and material) that God has placed in their hands to bless, not only Muslims communities, but also Nigerian ethno-religionists.

Critically speaking, one may ask: How is the praxis of community and civil societal actions for peacebuilding *staurocentric*? It must be understood that not everyone wants peace. There are elements in the society who seek to work against peace, and one of the ways they do so is to oppose those who are actively involved in peacebuilding. Imam Ashafa and Pastor James Wuye

---

75. Focus Group #1:394–398.

76. *Langa* is a local game in northern Nigeria played by children and youth, in which one player folds one of his/her legs and then runs with the other leg. Whenever someone else is able to dislodge the folded leg, then the former is out of the game.

77. Focus Group #1:505–519.

78. Weybrecht, "Adamawa Peacemakers Initiative and the American University of Nigeria."

expressed the opposition they encounter in their own efforts engaging in community and civil societal actions for peace. Those who work for peace may be faced with dangers and death threats.

In chapter 6 we highlighted the example of the Imam who hid over two hundred Christians in his home and mosque to protect them from being killed by Muslim attackers and a seminary that protected Muslims (subsection 6.2.2), and in section 8.1.1 above we argued that there exists a *staurocentric* element involved in seeking to protect a religious other being targeted for acute violence. A 'Muslim Samaritan' protecting a non-Muslim being targeted for acute violence could result to the death of the 'Muslim Samaritan.' The reverse is also true. A Christian protecting a Muslim being targeted for attack by Christian youths could result to attack on the peace-loving Christian. Thus, the dangers of death surrounding those who work for peace abound—irrespective of the ways they may adopt for building peace. For followers of Jesus, the dangers of death, however, must not deter us from involvement in peacebuilding actions at the community level. In fact, in the *kerygma* of *staurocentric* pathways, it must be proclaimed that involvement in peacebuilding may imply attacks from the hands of those who hate peace, but the assurance of Jesus's resurrection life can transform death to life, violence to peace, and hurts to healing.

8.2.5 The Church as a Prophetic Voice at the Nigerian Public and Political Square

Does taking *staurocentric* pathways imply being apolitical—removed and withdrawn from participation in the political and public square? Some may hold that view and argue that our kingdom is not of this world (John 18:36). On the contrary, we argue that the *staurocentric* life of the church is called to become a prophetic voice in the public and political square of the context wherein she dwells.

Accomplished and prominent pentecostal theologian, Amos Yong, in his dense volume, *In the Days of Caesar*, observes that the Nigerian Pentecostal followers of Jesus awakened to engagement in the public and political square "in response to the fear of Islamization."[79] I add in this respect that no longer is it only the Nigerian Pentecostals who have been awakened to this reality, but indeed, the entire Nigerian Christian body. The realities of both Boko Haram and Fulani herdsmen attacks, their sacking of villages, and their occupation by Muslims coupled with tacit inaction of the current

---

79. Yong, *In the Days of Caesar*, 10.

Muslim-led presidency in Nigeria have heightened the awareness among all strands of Nigerian Christians to become politically involved.

Thus, Yong rightly asserts that "[t]here is an increasing recognition that political engagement by pentecostals [and I add: and by all strands of Nigerian Christians] is not a waste of time but is imperative given the volatile situation."[80] Yong's central argument in his volume is that "the many tongues of Pentecost [elicit] many political practices."[81] He further states that "the many tongues of Pentecost, precisely . . . represent a diversity of ethnic, linguistic, and cultural experiences, [which] also imply the redemption of many political practices."[82] We draw from Yong's robust argument—focused on formulating a political theology in dialogue with the global Pentecostal movement—to maintain that the goal of the church in Nigeria must not be fixated on winning elections in order to place Christians in the corridors of the Nigerian political power. The *staurocentric* approach and engagement in the public and political square that may ensure peace go far beyond such a limited perception.

In dialogue with Radical Orthodoxy, Yong argues in chapter 6 of *In the Days of Caesar* that the many tongues of Pentecost lead to many witnesses and, thus, pentecostal political praxis leads to prophetic politics.[83] The implications of prophetic politics, as Yong elucidates, entails: (a) the recognition and proclamation "that allegiances to the state are secondary to allegiances to God . . . [and] that no matter how the state conspires against, threatens, and even harms the community of believers, the prophets in the community pronounce that the state can do no more than what God has [ordained]"[84]; (b) holding "the state [accountable] to do what it is supposed to do: uphold the law"[85]; and (c) "explicit witness in the public square."[86] Besides these three "explicit. . . prophetic political postures and practices,"[87] Yong enunciates a few other practices which prophetic political praxis entails: mutual generosity and sharing in the community of believers, community organizing, and being agents of the civil society.[88]

---

80. Yong, *In the Days of Caesar*, 10 11.
81. Yong, *In the Days of Caesar*, 109.
82. Yong, *In the Days of Caesar*, 110.
83. Yong, *In the Days of Caesar*, 238–52.
84. Yong, *In the Days of Caesar*, 239–40.
85. Yong, *In the Days of Caesar*, 214.
86. Yong, *In the Days of Caesar*, 242.
87. Yong, *In the Days of Caesar*, 242.
88. Yong, *In the Days of Caesar*, 242–43.

I argue that even though Nigerian Christians possess an awakened interest and active involvement in the public and political square, the elements of prophetic political praxis that Yong enunciates are yet to manifest among the Nigerian Christians' praxis. More often than not, Christians in the corridors of Nigerian political power have instead been swept off their feet by the strong current of "stomach-politics syndrome"[89] characterizing the Nigerian political arena. I maintain that unflinching prophetic voices and praxis in Nigeria's public and political square from Nigerian followers of Jesus are yet to be heard. Certainly, some Nigerian followers of Jesus have wooed Nigerian Christians' votes to clinch a political or public position but we are yet to see undaunted prophetic voices making significant contributions that elicit societal transformation. This remains a challenge that the church in Nigeria must stand up to. To so do, a *staurocentric* posture is required—a posture that positions followers of Jesus to serve the public even when no interest accrues to them, a posture that makes one stand and speak the truth in the corridors of power even when it will cost one's position or even one's life.

The church as a prophetic voice at the Nigerian public and political square must not be understood as synonymous with electing Christians to the helm of major political offices. A *staurocentric* prophetic engagement in the public and political square does not imply pushing for and installing a Christian-dominated government, or establishing a Christian political nation on this side of the eschaton. Such dream must be left for Jesus to accomplish at his Second Advent.

One of our research participants highlighted this element, positing for "a multi-ethnic/political and religious society [in Nigeria] . . . where all people, regardless of their size have a voice so they can feel heard and respected."[90] The participant laments, however, that his own denomination "and most evangelical churches [in Nigeria] are not so good with political actions."[91] Thus, while we look forward to Jesus's Second Advent, his followers in every context are called to reflect Jesus's *staurocentric* life, not only on

---

89. What I call "stomach-politics syndrome" in Nigeria refers to politics driven by self-interest at the expense of the promotion of public good Yagboyaju and Akinola, "Nigerian State and the Crisis of Governance," 1–10. Some refer to it, though with a slightly different nuance, as the "politics of stomach infrastructure" Ojo, "Nigerians and the Politics of Stomach Infrastructure," or politics of the belly. The idea is drawn for Jean-François Bayart's book (1989) *L'État en Afrique: La Politique du Ventre* (*The State in Africa: The Politics of the Belly*—my translation), which "points to the propensity of politicians to hoard and greedily consume resources in things and people . . . " Thomas, *Politics of the Womb*, 3.

90. Dauda D1#1:298–299, 302–303.

91. Dauda, 311.

the micro-individual level, but also together as the "messianic community" on the macro-public and political level. Gregory Boyd, in his volume, *The Myth of a Christian Nation*, addresses this issue in regard to the United States of America, calling the idea of having a political Christian nation a "Constantinian idolatry."[92] Boyd's position resonates with one of the implications of Yong's prophetic politics, in that he maintains that: "we who profess allegiance to Jesus Christ must commit ourselves to proclaiming in action and word the truth that the kingdom of God *always* looks like him. Since our ultimate allegiance is not to our nation or institution, we should be on the front lines proclaiming that the history and activity of our nation has nothing to do with the kingdom of God."[93]

In sum, we maintain that one of the *staurocentric* pathways that the church in Nigeria must tread is becoming a robust prophetic voice in the Nigerian public and political square. To do so, the church must first reject and divest herself of all practices that do not reflect the self-giving life of the cross. When this becomes praxis, it will lead to the creation of an ethical culture that can influence the country on a macro level. One cannot create something he or she does not possess. Only life can beget life. The church will be incapacitated to imprint upon the Nigerian public and political square a culture that she does not yet possess and has not made her praxis.

8.2.6 Other Peacebuilding Practices

Besides the practices identified above, there are others we must also point out. First, hospitality—a theme we discussed in chapters 5 and 6 as one of the African concepts and means for peacebuilding—is a practice that must be revived in the church in Nigeria. Having previously discussed its constructive and critical integration in a segment above (8.1.2), we deem it superfluous to discuss it again. Here, we simply emphasis that it is one of the *staurocentric* practices that the church in Nigeria must revive and reintegrate its practice—extending hearts, heads, hands, and homes of hospitality to Muslims and vice-versa. The *staurocentric* element in regard to the praxis of hospitality lies (as noted in subsection 8.1.2) in the sacrifice it entails to intentionally make one's home and food *halāl* that Muslims will feel welcomed to receive the hospitality extended.

Second, empowering women's action for peace through the Church must not be neglected. We discussed the theme of women's role in African

---

92. Boyd, *Myth of a Christian Nation*, 111. Gregory Boyd's "Constantinian idolatry" resonates with John H Yoder's "Constantinian mistake," which I have previously alluded to.

93. Boyd, Boyd, *Myth of a Christian Nation*, 111.

contexts both in chapter 5 and 6 as well as in subsection 8.1.2 above—where we pointed out the *staurocentric* characteristic involved in their participation in peacebuilding. Here, we simply point to two Nigerian-born scholars' view on this. Thaddeus Umaru points to the role women can play in promoting peace in northern Nigeria, holding that "if women are empowered and given the opportunity, they are effective agents in the promotion of peace and reconciliation in the community . . . [they] are teachers of culture, values, language, and models of peace and in the community."[94] Similar to the combined effort of Christian and Muslim women in Liberia's women's peace action (discussed in chapter 5), Akintunde E. Akinade, highlights a Nigerian example called the "Interfaith Forum of Muslim and Christian Women's Association, also known as Women's Interfaith Council (WIC), established in Kaduna in 2010."[95]

Nigerian women do not have to wait for further pain and suffering before a grassroots peace movement emerges, particularly in northeastern Nigeria. I posit that women fellowships of churches (locally referred to as *zumunta mata* in northern Nigeria) can pioneer such a movement in northeastern Nigeria. But for this to happen, the onus rests upon the church in Nigeria to teach and encourage it through her *kerygmatic* ministries. Furthermore, Nigerian women fellowships of churches (*zumunta mata*) can employ contextual means similar to the "love walks" of Boyle Heights' women (mentioned under the discussion on gender perspectives in subsection 8.1.2) to play *staurocentric* and significant roles in contexts of violence.

Third, as the church in Nigeria engages in the practices enunciated above, we can hope that the Holy Spirit will inspire in the hearts of Jesus's followers in Nigeria many other *staurocentric* practices that can be undertaken to diffuse the aroma that Jesus's life begets. The role of the Holy Spirit to provoke prayer and hope for engagement in the practices enunciated and for new dimensions of the *staurocentric* motif must not be marginalized. Without delving into a discussion on the carrefour of prayer and hope vis-à-vis the *staurocentric* pathways, I simply mention that one of our research participants highlighted its place and need for peacebuilding. In a response to a focus group discussion on how the church in Nigeria might respond to acute violence, a female participant said:

---

94. Umaru, *Christian-Muslim Dialogue in Northern Nigeria*, 236.

95. Akinade, "Christian-Muslim Relations in Contemporary Nigeria," 156.

> I see the church responding to [violence] peacefully in the aspect of prayers . . . Some of our churches hold all-nights,[96] individuals [are] having prayers. Recently, Dr. M was telling us that ECWA as a church is calling attention on all of her members to be [involved] in three-days prayers and fasting for our dear sister Leah [Sharibu].[97] So it is another way I see the church actively doing that with the hope and faith that God is going to work, whether in the political level or at others levels."[98]

Thus, followers of Jesus must consider Holy Spirit-inspired prayer and hope as part of praxis for peacebuilding. All things considered, we maintain that a peacebuilding-contextual theology grounded upon the paradox of the cross will chart the path to enduring peace and ultimately triumph over violence.

This *staurocentric* model needs to be rediscovered, re-echoed, and applied to contextual theology. One motivating factor for engaging in the rediscovering, re-echoing, and application of the *staurocentric* model is the knowledge that violence does not have the final word. Instead, peace and healing procured paradoxically by the Suffering Servant—the Prince of Peace—will ultimately triumph. Miroslav Volf emphatically asserts that "[t]*he end of the world is not violence, but a nonviolent embrace without end.*"[99] Kärkkäinen reiterates the same assertion.[100] And John Dear agrees, asserting:

> Violence does not have the last word. Gospel nonviolence insists that God is transforming us all and will transform the violence and injustice in every human heart and every unjust structure into God's reign of love and peace. Indeed, Christ proclaims that the God of nonviolence has already won the victory, that violence has not only been overcome, it has already been transformed. This already-won victory of God through nonviolence gives us the hope and the faith to go forward in the lifelong struggle of transforming nonviolence.[101]

---

96. "All-nights" in Nigeria are prayer vigils that usually start around 9:00 p.m. and go until daybreak. It is a wide-spread practice in most Pentecostal and evangelical churches in Nigeria.

97. Leah Sharibu is one of the girls abducted by Boko Haram, who until the time of writing there has not been any evidence to show that she is still alive.

98. Focus Group #1:379–383.

99. Volf, *Exclusion and Embrace*, 300. Emphasis in italics is Volf's.

100. Kärkkäinen, *Hope and Community*, 5:181.

101. Dear, *God of Peace*, 196.

These scholars are simply asserting that through the mystery underlying Jesus's death and resurrection, violence has been overcome. Thus we cannot resort to different models in search of countering the violence we see in our world and era, for violence is overturned to peace and healing in the face of the cross. At the cross, peace, reconciliation and healing happen.

8.3 CONCLUSION: SYNTHESIS, IMPLICATION, AND SIGNIFICANCE

In this concluding chapter, I attempted to respond to the question of how the African cultural concepts and resources from Islam and Muslims' perspectives can be constructively and critically integrated for peacebuilding-contextual theology. In other words, I tried to unpack the practices that must underlie *staurocentric* pathways for the church in Nigeria while triangulating them (where possible) with enunciations from my research findings. Thus, in this concluding segment, we are left to sketch a synthesis of our pivotal thesis, outline its implication and significance, and finally point out what possible setbacks to the *staurocentric* peacebuilding-contextual model might be.

First, the synthesis of our argument: In the second chapter of this study I briefly sketched the historical trajectories that impinge upon Nigeria pitching-in acute violence. The concluding argument therein was that Nigeria's political and religious histories interact together to form a complex tapestry that engenders violence in the country. Chapter 3 went on to posit that the contexts of acute violence that beleaguer Nigeria necessitate, therefore, contextual means and methods for peacebuilding, which followers of Jesus and participants in God's mission in Nigeria can constructively and contextually employ to engage in peacebuilding given those contexts. Given the demographic divide between followers of Jesus and followers of Muhammad in Nigeria, I maintained in chapter 4 that it is essential for Nigerian followers of Jesus engaging in peacebuilding not to neglect concepts of peacebuilding resident in Islam and from the perspective of Muslims. Thus, chapter 4 argued that there exist within Islam concepts, resources, and tools that can be harnessed and employed in constructing pathways to peace. Peacebuilding in contexts of violence, such as Nigeria, will not only require the integration of religious concepts but also culturally relevant motifs autochthonous to the context. This understanding drove us, therefore, to argue in chapters 5 and 6 that African cultural concepts for peacebuilding are models that must be studied and understood, and then constructively and critically integrated into peacebuilding-contextual theology, not only in African contexts of violence but also in other non-African contexts of violence. Chapter 7 elucidated the theologico-theoretical framework around which I have built the thesis of this entire study, namely that *staurocentric* pathways remain the triune God's instrument for triumphing over violence, and thus, should be espoused by Jesus's followers in every era and context for peacebuilding in contexts of violence through constructive and critical integration of autochthonous contextual peacebuilding concepts. The "how?" of the practices is what the preceding section (8.2) above sought to sketch.

Second: insofar as it pertains to the implication of our encompassing thesis—that *staurocentric* pathways remain the triune God's instrument for triumphing over violence, and thus, should be espoused by Jesus's followers in every era and context for peacebuilding in contexts of violence through critical and constructive integration of autochthonous contextual peacebuilding concepts—we ask: What might be the possible implication and significance of this argument, particularly for the church in Nigeria? I attempt a response to this double-pronged question by first sketching a perceived implication within the current purview of the church in Nigeria.

The *staurocentric* proposal made in this study demands the communitarian action of the "messianic community" (to use John Yoder's expression). To constructively and critically employ the *staurocentric* model—at its carrefour with the African concepts of community (*ubuntu, gammo, gaya,* and *Mun ki mwan a vul* concepts) and concepts of peacebuilding in Islam—implies taking the Christian understanding of taking up one's cross and dying to oneself (Matt 10:38; Luke 9:23) from the current parochial epistemological limit to the individual to a broader epistemological horizon that involves the messianic community. In other words, dying to oneself and taking up one's cross daily to follow Jesus must no longer be restricted to an individual Christian's task but rather broadened to the understanding that the entire community of God's people is called to possess the same mindset to drink the cup of the cross. I am compelled to point to Mahatma Gandhi's view of the power that a community effort can exert to yield greater and palpable result. In the first volume of his *Non-Violence in Peace and War,* Gandhi writes:

> In this age of democracy[,] it is essential that desired results are achieved by the collective effort of the people. It will no doubt be good to achieve an objective through the effort of a supremely powerful individual, but it can never make the community conscious of its corporate strength. An individual's success will be like a millionaire doling free food to millions of starving people.[102]

---

102. Gandhi, *Non-Violence in Peace and War,* 1:342.

We may recall that in chapter 3 we highlighted Martin Luther King Jr.'s statement, how he thought prior to studying Gandhi's works "that the ethics of Jesus were only effective in individual relationships . . . [and how he held that] The 'turn the other cheek' philosophy and the 'love your enemies' philosophy were only valid, . . . when individuals were in conflict with other individuals; when racial groups and nations were in conflict a more realistic approach seemed necessary. But after reading Gandhi, [King Jr.] saw how utterly mistaken [he] was."[103] King Jr. maintains that it was through Gandhi's "emphasis on love and nonviolence that [he] discovered the method for social reform that [he] had been seeking for so many months."[104] In view of the power that communitarian action can elicit, one major implication I foresee is the need for the church (not only in Nigeria, but indeed, globally) to recalibrate or reconfigure her "I-Thou" to a "We-You" relational epistemology[105] in matters concerning taking *staurocentric* pathways.

We may, therefore, assert that the *staurocentric* motif invites the community of Jesus's followers (messianic community) to be prepared to participate with Jesus in his death and resurrection in the face of occasions of violence and injustice that may be directed against them. They are not to seek themselves for such occasions of violence, but rather give themselves practicing the various elements of *staurocentric* pathways, which in themselves entail dying to oneself. And should (in their process of walking the *staurocentric* paths) violence or injustice become the wage they are given in recommence from those whom they seek to love, then let the messianic community remember the one who has gone ahead of them to set the model—Jesus Christ—who while hanging on the cross prayed for (not against) his malefactors saying: "Father forgive them, for they know not what they do" (Luke 23:34).

One overarching significance of our pivotal thesis, in my estimation, is that by adopting the *staurocentric* model for peacebuilding, the church will be multiplying in exponential progression the effect of Jesus's death and resurrection. In other words, the same way that Jesus's self-giving and *staurocentric* approach has produced transformation in the lives of individuals and people groups in time and space despite all odds, should the church—the body of Christ—walk the path that Christ walked we can expect that the triune God will produce similar transformation in the lives of people

---

103. King, *Stride Toward Freedom: The Montgomery Story*, 84.

104. King, *Stride Toward Freedom: The Montgomery Story*, 84–85.

105. See Barbara J. Thayer-Bacon's discussion on "I/Thou relationships" Thayer-Bacon, *Relational "(e)Pistemologies,"* 115–25. Here, "I-Thou" relational epistemology refers to the individual dimension whereas "We-You" (plural) denotes the communitarian epistemology.

and communities who aggress the body of Christ. I have a sense that Jesus's *staurocentric* example is a model the triune God has made available for those who follow Jesus to employ for triumphing over violence and evil. Unfortunately, to a large extent, this tool appears to remain far underutilized, perhaps, following the "Constantinian mistake" and the "Crusades motif" that dominated the history of the church.

Lastly, though not the least, possible setbacks we perceive include: (a) the propensity for some to comprehend *staurocentric* pathways to imply fatalism and (b) the difficulty African followers of Jesus demonstrate in retrieving and reintegrating their traditional concepts into possible practices. As it pertains to the first, we insist that *staurocentric* pathways do not imply fatalism. Insofar as Jesus's self-giving on the cross to make reconciliation and healing possible is not fatalistic but rather the ordained purpose of the triune God to employ it as means to triumph over death, evil, sin, and violence, to that degree *staurocentric* pathways must *not* be characterized as fatalistic.

Furthermore, engaging in *staurocentric* pathways in the context of violence does not imply neglecting the grief, pain and suffering which violence engenders. Violence births grief, pain, and suffering; not only on the part of the victim, but also on that of the perpetrator. As we saw from the Amish example in chapter 7, the Amish people in Nickel Mines, realized early that the aftermath of Charles Carl Roberts IV's gun violence did not only inflict grief and pain on them (the Amish victims, their families and community), but also on Roberts IV's widow, his children, his parents, and other family relations of the Roberts. At both poles of violence, there exist grief, pain and suffering.

Such aftermath of violence must be acknowledged while engaging with a context of violence using *staurocentric* pathways. Jesus's self-giving on the cross did not imply that he was put on a sort of divine anesthesia. Rather, he embraced, endured and owned the pain, while looking forward to the resurrection. In fact, the scars of his crucifixion are believed to still remain on Jesus's resurrected and glorified body and they will remain as a testimony to the *staurocentric* experience he had during his passion and on the cross at Calvary. Those scars have become precious pearls (so to say) and they possess a reconciliatory and redemptive power. We can point to three clues to support this assertion.

Firstly, Jesus showed his nail-pierced hands to Thomas (John 20:24–29 cf. Luke 24:40 and John 20:20). Secondly, God's word that declares "by his wounds you have been healed" (Isa 53:5 cited in 1 Pet 2:24b) remains a living and active word. That is: the wounds that Jesus sustained on his human body during his passion become means for the healing (physical, psychological, and spiritual alike) of those for whose sake he bore those wounds. The third clue is from pneumatic encounters. While serving in North Africa, I met and heard the testimonies of a number of Jesus's followers from a Muslim background to whom Jesus had shown his nail-pierced hands in dreams or visions which added to other pneumatic encounters that led them to entrust their lives to Jesus and acknowledge him as Lord and Savior.[106]

In the same manner that Jesus embraced, endured and owned the pain of violence unjustly meted to him, his followers who are subjected to violence of injustice will have to learn to follow that same path of *staurocentric* embrace, endurance, and owning of the pain of violence which may come upon them. But they must do so with a forward-looking assurance to a triumph over the violence and to a glorious resurrection. As they do so—bearing the marks of their suffering in the pattern of Jesus's cross—they can be sure that as their Master's death and *staurocentric* scars birth reconciliation and triumph over violence, theirs also will do the same because of Jesus's own death and resurrection.

Pertaining to the second possible setback mentioned above, it defines the looming work of doing theology that still remains to be done in African contexts to wean African Christians from the theological breastmilk of the Western agents of mission who brought the message of the gospel to Africa discarding African means and methods and replacing them with Western means, even when those African means were in no way against the Scriptures. I maintain that it will remain a theological uphill task for African Christians to come to grasp with constructive integration of their traditional concepts that conform to the Scriptures, because having tasted the old wine presented to them by the House of Western theology, it's hard to accept that the new is better (Luke 5:39).

All things considered, I maintain that the *staurocentric* model remains the triune God's instrument for triumphing over violence, and thus, should be espoused by Jesus's followers in every era and context for peacebuilding in contexts of violence through constructive and critical integration of autochthonous contextual peacebuilding concepts.

---

106. I have highlighted some of these in a peer-reviewed article: Anyanwu, "Pneumatological Considerations."

Reference List

Abdel Haleem, Muhammad. *Understanding the Qur'an: Themes and Style.* New York: I.B. Tauris, 2001.
Abimbola, 'Wande. "Attitude of Yoruba Religion Toward Non-Yoruba Religion, The." In *Attitudes of Religions and Ideologies Toward the Outsider: The Other*, edited by Leonard J. Swidler and Paul Mojzes, 135–45. Lewiston, NY: Edwin Mellen, 1990.
Abou El Fadl, Khaled. *The Great Theft: Wrestling Islam from the Extremists.* New York: HarperSan Francisco, 2005.
———. "Islam and Violence: Our Forgotten Legacy." In *Islam in Transition: Muslim Perspectives*, edited by John J. Donohue and John L Esposito, 460–67. New York: Oxford University Press, 2007.
———. *The Place of Tolerance in Islam.* Boston: Beacon, 2002.
Abu Dhabi TV. *Bahraini Liberal Author Dhiyaa Al-Musawi: We Hang Our Thinkers on the Gallows of Ideology.* Abu Dhabi, UAE: Abu Dhabi TV, 2006. https://www.memri.org/tv/bahraini-liberal-author-dhiyaa-al-musawi-we-hang-our-thinkers-gallows-ideology-i-listen-music-and.
Abu, Dooshima. "The Imam Who Saved Christians from Muslim Gunmen." *BBC*, July 1, 2018. https://www.bbc.com/news/world-africa-44657339.
Abū Zayd, Naṣr Ḥāmid. *Rethinking the Qur'ān: Towards a Humanistic Hermeneutics.* Utrecht: University of Humanistics, 2004.
Abū Zayd, Naṣr Ḥāmid, et al. *Reformation of Islamic Thought: A Critical Historical Analysis.* Amsterdam: Amsterdam University Press, 2006.
Abu-Nimer, Mohammed. *Nonviolence and Peace Building in Islam: Theory and Practice.* Gainesville, FL: University Press of Florida, 2003.
Abu-Nimer, Mohammed, and S. Ayse Kadayifci-Orellana. "Muslim Peacebuilding Actors in the Balkans, Horn of Africa, and the Great Lakes Regions." Salam: Institute for Peace and Justice. Washington, DC: Clingendael Institute, 2005. http://salaminstitute.org/wp-content/uploads/2016/05/MuslimPeacebuildingActorsReport.pdf.

Abu-Nimer, Mohammed, and Ihsan Onur Yilmaz. "Islamic Resources for Peacebuilding: Achievements and Challenges." In *Islam and Peacebuilding: Gülen Movement Initiatives*, edited by John Esposito and Ihsan Onur Yilmaz, 39–61. Lanham, MD: Blue Dome, 2013.

Accad, Martin. *Sacred Misinterpretation: Reaching Across the Christian-Muslim Divide.* Grand Rapids: Eerdmans, 2019.

Achebe, Chinua. *Things Fall Apart.* New York: Anchor, 1994.

Adamson, Peter. *Philosophy in the Islamic World.* Oxford: Oxford University Press, 2016.

Adesoji, Abimbola. "The Boko Haram Uprising and Islamic Revivalism in Nigeria." *Africa Spectrum*, 45 (2010) 95–108.

Adetoun, Bolanle A. "The Role and Function of Research in a Divided Society: A Case Study of the Niger-Delta Region of Nigeria." In *Researching Conflict in Africa: Insights and Experiences*, 47–55. New York: United Nations University Press, 2005.

Afigbo, Adiele E. "The Age of Innocence: The Igbo and the Neighbours in Pre-Colonial Times." The 1981 Ahiajoku Lecture, 1981. http://ahiajoku.igbonet.com/1981/.

Afolabi, Babatunde Tolu. *The Politics of Peacemaking in Africa: Non-State Actors' Role in the Liberian Civil War.* Oxford: James Currey, 2017.

Agbiboa, Daniel Egiegba. "Boko-Haram and the Global Jihad: Do Not Think Jihad Is Over. Rather Jihad Has Just Begun." *Australian Journal of International Affairs* 68 (2014) 400–417.

Ahmed, Patience M. "Impact of Terror on Internally Displaced Persons in Nigeria." PhD diss., Fuller Theological Seminary, 2019. https://www.proquest.com/pqdtglobal/docview/2305530544/abstract/9FC9289402FB4091PQ/1.

Ahmed, Zainab Datti, et al. "Obstetrics Fistula Repairs in Kano, Northern Nigeria: The Journey so Far." *Annals of Tropical Medicine and Public Health* 6 (2013) 545.

Ajayi, J. F. Ade. *Christian Missions in Nigeria, 1841–1891: The Making of a New Élite.* London: Longmans, 1965.

Ajiboye, Olanrewaju Emmanuel. "Globalization and Africa's Development." In *The Development of Africa: Issues, Diagnoses and Prognoses*, edited by Olayinka Akanle and Jimi O Adesina, 307–22. Cham, Switzerland: Springer, 2018.

Akinade, Akintunde E. "Christian-Muslim Relations in Contemporary Nigeria: A Contextual Approach." In *World Christianity in Muslim Encounter: Essays in Memory of David A. Kerr*, edited by Stephen R. Goodwin, 2:336–44. London: Continuum, 2009.

———. *Christian Responses to Islam in Nigeria: A Contextual Study of Ambivalent Encounters.* New York: Palgrave Macmillan, 2014.

Al-Kāshānī, Tafsīr ʿAbd al-Razzāq. *Tafsīr ʿ Al-Kāshānī: Great Commentaries of the Holy Qurʾan Part 1 Surahs 1–18.* Translated by Feras Hamza. Amman, Jordan: Royal Aal al-Bayt Institute for Islamic Thought, n.d. http://www.altafsir.com/Books/kashani.pdf.

Al-Maḥallī, Jalāl al-Dīn, and Jalāl al-Dīn Al-Suyūṭī. *Tafsīr Al-Jalālayn.* Translated by Feras Hamza. Amman, Jordan: Royal Aal al-Bayt Institute for Islamic Thought, 2007. http://www.altafsir.com/Books/Al_Jalalain_Eng.pdf.

Anderson, Lisa. "Fulfilling Prophecies: State Policy and Islamist Radicalism." In *Political Islam: Revolution, Radicalism, or Reform?*, edited by John L. Esposito, 17–31. Boulder, CO: Lynne Reinner, 1997.

An-Naʿim, Abdullahi Ahmed. "A Kinder, Gentler Islam?" *Transition* no. 52 (1991) 4–16.

———. *Toward an Islamic Reformation: Civil Liberties, Human Rights, and International Law.* Syracuse, NY: Syracuse University Press, 1996.

Anyanwu, Oyedolapo. "Egbo-o Ho Ho! A Cry for Crisis Intervention: Women Arbitrating Peace in Rural Eastern Nigeria." *The Community Psychologist, A Publication of the Society for Community Research and Action (SCRA)* 46 (2013) 31–32.

Anyanwu, Uchenna D. "Pneumatological Considerations for Christian-Muslim Peacebuilding Engagement." *PNEUMA* 40 (2018) 326–44.

Appleby, R. Scott. *The Ambivalence of the Sacred: Religion, Violence, and Reconciliation.* Carnegie Commission on Preventing Deadly, Conflict. Lanham, MD: Rowman & Littlefield, 2000.

Ashafa, Muhammad Nurayn, and James Movel Wuye. *The Pastor and The Imam: Responding to Conflict.* Muslim/Christian Youth Dialogue Forum. Lagos, Nigeria: Ibrash, 1999.

Ashcroft, Bill, et al., eds. *The Post-Colonial Studies Reader.* New York: Routledge, 2006.

Atallah, Ramez. "Two Rows by the Sea: A Poem About Faith in the Face of Adversity." *United Bible Societies* (blog), 2015. https://www.unitedbiblesocieties.org/two-rows-men-poem-faith-face-adversity/.

Ateek, Tanory. "The Nonviolence of the Strong: Muslim Resources for Resistance." In *Resources for Peacemaking in Muslim-Christian Relations: Contributions from the Conflict Transformation Project,* edited by J. Dudley Woodberry and Robin Basselin, 37–57. Pasadena, CA: Fuller Seminary Press, 2006.

Augsburger, David W. *Dissident Discipleship: A Spirituality of Self-Surrender, Love of God, and Love of Neighbor.* Grand Rapids: Brazos, 2006.

Augustine, Daniela C. *The Spirit and the Common Good: Shared Flourishing in the Image of God.* Grand Rapids: Eerdmans, 2019.

Awojobi, Oladayo N. "The Socio-Economic Implications of Boko Haram Insurgency in the North-East of Nigeria." *International Journal of Innovation and Scientific Research* 11 (2014) 144–50.

Azumah, John Alembillah. "Boko Haram in Retrospect." *Islam and Christian-Muslim Relations* 26 (2015) 33–52.

———. *The Legacy of Arab-Islam in Africa: A Quest for Inter-Religious Dialogue.* New York: Oneworld, 2014.

Barrett, David B. *World-Class Cities and World Evangelization.* Birmingham, AL: New Hope, 1986.

Barry, Doug. "American University of Nigeria-Led Adamawa Peacemakers Initiative Receives International Award for Peace Work." PRWeb, 2016. https://www.prweb.com/releases/2016/12/prweb13919279.htm.

Battle, Michael. *Ubuntu: I in You and You in Me.* New York: Seabury, 2009.

BBC. "Nigerian Child Bride 'Poisons Groom.'" *BBC News,* 2014. https://www.bbc.com/news/world-africa-26978872.

Believers Portal. "Jews Are Apes, Christians Are Swine: Saudi Textbooks for Kids Read." *Believers Portal* (blog), 2017. https://believersportal.com/jews-apes-christians-swine-saudi-textbooks-kids-read/.

Bergman, Lars R., and Anna-Karin Andershed. "Predictors and Outcomes of Persistent or Age-Limited Registered Criminal Behavior: A 30-Year Longitudinal Study of a Swedish Urban Population." *Aggressive Behavior* 35 (2009) 164–78.

Berinyuu, Rev Abraham Adu. "Peace Building in Africa: Lessons from Truth Commission." *International Journal of Humanities and Peace* 20 (2004) 24–34.

Bernard, H. Russell. *Research Methods in Anthropology: Qualitative and Quantitative Approaches*. Lanham, MD: AltaMira, 2011.

Bevans, Stephen B. *Models of Contextual Theology*. Maryknoll, NY: Orbis, 1992.

The Bible Society of Egypt. "Special Scripture Distributions: Bibles4Egypt," 2015. http://bibles4egypt.com/two-rows-by-the-sea/.

———. *Two Rows by the Sea*. Cairo, Egypt, 2015. https://vimeo.com/127460692 (accessed: Oct. 24, 2019).

Bidima, Jean-Godefroy. *La Palabre: Une Juridiction de la Parole*. Paris: Michalon, 2017.

Bin Laden, Osama, and Ayman Ẓawāhirī. *The Al Qaeda Reader*. Edited by Raymond Ibrahim. New York: Doubleday, 2007.

Bingham, Rowland V. *Seven Sevens of Years and a Jubilee: The Story of The Sudan Interior Mission*. 3rd ed. Toronto: Evangelical, 1943. https://missiology.org.uk/pdf/e-books/bingham-r-v/seven-sevens-of-years_bingham.pdf.

Biu, A. P. Mai Sule. "A Brief History of Evangelism in the Eastern District." In *Fifty Years in Lardin Gabas, 1923–1973*, 104–6. Kaduna, Nigeria: Baraka, 1974.

Blinzler, Josef. *The Trial of Jesus; the Jewish and Roman Proceedings Against Jesus Christ Described and Assessed from the Oldest Accounts*. Westminster, MD: Newman, 1959.

Boer, Jan Harm. *Missionary Messengers of Liberation in a Colonial Context: A Case Study of the Sudan United Mission*. Amsterdam: Rodopi, 1979.

Bosch, David J. *Transforming Mission: Paradigm Shifts in Theology of Mission*. 20th Anniversary Edition. Maryknoll, NY: Orbis, 2011.

Bourne, Richard. *Nigeria: A New History of a Turbulent Century*. London: Zed, 2015.

Boutros-Ghali, Boutros. "An Agenda for Peace: Preventive Diplomacy, Peacemaking and Peace-Keeping." UN Security Council Forty-seventh Year, 1992. https://documents-dds-ny.un.org/doc/UNDOC/GEN/N92/259/61/pdf/N9225961.pdf?OpenElement.

Bowlby, John. *Attachment and Loss*. New York: Basic, 1982.

Bowlby, Richard. *Fifty Years of Attachment Theory*. The Donald Winnicott Memorial Lectures. London: Karnac, 2004.

Boyd, Gregory A. *Cross Vision: How the Cucifixion of Jesus Makes Sense of Old Testament Violence*. Baltimore, Maryland: Project Muse, 2017.

———. *The Crucifixion of the Warrior God: Interpreting the Old Testament's Violent Portraits of God in Light of the Cross*. Minneapolis: Fortress, 2017.

———. *The Myth of a Christian Nation: How the Quest for Political Power Is Destroying the Church*. Grand Rapids: Zondervan, 2006.

Bozkurt, Süphan, and Yetkin Yildirim. "Fethullah Gülen's Vision for Peace Through Education and Dialogue." In *The Gülen Hizmet Movement: Circumspect Activism in Faith-Based Reform*, 47–60. Newcastle upon Tyne, UK: Cambridge Scholars, 2012.

Bredin, Mark. *Jesus, Revolutionary of Peace: A Nonviolent Christology in the Book of Revelation*. Paternoster Biblical and Theological Monographs. Carlisle, UK: Paternoster, 2003.

Brock-Utne, Birgit. "Peace Research with a Diversity Perspective: A Look to Africa." *International Journal of Peace Studies* 9 (2004) 109–23.

Bruce, F. F. *The Acts of the Apostles: The Greek Text with Introduction and Commentary.* Grand Rapids: Eerdmans, 1990.
Burns, Alan. *History of Nigeria.* London: Allen & Unwin, 1969.
Cahill, Lisa Sowle. "Just Peacemaking: Theory, Practice, and Prospects." *Journal of the Society of Christian Ethics* 23 (2003) 195–212.
Campbell, John. "Boko Haram: Origins, Challenges and Responses." Norwegian Peacebuilding Resource Centre, 2014. http://www.peacebuilding.no/var/ezflow_site/storage/original/application/5cfoebc94fb36d66309681cda24664f9.pdf.
Campbell, John, and Matthew T Page. *Nigeria: What Everyone Needs to Know.* New York: Oxford University Press, 2018.
CAPRO Media. *From Africa to the World: The Capro Story.* Edited by Festus Ndukwe. Lagos, Nigeria: CAPRO Media, 2019.
Casper, Jayson. "Forgiveness: Muslims Moved as Coptic Christians Do the Unimaginable." *Christianity Today*, 2017. https://www.christianitytoday.com/news/2017/april/forgiveness-muslims-moved-coptic-christians-egypt-isis.html.
Cassidy, Jude, and Philip R. Shaver, eds. *Handbook of Attachment: Theory, Research, and Clinical Applications.* New York: Guilford, 2016.
Channer, Alan, dir. *The Imam and The Pastor.* FLT Films, 2006. https://www.cultureunplugged.com/play/2421/The-Imam-and-The-Pastor.
Chatterjee, Margaret. *Gandhi's Religious Thought.* Notre Dame, IN: University of Notre Dame Press, 1983.
Check, Nicasius Achu. "The Politics of Alternative Justice in Post-Genocide Rwanda: Assessing the Gacaca Community Justice System." In *Building Peace from Within: An Examination of Community-Based Peacebuilding and Transitions in Africa*, edited by Sylvester B. Maphosa et al., 137–52. Pretoria: Africa Institute of South Africa, 2014.
Chetty, K., and A. Govindjee. "Freedom of Religion of Children in Private Schools." *Tydskrif vir Regswetenskap* 39 (2014) 31–59.
Chibuko, Patrick Chukwudezie. "Globalization: A Questionable Option for Africa." *African Ecclesiastical Review (AFER)* 49 (2007) 3–18.
Christoffersen, Mogens Nygaard, et al. "An Upbringing to Violence? Identifying the Likelihood of Violent Crime Among the 1966 Birth Cohort in Denmark." *Journal of Forensic Psychiatry and Psychology* 14 (2003) 367.
Christoffersen, Mogens Nygaard, et al. "Violent Life Events and Social Disadvantage: A Systematic Study of the Social Background of Various Kinds of Lethal Violence, Other Violent Crime, Suicide, and Suicide Attempts." *Journal of Scandinavian Studies in Criminology and Crime Prevention* 8 (2007) 157–84.
Church of Christ in the Sudan, Eastern District, ed. *Fifty Years in Lardin Gabas, 1923–1973.* Kaduna, Nigeria: Baraka, 1974.
Clark, Philip. *The Gacaca Courts, Post-Genocide Justice and Reconciliation in Rwanda: Justice Without Lawyers.* Cambridge: Cambridge University Press, 2011.
CNN. "Death Toll Rises to 49 in Palm Sunday Bombings in Egypt." WPTV, 2017. https://www.wptv.com/news/national/isis-claims-responsibility-for-egypts-palm-sunday-church-bombings.
Cohen, D., and B. Crabtree. "Qualitative Research Guidelines Project." Robert Wood Johnson Foundation–Qualitative Research Guidelines Project | Grounded Theory, 2006. http://www.qualres.org/HomeGrou-3589.html.
Collins, Kenneth J., and Jason E. Vickers, eds. *The Sermons of John Wesley: A Collection for the Christian Journey.* Nashville: Abingdon, 2013.

Comolli, Virginia. *Boko Haram: Nigeria's Islamist Insurgency*. London: C. Hurst & Co., 2015.

Conzelmann, Hans. *Acts of the Apostles: A Commentary on the Acts of the Apostles*. Edited by Jay Epp Eldon and R. Matthews Christopher. Translated by James Limburg et al. Philadelphia: Fortress, 1988.

Corbin, Juliet M., and Anselm Strauss. "Grounded Theory Research: Procedures, Canons, and Evaluative Criteria." *Qualitative Sociology* 13 (1990) 3–21.

Crowder, Michael. *A Short History of Nigeria*. New York: F. A. Praeger, 1966.

Daneel, Marthinus L. *African Earthkeepers: Environmental Mission and Liberation in Christian Perspective*. Vol. 2. Pretoria: UNISA, 1999.

———. *African Earthkeepers: Interfaith Mission in Earthcare*. Vol. 1. Pretoria: UNISA, 1998.

———. *African Earthkeepers: Wholistic Interfaith Mission*. Maryknoll, NY: Orbis, 2001.

Danjibo, Nathaniel Dominic. "Islamic Fundamentalism and Sectarian Violence: The 'Maitatsine' and 'Boko Haram' Crises in Northern Nigeria." In *Institute of African Studies, University of Ibadan*, 1–21. Peace and Conflict Studies Paper Series. Ibadan: University of Ibadan, 2009.

Dear, John. *The God of Peace: Toward a Theology of Nonviolence*. Maryknoll, NY: Orbis, 1994.

Doke, Clement M. *The Southern Bantu Languages: Handbook of African Languages*. New York: Routledge, 2018.

Dubensky, Joyce S., and Tanenbaum Center for Interreligious Understanding. *Peacemakers in Action: Profiles in Religious Peacebuilding—Volume II*. New York: Cambridge University Press, 2016.

Durnbaugh, Donald F., ed. *The Brethren Encyclopedia*. Philadelphia: Brethren Encyclopedia, Inc, 1983.

Dyck, Cornelius J. *An Introduction to Mennonite History: A Popular History of the Anabaptists and the Mennonites*. 3rd ed. Scottdale, PA: Herald, 1993.

Ebaugh, Helen Rose. *The Gülen Movement: A Sociological Analysis of a Civic Movement Rooted in Moderate Islam*. London: Springer, 2010.

Ebuziem, Cajetan E. *Doing Ministry in the Igbo Context: Towards an Emerging Model and Method for the Church in Africa*. Bible and Theology in Africa 12. New York: Peter Lang, 2011.

Echekwube, Anthony O. *African Philosophy: A Pathway to Peace and Sustainable Development in Nigeria*. Nigerian Academy of Letters Annual Lecture, 2010. Lagos, Nigeria: Spero, 2010.

Echema, Austin. *Corporate Personality in Traditional Igbo Society and the Sacrament of Reconciliation*. Europäische Hochschulschriften. Reihe XXIII, Theologie; 0721–3409; Bd. 538. New York: Peter Lang, 1995.

Ecuyer, Zack. "Dr. Glen Stassen on Just Peacemaking." https://www.youtube.com/watch?v=TqU7oeiYyUo.

Ekanola, Adebola. "Yorùbá Conception of Peace." In *The Palgrave Handbook of African Philosophy*, edited by Afolayan Adeshina and Toyin Falola, 671–80. New York: Palgrave Macmillan, 2017.

Ekechi, Felix K. "The Medical Factor in Christian Conversion in Africa: Observations from Southeastern Nigeria." *Missiology* 21 (1993) 289–309.

———. *Missionary Enterprise and Rivalry in Igboland, 1857–1914*. London: Cass, 1972.

Elworthy, Scilla. "Dekha Ibrahim Obiturary: Schoolteacher in Rural Kenya who Became a Global Peacemaker." *The Guardian,* August 9, 2011. https://www.theguardian.com/global-development/2011/aug/09/dekha-ibrahim-abdi-obituary.

Enāyat, Ḥamīd. *Modern Islamic Political Thought: The Response of the Shīʻī and Sunnī Muslims to the Twentieth Century.* London: I.B. Tauris, 2005.

Engelsviken, Tormod, et al., eds. *The Church Going Glocal: Proceedings of the Fjellhaug Symposium 2010.* Regnum Edinburgh 2010 Series. Oxford: Regnum, 2011.

Esack, Farid. *On Being a Muslim: Finding a Religious Path in the World Today.* Oxford: Oneworld, 1999.

Esposito, John L., and Natana J. DeLong-Bas. *Shariah: What Everyone Needs to Know.* Oxford: Oxford University Press, 2018.

Esposito, John, and Ihsan Onur Yilmaz. *Islam and Peacebuilding: Gulen Movement Initiatives.* Lanham, MD: Blue Dome, 2013.

Eusebius. *The Ecclesiastical History of Eusebius Pamphilus and an Historical View of the Council of Nice.* Translated by Christian F Crusè and Isaac Boyle. Grand Rapids: Baker, 1979.

———. *Eusebius—The Church History.* Translated by Paul L. Maier. Grand Rapids: Kregel, 2007.

———. *The History of the Church from Christ to Constantine.* New York: Dorset, 1984.

———. *Life of Constantine.* Translated by Averil Cameron and Stuart G Hall. Clarendon Ancient History Series. Oxford: Clarendon, 1999.

Falana, Femi. "How Ex-Gov Modu Sheriff Sponsored Boko Haram." *Premium Times Nigeria,* September 14, 2014. https://www.premiumtimesng.com/news/top-news/167724-how-ex-gov-modu-sheriff-sponsored-boko-haram-falana.html.

Falola, Toyin. *Colonialism and Violence in Nigeria.* Bloomington, IN: Indiana University Press, 2009. http://public.eblib.com/choice/publicfullrecord.aspx?p=474474.

———. *A History of Nigeria.* Cambridge: Cambridge University Press, 2008.

———. *Violence in Nigeria: The Crisis of Religious Politics and Secular Ideologies.* New York: University of Rochester Press, 2009.

Fani-Kayode, Femi. "Lord Lugard's Magic and Flora Shaw's Spell." *Daily Post Nigeria,* September 8, 2015. https://dailypost.ng/2015/09/08/femi-fani-kayode-lord-lugards-magic-and-flora-shaws-spell/.

Farah, Ahmed Yusuf. "The Roots of Reconciliation." *Horn of Africa Bulletin* 6 (1994) n.d.

Farah, Ahmed Yusuf, and I. M. Lewis. *Somalia: The Roots of Reconciliation: Peacemaking Endeavours of Contemporary Lineage Leaders: A Survey of Grassroots Peace Conferences in "Somaliland."* London: ACTIONAID, 1993.

Fee, Gordon D. *Paul's Letter to the Philippians.* Grand Rapids: Eerdmans, 1995.

Fetterman, David M. *Ethnography: Step-by-Step.* Los Angeles: Sage, 2010.

Fiedler, K. *The Story of Faith Missions: From Hudson Taylor to Present-Day Africa.* Eugene, OR: Wipf & Stock, 2011.

Finley, Mark. "New Life for a Dying Nation: Forgiveness, Baptism." https://www.scribd.com/document/38607866/New-Life-for-a-Dying-Nation.

Finney, Mark T. "Servile Supplicium: Shame and the Deuteronomic Curse—Crucifixion in Its Cultural Context." *Biblical Theology Bulletin* 43 (2013) 124–34.

Fischer, Martina, ed. *Peacebuilding and Civil Society in Bosnia-Herzegovina: Ten Years After Dayton.* 2nd ed. Berlin: Lit Verlag, 2007.

Frend, W. H. C. *The Rise of Christianity.* Philadelphia: Fortress, 1984.

Fuest, Veronika. "Liberia's Women Acting for Peace: Collective Action in a War-Affected Country." In *Movers and Shakers: Social Movements in Africa*, 114–37. Leiden: Brill, 2009.

Gabriel, Achadu. "Genocide in Southern Kaduna: Senator La'ah Indicts El-Rufai." http://kingdomnewsng.com/381-genocide-in-southern-kaduna-senator-la-ah-indicts-el-rufai.

Gade, Christian B. N. "What Is Ubuntu? Different Interpretations Among South Africans of African Descent." *South African Journal of Philosophy* 31 (2012) 484–503.

Galtung, Johan. *Peace by Peaceful Means: Peace and Conflict, Development and Civilization*. Thousand Oaks, CA: Sage, 1996.

Gandhi, Mohandas Karamchand. *The Collected Works of Mahatma Gandhi Vol. 62*. New Delhi: The Publications Division, 2000.

———. *Gandhi on Non-Violence: Selected Texts from Mohandas K. Gandhi's Non-Violence in Peace and War*. Edited by Thomas Merton. New Direction Paperbook. New York: New Directions, 2007.

———. *Non-Violence in Peace and War Vol. I*. Ahmedabd, India: Navajivan, 1942.

Gangat, Sharmeen Akbani. "Islam: Religion of Peace or Violence?" http://www.womensmediacenter.com/feature/entry/islam-religion-of-peace-or-violence.

Gann, Lewis H., and Peter Duignan. *Burden of Empire: An Appraisal of Western Colonialism in Africa South of the Sahara*. New York: Frederic A. Praeger, 1967.

Gates, Henry Louis, Jr., and Anthony Appiah Kwame, eds. *Encyclopedia of Africa*. New York: Oxford University Press, 2010.

Gathogo, Julius. *Christ's Hospitality from an African Theological Perspective: Lessons from Christ's Ideal Hospitality for Africa*. Saarbrucken: Lambert Academic, 2011.

Gbowee, Leymah. "Effecting Change through Women's Activism in Liberia." *IDS Bulletin* 40 (2009) 50–53.

Gbowee, Leymah, and Carol Lynn Mithers. *Mighty Be Our Powers: How Sisterhood, Prayer, and Sex Changed a Nation at War*. New York: Beast, 2013.

Gerson, Allan. "Peace Building: The Private Sector's Role." *The American Journal of International Law* 95 (2001) 102–19.

Goldingay, John, and David F. Payne. *A Critical and Exegetical Commentary on Isaiah 40–55*. Vol. 2. London: T. & T. Clark, 2006.

Green, Marci, and Scholes Marc, eds. *Attachment and Human Survival*. London: Karnac, 2004.

Gülen Movement. "What Is the Gülen Movement." http://www.gulenmovement.com/gulen-movement/what-is-the-gulen-movement.

Gutip, Nanwul. *Church of Christ in Nations: COCIN Birth and Growth*. Jos, Nigeria: COCIN, 2017.

Hankela, Elina. *Ubuntu, Migration, and Ministry: Being Human in a Johannesburg Church*. Leiden: Brill, 2014.

Harmsen, Egbert. "Islam, Civil Society and Social Work: Muslim Voluntary Welfare Associations in Jordan Between Patronage and Empowerment." Doctoral thesis, Universiteit Utrecht, 2008.

Johannes Harnischfeger. *Democratization and Islamic Law: The Sharia Conflict in Nigeria*. Frankfurt/New York: Campus, 2008.

Hastings, Adrian. *The Church in Africa, 1450–1950*. Oxford: Clarendon, 1994.

Hedges, Paul. *Controversies in Interreligious Dialogue and the Theology of Religions*. London: Hymns Ancient & Modern, 2010.

Hengel, Martin. *Crucifixion in the Ancient World and the Folly of the Message of the Cross*. Philadelphia: Fortress, 1977.
Hiebert, Paul G. "Critical Contextualization." *Missiology* 12 (1984) 287–96.
Hiskett, Mervyn. *The Sword of Truth: The Life and Times of the Shehu Usuman Dan Fodio*. Evanston, IL: Northwestern University Press, 1994.
Hoechner, Hannah. *Searching for Knowledge and Recognition: Traditional Qur'anic Students (Almajirai) in Kano, Nigeria*. University of Ibadan: French Institute for Research in Africa / Institut Français de Recherche en Afrique (IFRA-Nigeria), 2013.
Hogben, S. J. *An Introduction to the History of the Islamic States of Northern Nigeria*. Ibadan: Oxford University Press, 1967.
Holmes, Jeremy. *John Bowlby and Attachment Theory*. London: Routledge, 1993.
Hord, Fred L, and Jonathan Scott Lee, eds. *I Am Because We Are: Readings in Black Philosophy*. Amherst, MA: University of Massachusetts Press, 1995.
Housley, Norman. "The Crusades and Islam." *Medieval Encounters* 13 (2007) 189–208.
Hugo, Pieter, and Susan Dominus. "Portraits of Reconciliation." *The New York Times*. June 4, 2014, https://www.nytimes.com/interactive/2014/04/06/magazine/06-pieter-hugo-rwanda-portraits.htm.
Huntington, Samuel P. *The Clash of Civilizations and the Remaking of World Order*. New York: Simon & Schuster, 1996.
Ibn 'Abbās, 'Abdullāh, and Muḥammad Al-Fīrūzabādī. *Tanwīr Al-Miqbās Min Tafsīr Ibn 'Abbās*. Translated by Mokrane Guezzou. Amman, Jordan: Royal Aal al-Bayt Institute for Islamic Thought, 2007. https://archive.org/details/TanwirAl-MiqbasMinTafsirIbnAbbasEng.
Ibn Kathir, Hafiz. *Tafsīr Ibn Kathir*. Translated by Sheikh Safiur-Rahman Al-Mubarakpuri. Riyadh: Darussalam, 2016.
Ibrahim Abdi, Dekha. "A Discussion with Dekha Ibrahim, Founder, Wajir Peace and Development Committee, Kenya." Interview by Katherine Marshall, 2010. https://berkleycenter.georgetown.edu/interviews/a-discussion-with-dekha-ibrahim-founder-wajir-peace-and-development-committee-kenya.
Ibrahim, Raymond. "Lies about Islamic Taqiyya (Dissimulation)." Gatestone Institute, September 28, 2015. http://www.gatestoneinstitute.org/6587/carson-taqiyya-dissimulation.
Ijaiya, M. A., et al. "Vesicovaginal Fistula: A Review of Nigerian Experience." *West African Journal of Medicine* 29 (2010) 293–98.
Imam Tawhidi. *Imam Tawhidi—Persecution of Christians in Egypt*. https://www.youtube.com/watch?v=bec7tpBqR-U.
Institute for Economics and Peace. "Global Terrorism Index 2015: Measuring and Understanding Global Terrrorism." http://economicsandpeace.org/wp-content/uploads/2015/11/Global-Terrorism-Index 2015.pdf.
Irvin, Dale T., and Scott Sunquist. *History of the World Christian Movement: Earliest Christianity to 1453*. 3 vols. Maryknoll, NY: Orbis, 2001.
Isichei, Elizabeth Allo. *A History of Nigeria*. London: Longman, 1983.
Ite, Aniefiok E., et al. "Petroleum Exploration and Production: Past and Present Environmental Issues in the Nigeria's Niger Delta." *American Journal of Environmental Protection* 1 (2013) 78–90.
James, I. "Lake Chad as an Instrument of International Co-Operation." In *Borderlands in Africa: A Multidisciplinary and Comparative Focus on Nigeria and West Africa*, edited by A. I Asiwaju and P. O Adeniyi, 309–11. Lagos, Nigeria: University of Lagos Press, 1989.

Jesudasan, Ignatius. *A Gandhian Theology of Liberation*. Maryknoll, NY: Orbis, 1984.

Johnson, Todd M., and Gina A. Zurlo. "World Christian Database." World Christian Database: Center for the Study of Global Christianity, 2018. http://www.worldchristiandatabase.org.proxy.gordonconwell.edu/wcd/home.asp.

———, eds. *World Christian Encyclopedia: Third Edition*. Edinburgh: Edinburgh University Press, 2019.

Josephus, Flavius. *Antiquities of the Jews*. Grand Rapids: Christian Classics Ethereal Library, n.d.

———. *Flavius Josephus: Translation and Commentary Vol. 1b, Judean War 2*. Edited by Steve Mason and Honora Chapman. Leiden: Brill, 2008.

Kadayifci-Orellana, S. Ayse. "Peacebuilding in the Muslim World." In *The Oxford Handbook of Religion, Conflict, and Peacebuilding*, edited by Atalia Omer et al., 430–69. New York: Oxford University Press, 2015.

Kalu, Ogbu, ed. *African Christianity: An African Story*. Trenton, NJ: Africa World, 2007.

———. "Christianity in Africa." In *Christianity: The Complete Guide*, edited by John S Bowden, 2–12. London: Continuum, 2005.

———. *The History of Christianity in West Africa*. New York: Longman, 1980.

Kamali, Mohammad Hashim. *The Dignity of Man: An Islamic Perspective*. Cambridge: The Islamic Texts Society, 2002.

———. *The Middle Path of Moderation in Islam: The Qur'anic Principle of Wasatiyyah*. New York: Oxford University Press, 2015.

Kärkkäinen, Veli-Matti. *Christ and Reconciliation*. Constructive Christian Theology for the Pluralistic World 1. Grand Rapids: Eerdmans, 2013.

———. *Hope and Community*. A Constructive Christian Theology for the Pluralistic World 5. Grand Rapids: Eerdmans, 2017.

Kendhammer, Brandon, and Carmen McCain. *Boko Haram*. Ohio Short Histories of Africa. Athens, OH: Ohio University Press, 2018.

Kenny, Joseph. *Philosophy of the Muslim World: Authors and Principal Themes*. Washington, DC: Council for Research in Values and Philosophy, 2003.

———. "Sharīa and Christianity in Nigeria: Islam and a 'Secular' State." *Journal of Religion in Africa* 26 (1996) 338–64.

———. *The Spread of Islam through North to West Africa, 7th to 19th Centuries: A Historical Survey with Relevant Arab Documents*. Lagos: Dominican, 2000.

Khadduri, Majid. *The Islamic Conception of Justice*. Baltimore, MD: Johns Hopkins University Press, 1984.

Kieh, Goerge Klay, Jr. "Combatants, Patrons, Peacemakers, and the Liberian Civil Conflict." *Studies in Conflict and Terrorism* 15 (1992) 125–43.

———. *Ending the Liberian Civil War: Implications for United States Policy Towards West Africa*. Washington, DC: Transafrica Forum, 1996.

———. *First Liberian Civil War: The Crises of Underdevelopment*. New York: Peter Lang, 2008.

———. *Zones of Conflict in Africa: Theories and Cases*. Westport, CT: Praeger, 2002.

King, Martin Luther, Jr. "Nonviolence and Racial Justice." *Friends Journal: A Quaker Weekly* 4 (1958) 442–44.

———. *Stride Toward Freedom: The Montgomery Story*. Boston: Beacon, 2010.

Kirkup, James. "Democracy Is Route to Peace in Middle East, Says David Cameron." *The Telegraph*, 2011. http://www.telegraph.co.uk/news/worldnews/middleeast/8339054/Democracy-is-route-to-peace-in-Middle-East-says-David-Cameron.html.

Kittel, Gerhard, and Gerhard Friedrich, eds. *Theological Dictionary of the New Testament*. Translated by Geoffrey W Bromiley. Grand Rapids: Eerdmans, 1982.

Koonings, Kees, and Dirk Kruijt. *Megacities: The Politics of Urban Exclusion and Violence in the Global South*. New York: Zed, 2009.

Korieh, Chima J., and Raphael Chijioke Njoku. *Missions, States, and European Expansion in Africa*. New York: Routledge, 2007.

Krabill, James R. "Biblical Approaches to Peace." In *(Un)Common Sounds: Songs of Peace and Reconciliation Among Muslims and Christians*, edited by Roberta Rose King and Sooi Ling Tan, 87–103. Eugene, OR: Cascade, 2014.

Krawietz, Birgit, and Georges Tamer, eds. *Islamic Theology, Philosophy and Law: Debating Ibn Taymiyya and Ibn Qayyim al-Jawziyya*. Berlin: Walter de Gruyter, 2013.

Kraybill, Donald B., et al. *Amish Grace: How Forgiveness Transcended Tragedy*. San Francisco, CA: Jossey-Bass, 2007.

Kukah, Matthew Hassan, and Kathleen McGarvey. "Christian-Muslim Dialogue in Nigeria: Social, Politcal and Theological Discussions." In *Fractured Spectrum: Perspectives on Christian-Muslim Encounters in Nigeria*, edited by Akintunde E. Akinade. New York: Peter Lang, 2013.

Küster, Volker. *Theologie im Kontext: Zugleich ein Versuch über die Minjung-Theologie*. Studia Instituti Missiologici Societatis Verbi Divini. Nettetal, Germany: Steyler, 1995.

Lamb, Christopher. "Abrogation: Muslim and Christian." In *World Christianity in Muslim Encounter: Essays in Memory of David A. Kerr*, 2:16–26. London: Continuum, 2009.

Langmead, Ross. "Reconciliation at the Heart of God and Mission." Myanmar Institute of Theology, 2014. http://rosslangmead.50webs.com/rl/Downloads/Resources/ReconciliationNov12.pdf.

———. "Transformed Relationships: Reconciliation as the Central Model for Mission." *Mission Studies: Journal of the International Association for Mission Studies* 25 (2008) 5–20.

Latourette, Kenneth Scott. *A History of Christianity: Beginnings to 1500, Vol. I*. Peabody, MA: Prince, 2003.

Lederach, John Paul. *Preparing for Peace: Conflict Transformation Across Cultures*. Syracuse, NY: Syracuse University Press, 1995.

Lederach, John Paul, and Angela Jill Lederach. "Let Us Talk: African Contributions to Peacebuilding." In *Building Peace from Within: An Examination of Community-Based Peacebuilding and Transitions in Africa*, edited by Sylvester B. Maphosa et al., 36–52. Pretoria: Africa Institute of South Africa, 2014.

———. *When Blood and Bones Cry Out: Journeys Through the Soundscape of Healing and Reconciliation*. Oxford: Oxford University Press, 2010.

Leedy, Paul D., and Jeanne Ellis Ormrod. *Practical Research: Planning and Design*. Boston: Pearson, 2016.

Leong, Frederick T. L., et al., eds. *Internationalizing the Psychology Curriculum in the United States*. New York: Springer, 2011.

Levinson, David. *Ethnic Groups Worldwide: A Ready Reference Handbook*. Phoenix, AZ: Oryx, 1998.

Liotta, P. H, and James F Miskel. *The Real Population Bomb: Megacities, Global Security and the Map of the Future*. Washington, DC: Potomac, 2012.

Little, David, and Tanenbaum Center for Interreligious Understanding, eds. *Peacemakers in Action: Profiles of Religion in Conflict Resolution*. New York: Cambridge University Press, 2007.

Lloyd, Simon. "The Crusading Movement 1096–1274." In *The Oxford History of the Crusades*, edited by Jonathan Riley-Smith, 35–67. Oxford: Oxford University Press, 1999.

Loimeier, Roman. *Islamic Reform and Political Change in Northern Nigeria*. Evanston, IL: Northwestern University Press, 1997.

Love, Rick. *Glocal: Following Jesus in the 21st Century*. Eugene, OR: Wipf and Stock, 2017.

Lugard, Frederick Dealtry. *The Dual Mandate in British Tropical Africa*. Edinburgh: William Blackwood, 1922.

Mahmud, Muhammad. "Almajiri: Beyond the Rhetorics." http://www.gamji.com/article8000/NEWS8006.htm.

Maiangwa, Benjamin. "Killing in the Name of God? Explaining the Boko Haram Phenomenon in Nigeria." *The Journal of Social, Political, and Economic Studies* 38 (2013) 55–79.

Maina, Wilson Muoha. *Historical and Social Dimensions in African Christian Theology: A Contemporary Approach*. Eugene, OR: Wipf & Stock, 2009.

Mamdani, Mahmood. *When Victims Become Killers: Colonialism, Nativism, and the Genocide in Rwanda*. Princeton, NJ: Princeton University Press, 2014.

Mandryk, Jason. *Operation World*. Colorado Springs, CO: Biblica, 2010.

Mantzikos, Ioannis. "Boko Haram Attacks in Nigeria and Neighbouring Countries: A Chronology of Attacks." *Perspectives on Terrorism* 8 (2014) n.d.

Maphosa, Sylvester B., et al., eds. *Building Peace from Within: An Examination of Community-Based Peacebuilding and Transitions in Africa*. Pretoria: Africa Institute of South Africa, 2014.

Martin, Ralph P. *Carmen Christi: Philippians Ii. 5-11 in Recent Interpretation and in the Setting of Early Christian Worship*. Cambridge: Cambridge University Press, 2005.

Mbanda, Laurent., and Steve Wamberg. *Committed to Conflict: The Destruction of the Church in Rwanda*. London: SPCK, 1997.

Mbaya, Isheku P. K. "A Brief History of the Coming of the Church of the Brethren Mission into Lardin Gabas North-Eastern State of Nigeria." In *Fifty Years in Lardin Gabas, 1923–197*, 3–6. Kaduna, Nigeria: Baraka, 1974.

Mbefo, Luke N. "Theology and Inculturation: The Nigerian Experience." *Cross Currents* 37 (1987) 393–403.

Mbembe, Joseph-Achille. *On the Postcolony*. Berkeley, CA: University of California Press, 2001.

Mbiti, John S. *African Religions and Philosophy*. Garden City, NY: Doubleday, 1970.

McGavran, Donald A. *Understanding Church Growth*. Grand Rapids: Eerdmans, 1980.

Mikailu, Naziru. "Making Sense of Nigeria's Fulani-Farmer Conflict." BBC, 2016. http://www.bbc.com/news/world-africa-36139388.

Moila, Moeahabo P. *Challenging Issues in African Christianity*. Pretoria: C.B. Powell Bible Centre, 2005.

Montanari, Franco. *The Brill Dictionary of Ancient Greek*. Edited by Madeleine Goh and Chad M Schroeder. Leiden: Brill, 2015.

Morris, Catherine. "What Is Peacebuilding? One Definition." http://www.peacemakers.ca/publications/peacebuildingdefinition.html.

Moyo, Sam, and Mine Yoichi, eds. *What Colonialism Ignored: African Potentials for Resolving Conflicts in Southern Africa*. Bamenda, Cameroon: Langaa Research, 2016.

Muhammad, Garba. "Four Killed as Youth Attack Shiites in Kaduna." *Premium Times Nigeria*, 2016. http://www.premiumtimesng.com/news/headlines/212579-four-killed-youth-attack-shiites-kaduna.html

Muir, Jim. "Nigeria's Boko Haram Pledges Allegiance to Islamic State." *BBC*, 2015. http://www.bbc.com/news/world-africa-31784538.

Mulders, Arne. "Crushed but Not Defeated: The Impact of Persistent Violence on the Church in Northern Nigeria." Open Doors International, 2016. http://www.opendoorsuk.org/persecution/worldwatch/nigeria/documents/nigeria-report-48.pdf.

Murray, Jocelyn, ed. *Cultural Atlas of Africa*. New York: Facts on File, 1981.

Mutisi, Martha. "Addressing Ethno-Political Conflicts Through the Concept of Abanyarwanda: A Case of 'Ethnic Amnesia' in Rwanda?" In *Building Peace from Within: An Examination of Community-Based Peacebuilding and Transitions in Africa*, edited by Sylvester B. Maphosa et al., 119–36. Pretoria: Africa Institute of South Africa, 2014.

Mwaruvie, John Mwaniki. "Mission of the Church in Africa: Peacemaking and Restorative Justice." *African Ecclesial Review* 50 (2008) 266–83.

Nkwede, Joseph Okwesili, et al. "Effects of Boko Haram Insurgency on the Socio-Economic Development in Nigeria." *International Journal of Sustainable Development (OIDA)* 08 (2015) 59–72.

Nolt, Steven M. *The Amish: A Concise Introduction*. Baltimore, MD: Johns Hopkins University Press, 2016.

Nutting, Anthony. *Scramble for Africa: The Great Trek to the Boer War*. London: Constable, 1970.

Obasi, Nnamdi. "New Risks on Nigeria's Shiite Fault Line." *International Crisis Group—In Pursuit of Peace* (blog), 2015. https://www.crisisgroup.org/africa/west-africa/nigeria/new-risks-nigeria-s-shiite-fault-line.

O'Brien, Peter Thomas. *The Epistle to the Philippians: A Commentary on the Greek Text*. Grand Rapids: Eerdmans, 1991.

Odo, Linus Ugwu. "Boko Haram and Insecurity in Nigeria: The Quest for a Permanent Solution." *African Research Review* 9 (2015) 47–61.

Ojo, Jide. "Nigerians and the Politics of Stomach Infrastructure." *IFES Nigeria: Political Finance Newsletter* 5 (2014) 1–2.

Okoro, Efehi Raymond. "Terrorism and Governance Crisis: The Boko Haram Experience in Nigeria." *African Journal on Conflict Resolution (AJCR)* 14 (2014) 103–28.

Oloyede, Is haq O. "In Search of a Peaceful Society." Presented at the University of Lagos Muslim Alumni Luncheon, Lagos, Nigeria, 2000.

———. "Secularism and Religion: Conflict and Compromise (An Islamic Perspective)." *Islam and Modern Age* 18 (1987) 21–38.

———. "That All May Be One." In *Islamic Perspectives on Contemporary Issues*, edited by Misbau O. Junaid, 37–44. Lagos: University of Lagos, 1999.

Omar, Abdul Rashied. "Islam Beyond Tolerance: The Qur'anic Concept of Ta'aruf." *Brethren Life and Thought* 53 (2008) 15–20.

Omega Fire Ministries. *Apostle Suleman Speaks On Biafra, Southern Kaduna Killings; Tells Members to Kill Fulani Herdsmen,* 2017. https://www.youtube.com/watch?v=crkQJLKwWmo.

Omoruyi, Omo. "The Origin of Nigeria: God of Justice Not Associated with and Unjust Political Order—Appeal to President Obasanjo Not to Rewrite Nigerian History. (PART 1)." *ReworkNigeria* (blog), 2010. http://reworknigeria.blogspot.com/2010_01_19_archive.html.

Onuoha, Freedom. "Porous Borders and Boko Haram's Arms Smuggling Operations in Nigeria." Al Jazeera Center of Studies, 2013. http://studies.aljazeera.net/ResourceGallery/media/Documents/2013/9/8/20139810737330580Porous%20Borders_bokoharam.pdf.

Ormerod, Neil, and Shane Clifton. *Globalization and the Mission of the Church: Ecclesiological Investigations.* London: T. & T. Clark, 2009.

OSAGI, Office of the Special Adviser on Gender Issues and Advancement of Women. "Landmark Resolution on Women, Peace and Security: Security Council Resolution 1325." http://www.un.org/womenwatch/osagi/wps/.

Oyebamiji, Isaac O. *Travail and Triumph: The Story of CAPRO.* Jos, Nigeria: Tishbeth, 2012.

Paden, John N. *Muslim Civic Cultures and Conflict Resolution: The Challenge of Democratic Federalism in Nigeria.* Washington, DC: Brookings, 2005.

Paffenholz, Thania, and Kristina Lundqvist. *Community-Based Bottom-up Peacebuilding: The Development of the Life and Peace Institute's Approach to Peacebuilding and Lessons Learned from the Somalia Experience (1990–2000).* Uppsala: Life & Peace Institute, 2006.

Pakenham, Thomas. *The Scramble for Africa: White Man's Conquest of the Dark Continent from 1876 to 1912.* New York: Random, 1991.

Palmer, Herbert R. *Sudanese Memoirs: Being Mainly Translations of a Number of Arabic Manuscripts Relating to the Central and Western Sudan.* London: Frank Cass, 1967.

Parliamentary Assembly of Bosnia–Herzegovina. "Law on Freedom of Religion and Legal Position of Churches and Religious Communities in Bosnia and Herzegovina, Pub. L. No. Official Gazette of Bosnia and Herzegovina No. 5/04; Sarajevo (2004)." http://www.mrv.ba/upload/attachments/law_on_religion_VO1.pdf.

Paul VI, Pope. "Eucharistic Celebration at the Conclusion of the Symposium Organized by the Bishops of Africa: Homily of Paul VI." Vatican City: Libreria Editrice Vaticana, 1969. https://w2.vatican.va/content/paul-vi/en/homilies/1969/documents/hf_p-vi_hom_19690731.pdf.

Perham, Margery. "Frederick Lugard: British Colonial Administrator." Encyclopedia Britannica, 1998. https://www.britannica.com/biography/Frederick-Lugard.

———. *Native Administration in Nigeria.* London: Oxford University Press, 1937.

Perkins, Judith. *The Suffering Self: Pain and Narrative Representation in Early Christian Era.* London: Routledge, 1995.

Ploughshares, Project. "Nigeria (1990—First Combat Deaths)," 2012. http://ploughshares.ca/pl_armedconflict/nigeria-1990-first-combat-deaths/.

Pohl, Christine D. *Living into Community: Cultivating Practices That Sustain Us.* Grand Rapids: Eerdmans, 2012.

Pöntinen, Mari-Anna. *African Theology as Liberating Wisdom: Celebrating Life and Harmony in the Evangelical Lutheran Church in Botswana.* Leiden: Brill, 2013.

Quetteville, Harry de. "Christians Still 'Swine' and Jews 'Apes' in Saudi Schools." *The Telegraph*, 2006. http://www.telegraph.co.uk/news/worldnews/middleeast/saudiarabia/1522286/Christians-still-swine-and-Jews-apes-in-Saudi-schools.html.

Quinn, Charlotte A., and Frederick Quinn. *Pride, Faith, and Fear: Islam in Sub-Saharan Africa*. New York: Oxford University Press, 2003.

Ray, Benjamin C. *African Religions: Symbol, Ritual, and Community*. Upper Saddle River, NJ: Prentice Hall, 2000.

Reisacher, Evelyne A. *Joyful Witness in the Muslim World: Sharing the Gospel in Everyday Encounters*. Mission in Global Community. Grand Rapids: Baker Academic, 2016.

———. "The Process of Attachment Between the Algerians and French within the Christian Community in France." PhD diss., Fuller Theological Seminary, 2001.

Renard, John. *Islam and Christianity: Theological Themes in Comparative Perspective*. Berkeley, CA: University of California Press, 2011.

———, ed. *Islamic Theological Themes: A Primary Source Reader*. Oakland, CA: University of California Press, 2014.

Renders, Marleen. *Consider Somaliland: State-Building with Traditional Leaders and Institutions*. African Social Studies Series 26. Leiden: Brill, 2012.

Reticker, Gini. *Pray the Devil Back to Hell*. Documentary, 2008.

Richardson, Don. *Peace Child*. Ventura, CA: Regal, 1976.

Riley-Smith, Jonathan. *The Crusades, Christianity, and Islam*. New York: Columbia University Press, 2011.

———. *The Crusades: A History*. 2nd ed. New Haven, CT: Yale University Press, 2005.

———, ed. *The Oxford History of the Crusades*. Oxford: Oxford University Press, 1999.

———, ed. *The Oxford Illustrated History of the Crusades*. Oxford: Oxford University Press, 1995.

Robinson, Ronald, et al. *Africa and the Victorians: The Official Mind of Imperialism*. 2nd ed. London: Macmillan, 1981.

The Royal Aal Al-Bayt Institute for Islamic Thought. *Common Word Between Us and You, A*. MABDA · English Monograph Series 4. Amman, Jordan: The Royal Aal Al-Bayt Institute for Islamic Thought, 2009. http://rissc.jo/docs/Common_word.pdf.

———. *Common Word Between Us and You: 5-Year Anniversary Edition, A*. MABDA · English Monograph Series 20. Amman, Jordan: The Royal Aal al-Bayt Institute for Islamic Thoughtz, 2012. http://rissc.jo/docs/20-acw/20-ACW-5.pdf.

Rucyahana, John, and John Riordan. *The Bishop of Rwanda*. Nashville: Thomas Nelson, 2007.

Runciman, Steven. *A History of the Crusades*. London: Penguin, 1965.

Sahih International, trans. *Al-Qur'an al-Kareem—* القرآن الكريم. Jeddah, Saudi Arabia: Saheeh International, 1997.

Sanneh, Lamin, and Joel Carpenter, eds. *The Changing Face of Christianity: Africa, the West, and the World*. New York: Oxford University Press, 2005.

Schoeman, Marelize. "The African Concept of Ubuntu and Restorative Justice." In *Reconstructing Restorative Justice Philosophy*, edited by Theo Gavrielides and Vasso Artinopoulou, 291–310. Farnham, UK: Ashgate, 2013.

Schreiter, Robert J. *Reconciliation: Mission and Ministry in a Changing Social Order*. Maryknoll, NY: Orbis, 1992.

Senior, Donald. *Why the Cross?* Edited by Joel B Green. Reframing New Testament Theology. Nashville: Abingdon, 2014.

Setton, Kenneth M. *A History of the Crusades*. 2nd ed. Madison, WI: University of Wisconsin Press, 1969.

Shah-Kazemi, Reza. *The Spirit of Tolerance in Islam*. London: I.B. Tauris, 2012.

Shenk, David W. *Christian. Muslim. Friend.: Twelve Paths to Real Relationship*. Harrisonburg, VA: Herald, 2014.

Shenk, Wilbert. "Contextual Theology: The Last Frontier." In *The Changing Face of Christianity: Africa, the West, and the World*, edited by Lamin Sanneh and Joel Carpenter, 191–212. New York: Oxford University Press, 2005.

Smith, Gary V. *The New American Commentary: An Exegetical Exposition of Scripture Vol. 15B Isaiah 40–66*. Nashville: B&H, 2009.

Smock, David R., ed. *Religious Contributions to Peacemaking*. New York: Nova Science, 2010.

Spencer, M. "Border and State Insecurity." In *Countering Terrorism and Insurgency in the 21st Century: International Perspectives*, edited by James F Forest, 2:109–26. Westport, CT: Praeger, 2007.

Stackhouse, Max L. *Apologia: Contextualization, Globalization, and Mission in Theological Education*. Grand Rapids: Eerdmans, 1988.

Stark, Rodney. *The Triumph of Christianity: How the Jesus Movement Became the World's Largest Religion*. New York: HarperOne, 2011.

Stassen, Glen Harold. *Just Peacemaking: The New Paradigm for the Ethics of Peace and War*. Cleveland: Pilgrim, 2008.

———. *Just Peacemaking: Ten Practices for Abolishing War*. Cleveland, OH: Pilgrim, 1998.

———. "The Unity, Realism, and Obligatoriness of Just Peacemaking Theory." *Journal of the Society of Christian Ethics* 23 (2003) 171–94.

Stewart, David W., and Prem N. Shamdasani. *Focus Groups: Theory and Practice*, 2015.

Strauss, Anselm L., and Juliet M. Corbin. "Grounded Theory Methodology." In *Handbook of Qualitative Research*, edited by Norman K. Denzin and Yvonna S. Lincoln, 217–85. Thousand Oaks, CA: Sage, 1994.

Sulaiman, Ibraheem. *A Revolution in History: The Jihad of Usman Dan Fodio*. London: Mansell, 1986.

———. "The Moment of Truth in Nigeria: Truth Is That You Can Build Nothing on the Debris of Western Imperialism." *Impact International* n.d. (1984) 13–26.

"Sunnah.Com." http://sunnah.com/.

Swinton, John, and Harriet Mowat. *Practical Theology and Qualitative Research*. London: SCM, 2016.

Ṭāhā, Maḥmūd Muḥammad. *The Second Message of Islam*. Translated by Abdullahi Ahmed An-Naʿim. Syracuse, NY: Syracuse University Press, 1987.

Taiwo, Olufemi. *How Colonialism Preempted Modernity in Africa*. Bloomington, IN: Indiana University Press, 2010.

Tasie, G. O. M. *Christian Missionary Enterprise in the Niger Delta 1864–1918*. Leiden: Brill, 1978.

Tawadros II, Pope. "The 2017 Papal Message of the Glorious Feast of the Resurrection." *St. Mary and St. Antonios Coptic Orthodox Church* (blog), 2017. https://copticchurch.org/the-2017-papal-message-of-the-glorious-feast-of-the-resurrection/.

Tennent, Timothy C. *Theology in the Context of World Christianity: How the Global Church Is Influencing the Way We Think about and Discuss Theology*. Grand Rapids: Zondervan, 2007.

Thayer-Bacon, Barbara J. *Relational "(e)Pistemologies."* New York: Peter Lang, 2003.

Thomas, Lynn M. *Politics of the Womb: Women, Reproduction, and the State in Kenya.* Berkeley, CA: University of California Press, 2003.

"A Threat to the Entire Country." *The Economist*, 2012. http://www.economist.com/node/21563751#print.

Thurston, Alexander. *Boko Haram: The History of an African Jihadist Movement.* Princeton, NJ: Princeton University Press, 2019.

Tibi, Bassam. *Islamism and Islam.* New Haven, CT: Yale University Press, 2012.

Tidrick, Kathryn. *Gandhi: A Political and Spiritual Life.* London: Verso, 2013.

Tongeren, Paul J. M. van, Malin Brenk, and Marte Hellema, eds. *People Building Peace II: Successful Stories of Civil Society.* Project of the European Centre for Conflict Prevention. Boulder, CO: Lynne Reinner, 2005.

Townsend, Tim. "Forgiving the Unforgivable in Rwanda." CNN Belief Blog, 2014. http://religion.blogs.cnn.com/2014/04/13/ministering-to-evil-and-forgiving-the-unforgivable-in-rwanda/.

Turaki, Yusufu. *An Introduction to the History of SIM/ECWA in Nigeria, 1893–1993.* Nigeria: Yusufu Turaki Foundation, 1993.

Tutu, Desmond. *No Future Without Forgiveness.* New York: Doubleday, 2000.

Tyerman, Christopher. *Fighting for Christendom: Holy War and the Crusades.* Oxford: Oxford University Press, 2004.

———. *God's War: A New History of the Crusades.* Cambridge, MA: Harvard University Press, 2006.

Ukpong, Justin S. *African Theologies Now: A Profile.* Eldoret, Kenya: Gaba-AMECEA, 1984.

———. "Contextualisation: A Historical Survey." *African Ecclesiastical Review (AFER)* 29 (1987) 278–86.

Umaru, Thaddeus Byimui. *Christian-Muslim Dialogue in Northern Nigeria: A Socio-Political and Theological Consideration.* Philadelphia: Xlibris, 2013.

Vanier, Jean. *Community and Growth.* New York: Paulist, 1989.

Voice of America. "Nigerian Child Bride Accused of Killing Husband to Be Freed." *Voice of America*, 2015. https://www.voanews.com/africa/nigerian-child-bride-accused-killing-husband-be-freed.

Volf, Miroslav. *The End of Memory: Remembering Rightly in a Violent World.* Grand Rapids: Eerdmans, 2006.

———. *Exclusion and Embrace: A Theological Exploration of Identity, Otherness, and Reconciliation.* Nashville: Abingdon, 1996.

Volf, Miroslav, et al., eds. *Common Word: Muslims and Christians on Loving God and Neighbor, A.* Grand Rapids: Eerdmans, 2010.

Wallis, Andrew. *Silent Accomplice: The Untold Story of France's Role in the Rwandan Genocide.* London: I.B. Tauris, 2006. http://public.eblib.com/choice/publicfull record.aspx?p=677136.

Walls, Andrew F. *The Cross-Cultural Process in Christian History: Studies in the Transmission and Appropriation of Faith.* Maryknoll, NY: Orbis, 2002.

Wariboko, Nimi. "Christian-Muslim Relations and the Ethos of State Formation in West Africa." In *Dynamics of Muslim Worlds: Regional, Theological and Missiological Perspectives*, edited by Evelyne A. Reisacher, 57–81. Missiological Engagement. Downers Grove, IL: IVP Academic, 2017.

Waters, Malcolm. *Globalization.* New York: Routledge, 2001.

Werner, Dietrich, et al., eds. *Handbook of Theological Education in World Christianity: Theological Perspectives, Regional Surveys, Ecumenical Trends*. Eugene, OR: Wipf & Stock, 2010.

Weybrecht, Giselle. "Adamawa Peacemakers Initiative and the American University of Nigeria," 2016. https://primetime.unprme.org/2016/07/04/adamawa-peacemakers-initiative-and-the-american-university-of-nigeria/.

Whiteman, Darrell L. "Contextualization: The Theory, the Gap, the Challenge." *International Bulletin of Missionary Research* 21 (1997) 2–7.

Wilken, Robert Louis. *The First Thousand Years: A Global History of Christianity*. New Haven, CT: Yale University Press, 2012.

Williams, Daniel, and Eric Guttschuss. "Spiraling Violence: Boko Haram Attacks and Security Forces Abuses in Nigeria." New York: Human Rights Watch, 2012. https://www.hrw.org/sites/default/files/reports/nigeria1012webwcover_0.pdf.

Williams, Demetrius K. *Enemies of the Cross of Christ: The Terminology of the Cross and Conflict in Philippians*. London: Sheffield Academic, 2002.

Williams, Rowan. "What Is Christianity?" Dr. Rowan Williams 104th Archbishop of Canterbury, 2005. http://rowanwilliams.archbishopofcanterbury.org/articles.php/1087/what-is-christianity.

Woodberry, J. Dudley, and Robin Basselin, eds. *Resources for Peacemaking in Muslim-Christian Relations: Contributions from the Conflict Transformation Project*. Pasadena, CA: Fuller Seminary Press, 2006.

Yagboyaju, Dhikru Adewale, and Adeoye O. Akinola. "Nigerian State and the Crisis of Governance: A Critical Exposition." *Sage Open* 9 (2019) 1–10.

Yoder, John Howard. *Nevertheless: The Varieties and Shortcomings of Religious Pacifism*. Scottdale, PA: Herald, 1992.

———. *The Politics of Jesus: Vicit Agnus Noster*. 2nd ed. Grand Rapids: Eerdmans, 1994.

———. *The War of the Lamb: The Ethics of Nonviolence and Peacemaking*. Edited by Glen Harold Stassen et al. Grand Rapids: Brazos, 2009.

Yong, Amos. *Hospitality and the Other: Pentecost, Christian Practices, and the Neighbor*. Maryknoll, NY: Orbis, 2008.

———. *In the Days of Caesar: Pentecostalism and Political Theology*. Grand Rapids: Eerdmans, 2010.

———. *The Spirit Poured out on All Flesh: Pentecostalism and the Possibility of Global Theology*. Grand Rapids: Baker Academic, 2005.

Zaikman, Yuliana, et al.. "The Influence of Early Experiences and Adult Attachment on the Exhibition of the Sexual Double Standard." *Sexuality and Culture: An Interdisciplinary Quarterly* 20 (2016) 425–45.

Zunkel, C. Wayne. "Church Growth: 'Not Another Evangelistic Fad.'" *Brethren Life and Thought* 25 (1980) 223–36.

Index

Abanyarwanda concept, 161–63, 192, 220, 241
Aba Women's Riot of 1929, 164, 167
Abdullah bin Umar, 110
'Abdur Rahman bin Abi Laila, 109
Abel Haleem, Muhammad, 97
Abimbola, 'Wande, 180
Abou El Fadl, Khaled, 11, 98–99, 107, 112–13, 117, 136–38, 149, 237–38
abrogation *(naskh)*, 119–20
Abu, Dooshima, 177
Abu Hamid, Ibrahim, 129
Abu Huraira, 111, 113
Abuja, 19
Abu-Nimer, Mohammed, 110–12, 131, 139, 238
Abū Zayd, Nasr, 99
Abū Zayd, Naṣr Ḥāmi, 64, 103
Accad, Martin, 96, 142
Accountability Committee, Nickel Mines, 230
Accra, Ghana, 164–67
Achebe, Chinua, 172
acute violence, 10–11, 23, 53–54, 66, 70, 235, 237
    background to study, 1–3
    carrefour of Nigeria's political and religious histories, 61–69

    Christ's followers' response to, 200, 213–18
    and colonialism, 29–30
    community power, 181–83
    contexts of for peacebuilding in Nigeria, 55–61
    contextual theology, 85–86
    dan Fodio's jihad, 39
    gun violence, 227–31
    hospitality as an African means for peacebuilding, 242
    Jesus's cross, 196, 205
    justice and peacebuilding, 111
    major areas of, 12
    Muslim Samaritan, 238
    preventive peacebuilding, 152
    research procedure, 18–20
    scope of study, 13–14
    seeking to protect a religious other from, 268
    sexual violence and abuse, 168
    significance of study, 14–16
    statement of research problem, 4–5
    staurocentric forgiveness, 218–31
    staurocentric practices for the church in Nigeria, 7, 255–74
    See also Boko Haram; Fulani herdsmen; Islamist acute violence; nonviolent resistance philosophies

Index

Adamawa Peacemakers Initiative (API), 265–67
Adamawa State, 12–13, 19, 265–66
Adeeb, Amr, 226
Adetoun, Bolanle, 59
Adhhémar of Monteil, 210
adl (justice), 110–11, 116, 131, 139, 238
Afigbo, Adiele E., 78–79, 136
Afolabi, Babatunde Tolu, 166–67
African American Black theology, 82
African concepts for peacebuilding, 6, 14, 16–17, 20, 254–55
  Abanyarwanda concept, 161–63, 192, 220, 241
  carrefour with peacebuilding-contextual theology, 192, 257
  community festivals, 171, 181, 185–87, 192, 241
  community power in, 181–85
  cross-clan marriages, 154–56, 171, 185, 190–92, 241, 243, 253–54
  Gacacha court system, 158–63, 192, 220, 241–42
  hospitality, 112–14, 131, 171, 174–81, 185, 192, 238, 241–42, 248–52, 271
  Jesus's *staurocentric* model, 244–45
  Liberian women, 163–69
  nabadraadin–guurti concept, 153–57, 173, 190, 192, 241–42, 257
  nzu concept, 171–74, 185, 189, 192, 241–42, 250–51
  ubuntu, 118, 146–53, 153n24, 155, 185, 192, 241, 245–47, 261, 264
African contexts of violence, 81, 93, 145, 171, 193, 254
African contextual theologies, 6, 70, 80, 81–87, 247. *See also* nonviolent resistance philosophies
African cultures and contexts, 76–77, 82, 86, 147, 174–75, 185, 192
African Earthkeepers (Daneel), 263
African Muslims, 117–24, 131–35
African national movements, 25
African political states, 158
African Religions (Ray), 31
African Religions and Philosophy (Mbiti), 146
African traditional community, 247–48
African traditional ethics of the stranger. See *nzu* concept
African traditional religions. *See* ethno-religious practices
African worldview of the individual. See *ubuntu*
Agape organization, 258
agency of community festivals and rituals, 171, 181, 185–87, 192, 241
Agenda for Peace (Boutros-Ghali), 8
Aḥādīth (traditions of the prophet of Islam), 97, 98, 107–17, 118, 139, 141
ahimsa (nonviolence). *See* nonviolent resistance philosophies
Ahmed (participant), 41–42, 41n70, 174–75
Akinade, Akintunde E., 55, 176–77, 272
"A Kinder, Gentler Islam?" (An-Naʻim), 122
àlààfíà, 180–81
Al-Azhar University, 129–30
Al-Bara, 108
Al-Bukhari, Sahih, 108–12
Alexandria, Egypt, 225
al-Faisal, Turki, 129
Al-Jalayan, 101
al-Ka'b, Abu Shuraih, 113
Al-Kameni, 42
Al-Kāshānī, Tafsīr ʿAbd al-Razzāq, 100–101
Allahcracy, 11, 11n36, 128
al-majiri phenomenon, 30–31, 38, 43–45, 67–68, 183–84, 259, 261
Al-Musawi, Dhiyaa, 102–3, 128, 142n163
Aloma, Idris (Kin), 32
Al-Shabaab, 56, 68
Amadu (participant), 178
American University of Nigeria (AUN), 265
Americo-Liberians, 167–68
Amish, 88, 219, 227–31
Amish Grace (Kraybill), 227

Index

Amish Studies, 228
Anabaptists, 6, 70, 87–90, 228–30, 246, 264
Anas bin Malik, 114
Anderson, Lisa, 56
Andraus (participant), 178
Anglicans, 46, 75–76
Angola, 259
Aniagolu, A. N., 38
An-Naʻim, Abdullahi Ahmed, 114, 119–22, 124
Ansaru group, 3
Anthony, E. A., 49
Anyanwu, Oyedolapo, 187–88
apartheid, 82, 147, 149, 152, 192
applying *ubuntu*, 150–51
Arab Spring, 224
Archbishop of Verhbosan-Sarajevo, 126
Arusha Courts, 159, 162, 192
Ashafa, Muhammed, 101, 124, 133–35, 239, 265, 267–68
Ateek, Tanory, 106n34, 108
attachment theme, 180, 180n37, 187, 267
Attalah, Ramez, 225
At-Taqiyya fiʼl-Islam (Murkaram), 117
Attitudes of Religions and Ideologies Toward the Outsider (Swidler and Mojzes), 180
Augsburger, David, 252–53
Augustine, Daniela, 258
authentic theology, 73–74
auto-determination, 26
Ayuba (participant), 262–63
Azumah, John, 41, 67

Banfield, Alex W., 49
baptism, 228–29
base animal drives, 63–66, 121, 239
Bateman, Ambrose, 49
Battle, Michael, 149
Bauchi State, 12
BBC News online, 41
Bello, Muhammad, 33
belongingness, 16, 16n43, 27, 161
beneficence or goodness (*iḥsan*), 110–11, 139–40, 224, 238
Benue, Nigeria, 3

Berbers of the central Atlas Mountains, 75
Berbers of the Rif, 75
Berinyuu, Abraham Adu, 8
Berlin Conference of 1884–1885, 27, 60
Bernard, H. Russell, 20, 21
Bevans, Stephen, 72–73, 78
Biafra, 26, 79
Bible Society of Egypt, 224–25
Bibles4Egypt.com, 225
bibliographical research, 7, 13, 17, 18
Bida, 48
Bidima, Jean-Godefroy, 156–57
Bingham, Rowland V., 47–49
The Bishop of Rwanda (Rucyahana), 159–62
Blinzler, Josef, 197–98
Boer, Jan Harm, 50
Boi, 50
Boko Haram, 1–3, 4, 12, 14, 18, 19, 30–31, 33, 38–42, 44, 45, 53, 56, 60, 67–68, 122, 151, 263, 268, 273n97
Boonstra, Shawn, 221
Borno State, 12–13, 14, 19, 40, 42, 52–53, 52n116, 178, 181n44, 190
Boroma Conference, 156
Bosch, David, 72
Bosnia-Herzegovina (BiH), 126–30, 240, 258
Bosnia-Herzegovina Law on Religious Freedom, 130, 240
Bourne, Richard, 1, 25–26
Boutros-Ghali, Boutros, 8
Boyd, George A., 89–90, 217, 271
Boyle Heights, 252–53, 272
Bredin, Mark, 93
The Brethren Encyclopedia, 52
British colonialism, 1, 5, 24, 30, 57, 60, 61–62, 93–94, 157. *See also* missionary efforts
Brock-Utne, Birgit, 147–48, 157
brokenness, 114n64, 233–35, 238
Bruce, F. F., 200, 202n24
Buhari, Muhammadu, 2, 79
Building Peace from Within (Mutisi), 153, 160–61
Bukuru, Plateau State, 50–51

Bura people, 51–52, 178
Burke, Homer L. and Marguerite, 51
Burns, Alan, 31
Burt, John, 49

Cahill, Lisa S., 92–93, 246–47
Cain and Abel, 103–5, 108, 139
Cameron, David, 127
Cameroun, 41, 53, 60, 151
Campbell, John, 42
Canada, 48, 50, 228
carrefour
    of African concepts with peacebuilding-contextual theology, 192–93
    Christian-Muslim carrefour for peacebuilding, 136–41
    and forgiveness, 257
    of Nigeria's political and religious histories, 61–69
    obedience and suffering, 198
    staurocentric carrefour with peacebuilding, 231–35, 237–55
Carson, Ben, 117
Cartesian epistemology, 146–47
Casper, Jayson, 226
Caxito, Angola, 259
Cerić, Mustafa, 126–27
Chad, 41, 60, 151
Chapman, Honora, 195
charity (*sadaqa*), 111–14
Check, Nicasius Achu, 159–60
Chibok, 40, 52, 254n42
Chibuko, Patrick, 80
children, 43–45, 102, 182–85, 188–91, 228–30
Chirac, Jacques, 135
Christianity, 13
    African contextual theologies, 81
    artisans of peacebuilding, 85, 239
    Christian-Muslim carrefour for peacebuilding, 135, 136–43
    Christian-Muslim engagement, 55–69, 197, 211–12, 214–16, 254, 265
    Christian-Muslim women, 165, 272
    community festivals, 186
    Constantine and the Crusades, 203–13
    contextual theology, 71–77
    cross in contexts, 213–18
    Egyptian Copts, 219, 225
    and hospitality, 176–80, 248–55
    and Islam in Nigeria's religious history, 30–54
    loving and blessing Muslim communities, 258–64, 268
    missionary efforts, 28–29, 45–54, 72, 81
    Nigeria's religious history, 69
    public and political square, 269–70
    and Scripture, 104–5, 196–97
Christian-Muslim Dialogue in Northern Nigeria (Umaru), 37
church in Nigeria, 2, 12–13
    al-majiri phenomenon, 68
    Christianity in Nigeria's religious history, 45–54
    missiological significance of study, 15–17
    research methodology, 17–19
    research problem, 4–7
    scope of study, 13–14
    staurocentric practices for, 255–74
Church Missionary Society (CMS), 46, 69
Church of Christ in Nations (COCIN), 3–4, 12–13, 18, 31, 46–47, 49–51, 53
Church of Christ in Nigeria. *See* Church of Christ in Nations (COCIN)
Church of England, 46, 69
Church of Nigeria (Anglican Communion), 46
Church of the Brethren. *See* Ekklesiyar Yan'uwa a Nigeria (EYN)
citation from transcribed interviews, 20–21
civil societal actions, 264–68
civil war, 25–26, 50
The Clash of Civilizations (Huntington), 80
Clermont, France, 209–10
Clifton, Shane, 77

Coalition for Peace in Africa, and Action for Conflict Transformation, 132
Coatesville Savings Bank, 230
coding themes, 20
coherence theory, 10, 85–86, 245
colonialization, 26–27, 29, 60, 157, 158, 162. *See also* British colonialism
colonial mission schools, 260–61
"A Common Word" (ACW), 140–41
community, 140, 146–53, 155–56, 181–85, 192, 245–48, 252, 261, 264–68
Community Psychologist, 187
Comolli, Virginia, 33–34, 39–40, 43–44, 64–67, 183
compassion *(raḥma)*, 110, 114–16, 139–40, 238
Comprehensive Peace Agreement (CPA), 166
conflict, 1–2, 34–37, 40–41
Conflict Prevention Prize, 134
Constantine and the Crusades, 203–13, 256
Constantinian idolatry, 271
Constantinian mistake, 203–4, 208, 256
constructive theology, 85, 244
contexts of acute violence for peacebuilding in Nigeria, 55–61
contextuality and globalization, 77–80, 83, 86–87
contextuality as principle element, 53–54
contextual theology, 71–80, 83–88
conversions, 127, 142–43, 205, 209, 234
conviction, 2, 127, 131, 143
convocation, 198, 215, 217, 219, 255
Conzelmann, Hans, 200
Coptic Christians, 129, 219, 224–27
corruption, 63, 106, 220
Council for Foreign Affairs, 58
Creative Court, 223–24
cross. See *staurocentric* pathways and practices
cross as locus, Anabaptists, 88–90, 264
cross-clan marriages, 154–56, 171, 185, 190–92, 241, 243, 253–54
crucifixion, 9, 195–201, 213

cruciform hermeneutic, 90
crude oil, 58–59
Crusades, 138, 203, 205, 209–18, 256
The Crusades, Christianity, and Islam (Riley-Smith), 216
Crusé, Christian F., 203
cultural context of globalization, 77–80
culture and context, 72–75, 79
culture of hatred, 102–3

Damaturu, 13
Dampar, 50
Daneel, Marthinus L., 263
dan Fodio, Usman, 5, 30, 31–37, 39–40, 57, 62–66, 68–69, 78, 123
Danjibo, Nathaniel, 38, 43–44
Dapchi, 40, 254n42
Dauda (participant), 177–78, 262–63
Dear, John, 273
demographic majority and minority context, 214–19, 255
Descartes, René, 146–47
desertification, 262
The Dignity of Man (Kamali), 115
Disarmament, Demobilisation and Reintegration (DDR) process, 166
Disaster Relief Ministry, 262
disintegrated Nigeria, 14
Disney, Abigail, 164
Dissident Discipleship (Augsburger), 252–53
diversity and difference, 30–31, 62, 84–85, 99–100, 123, 136, 158, 208
doing/being good *(khayr)*, 111, 131
Donga, 50
The Dual Mandate in British Tropical Africa (Lugard), 28
Dyck, Cornelius J., 88
Dynamics of Muslim Worlds (Wariboko), 29

East Africa, 55, 68, 82, 132, 157
Ebaugh, Helen Rose, 131
Ebuziem, Cajetan, 78
Echekwube, Onyebuchi, 153
Echema, Austin, 250

Index

Economic Community of West African States (ECOWAS), 164–65
education, 28–29, 42, 43, 128–30, 132, 150, 153, 168, 238, 252, 260
Egbe, 49
egbo-o ho ho concept, 171, 185, 187–89, 191–92, 241, 243, 251
Egypt, 129, 219, 224–27
Ekanola, Adeshina, 180–81
Ekklesiyar Kristi a Nigeria (EKAN), 51
Ekklesiyar Kristi a Sudan (EKAS), 51
Ekklesiyar Yan'uwa a Nigeria (EYN), 3–4, 12–13, 18, 31, 47, 52–53, 262
Elbadawi, Ibrahim A., 83
elders. See *ergada* (traveling elders); *gurrti* (council of elders)
Eliphaz the Temanite, 65
El-Rufa, Malam Nasir, 79
Elworthy, Scilla, 133
emancipation, 26
Enāyat, Ḥamid, 104–5
encounter of Islam with Christianity, 5, 62, 68–69
End of Memory (Volf), 64, 216
entrusting oneself to God, 200
Enugu State, 3
ergada (traveling elders), 153–54, 192, 241–42
Esack, Farid, 118–19, 122, 124
ethnic conflicts, 2, 57–58. See also Rwanda/Rwandan genocide
ethnographic research in Nigeria, 170–91
ethnolinguistic concepts, 24, 241, 244, 245
ethnolinguistic groups, 23, 57, 145, 145n1, 158, 170–71, 174, 178, 180, 190, 192
Ethnologue, 57
ethno-religious practices, 31, 35, 39, 54, 69
Europeanized Africans, 28
European partition of Africa, 24, 27, 57, 60, 157, 158
Eusebius, 203, 206

Evangelical Church Winning All (ECWA), 3–4, 12–13, 18, 31, 46–49, 53, 260
evil, 63–64, 95, 114n64, 138, 196, 200–203, 205, 215–17, 219, 220, 224, 255
extracting recurring structural themes, 20

Faheem, Naseem, 225–26
faith conviction, 131
Falana, Femi, 42
Falola, Toyin, 1, 24–25, 27–28, 31, 34, 46, 62, 67
family unit, 150
Fani-Kayode, Femi, 27
Farah, Ahmed Yusuf, 154–55
Federal Republic of Nigeria, 23, 24
Fee, Gordon, 198
Fellowship of the Churches of Christ in Nigeria. See Tarrayar Ekklesiyoyin Kristi a Nigeria (TEKAN)
festivals and rituals as means for peacebuilding, 171, 181, 185–87, 192, 241
Fetterman, David, 21
fieldwork, 17–21, 31, 53, 68, 155, 170
Finely, Mark, 221–23
Finney, Mark T., 195–96
First Crusade, 210
First Message of Islam, 120–21, 129, 239
Flomo, Vaiba, 165, 167
focus groups, 4, 13, 17–22, 155, 170–71, 171n1, 179, 179n34, 182–87, 190, 250, 256–58, 262–63, 266–67, 272–73
Folk Islam, 74
Fondation Chirac, 134
food, 179–80, 249–50, 249n29, 263, 271. See also hospitality
forced marriage, 29–30, 262
foreign policies of nation-states, 151–52
forgiveness *(samah)*, 131, 160, 162–63, 192, 199–200, 218–24, 226–27, 229–31, 233, 242–43, 245–46, 257–58
Fractured Spectrum (Akinade), 25

Index   303

France, 24, 209–10, 219
Freedom House, 129
freedom of religion, 127–28, 207, 240, 260
Fuest, Veronika, 168–69
Fulani herdsmen, 2–3, 4, 56–57, 79–80, 84, 122, 262, 268
Fuller Theological Seminary, 18, 73n11

Gabe, Christian B. N., 147–48
Gacacha court system, 158–63, 192, 220, 241–42
Gahigi, Steven, 220–21
Galtung, Johan, 7–8, 10–11
gammo and *gaya* concepts, 171, 181–85, 192, 241–42, 245, 247, 261, 264
Gandhi, Mahatma, 70, 87–88, 93–94
A Gandhian Theology of Liberation (Jesudasan), 94
Gandhi on Non-violence (Merton), 93
gang violence, 252–53
Garkida, 51–52
Gathogo, Julius, 250–51
Gazargamu, 32
Gbowee, Leymah, 163–68, 192
General Assembly, Egbe, 49
General Assembly of the Church of the Brethren, 52
geographical locus of *ubuntu*, 150–51
Germany, 24, 157, 220
Gerson, Allan, 2, 83–84
Gindiri, Plateau State, 50
Gindiri Theological Seminary (COCIN), 18
Glavda people, 190–91
globalization, 70–71, 76–80, 86–87, 92, 130, 139, 151, 247
global Muslim community (*umma*), 103, 116, 125–35
Global South, 73, 87
glocal, 81, 86–87
Glocal (Love), 86–87
God. *See* triune God
God-human relationship, 234
Goldingay, John, 231, 233
Good Samaritan, 105, 139
gospel, 16, 53–54, 71–76, 80, 82, 202–3, 208, 259–60

government intervention, 1–2, 83–84
Gowans, Margaret Craig, 47–48
Gowans, Walter, 47–48
grassroots movements, 35, 91, 135, 142, 153–54, 167–68, 251–52, 257, 272
The Great Theft (Abou El Fadl), 112–13
Grounded Theory research, 17
The Guardian, 67, 133
Gülen, Fethullah, 130–31, 136, 239–40
Gülen Movement, 130–31
The Gülen Movement (Ebaugh), 131
Gumi, Abubakar, 35, 40, 123
gun violence, 227–31
gurrti (council of elders), 153–57, 160, 173, 184, 189, 191, 192, 241–42
Gutip, Nanwul, 50
Gwoza Local Government Area, 190

Hadith. *See Aḥādīth* (traditions of the prophet of Islam)
ḥalāl, 179, 249–50, 271
Hamas, 68
Hankela, Elina, 147
Hargeisa, Somalia, 153
Hargeysa Women Community, 155
Harmsen, Egbert, 112
Hausas, 24–25, 28, 32–36, 38–39, 43, 62–63, 66, 69, 75, 79, 180, 182
hawks *(egbe)*, 189
healing, 221, 232–35, 273–74
healthcare facilities, 259, 262–63
Hebrew parallelism, 231–32
Hedges, Paul, 176–77
Helser, Albert David, 51–52
Helser, Lola B., 51–52
Hengel, Martin, 196–97
heretics, 103
Hiebert, Paul, 73
hijra, 43
ḥikma (wisdom), 110, 116, 238
Hiskett, Mervyn, 32, 33
Holy Spirit, 16, 140, 208, 212n56, 234–35, 257, 261, 272–73
Horn of Africa, 82, 153, 157
Horn of Hope Vision for Peace Community Development of Nigeria (HOHVIPAD), 265

hospitality, 112–14, 131, 171, 174–81, 185, 192, 238, 241–42, 248–51, 271
Hospitality and the Other (Yong), 176, 250
houses in African villages, 181–82
Housley, Norman, 211
Hugo, Pieter, 223–24
Human Subject Research Committee (HSRC), 18, 21
humility, 198–201, 218, 224
Huntington, Samuel P., 80, 130
Hutus, 158–59, 161
hymn of Christ, 198–99, 201, 215, 233

Ibn 'Abbās, Abdullāh, 100–101
Ibn Kathir, Hafiz, 106, 139
Ibrahim Abdi, Dekha, 132–33
Idowu, Bolaji, 251
Igbos, 24–25, 26, 75, 78–79, 171–74, 180, 189, 242
iḥsan (beneficence), 110–11, 116, 136, 139–40, 238
imago Dei, 148–50, 241, 245, 250
Imo State, 139, 187
incarnation, 10, 199–201
inculturation theology, 81
in-depth interviews, 4, 17, 18, 20, 21
indigenous concepts of peacebuilding, 157, 241
indigenous hospitality rituals, 175
indigenous languages, 57
indigenous Liberians, 167–68
indigenous missionary movements, 54
indigenous non-Muslims, 35
Indigenous People of Biafra (IPOB), 26
individual, African worldview of, 146–49. See also *ubuntu*
individual interviews, 4, 17–22, 170
indoctrination, 128–29
Informed Consent Letter, 20n49, 21
injustice, 58, 63, 82, 91, 112, 152, 157, 168, 188, 200, 203, 205, 215–17, 218, 245, 256, 258
"In Search of a Peaceful Society" (Oloyede), 123–24
Institutional Review Board (IRB) protocol, 18

inter-clan marriages. *See* cross-clan marriages
inter-group relationships, 78–79, 136
Internally Displaced Persons (IDPs), 15, 40, 53, 260, 263
international actors, 60
International Islamic University, 211
International Journal of Peace Studies, 148
interpersonal relationships, 150–53
Inter-Religious Council of Bosnia-Herzegovina, 126–28
In the Days of Caesar (Yong), 268–70
intra-religious conflicts, 57–58, 122–23, 126
An Introduction to Mennonite History (Dyck), 88
in vivo coding, 20
Iran, 58
Iraq, 58, 68. *See also* ISIS (Islamic State in Iraq and Syria)
Irvin, Dale T., 204, 207–8
Isaiah, 231–33
Islam
  artisans of peace within the Muslim *umma*, 125–35
  carrefour of Nigeria's political and religious histories, 62–69
  and Christianity in Nigeria's religious history, 30–54
  constructive theology, 244
  contexts of acute violence for peacebuilding in Nigeria, 55–61
  contextualization, 74
  Islamic and African cultural concepts at the *staurocentric* carrefour, 237–41
  in northern Nigeria, 5, 28, 30–42, 175, 177–78
  peacebuilding from African Muslims' perspectives, 118–24
  peacebuilding in the Islamic scriptures, 97–117, 137–38
  Yoruba practice of hospitality, 180
Islamabad, Pakistan, 211
Islam and Peacebuilding (Abu-Nimer and Yilmaz), 131

Index

Islam and the Modern Age (Oloyede), 124
The Islamic Conception of Justice (Khadduri), 111
Islamic law *(shari'a)*, 14, 29, 33, 35–37, 54, 62–63, 67, 97–99, 124, 253
Islamic State in Iraq and Syria (ISIS), 41, 56, 68, 224
Islam in Transition (Donohue and Esposito), 107
Islamist acute violence, 2–3, 4–5, 10–11, 12–13, 14, 16, 19, 30–42, 43–45, 47, 53, 56–57, 56n127, 66–69, 82, 85–86, 103–7, 111, 116–17, 118–22, 129–30, 138, 141, 174, 177, 192, 238–39, 247–48, 252–54, 255, 265
Islamization, 79, 268
Italians, 157

Jabir bin ʿAbdullah, 109
jahiliyya (pre-Islamic ignorance), 118
Jama'atu Ahlis Sunnah Lidda'awati w'al Jihad. *See* Boko Haram
Jerusalem, 210, 216
Jesudasan, Ignatius, 93–94
Jesus, Revolutionary of Peace (Bredin), 93
Jesus's followers, 80, 82–83, 96
  carrefour of Christian and Islamic traditions, 137–42
  community and civil societal actions, 264–68
  Constantine and the Crusades, 203–18
  Holy Spirit, 140, 272–73
  and hospitality, 174–81, 248–55
  kerygma of staurocentric pathways, 256–57
  loving and blessing Muslim communities, 258–64
  public and political square, 268–71
  public declaration of forgiveness, 257–58
  staurocentric mindset, 199–203, 218–27, 233–35, 255–56
  See also nonviolent resistance philosophies

Jews, 16n43, 102–6, 109, 128, 142, 211, 253
Jibreel (participant), 182, 184, 259, 263–64
jihad, 45, 63–68, 137–38, 149, 239. *See also* Boko Haram; dan Fodio, Usman; First Message of Islam; Fulani herdsmen
Joash, 143
John the Apostle, 140
Jos ECWA Theological Seminary (JETS), 18
Josephus, Flavius, 195
Joyful Witness in the Muslim World (Reisacher), 180
justice *(adl)*, 110–11, 116, 131, 139–40, 238
Just Peacemaking theory, 70, 87–88, 90–93, 246–47
just war theory, 90–92

Kadayifci-Orellana, S. Ayse, 125
Kaduna State, 3, 12, 44, 58, 79, 272
Kähler, Martin, 72
Kalu, Ogbu, 27
Kamali, Mohammad Hashim, 115–16, 238
Kampala, Uganda, 248
Kanem-Borno empire, 31–32
Kano State, 12, 58
Kärkkäinen, Veli-Matti, 4, 10, 72–73, 73n11, 85, 85n50, 244, 248–49, 273
Kenny, Joseph, 35
kenosis principle, 9, 104n29, 137, 198, 245
Kent, Thomas, 47–48
Kenya, East Africa, 132–33
kerygmatic approach, 96, 142, 256–57, 263–64, 268, 272
Khadduri, Majid, 111, 139
Kieh, George Klay Jr., 163
Kigali, Rwanda, 162, 224
King, Martin Luther Jr., 70, 87–88, 94–95
King Solomon, 116
Krabill, James R., 15
Kraybill, Donald B., 230

kuffār (infidels), 102, 118
Kukah, Matthew Hassan, 25
Kulp, Harold Stover, 51–52
Kulp, Ruth Royer, 51
Kulp Theological Seminary, 18, 52–53
Kumm, Karl W., 49–50
Kuzmič, Peter, 258
Kwara State, 49
Kwarhi, 18, 52–53

labarum, 207
Lagos, Nigeria, 48
Lancaster, Pennsylvania, 227–31
Langmead, Ross, 234
Langtang, 50
languages, 24, 57, 147–48, 147n8
La Palabre (Bidima), 156–57
larger community, 150–51
Latourett, Kenneth Scott, 207
"Law on Freedom of Religion and Legal Position of Churches and Religious Communities in Bosnia and Herzegovina," 127–28
Lederach, Angela, 153–54
Lederach, John P., 7–8, 153–56, 190
leprosarium, 52
liberal democracy, 29
liberation theology, 81–82
Liberia/Liberian women, 163–69, 191, 241–43, 251, 252, 272
Liberians United for Reconciliation and Democracy (LURD), 165
Liberian Women Initiative (LWI), 166–67
Living into Community (Pohl), 248
Loimeier, Roman, 34–35, 39
love, 9, 16, 76, 89, 93–94, 130–31, 139–43, 172–74, 179, 203, 205, 207, 209, 211, 223–24, 239–40, 258–64, 266
Love, Rick, 86–87
loving and blessing Muslim communities, 258–64
Luanda, Angola, 259
Lugard, Frederick John Dealtry, 24, 27–30, 50
Luke, 139, 199–203

Luke-Acts narrative, 250
Lutherans, 46–47

maḏāhib (Islamic schools of thought), 34
madrasas, 44
Maiduguri, Borno State, 13, 42
Maina, Wilson, 84
Maitatsine group, 3, 38, 43, 45
Mangu Leprosy Settlement, 50
"Manifestations of *Wasaṭiyyah*" (Kamali), 116
Mano River Women Peace and Security Network (MARWOPNET), 166
Mantzikos, Ioannis, 1
Margi people, 52n116, 181–82, 185–86
Mar Girgis Cathedral, Tanta, 225
Marshall, Katherine, 132
martyrdom, 105n31, 204, 209, 225–31
Martyrs Mirror, 228, 230
Marwa, Muhammad, 38, 43–44
Mason, Steve, 195
Mass Action for Peace (MAP), 167
Masterton, Christiana, 52
Maxentius, 206
Maxwell, Lowry, 49
Mbaya, Isheku P. K., 51–52
Mbefo, Luke, 81
Mbiti, John S., 30, 146, 146n3, 153n24, 251, 267
McGarvey, Kathleen, 25
McGavran, Donald, 16
Meccans, 108–9
Mennonites, 88–89, 229, 230n111
Mennonite World Conference, 89
merchants of death, 59–60
Merton, Thomas, 93
messianic community, Yoder, 88, 95, 246, 264, 271
Methodists, 46, 69, 75, 217
Metropolitan of Dabar-Bosna Nikolaj, 126
The Middle Path of Moderation in Islam (Kamali), 115–16
migration, 43, 139, 189, 247, 252
military force, 1–3, 83, 124, 198, 217–18
Ministry of Human Rights, 128
Miskett, Mervyn, 67

missio Dei, 10, 15, 234
missionary efforts, 28–29, 45–54, 81
Miyetti Allah. *See* Fulani herdsmen
Molai Leprosy Settlement, 50
"The 'Moment of Truth' in Nigeria" (Sulaiman), 67
Monrovia, Liberia, 164–66
Morocco, 75, 212
Morris, Catherine, 8
Movement for the Actualization of the Sovereign State of Biafra (MASSOB), 26
Movement for the Emancipation of Niger Delta (MEND), 26
Movement for the Survival of Ogoni People (MSOP), 26
Mubi, 52
Muhammad, 96, 97, 107–11, 113–15, 119
Mukaram, Sami, 117
Mun ki mwan a vul (we walk two by each other's side) concept, 185, 245, 247, 261, 264
music, 75–76
Muslim-Christian Dialogue Forum (MCDF), 135, 265
Muslims, 6, 54, 96
   al-majiri phenomenon, 43–45, 183
   artisans of peace in non-African contexts, 126–32
   artisans of peace within the Muslim *umma*, 125–35
   Christian-Muslim carrefour for peacebuilding, 135, 136–43
   Christian-Muslim engagement, 55–69, 197, 211–12, 214–16, 254, 265, 272
   Christian-Muslim women, 165
   community festivals, 186
   in Egypt, 224–27
   and forgiveness, 257
   and hospitality, 174–80, 248–50
   vs. Islamists, 11
   loving and blessing of communities, 258–64
   in Nigeria's religious histories, 31–45
   in northern Nigeria, 28–29, 39–42

   peacebuilding from African Muslims' perspectives, 118–24, 132–35
   peacebuilding in the Islamic Scriptures, 97–117
   scope of study, 13
   statement of research problem, 4–5
   staurocentric carrefour for peacebuilding, 237–41
   and *ubuntu*, 246–47
   See also Fulani herdsmen; Islam; non-Muslims
Muslim Samaritan, 238, 268
Mussaqui, António, 259
Mutisi, Martha, 160–62
Mwaruvie, John Mwaniki, 1, 7, 83–84
Mwughavul, 185
The Myth of a Christian Nation (Boyd), 271

nabadraadin-guurti concept, 153–57, 173, 190, 192, 241–42, 257
narrative data, 17, 19–20, 68, 86, 155, 170, 192, 235, 237, 241–42
Nasarawa State, 3
National Patriotic Front (NPFL), 163
nation-building, 162, 167, 189, 247
nation-states, 151–52
neighbor theme, 78, 105, 114, 138–43
Nevertheless (Yoder), 88
New Testament, 140, 178, 197, 202n24
New York Times, 141, 223–24
Nguni languages, 147, 147n8. *See also ubuntu*
Nickel Mines, 227–31
Niger-Delta context, 26, 58–59
Nigeria
   contexts of acute violence for peacebuilding in, 55–61
   contextuality and globalization, 78–80
   cross-clan marriage, 254
   grassroots movements, 251–52
   Muslims in, 118–24
   peacebuilding concepts from the ethnographic research in, 170–91

political history of, 5, 23–54, 61–69, 274
power of community in, 245–48
religious histories of, 5, 12–13, 23–24, 30–54, 61–69
staurocentric practices for the church in, 255–74
See also northeastern Nigeria; northern Nigeria
Nigeria (Campbell and Page), 42
Nigerian Directorate of State Services (DSS), 79
Niger Republic, 41, 60, 151
no-conflict contexts, 153
Nolt, Steven M., 230
non-African contexts, 125–32, 171, 254–55
non-Christian religious contexts, 4, 85, 244
Non-Governmental Organizations (NGOs), 2, 83–84, 265
non-Muslims, 4–5, 13, 35, 39, 79, 102, 107, 110, 112–13, 117, 118–19, 123–24, 126, 133, 135, 238–40, 253, 263, 268. See also Christianity
nonviolent resistance philosophies, 70, 273
    Amish grace and forgiveness, 231
    of Gandhi and King, 70, 93–95
    and Islam, 108
    Just Peacemaking theory, 70, 90–93
    nonviolence peacebuilding ethics, Anabaptists, 6, 70, 87–90, 246
non-Western contexts and traditions, 72–73
North Africa, 31–32, 55–56, 82, 102, 145n1
northeastern Nigeria, 3–5, 12, 13–14, 18, 39–40, 52, 155, 182, 185, 190–91, 243, 254, 272. See also Adamawa State; Borno State
northern Nigeria, 5, 12–13, 17, 19, 28, 30–42, 43–45, 47, 49–51, 53, 60, 62–69, 122–23, 133, 175–77, 183, 259–60, 262–63, 265, 266, 272

not harming, 113
Nzeka (participant), 172–73
nzu concept, 171–74, 185, 189, 192, 241–42, 250–51

obedience, 198–99, 201, 233, 245n16
O'Brien, Peter T., 215
Official Gazette No. 5/04, 127
Ohio, 228
Olodumare: God in Yoruba Belie (Idowu), 251
Oloyede, Is-haq Olanrewaju, 123–24
Omar, Rashied, 98, 110
On Being a Muslim (Esack), 118–19
Onuoha, Freedom, 60–61
Ormerod, Neil, 77
the other, 4, 9, 98–103, 109, 113–14, 117, 118–19, 123–24, 127, 130, 138–43, 175n18, 178, 215–18, 238–40, 255–56, 261–64. See also *ubuntu*
The Oxford Handbook of Religion, Conflict, and Peacebuilding (Kadayifci-Orellana), 125

pacifism, 88, 90–92
Paden, J. N., 39–40, 122
pagan world, 209
Page, Matthew T., 42
Palmer, Herbert R., 32
Parliamentary Assembly of Bosnia and Herzegovina, 127
participant observation, 17
partitioning of Africa, 27, 57
The Pastor and the Imam (Ashafa and Wuye), 133–34
Pategi, 49
Paul (apostle), 65, 196, 198, 201–3, 215, 226, 233, 249
Paul VI (pope), 248, 251
Payne, David, 231, 233
peacebuilding actors, 125–26, 133, 251–52
peacebuilding and peacebuilding-contextual theology, 2, 54, 68–69
    African contextual theologies and, 81–87

Index

from African Muslims' perspectives, 118–24, 132–35
agency of community festivals and rituals, 185–87
artisans of peace within the Muslim *umma*, 125–35
carrefour of African concepts with, 192–93
Christian-Muslim carrefour for peacebuilding, 136–43
community and civil societal actions, 264–68
community power in, 181–85
constructive and critical integration for, 243–45
contexts of acute violence for, 55–61
contextuality and globalization, 77–80
cross-clan marriages, 190–91
defined, 10
egbo-o ho ho concept, 187–89
from the ethnographic research in Nigeria, 170–91
Gacacha concept, 157–63
and hospitality, 174–81
in the Islamic scriptures, 97–117
Liberian women, 163–69
loving and blessing Muslim communities, 258–64
peacebuilding defined, 7–9
public and political square, 268–71
scope of study, 13–14
significance of study, 14–17
statement of research problem, 4–7
staurocentric carrefour with, 231–35, 237–55
staurocentric pathways to, 194–235
as a stream of contextual theology, 83–88
traditions of nonviolence ethics, 87–95
and *ubuntu*, 146–53
women's role in, 163–69, 251–55, 271–73
See also nonviolent resistance philosophies
peace education, 150, 153, 238

Peacemakers in Action, 134–35
Pennsylvania, 227–31
Pentecostal church, 266–67, 268–69, 273n96
People Oriented Development (POD), 260, 263
Perham, Margery, 164
Perkins, Judith, 213–14
Peter (apostle), 137, 200
Philip, 203
The Plagrave Handbook of African Philosophy, 181
Plateau State, 12, 19, 49–51, 178
pluralism, 99, 130
plurality, 4, 84–85
POD (People Oriented Development), 260, 263
Pohl, Christine D., 248
political governing actors, 83–84
political history of Nigeria, 5, 23–54, 61–69, 274
political Islam, 39, 56–57
Political Islam (Anderson), 56
political power, 57, 84, 217–18, 269–70
political square, 268–71
political violence, 1, 15. *See also* political history of Nigeria
politics, prophetic, 268–71
The Politics of Jesus (Yoder), 89
porosity of borders, 60–61
positivist tradition, 21
post-civil war revival, 54
power and control, 65–66
power of community, 171, 181–85, 192, 245–48, 252, 261, 264. *See also* hospitality
Pray the Devil Back to Hell (film), 164–65
Presbyterians, 46, 69, 75
preventive peacebuilding, 8, 16, 152
private sector, 2
probing questions, 20
prophetic politics, 268–71
pseudonyms, 20–21, 41n70, 171n1
public and political square, 268–71
public declaration of forgiveness, 257–58

Index

Qādiriya, 34–35, 123
Quetteville, Harry de, 129
Qur'ān, 64–65, 97–117, 118–22, 124, 131, 133, 136–39, 142, 197, 237–40, 253

Rabat, Morocco, 212
Radical Orthodoxy, 269
raḥma (compassion), 110, 114–16, 139–40, 238
Ray, Benjamin C., 30–31
reconciliation, 9, 135, 147, 154–56, 159–63, 220–21, 233–35, 247, 265, 274. See also *ubuntu*
recorded interviews, 20
Red Cross Society, 212
redemption, 9, 15–16, 196, 212–13, 220
refugees, 53, 132, 151
Reisacher, Evelyne A., 180
religious freedom, 127–30, 240
religious histories of Nigeria, 5, 12–13, 23–24, 30–54, 61–69
religious identity, 2, 40, 66–67, 178
religious other, 235, 242, 261, 264, 268
religious teachings and symbols, 62, 68
Renard, John, 105–6
Renders, Marleen, 154–57
research methodology, 17–22
research problem, 4–7
research procedure, 18
restorative justice, 152, 162–63, 224, 245. See also *Gacacha* court system
resurrection, 5, 9, 10, 16, 88, 95, 137, 197, 202–5, 212–13, 215, 226–27, 256, 268, 274
Reticker, Gini, 164–69
retributive justice, 159, 162–63, 224, 242
A Revolution in History (Sulaiman), 32
Riley-Smith, Jonathan, 211, 216
Riyad as-Salihin, 113
Roberts, Charles Carl IV, 227–31
Robertson, R. L., 52
Robinson, Charles, 49
Roman Catholic Church, 46, 69, 75, 138, 231
Roman Catholic Mission (RCM), 69
Roman Empire, 205, 214

Romans, 195–97
RPF (Rwanda Patriotic Front), 161
Rucyahana, John, 159–62, 220–21
Rugelinyange, Amon, 221–22
rural-urban migration, 189, 247–48, 252
Russia, 151–52
Rwanda Patriotic Front (RPF), 161
Rwanda Prison Fellowship, 220–21
Rwanda/Rwandan genocide, 57, 151, 157–63, 192, 219, 220–24, 241–42, 247

Sacred Misinterpretation (Accad), 96
sadaqa (charity), 111–14
Sahel (regions south of the Sahara), 32, 80, 82
Sahih Muslim, 113, 120
Saifawa dynasty, 32
Salamatu (participant), 182, 185–86
Salam: Institute for Peace and Justice, 125
sanctity of human life, 106, 110, 114
Sarkozy, Nicolas, 134
Saud al-Faisa, 129
Saudi Arabia, 40, 129
Saul, 202–3
Schoeman, Marelize, 152
schools, 42, 46, 50, 259–61
Schreiter, Robert J., 11
Second Advent, 202, 215, 270–71
Second Message of Islam, 121, 239
The Second Message of Islam (Ṭāhā), 119–22, 239
self-giving, 200–201, 215, 218, 224, 233, 238–43, 245, 252, 261, 263, 271
Selfu, Adele, 222–23, 246, 257
Senior, Donald, 201
Servant poems in Second Isaiah, 231–33
Serving in Missions (SIM), 47–49
sexual violence and abuse, 168
Shagari, Alhaji Shehu, 38
shahāda (confession of faith), 36, 74
Shah-Kazemi, Reza, 115, 238
shalom, 8, 15, 152, 180, 209. See also peacebuilding-contextual theology
Shamdasani, Prem N., 22

Index

shari'a (Islamic law), 14, 29, 33, 35–37,
    54, 62–63, 67, 97–99, 124, 253
sharing of food, 179–80, 249–50
Shaw, Flora, 24
Shea, Nina, 128–29
Shekau, Abubakar, 41
Shenk, Wilbert, 10, 87
Sherriff, Alhaji Ali Modu, 42
Shi'ite Muslims, 34–35, 55–58
Shilha, 75
Simons, Menno, 88, 229
sinking boreholes, 259–60, 263
Sirleaf, Ellen Johnson, 168
Smith, Gary V., 231
social justice, 168, 188
Sokoto Caliphate, 33–34
Sokoto Sultanate, 66, 123
Somalia, 56, 132, 153–57
Somalia: The Roots of Reconciliation
    (Farah and Lewis), 154
Somaliland, 153–57, 190–91, 192,
    241–43. See also *gurrti* (council
    of elders)
South Africa, 82, 147, 149, 152, 192, 247
South African Black theology, 81–82
South America, 228
spiritual dimension of peace, 63n145,
    235
sports and games, 186–87, 266–67
Stackhouse, Max, 244
Stark, Rodney, 204, 209
Stassen, Glen Harold, 70, 87–88, 90–93,
    246–47
"Statement of Shared Moral
    Commitment," 126–27
Statement the Inter-Religious Council of
    Bosnia-Herzegovina (IRC-BiH),
    126–28
staurocentric pathways and practices, 7,
    9, 64, 192–93
    Amish community, 227–31
    Anabaptist locus on the cross, 89
    carrefour with peacebuilding, 231–
        35, 237–55
    for the church in Nigeria, 255–74
    Constantine and the Crusades,
        203–18
    Coptic Christians in Egypt, 224–27
    elements characteristic of, 199–203
    and forgiveness, 162–63, 218–31
    gender perspectives, 252–53
    in Greco-Roman times, 195–203
    and hospitality, 249–51
    Islamic and African cultural
        concepts, 237–41
    Jesus's overturning the meaning of,
        197–99
    and peacebuilding-contextual
        theology, 10, 104, 104n29,
        194–235
    research procedure, 20
    Rwanda/Rwandan genocide, 220–24
    scope of study, 13
    significance of the study, 15–17
    statement of research problem, 4–5
    and *ubuntu*, 245–46
Stephen, 199–203
Stewart, David W., 22
Stirrett, Andrew P., 49
St. Mark's Cathedral, 225–26
straight path theme, 100–101
Stride Toward Freedom (King), 94–95
Sudan, 47–49
Sudan Interior Mission (SIM), 47–49,
    52, 69
Sudan United Missions (SUM), 46,
    49–52, 69
suffering and obedience, 198–99, 233
The Suffering Self (Perkins), 213
Suffering Servant, 231–33, 273
Sufi brotherhoods, 35, 123
Sulaiman, Ibraheem, 32–33, 35–37, 57,
    63–64, 67
Sunan Abi Dawud, 107–8, 113
sunna, 113–14
Sunni Muslims, 55, 57–58
Sunquist, Scott W., 204, 207–8
The Sword of Truth (Hiskett), 32
Sword verse of the Qur'ān, 119n87, 121,
    239
symbol, cross as, 208, 212–13. See also
    religious teachings and symbols;
    staurocentric pathways and
    practices
syncretism, 35–36, 39, 75–76, 123
Syria, 58, 68, 151, 211

312 Index

ta'āruf (embrace of the other), 98–99, 101, 109–10, 113–14
tafāsir, 101
Tafsīr al-Jalalayn, 98, 100
Ṭāhā, Maḥmūd Muḥammad, 63n146, 119–22, 124, 239
Tanwīr al-Miqbās min Tafsīr Ibn 'Abbās, 100, 104
taqiyya, 117, 142
Taraba State, 12
Tarrayar Ekklesiyoyin Kristi a Nigeria (TEKAN), 51
Tawadros II (pope), 226–27
Tawhidi, Shaikh M., 129, 239
Taylor, Albert, 49
Taylor, Charles, 163–65
Tennent, Timothy C., 73
Theodosius, 205
Theological College of northern Nigeria (TCNN), 51
theological epistemology, 74–75
Things Fall Apart (Achebe), 172
Tijāniya, 34–35, 123
The Times of London, 24
'Titi tuku 'a rumbwa mai,' 181
Toward an Islamic Reformation (An-Na'im), 114
Townsend, Tom, 220–21
transcribed research interviews, 20–21, 170–71
transgression and iniquities, 232
transnational groups, 61
tree-planting, 259, 262–63
trinitarian theological model, 9, 10, 16
triune God, 2, 7–10, 15–16, 54, 76, 89, 135, 196, 213, 223–24, 234–35
Turaki, Yusuf, 46–48
Turkey, 130–31
Tutsis, 151, 158–59, 161–62, 219, 223
Tutu, Desmond, 147–50, 162, 224, 245–46
Twa, 158, 161
Two Rows by the Sea (Atallah), 224–25
Tyerman, Christopher, 210–11
Tyriaka (participant), 20–21, 171–74, 171n1, 247

ubuntu, 118, 146–53, 153n24, 155, 185, 192, 241, 245–47, 261, 264
Ukpong, Justin, 71, 74, 81–82, 146–47
Ukraine, 151–52
Umaru, Thaddeus Byimui, 37, 272
umma (global Muslim community), 103, 116, 125–35
Umudim, Imo State, 187–88
unequal yoke, 253–54
United Nations (UN), 159, 162
United Nations Commission for Refugees, Geneva, 266
United Nations Security Council, 60, 251–52
United States of America, 50, 69, 82, 151, 214, 219, 227–31, 271. See also missionary efforts
universal ethics of the stranger, 171–74, 192, 241–42, 250–51
"Universality of Human Rights" (An-Na'im), 122
unstructured interviews, 17, 19–21
upbringing of children, 182–84
urban areas, 247, 252, 259. See also rural-urban migration
Urban II (pope), 209–11
Usamah ibn Zaid, 114–15
"The Use of Money" (Wesley), 217
U.S. Presidential elections of 2016, 117

Vanier, Jean, 248
Vesicovaginal Fistula (VVF) cases, 262
Victory Presbyterian Church, 259
violence. See acute violence; Islamist acute violence; nonviolent resistance philosophies
Virgwi, 52
Volf, Miroslav, 64, 216, 273
Vom Christian Hospital, 50

Wahhabi Islam, 40, 129
Wajir Peace and Development Committee, 132–33
Wallis, Andrew, 60
Walls, Andrew, 26–27
Wariboko, Nimi, 29, 31
The War of the Lamb (Yoder), 89

Waters, Malcolm, 77
Wathiqat ahl al-Sudan, 33, 36
Weaver-Zercher, David L., 230
Wesley, John, 217
Western church, 87
Western missionary enterprise, 28–29, 45–54, 69, 75–76, 81
Western theologies, 17, 72–74, 81–82
West Nickel Mines School, 227–31
Whiteman, Darrell, 71–72
Wilken, Robert, 204, 205, 207n38, 214
Williams, Demetrius K., 199
Williams, Rowan, 211
Windibiziri, David L., 176
wisdom (*ḥikma*), 110, 116
women, 154–56, 163–69, 187–93, 241–43, 251–54, 262, 271–73
women fellowships of churches (*zumunta mata*), 272
Women in Peacebuilding Network (WIPNET), 165–66
Women's Interfaith Council (WIC), 272
Woodberry, J. Dudley, 138, 145, 149
World Bank's Development and Research Group Conference, 83
World Christian Database, 25n8, 214, 255
World Christian Encyclopedia, 214, 255
Wukari, 50
Wuye, James, 124, 133–35, 239, 265, 267–68

Yaji of Kano, 32
Yale Center for Faith & Culture response, 141
Yan Izala, 34–35, 123
Yazidis, 68
Yilmaz, Ihsan Onur, 131
Yobe State, 12–13, 19, 40
Yoder, John Howard, 88–89, 95, 208, 246, 264
Yola, Adamawa State, 13, 265
Yong, Amos, 68, 176, 250, 268–71
Yorubas, 24–25, 75, 180–81
Yusuf, Muhammed, 41–42, 44

Zaghawa, 32
Zimbabwe, 263
zumunta mata (women fellowships of churches), 272
Zuruaga (participant), 178, 251, 257

www.ingramcontent.com/pod-product-compliance
Lightning Source LLC
Chambersburg PA
CBHW061427300426
44114CB00014B/1568